REAL WORLD FREEHAND 3

Real World
FreeHand 3

by
Olav Martin Kvern

AN OPEN HOUSE BOOK

PEACHPIT PRESS, INC.

To Leslie Renée Simons, with love.

REAL WORLD FREEHAND 3
Olav Martin Kvern

PEACHPIT PRESS, INC.
2414 Sixth St.
Berkeley, CA 94710
(415) 527-8555
(415) 524-9775 (fax)

ISBN 0-938151-29-0

0 9 8 7 6 5 4 3 2

Printed and bound in the United States of America

If I weren't one of the authors of Aldus Free-Hand, I'd want this book to teach me how to use it. Actually, I'd want Ole to teach me, but he lives two thousand miles away. And he probably would get pretty tired of showing me the tricky parts over and over and over. With *Real World FreeHand* I have his advice and insight any time I need them.

When we started on FreeHand nearly five years ago, we had a vision of an easy–to–use, yet extraordinarily powerful graphics program. We wanted it to be usable by both novices and professional designers, and give results limited only by a person's artistic ability. It should be as intuitive as a pencil, but as powerful as a mind link to a hallucination machine. We've come a long way in those five years. Of course, we aren't quite up to the level of our vision yet. But it wouldn't have been much of a vision if we could achieve it in just five years of programming.

We had another vision too—one of talented artists working with computers, multiplying their abilities a hundredfold, and avoiding the dull, routine work of aligning things that simply refused to align; of specifying type, then setting the job aside while waiting for the galleys to come back from the typesetting house; of doing what our first ad agency did—cutting that type apart letter by letter and hand setting it with just the right spacing; of hearing the client ask to change a word in the middle of one of those blocks when the final extended deadline is tomorrow morning. With FreeHand, everything is malleable until the moment when a scanning laser beam starts to reveal the billions of pixels that make up your page on the drum of a laser printer or to the film of an imagesetter.

We also thought everybody ought to have a chance to undo their mistakes. Any mistakes. A bunch of mistakes. Imagine how much bolder you could be in real life if you had a chance to undo some of your blunders. Call your broker and tell him to undo that stock you sold last week. Go back two years and change your mind about marrying that bum who just passed out on the couch. You can't do it in real life, but you sure can with FreeHand. It is an underappreciated fact that FreeHand lets you undo more than just the easy things. FreeHand is the only program I have ever seen that lets you undo *every* editing operation, as many as 99 operations back.

I am really happy with what we finally achieved in FreeHand 3 (née RoadRunner). Our RoadRunner development team worked for two years getting it to feel right (thanks, Rusty, Pete, Steven, Samantha, Alan, Kevin, and Andrew). They worked for months on fixing bugs that companies who don't care as much about perfection as Altsys and Aldus would have shipped with. They kept improving it even after it was good enough, kept working on it until they were sick of it, in fact. I think there are three factors in our success: we really care about doing the best job we know how, we have several very smart software engineers working on it, and we have some awesomely talented users who continue to tell us how to make it even better.

Reading the drafts of this book is a lot like reading a biography of your own daughter. The writer talks about her accomplishments. Her beauty. Her charm. Her high-pitched whiny voice. Well, no writer is perfect. Fortunately, Ole laughs with us on those few occasions where the reality differs from the vision. And he goes on to explain those hard parts step by step in a way that almost anybody can understand.

I've reconsidered my first sentence. I want this book, even though I did write a lot of FreeHand. *Real World FreeHand* is a great study guide: we'll continue to improve the parts of FreeHand Ole finds great, and we'll rework the parts Ole finds need lots of explaining. Reader, you've made two good choices. Crank up FreeHand and get started with *Real World FreeHand*. I think you'll have fun with both.

Jim Von Ehr
President and CEO,
Altsys Corporation

Introduction

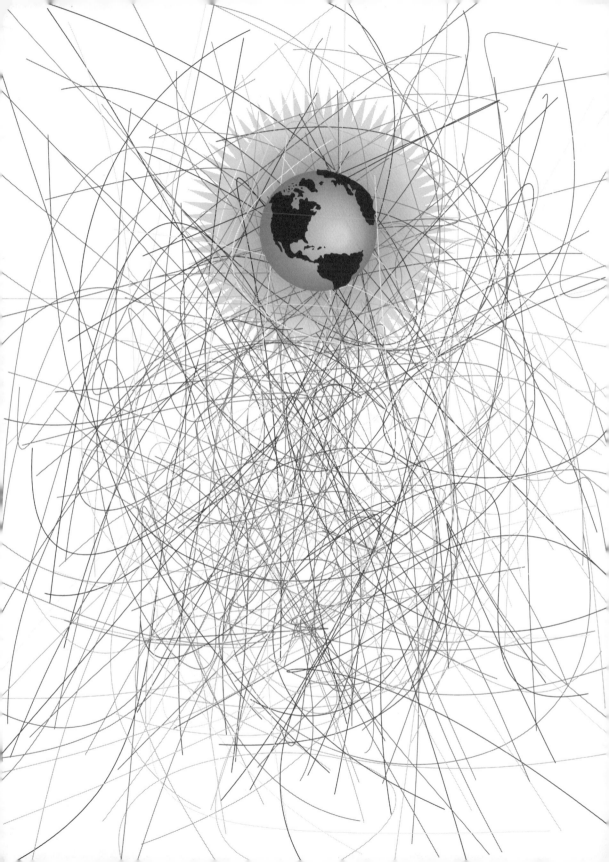

"Here's a message from someone asking when we'll be writing *Real World FreeHand.*"

"Should we?"

"I'm way too busy. You do it."

"Are you kidding? I nearly died last time."

After Steve Roth and I wrote *Real World PageMaker,* various people wrote to us asking when we'd be doing *Real World FreeHand.* We laughed at the idea long enough to start taking it seriously. This time, Steve's on board as my editor, and I'm slugging out the copy. This should free me from at least some of his infernal bickering and silly notions (*that's Mr. Silly Notions to you, bub.* SR), while giving me the benefit of his sage editorial advice. We'll see.

Why should you listen to what I have to say about working with FreeHand? I bring to this book my experience as an illustrator (I've worked as a technical, medical, archaeological, and veterinary illustrator, as well as a general-purpose book and magazine illustrator), as a designer, and as a typesetter.

Specifically, however, I bring my experience as a FreeHand user. I really have been through the long shifts (some of them longer than 40 hours) trying to get FreeHand files to print. On most of those late nights and early mornings, I could have been home in bed if I'd known just one key piece of information. But I didn't. There was no one to tell me.

I'm here to tell you. If some piece of information in this book saves you one late night, or gets your file to print on the first pass through the imagesetter instead of the second or third, I will have succeeded in my purpose.

Where I'm Coming From

There's a bias to this book. FreeHand is marketed and sold as an illustration program, and I think that's great—my background, after all, is in illustration. But I think of FreeHand as both a great illustration program, and a fantastic page-layout program for short, complex documents. So when I'm talking about a FreeHand file, I call it a *publication*, not an *illustration*.

I did consider doing the page layout for this book in FreeHand, just to make my point, but chickened out. Writers on tight schedules need spelling checking, table of contents generation, and indexing features, so I stuck with PageMaker for my page layout. The title pages for each chapter and the color pages are all FreeHand publications, though.

Finally, I'm a curmudgeon. But I'm a friendly curmudgeon. Most of the people who read my writing tell me that it's friendly, approachable, and funny. But there are a few who—somehow—find it patronizing, arrogant, and harsh. I don't want to sound that way at all! (Well, not patronizing and harsh, anyway.) No matter how obnoxious I might sound, please keep in mind that I'm just trying to help.

Once, a janitor found me pounding on a Linotronic film processor (an ML-314, for you hardware tweaks) with a wastebasket at 4:00 A.M. I'd been up for more than 36 hours, and it'd just eaten a job that'd taken six hours to run on an imagesetter. I wrote this book in the hope that I could save others from repeating this scene.

Organization

This book's pretty simple: first, I'll show you how to get things into FreeHand; next, I'll talk about how to work with elements in FreeHand; and, finally, I'll tell you how to get your work out of FreeHand. Then, in Chapter 8, "PostScript," I'll show you how to extend FreeHand and make it do more than it could do when it came out of the box.

What's New in FreeHand 3. This section is for people who've been using FreeHand 2 and want to know what's changed since then. Here, I've covered many (though not—as the Altsys engineers reviewing this book proudly pointed out—most) of the new features in FreeHand 3. The section works like an expanded table of contents: there's a quick overview of each new feature, followed by a page number where you can find further information.

Chapter 1: FreeHand Basics. This chapter is your orientation to the world of FreeHand. In it, I describe the publication window, selecting objects, moving objects, working with FreeHand's toolbox, and an overview of the way that you create and import elements into Free-Hand (including basic path drawing).

Chapter 2: Drawing. This is all about using FreeHand's drawing tools—from creating and joining paths to applying lines and fills, creating styles, working with blends, creating charts and graphs, and drawing using perspective. This chapter expands on the discussion of drawing paths and adjusting curve handles that started in Chapter 1, "FreeHand Basics."

Chapter 3: Text and Type. This chapter deals with working with text in FreeHand—how to enter, edit, and format text. It covers wrapping text around graphics, specifying type, FreeHand's type effects, joining text to a path, and converting text into paths.

Chapter 4: Importing and Exporting. FreeHand doesn't exist in a vacuum. You need to be able to import images from scanners and color image-editing programs, or to be able to import EPS graphics from other PostScript drawing programs. This chapter shows you how, and where FreeHand fits in with your other applications. Topics include working with TIFFs, importing PICTs, importing formatted text, importing EPSs created in other programs, importing 3-D graphics, converting FreeHand EPSs to Illustrator 1.1 EPS format, and converting FreeHand EPSs to Super 3D text format so that you can draw things in Freehand and then turn them into 3-D objects in Super 3D.

Chapter 5: Transforming. This chapter shows you how to manipulate FreeHand elements you've drawn, typed, or imported, and describes how to use the skewing, scaling, rotation, and reflection tools.

Chapter 6: Color. In this chapter, I cover creating and applying colors in FreeHand. This chapter also discusses color models, the history of color printing, creating duotones, and controlling the conditions under which you view and create color publications.

Chapter 7: Printing. It don't mean a thing if you can't get it on paper or film. Here's how to do that, plus a bunch of tips that'll save you money at your imagesetting service bureau and your commercial printer. In this chapter, I also talk about the various options contained in FreeHand's Print and Print options dialog boxes and how they affect your publications.

Chapter 8: PostScript. In many ways, this chapter is the heart of the book. In it, I show you how to use PostScript when working with Free-Hand, and how to add features to FreeHand. I wrote this chapter because I want to demythologize the process of adding PostScript lines and fills to FreeHand. You don't have to have an engineering degree, or be a rocket scientist, to add unique touches to FreeHand that'll make it truly your own program. This chapter shows you how.

Conventions

I've always wanted to write a book that didn't have a section on "Conventions." I should be good enough at what I do that you don't have to do anything more than read the text and look at the figures to get the point. But I do have a few idiosyncracies of terminology I think need going over.

- Text edit box. You know, a box in a dialog box you type text in.

- Submenu. One of those annoying little menus that pops off the side of legitimate menu items.

- Pop-up menu. One of those annoying little menus that pops up from something that should be a text edit box.

- Object info dialog box. FreeHand is full of dialog boxes containing information (position, size, etc.) about FreeHand elements. There's one for every type of object that you can create in or import into FreeHand, and a couple of special ones beyond that. I call them all object info dialog boxes.

Disclaimer

Some of the techniques in this book involve modifying either FreeHand's subsidiary files (like PPDs) or modifying FreeHand itself. While I've tried to make the procedures (in these cases, anyway) as complete and accurate as possible, you need to be aware that you're proceeding entirely at your own risk. Given that, there are a few things you can do to make everything less risky.

Work on Copies of Files. If you don't keep your original files in their original state, how can you ever go back to where you started? Always back your files up before you try altering them.

Remember That Not Everyone Will Have Your System. You can't expect your friends and your imagesetting service bureau to be absolutely up-to-date with your current modifications if you don't give them to them. Therefore, if your publication requires a custom page size you've written into a PDX, make sure that your imagesetting service bureau has the PDX.

Clean up after Yourself. If you change any of FreeHand's PostScript printing routines in a printer's RAM, make sure that you change them back to their original state before anyone else sends a job to that printer or imagesetter. Nothing is more embarrassing for you or as much of a bother to everyone else as having your name and "DRAFT" print across all of the jobs printed on a particular printer because you forgot to change *showpage* back to its original definition. This, in fact, is a great way to provoke the villagers to come after you with torches and pitchforks.

Don't Call Aldus Technical Support If Something You Read in This Book Doesn't Work. They're the best in the business, but they didn't write this book and shouldn't be expected to support it. This book is not an Aldus product, and Aldus Corporation has no control over its content. I'm not kidding. Write to me, instead. My physical and electronic mail addresses are listed in Appendix B, "Resources."

Acknowledgments

Congratulations to everyone at Altsys for producing such an amazing, creativity-enhancing tool: Kevin Crowder, Peter Mason, Rusty Williams, Steven Johnson, Samantha Seals, Alan Sibley, John Ahlquist, James Brasure, Parry Kejriwal, Mark Skaggs, David Spells, Brian Welter, and, especially, to Jim Von Ehr for his inspiring foreword.

Congratulations, too, to everyone at Aldus, for their contribution to FreeHand and to this book, especially to: Harry C. Edwards, J. Scott Campbell, Jan C. Wright (my left brain), Bill Knight, Nichole J. Vick, Mary Hauslauden, jwhiting, Laura Perry, Jeff Rowley, Diane Catt, Janet Williams, Pam Trebon, Beth Norton, Joe Friend, Reuben Lam, and Michele Gilles. Many thanks to the amazing Phil Gaskill for his typographic suggestions, and to Jeff Harmon (of the Aldus auto racing team), David Joslin, and Abbo Peterson (for his help with PrePrint).

I have had nothing but admiration for Tracy Tobin and her work since she and I worked together on the FreeHand 2.0 documentation, and many of the tips and techniques in this book were outright stolen from her (all the rest were stolen from Conrad Chavez).

Special thanks to David Blatner of Parallax Productions and Greg Stumph, two PostScript wizards whose work enriches this book tremendously. Don't forget that you can contact these guys and put them to work writing the PostScript effects you're dreaming of (you can find their addresses in Appendix B, "Resources").

Doug Peltonen of PrePress Associates helped out tremendously with the sections on color (though I may have mangled his advice in translation).

Thanks to the Seattle Gilbert and Sullivan Society, and their photographer, Ray O. Welch, for giving me permission to use some of their archival photographs as example images.

Thanks to Robert Dietz of Ted Mader and Associates, who produced the incredible cover using FreeHand.

Thanks to Ted Nace for being a great publisher (and the only publisher I've ever had to loan money so he could take me out to dinner), and to my editor and good buddy, Steve Roth, for all of his help whipping this puppy into shape. I couldn't have gotten through without Susie Hammond's attention to detail and grammar ("This isn't a sentence—it's an exasperation!"). And Ron Drummond's work on the index may have saved my life.

As usual, Chuck Cantellay, Peter Curry, Adam Buckner, and the rest of the staff of Seattle ImageSetting helped tremendously in getting the book out of their Linos.

Finally, thanks to my wonderful wife, Leslie Renée Simons, for her encouragement, understanding, and support.

Olav Martin Kvern
Seattle, 1991

What's New in FreeHand 3?

FreeHand 3

sports a variety of performance enhancements and new features over FreeHand 2. In this section, I'll quickly describe many of the most significant new features. If you want to know more about the feature, turn to the page number that ends each description.

This list is, of course, a subjective view—the Altsys engineers reviewing this manuscript let me know that I'd missed a few, and attached their list of 150 (150!) new features. I figure I'm doing pretty well if I can cover even 10 percent of their amazing work in this "What's new" section.

User Interface Changes

The most obvious differences between FreeHand 2 and FreeHand 3 are in the area of the program's user interface. In version 3, FreeHand has floating palettes for assigning colors, graphic styles, and layers.

To edit any of the items displayed in any of these floating palettes, double-click on the name of the item in the palette. If you want to change the position of the item in the palette, drag the item to a new position inside the palette. For more on working with the palettes, see page 45.

The Layers Palette In FreeHand 2, it was often difficult to tell which layer a particular object or group of objects occupied, and it was impossible to specify certain layers not to print. FreeHand 3's Layers palette makes working with layers easy, and also adds the ability to make layers either foreground (printing) or background (nonprinting) layers. FreeHand 3 gives you control over whether foreground or background layers (or both) are active and visible. For more on using the Layers palette, see page 46.

One of the most wonderful layers in the Layers palette is Free-Hand's Guides layer—which holds all of your rule guides and can be placed behind—or in front of—any other layer. For more on using the Guides layer, see page 49.

The Styles Palette

Graphic styles are named collections of attributes (line weight and pattern, color, fill, and overprinting instructions, to name a few). Free-Hand 2 had a rudimentary version of graphic styles, but FreeHand 3 takes the concept of graphic styles further, providing an environment almost as rich and powerful as PageMaker's paragraph styles. For more on the Styles palette, see pages 50 and 122.

The Colors Palette

Many FreeHand users got tired of pulling down a menu to apply colors they'd already defined to objects they'd selected. The Colors palette simplifies the process of applying colors to an object: just select the object, click on the color in the Colors palette, and FreeHand applies the color to the object. For more on the Colors palette, see page 51.

Visible Grid

FreeHand 2's "Snap-to" grid was great, but you couldn't see it. Free-Hand 3 features both a visible and an invisible grid. You can display the visible grid on your page in whatever color you want, in whatever increments you want. For more on FreeHand's grids, see page 18.

Nudge Keys

You can press the arrow keys to move selected objects in specific increments, which you can specify in the Preferences dialog box. See page 254.

Improved Performance

FreeHand 3 is faster, smoother, and more stable than FreeHand 2. FreeHand 3 also has more performance-related preferences, which you can use to tailor FreeHand's behavior to your particular ways of working. For more on preferences, see page 20.

Smooth Drawing

FreeHand 3 redraws the screen faster, and with less flicker, than Free-Hand 2. If you have enough RAM, you'll see objects and points drag smoothly across the screen as you work with them. For more on smooth drawing, see page 5.

Faster Printing

Having nursed most of the Freehand 2.0 documentation out of a version 47.1 ROM Linotronic 300, I wasn't looking forward to trying to print using FreeHand 3. Call me a pessimist. I was pleasantly surprised by FreeHand's improved printing speed. I haven't run any benchmarks, but it's my impression that FreeHand 3 prints things—especially TIFFs—in around half the time it took FreeHand 2. Some operations, such as using clipping paths to crop TIFFs, were impractical in FreeHand 2 because of the time it took them to print. In FreeHand 3, this is no longer true (though you should, still, exercise caution when using clipping paths). For more on FreeHand 3's printing, see page 341.

Improved Precision

FreeHand 3's smallest unit is .0001 of a point. This is a huge improvement over the .1-point precision available in FreeHand 2.

PPD/PDX Support

FreeHand now supports Adobe's PPDs (PostScript Printer Description) and PDX (Printer Description Extension) files, in addition to the APD (Aldus Printer Description) files FreeHand 2 used to customize printing for specific printer models. PPD/PDXs improve on APDs by containing sets of screen angle and line screen combinations which minimize moiré patterns when you're printing color separations. For more on PPDs/PDXs, see page 360.

Automatic Trapping

FreeHand 3 also improves on FreeHand 2's color separation capabilities by offering a new field—"Spread size" in the Print options dialog box. "Spread size" spreads basic lines and fills over any background objects, thereby trapping the object (by creating a spread). For more on trapping, see page 319.

Working with Elements

FreeHand 3 features some new ways to work with objects you've drawn, typed, or imported. They make the program more fluid. Think less, draw more, I always say.

Subselection Inside Groups

Working with objects inside a group used to be tough (you had to ungroup the group to act on an object inside the group), but, in Free-Hand 3, you can hold down Option and select an individual item inside a group and change it—without ungrouping, just as you would if it weren't inside the group. When you're through editing the object, it's still inside the group. For more on subselecting objects inside groups, see page 43.

Control-click Through Stacked Objects

In FreeHand 2, I always wished there was a way to select through an object to reach the objects behind it without manipulating layers or stacking order. In FreeHand 3, hold down Control and click to select through objects. For more on selecting through objects, see page 43.

Multiple Ungroup

In FreeHand 2, you had to ungroup, then deselect, then select again, then ungroup, and so on when you wanted to completely ungroup assemblages of objects containing more than one group. In FreeHand 3, you can just keep on pressing Command-U to ungroup until theere's nothing left to ungroup. See page 255.

Snap to Point

FreeHand 2 featured the ability to snap to ruler guides or to an invisible grid. FreeHand 3 adds "Snap to point," which snaps points, paths, and objects to nearby objects when you're drawing or dragging. For more on "Snap to point," see page 24.

Reblending

In FreeHand 2, you could blend any two objects you wanted, but if you wanted to change the blend you had to delete the intermediate blend objects and start over. In FreeHand 3, you can adjust the blend *after it's blended.* This amazes me. For more on reblending, see page 100.

Paste Behind

FreeHand 3 can paste an object you've cut to the Clipboard behind objects on the current layer (that is, it's sent to the bottom of the stacking order). To paste an object behind the objects on the current layer, press Command-Shift-V (or you can hold down Shift as you choose "paste" from the Edit menu).

Note that this feature does not paste the objects on the Clipboard immediately behind the object you've got selected when you paste.

Working with Graphics

FreeHand 3 adds a number of new features for working with graphics. Once again, everything in FreeHand 3 is smoother and more intuitive than in FreeHand 2.

Display Curve Levers

In FreeHand 2, it could be difficult to tell which curve handle applied to which point. In FreeHand 3, it's easy—thanks to curve levers, straight lines which connect each curve handle to its point. For more on curve levers, see page 22.

Combined Fill and Line Dialog Boxes

In FreeHand 2, you had to work with one dialog box to specify an object's fill, and then use another dialog box to specify that object's line properties. In FreeHand 3, these dialog boxes have been combined into the enormous Fill and line dialog box. Select an object and press Command-E to display the Fill and line dialog box.

Not everyone thinks this is an improvement, though I do. Still, it is new. For more on the Fill and line dialog box, see pages 108 and 115.

Arrowheads and Tailfeathers

A new attribute of open paths is that you can apply arrowheads and tailfeathers to them. Draw a path, press Command-E to display the Fill and line dialog box, and pick an arrowhead/tailfeather combination. For more on these items, see page 110.

Color TIFF Separation

FreeHand 3 can separate color TIFF images. You can either import the TIFF and separate it with FreeHand, or you can preseparate the image and place it in FreeHand as an EPS file (including DCS files saved in either the binary or ASCII format), or you can place the image, manipulate it, and link to a high-resolution version of the image on an OPI separation system. Sound flexible? It is. Practically, however, preseparating your color images using Adobe Photoshop, Letraset

Color Studio, or Aldus PrePrint 1.5 is the best way to go. For more on separating color images, see page 335.

Improved Custom Lines and Fills

FreeHand 2 shipped with lots of great line and fill effects, but no one ever used them. Why? You had to type code in the PostScript dialog box, and you couldn't see what the line or fill looked like until you printed. You still can't see the effect on screen, but FreeHand's new Custom fills and lines make applying these unique effects much easier. Having these fills built-in also means that you don't have to worry about a USERPREP or ADVANCEDUSERPREP file—it's all inside of Free-Hand. For more on custom lines and fills, see pages 113 and 115.

Improved Handling of Linked TIFF Files

FreeHand 3 improves on FreeHand 2's handling of linked TIFF images in two ways. First, if you're opening a FreeHand file containing a linked image which FreeHand can't find, FreeHand 3 displays an alert and helps you locate the image. Next, FreeHand's Export dialog box now contains the option, "Include TIFF images," so that you can choose to include the TIFF in your EPS file (this is necessary, but watch out! TIFF files can be huge). If you're creating a file that'll be separated by an OPI separation program (such as Aldus PrePrint), uncheck this option—your separation program will be able to link to the images, thanks to the OPI information in the file.

Graphics Styles

I've talked myself blue in the face about using paragraph styles in Microsoft Word and in PageMaker, and I can see that I'll be doing the same for FreeHand 3's graphic styles. Simply put: styles are the handiest tool you have for trying out several design alternatives quickly, for saving the day when last-minute changes are required, and for speeding up the process of designing, laying out, or creating illustrations. For more on graphic styles, see page 122.

Composite Paths

In FreeHand 2, it was difficult to cut holes in shapes to let whatever was behind them show through. You usually ended up using a "Paste inside" operation to get the effect you wanted, which made your job take longer (like days longer) to print. FreeHand 3's "Composite paths" makes creating closed paths with holes in them easy. Select two closed paths and press Command-J (or choose "Join elements" from the Element menu) and FreeHand turns the two paths into a single, composite path. The areas where the insides of the two paths overlap becomes transparent. See page 92.

Apply Attributes to Groups

When you've got a group selected, you can apply a fill, line, or color to every path inside that group (you can also apply colors to any imported TIFF or paint-type images inside the group).

Retract Handles

When you needed to retract curve handles in FreeHand 2, you'd have to drag the curve handles inside a point. At many screen magnifications, this could be tough to do. In FreeHand 3, you can select the point and then retract one or both curve handles by pressing buttons in the Path/point dialog box and pressing Return. See page 80.

Improved Knife Tool

FreeHand 2's knife tool often shifted paths as you split them. FreeHand 3's knife tool (mostly) doesn't, and it's certainly a lot easier to hit the line or point you want to cut with the tool than it was in FreeHand 2. For more on the knife tool's new behavior, see page 87.

Better Line Tool

When you drew a line using the line tool in FreeHand 2, you produced a special sort of line that was, in general, more trouble than it was worth. You almost always had to ungroup it (to convert it to a normal path) to do anything with it. When you draw a line with FreeHand 3's line tool, the line you produce behaves exactly as if you'd drawn it using the corner tool. See page 72.

Working with Text

FreeHand 3's text handling features have also improved since FreeHand 2, though, perhaps, not as much as the product has improved in other areas. Yes, you still have to edit text in a dialog box (I actually prefer it, but I understand I'm in a minority), but there are some other new features you should take a look at.

Display Text Effects

In FreeHand 2, you had to take it on faith that your text effects would print, because they weren't displayed on screen. This meant that you had to print your publication to see what you were doing. In FreeHand 3, you can see your text effects—heavy, oblique, zoom text, shadow, inline, and outline—on screen as you work with your publication. See pages 22.

Inline Text Effect

FreeHand 3 adds a new text effect, "Inline," to the list of effects you have available. See page 172.

Vertical Text Alignment

FreeHand 3 adds a new text alignment, "Vertical," to the four alignments ("Align left," "Align center," "Align right," and "Justify") featured by FreeHand 2. "Vertical," as you'd expect, stacks characters up vertically. It's easier than putting a carriage return between all of the characters in a text block to get the same effect. See page 175.

Convert Text to Paths

FreeHand 3 can turn any Type 1 PostScript font (and any Type 3 Post-Script font created with Altsys' Fontographer) into FreeHand paths. To convert characters to paths, select the text block (or blocks) you want to convert, and choose "Convert to paths" from the Type menu.

Once characters are converted to paths, you can edit them as you would any FreeHand path, which means that you can stretch, twist, and redraw characters however you want. This is especially useful when you want to create a logo by altering or merging the shape of character outlines, or when you want to fill some text with a graduated fill or a scanned image.

FreeHand's got to be able to locate the outline (or printer) fonts for the characters you're trying to convert, or "Convert to paths" won't work. See page 190.

Easier Ways to Join Text to a Path

When you join a text block containing at least two paragraphs to an ellipse you've drawn with the ellipse tool, the first paragraph in the text block gets centered across the top of the ellipse and the second paragraph gets centered across the bottom of the ellipse. For more on joining text to basic shapes, see page 184.

Easier Editing for Text on a Path

In FreeHand 2, you couldn't change the format of text that you had joined to a path without selecting the path, pressing Command-I to display the Text on a path dialog box, pressing the Edit button, and then selecting and formatting the text. In FreeHand 3, you can select the paths and then change the text formatting using the selections on the Type menu or in the Type specifications dialog box. See page 187.

Greeking

FreeHand's Preferences dialog box gives you the ability to display greeking—gray bars that simulate text—instead of waiting for all of the text in your publication to redraw. As you'd expect, this speeds up your screen display. See page 20.

Improved Handling of Missing Fonts

As you open the publication, FreeHand 3 tells you if the publication contains fonts not installed on your system. This is very handy, especially for imagesetting service bureaus. When FreeHand can't find a font, it substitutes Courier, making it very obvious where the substitution's taken place. See page 167.

Other New Features

Here are a couple of things that I couldn't fit in anywhere else. The first one's very nice, and the second one's about the most important—and least documented—new feature in FreeHand 3.

Online Help

FreeHand 3 features a new, context-sensitive help system put together by jwhiting and Greg Stumpf. Press Command-Shift-?, and the cursor turns into a question mark (?). Choose a menu item or tool with the question mark, and FreeHand displays a screen of information about that feature. When you've got a dialog box open, press the same keys to display a help screen about that dialog box. If your keyboard has a Help key, you can press that key instead of pressing Command-Shift-? but I find myself hitting "Help" all the time when all I want to do is press Delete.

External Resource Files

You can extend or alter FreeHand 3 by creating external resource files. When you start FreeHand, it checks the Aldus folder in your system folder for the presence of any files with the file type FHX3. If it finds them, it loads the resources inside them, and uses those resources as it would any other resources inside the program. When FreeHand finds an external resource file with the same resource ID as one inside the application, it uses the external resource.

You can use this feature to alter or extend FreeHand however you like. Altsys has already released their first major external resource file "EPS Exchange" (which gives FreeHand the ability to export in the Illustrator 3.0 and Illustrator '88 EPS formats), and you can expect other developers to take advantage of this new power. I know I have. For more on external resource files, see page 412.

FreeHand Basics

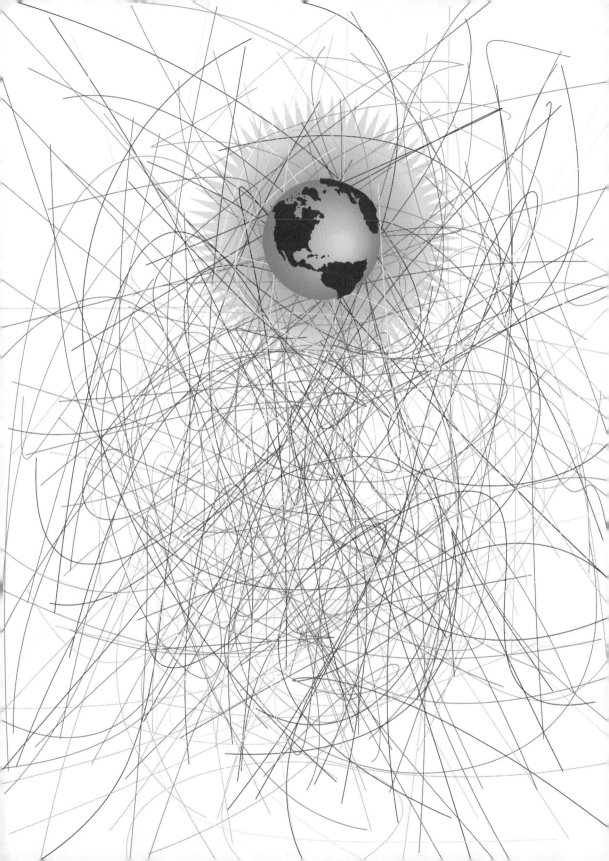

If you've been watching the computer news lately, you've probably seen quite a bit about virtual reality—about cyberspace cowboys breaking into banks in Tokyo, underworld dealings for glittering pyramids of military data, and so on. Something the press hasn't caught on to yet is that every computer program is a virtual reality of some sort.

In this chapter, I'll tell you how you can expect FreeHand to look and behave, and I'll try to give you my conceptual overview of the virtual reality that is FreeHand. There'll be lots of definitions of terms (how can you know what I'm talking about unless we're using the same vocabulary?) and "maps" of FreeHand's screen (how can you tell where you're going unless you know the lay of the land?). Some of the concepts and practices covered here are covered in greater depth in other chapters. In those cases, I'll provide a cross reference to the more detailed explanation.

I'll also be going through techniques for changing the way Free-Hand looks and behaves, because I believe that the tools you use should fit your working habits. Someday, all of our software will be completely modular and completely customizeable, but, until that day arrives, there's always ResEdit.

At the end of the chapter, I'll run through my list of rules for using FreeHand. Take them or leave them; there are many different ways to approach FreeHand, and my methods are not necessarily the ones that'll work best for you. Some of my habits are rooted in the dim past (giant ground sloths, woolly mammoths, and Linotronic L300s with

PostScript version 47.1 RIP IIs roamed the earth) and may not apply in the shiny, new world of infinite imagesetter RAM and faster-than-light RIPs we'll be living in when this book actually reaches the bookstores.

Page and Pasteboard

When you open or create a FreeHand publication, you view and work on the publication in the publication window (see Figure 1-1). Like its sibling PageMaker, FreeHand is modeled around the concept of a page—an area on which you place graphic elements. The page floats in the middle of the pasteboard—an area you can use for temporary storage of the elements you're working with.

Objects can extend past the edge of the page, into an area of the pasteboard that's defined as the bleed. The publication's bleed is shown in the publication window by a dotted line surrounding the page.

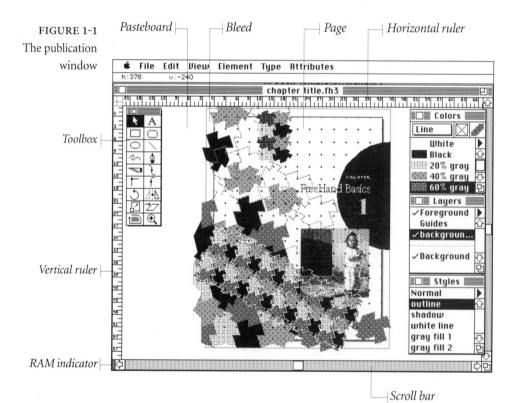

FIGURE 1-1
The publication
window

Pasteboard
Bleed
Page
Horizontal ruler
Toolbox
Vertical ruler
RAM indicator
Scroll bar

The size of the bleed, the page size, and the size of the paper in your printer affect each other. In FreeHand, the page size you define in the Document setup dialog box should be the same as the final size of the document's page after it's been printed by a commercial printer. You define the paper size—the physical size of the paper in your printer—in the Print options dialog box. When you're printing to an imagesetter, the paper size is a defined area on the imagesetter's film roll.

If your publication's page size (without the bleed) is the same as the paper size you've chosen in the Print options dialog box, you can expect FreeHand to neatly clip off the bleed area you've specified. Choose a larger paper size in the Print options dialog box than your publication's page size if you want to print bleeds—choose "Letter.Extra" when you're printing a letter-size publication with a bleed, for example. If you're interested in creating new paper sizes for imagesetters (I don't know of any laser printer that can handle custom paper sizes), see "Rewriting PPDs and PDXs" in Chapter 7, "Printing."

You can have as many publications open as FreeHand can fit into your machine's RAM. You move between open publications by choosing their file names from the Windows submenu off the View menu or by clicking on their windows, just as you'd switch between applications in MultiFinder (see Figure 1-2).

FIGURE 1-2
Windows submenu

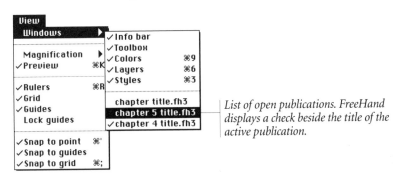

List of open publications. FreeHand displays a check beside the title of the active publication.

RAM Indicator

At the lower-left corner of the publication window is FreeHand's RAM indicator. If you have enough RAM available for FreeHand's new "smooth drawing" feature (see "Smooth Drawing" in "What's New in FreeHand 3?"), the RAM indicator is gray. If the RAM indicator is half gray, you'll be able to use smooth drawing some of the time, and if the RAM indicator is white, there's not enough RAM available to use smooth drawing at all. If your RAM indicator is white, and you have plenty of RAM, try increasing the amount of RAM available to Free-Hand. Note that this RAM allocation only applies if you're using MultiFinder (or System 7).

If you're using the (pre-System 7) Finder, and FreeHand's RAM indicator is still white even though you think you have lots of RAM, you'll need to find out what's taking up all of your memory. Suspect INITs and cdevs first—they're usually the culprits.

To increase the amount of RAM, quit FreeHand. Once you're in the MultiFinder, locate and select your copy of FreeHand and press Command-I. The Finder displays a dialog box containing information about FreeHand. In the lower-right corner of the dialog box you'll see the Application Memory Size text edit box. Type a larger number in this text edit box ("3000" is a good place to start) and press Command-W to close the dialog box. The next time you start FreeHand, you'll have more RAM to work with (see Figure 1-3).

FIGURE 1-3
Increasing the amount
of RAM allocated to
FreeHand

Select the Aldus
FreeHand 3.0 icon and
press Command-I.

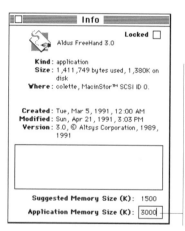

*Type a new
number here
and close this
dialog box by
pressing
Command-W.
The next time
you start
FreeHand, it'll
run in a larger
memory
partition.*

FreeHand's Toolbox and Palettes

Above the page and pasteboard float the FreeHand Toolbox, Info bar, and any of three palettes: Layers, Colors, and Styles. The Toolbox is where you choose what tool you want to work with (see Figure 1-4).

Across the top of the publication window is the Info bar. The Info bar displays information about the current state of the selected object and the position of the cursor or selected object. You can move or hide the Info bar, but you can't resize it (see Figure 1-5).

The palettes are an integral part of FreeHand's new user interface, and are the key to working with layers, colors, and styles (see Figure 1-6). Each palette has an attached submenu. Position the cursor over the arrow at the top of the palette and hold down the mouse button to display the submenu.

FIGURE 1-4
FreeHand's Toolbox

FIGURE 1-5
FreeHand's Info bar

Info bar showing that you've got nothing selected, and that your cursor is off the page. "h" shows the horizontal position of the cursor; "v" shows the vertical position of the cursor. FreeHand measures these coordinates from the publication's current zero point.

When you rotate an object, the Info bar looks like this. "ch" shows the horizontal center of the object; "cv" shows the vertical center; "angle" shows you the angle of rotation.

FIGURE 1-6
FreeHand's floating
palettes

To use the submenus attached to FreeHand's palettes...

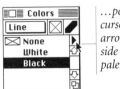 *...position the cursor over the arrow on the side of the palette...*

 *...and make a choice from the submenu.*

Rulers

Command-R displays or hides FreeHand's rulers, handy measuring tools that appear along the top and left sides of your publication window (see Figure 1-7). They're marked off in the units of measurement specified in the Document setup dialog box. The actual increments shown on the rulers vary with the current page view; you'll see more ruler tick marks and finer increments at 800% size than you'll see at 12.5% size.

FIGURE 1-7
FreeHand's rulers

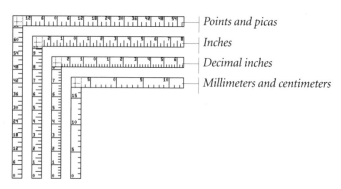

Points and picas
Inches
Decimal inches
Millimeters and centimeters

As you move the cursor, dotted lines in the rulers (called shadow cursors) display the cursor's position relative to the rulers (see Figure 1-8).

The point where the ruler guides intersect is called the zero point (see Figure 1-9). The zero point marker (two intersecting, dotted lines

FIGURE 1-8
Shadow cursors

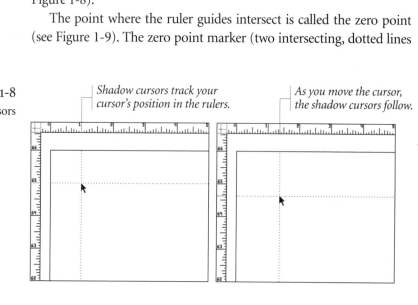

Shadow cursors track your cursor's position in the rulers.

As you move the cursor, the shadow cursors follow.

inside the zero point) is used for resetting the point from which the rulers start measuring (also called the 0,0 point).

To move the zero point, point at the zero point marker, press the mouse button, and then drag the zero point marker to a new position. As you drag, intersecting dotted lines show you the position of the zero point. When you've moved the zero point to the location you want, release the mouse button. The rulers now mark off their increments based on a new starting point (see Figure 1-10).

If you need to reposition only the horizontal or vertical ruler's zero point, just drag the zero point marker along the other ruler—the one you don't want to change—until the zero point is where you want it (see Figure 1-11).

FIGURE 1-9
Zero point

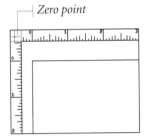

FIGURE 1-10
Repositioning
the zero point

FIGURE 1-11
Repositioning only one
of the zero points

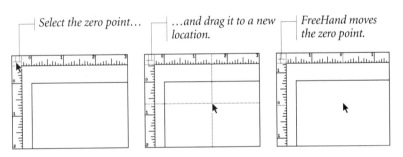

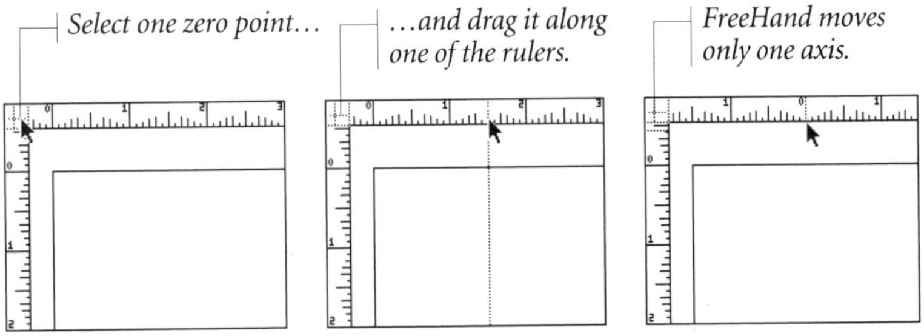

Ruler Guides

Ruler guides are nonprinting guidelines you use when you're aligning items on a page. To position a vertical or horizontal ruler guide, position the cursor over one of the rulers, press the mouse button, and then drag the cursor onto the page or pasteboard. As you drag the cursor off the ruler, a dotted line follows the cursor, showing you the position of your new ruler guide. When the dotted line falls where you want it, release the mouse button. FreeHand positions a new ruler guide at this position (see Figure 1-12).

FIGURE 1-12
Positioning
a ruler guide

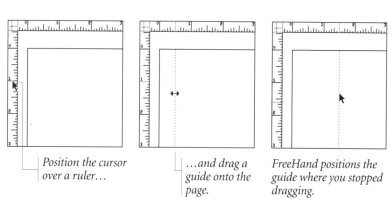

Position the cursor over a ruler...

...and drag a guide onto the page.

FreeHand positions the guide where you stopped dragging.

There's no limit to the number of ruler guides you can use in a publication.

When you want to remove a ruler guide, just position the pointer tool above the ruler guide, hold down the mouse button, and drag the ruler guide off the page or over another ruler guide (see Figure 1-13). If

FIGURE 1-13
Removing a ruler guide

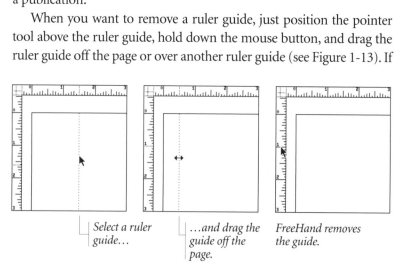

Select a ruler guide...

...and drag the guide off the page.

FreeHand removes the guide.

you can't select the ruler guide, you've probably got "Lock guides" turned on. Turn it off by choosing "Lock guides" from the View menu.

Ruler guides are especially useful in conjunction with the Snap to guides option (turn this option on and off with Command-;). When you've got "Snap to guides" turned on, objects within a certain distance (which you specify in the Preferences dialog box) automatically snap into alignment with the ruler guide (see Figure 1-14, and for more on snapping in general, see "Snap-to Distance" later in this chapter).

To see how "Snap to guides" works, turn on "Snap to guides," draw a box, position a ruler guide, and drag the box toward the guide. When the box gets within a certain distance of the guide, it snaps to the guide. You can almost feel the magnetic pull of the guide in the mouse as you move the box closer to the guide. There's nothing actually affecting the movement of your mouse, of course, but it's a useful illusion.

FIGURE 1-14
"Snap to guides"

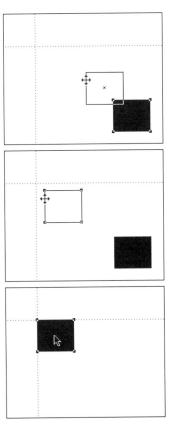

When you're dragging an object with "Snap to guides" turned on, nothing happens…

…until you drag the object within a certain distance of a ruler guide. At this point, the guides seem to pull the object toward them…

…until the object snaps to the guide (or guides).

Moving Around in Your Publication

FreeHand offers many ways to change your view of the publication. The most obvious way is to use the scroll bars. These days, it's a wonder any Macintosh applications still have scroll bars. I'm glad that they're there, but, ordinarily, I use zooming (that is, changing magnifications of the view of the publication) to move from one area of the page or pasteboard to another. The View menu offers several different magnifications and several keyboard shortcuts (see Table 1-1).

All of these commands except "Fit in window" center the currently selected object in the publication window. If there's no object selected, these shortcuts zoom in or out based on the center of the current view. "Fit in window" centers the publication in the publication window. This makes "Fit in window" the perfect "zoom-out" shortcut.

TABLE 1-1
Magnifications and
their shortcuts

View	Command
Fit in window	Command-W
12.5%	None
25%	None
50%	Command-5
75%	Command-7
100%	Command-1
200%	Command-2
400%	Command-4
800%	Command-8

Another zooming method: choose the magnifying glass, point at an area in your publication, and click. FreeHand zooms to the next larger view size (based on your current view—from 100% to 200%, for example), centering the area you clicked on in the publication window. Hold down Option and the magnifying glass tool changes to the reduction glass tool. Click the reduction glass tool and you'll zoom out to the next smaller view size. Hold down Command-Spacebar to change any tool into the "zoom-in" magnifying glass; or hold down Option-Command-Spacebar to change any tool into the "zoom-out" reduction glass (see Figure 1-15).

FIGURE 1-15
Magnifying glass

Press Command-Spacebar to turn any tool into the Magnifying glass and click to zoom in to the next magnification level.

FreeHand zooms to the next magnification level. To zoom back out, hold down Command-Option-Spacebar to turn any tool into the reduction glass, and click again.

You can also move your view of the publication using the grabber hand. If you hold down the Spacebar, and then hold down the mouse button, the cursor turns into the grabber hand. As long as you keep the mouse button down, you can slide the publication around in the publication window (see Figure 1-16).

Never forget that you can change your view by dragging objects off the screen. If you know an object should be moved to some point below your current view, just select the object and drag the cursor off the bottom of the publication window. The publication window scrolls as long as the cursor is off the bottom of the screen and the mouse button is down. Sometimes it's the best way to get something into position (see Figure 1-17).

FIGURE 1-16
Grabber hand

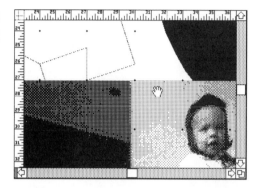

Hold down Spacebar with any tool selected to turn the cursor into the grabber hand.

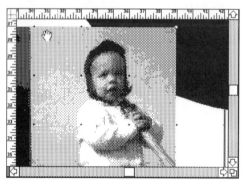

Use the grabber hand to drag your publication around in the publication window.

FIGURE 1-17
Moving by dragging

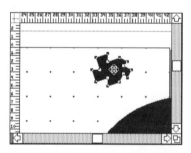

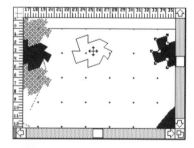

As you drag an object, FreeHand scrolls the current window to keep up with your dragging.

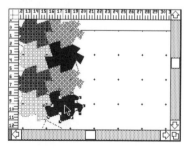

Tip:
What's the Most
Accurate View in
FreeHand?

Lots of FreeHand users have noticed that elements seem to shift slightly as they zoom in and out, and have wondered which magnification is the most accurate. It's simple: it's the 800% view. Interestingly, the "Fit in window" view is pretty good, too. If something's a point off in the 800% view, it sometimes looks like it's about a mile away in the "Fit in window" view. Which is good. You want to know when lines aren't where you want them, so a little exaggeration is a good thing. The final arbiters of accuracy are the numbers in the object info dialog boxes. If points don't seem to line up, select them by turn and look at their object info dialog boxes. By comparing their numeric positions, you'll know exactly where they are, and whether they're where you want them.

Viewing Modes

Another way to change your view of the page is to choose to view the page in Preview or Keyline mode. In Preview mode, FreeHand renders the objects you've drawn as they'll be printed. In Keyline mode, Free-Hand shows you only the outlines of the objects on the page (see Figure 1-18).

Both views have advantages and disadvantages. Preview is handy because you can see something resembling the printed publication, but takes longer to display on the screen; Keyline view redraws quickly but doesn't usually resemble the printed publication. It's easier to select points in Keyline view, and it's easier to select objects in Preview mode. You'll find yourself switching between Preview and Keyline often. The keyboard shortcut for toggling between Keyline and Preview modes is Command-K.

FIGURE 1-18
Preview and
Keyline views

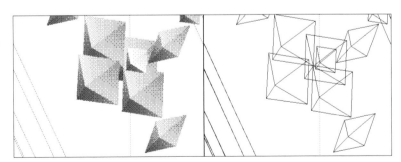

Preview mode shows you the objects in your publication as they'll be printed.

Keyline mode shows you only the outlines of the objects in your publication, and renders imported images as boxes with an "x" through them.

Working with the Document Setup Dialog Box

The first thing you do when creating a publication is to set up your page using the Document setup dialog box (see Figure 1-19). You can always return to the Document setup dialog box and make changes, if you need to; changing the values here only changes the underlying page and its associated settings, and won't change anything you've drawn or imported.

FIGURE 1-19
Document setup
dialog box

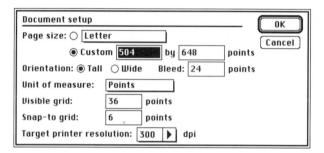

Page Size. Generally, you'll want to enter the page size you want for your printed publication. I see far too many people (especially those who should know better) laying out single business cards in the middle of a 51-by-66-pica (that's 8.5-by-11-inch) page. Try not to do this; it wastes film and time when you go to your imagesetting service bureau (if you own an imagesetter yourself, it's even more important). If you need to have elements extend beyond the edge of the page, use the Bleed option, described later in this section.

You can specify any page size from 6 by 6 picas (1 inch square) to 240 by 240 picas (40 inches square). However, as you specify your page size, remember the paper sizes available for the printer you'll be using for your final printing. Linotronic L300s, for example, have a film roll that, while very long, is only 11.7 inches wide (11.9 inches on newer models). When you need the larger page sizes, you can always look for an imagesetter with a wider film roll, or you can print tiles (selected parts) of your publication and paste them together. Tiling is ugly, and I try to avoid it. There are often better ways to create large layouts (I tend to create them small, print them at high resolution, then enlarge them using conventional photographic methods).

Orientation. Choose "Tall" if your publication is taller than it is wide, and choose "Wide" if the reverse is true. Once again, try to keep the printer you'll be using for your final printing in mind. In some cases, you might find yourself laying things out sideways to get them onto a film roll's limited width (though you can flip the printing orientation of your publication by rewriting the APD or PPD file you're using).

Bleed. Enter the amount of space you want to print that extends beyond the edge of the page. The value you enter here is added to all four sides of the page. Again, keep the page sizes of your final output device in mind as you enter the bleed area. If your publication's page size is 10 by 12 picas and your imagesetter's page size is 11 by 13 picas, the largest bleed area you'd be able to use is 6 points (though you could always rewrite the APD or PPD file you're using to accommodate a larger bleed).

Unit of Measure. Choose your favorite unit of measure from the pop-up menu. I prefer points and/or picas, because they're the measurement system of type, and type is the backbone of all of my designs, but I'll try not to be a fascist about it. You can always override the current unit of measure for setting your type in dialog boxes, as shown in Table 1-2.

Value you want	Type this in the dialog box
7 inches	7i
22 points	0p22
11 picas	11p
6 picas, 6 points	6p6
23.4 millimeters	23.4m

TABLE 1-2
Overriding units
of measure

Visible Grid. A new feature in FreeHand 3 is the ability to display a nonprinting grid on your page. Enter a value in the Visible grid text edit box, and FreeHand positions a grid (represented by cross hairs at grid intersections) on the page, starting the grid at the 0,0 point on the ruler guides (see Figure 1-20). If you move the zero point of the ruler guides, the visible grid moves, too.

FIGURE 1-20

Visible grid

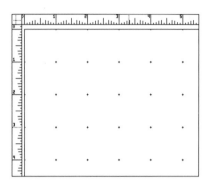

Snap-to Grid. This grid is essentially the same as FreeHand 2's Grid size setting. It creates an invisible grid on your page, starting the grid at the lower-left corner of the page (see Figure 1-21). The Snap-to grid, like the visible grid, moves when you move the zero point.

Objects snap to this grid when the Snap to grid command (from the View menu) is active. While this grid is not necessarily the same thing as the visible grid, you'll often want to set your Snap-to grid to the same units as your visible grid so that you can see what you're snapping to. For more on snapping in general, see "Snap-to Distance" later in this chapter.

FIGURE 1-21

Invisible grid

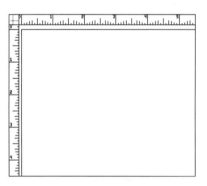

You can't see it, but it's there—FreeHand's Snap-to grid is one of the handiest tools in the application. Because you can't see it, it's a good idea to set up your visible grid so that it has some relation to the Snap-to grid.

Target Printer Resolution. Type a value here for the resolution of the printer you intend to use for final output of this publication, or choose a value from the defaults listed in the pop-up menu. FreeHand uses this value for sizing bilevel bitmaps to the resolution of the output device ("magic stretching," to you PageMaker fans out there). For more on why you need to stretch bilevel bitmaps to your printer's resolution, see "Resizing Images to Your Printer's Resolution" in Chapter 4, "Importing and Exporting."

Using the Page Setup Dialog Box

The Page setup command brings up the Apple LaserWriter driver's dialog boxes and printing options. Almost every command in these dialog boxes is overridden by your settings in FreeHand's Print and Print options dialog boxes, assuming you're printing to a PostScript printer.

There's still one incredibly important setting you've got to specify in these dialog boxes, however. Choose "Page setup..." from the File menu to bring up the LaserWriter Page Setup dialog box. Click the Options button. The LaserWriter Options dialog box appears. Click the Unlimited downloadable fonts in a document check box (if it's already checked, leave it checked), and then press Return twice to close the dialog boxes (see Figure 1-22).

FIGURE 1-22

Turning on the Unlimited down-loadable fonts in a document option

Choose "Page setup..." from the File menu.

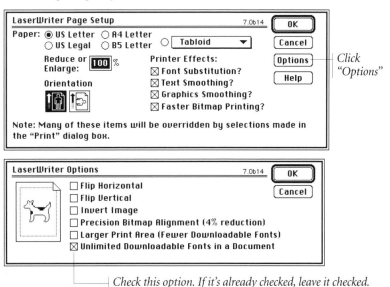

Check this option. If it's already checked, leave it checked.

Many jobs that FreeHand would otherwise print have been cancelled because this simple option was not turned on. If your job isn't printing, try turning this option on. Better yet, turn it on in your default file so that you don't have to turn it on in every publication (see "Setting FreeHand's Defaults," later in this chapter).

Preferences

FreeHand 2 had lots of different preferences settings that people never understood or used, and FreeHand 3 has even more. It's worth learning what the different choices are, however, because the Preferences dialog box is the one place inside FreeHand where you can truly fine-tune FreeHand's performance and behavior (see Figure 1-23).

FIGURE 1-23
Preferences dialog box

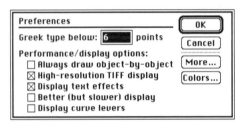

Greek Type Below *N* Points. This option displays type as a gray bar if it's shorter, in pixels, than the point size you enter. As you zoom close to the text, you'll see the characters in the text block again (see Figure 1-24). This happens because the type's taller, in pixels, at larger magnifications. The size of the type, in points, hasn't actually changed. So why does the dialog box say "points?" Beats me.

The advantage of using this option is that greeked type redraws much faster than the actual characters, thereby speeding up your screen display. This option applies to both Preview and Keyline views.

FIGURE 1-24
Greeked type

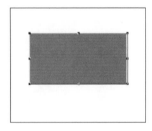

24-point type at 100% view; "Greek type below…" set to 6 points.

24-point type at 100% view; "Greek type below…" set to 100 points.

Tip:
Greek All (or
Almost All)

You can always choose to greek all (almost, anyway…) of the text in your document at most views by entering "200"—the largest value you can enter—in the Greek type below text edit box. This will greek all type below 200 points at the 100% view, and all type below 400 points at most Fit in window views (the exact magnification of the Fit in window view depends on the size of your page).

Always Draw Object-by-object. From your Macintosh's point of view, you're very slow. And you don't do very much work. FreeHand makes use of the spare time between your mouse clicks and keystrokes drawing all of the objects in your publication—off screen, where you can't see them. Then, when you do something that requires FreeHand to redraw the screen, it blasts them onto the screen at once. This results in faster screen display of your publication.

The only drawback to the off-screen drawing technique is that it consumes more memory than drawing each object individually when redrawing the screen. Therefore, any time RAM is limited, FreeHand draws object-by-object. There is no difference in display quality between the two options.

If you're running FreeHand with less than 1.5MB of RAM allocated to it, check this option.

High-resolution TIFF Display. If you check this option, FreeHand gets its information about how to render a TIFF from the original TIFF file that's linked to your FreeHand publication, which means that Free-Hand renders the best possible display of the TIFF image for your current magnification level. With this option off, FreeHand constructs a low-resolution screen version of the image and uses it for display at all magnification levels (see Figure 1-25).

FIGURE 1-25
High- and low-resolution TIFF display options

Low-resolution TIFF display   *High-resolution TIFF display*

The tradeoff? Speed of screen redraw. High-resolution TIFF images can take forever to draw on your screen. Given this, it's a good idea to leave this option unchecked until you absolutely must see the TIFFs at their best resolution.

Display Text Effects. The Display text effects option displays any of FreeHand's text effects you've applied to text blocks in your publication. If you don't turn this option on, you'll see the text displayed at the correct size and leading, but without the effects. If the text effects extend beyond the text block (zoom text can, for example), the selection rectangle shows the extent of the text and the effects when you move the text block. Turning this option on shows you your text effects, but slows down your screen display (see Figure 1-26).

FIGURE 1-26
Display text
effects option

"Zoom text" effect with
"Display text effects" on

"Zoom text" effect with
"Display text effects" off

Better (but Slower) Display. When the Better (but slower) display option is turned off, FreeHand draws graduated and radial fills on screen more rapidly, using fewer gray steps to render them. Turn it on to see a better representation of your fills on screen. This option has no effect on the printing of the fills.

Display Curve Levers. When the Display curve levers option is on, FreeHand displays a straight line connecting any curve control handles attached to a selected point. FreeHand also displays curve levers attached to the line segment from the points both preceding and following the selected point along the path (see Figure 1-27).

FIGURE 1-27
Display curve
levers option

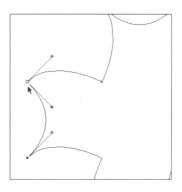

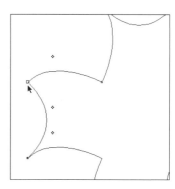

"Display curve levers" on   *"Display curve levers" off*

With this option off, you just see the curve control handles, not the levers connecting them to points on the path.

It's best to turn this option on, because, at higher magnification, it's good to be able to see if points have curve handles that might be off the current display. It also makes it easier to see which curve handles apply to which point.

More Preferences

Click the More... button in the Preferences dialog box to display the More preferences dialog box (see Figure 1-28). I'm hoping that Free-Hand 4 will have a Yet more preferences dialog box, or a Son of more preferences dialog box. The possibilities are endless.

Number of Undo's. This option sets the number of actions held in FreeHand's "Undo" queue. Enter smaller numbers here if you find you don't use that many levels of "Undo," or want to save memory. Enter larger numbers here if you change your mind a lot and don't like the

FIGURE 1-28
More preferences
dialog box

More preferences	OK
Number of undo's:	8
Snap-to distance:	3 pixels
Cursor key distance:	0.5 points
Guides color:	
Grid color:	
☒ Changing elements changes defaults	
☒ Save palette positions	

idea of using "Save as…" and "Revert" when you're experimenting with possibilities. Remember, however, that each level of "Undo" adds to the amount of RAM that FreeHand uses (the amount of RAM consumed depends on the action). You can enter any number from 1 to 99 in this text edit box.

Snap-to Distance. FreeHand has lots of different "Snaps." There's "Snap to guides," "Snap to point," "Snap-to distance," "Snap to grid," and, for good measure, "Snap-to grid." Is there an echo in here? I'll explain.

"Snap to point" is a command on the View menu, and makes Free-Hand points snap together when you get within a certain distance of them. "Snap to guides" is also a command on the View menu, and snaps objects to ruler guides when you drag the object within a certain distance of them. "Snap to grid" is also a command on the View menu, and makes objects snap to an underlying grid—the "Snap-to" grid (which you define in the Document setup dialog box).

The number you enter in the Snap-to distance text edit box sets the distance (in screen pixels), that all of the "Snap" commands rely on. Set the Snap-to distance option to 5 pixels, and the next time you drag an object within 5 pixels of an active "Snap" point (point, ruler guide, or grid intersection), FreeHand snaps the object to that point.

If you just can't seem to get one point to land on top of another so that you can close a path or connect the end of one path to the end of another (see "Open and Closed Paths" in Chapter 2, "Drawing," for more on closing paths), try increasing the number in the Snap-to distance text edit box. If, on the other hand, you're having a hard time keeping points from snapping together, enter a smaller number in the Snap-to distance text edit box.

Cursor Key Distance. The Cursor key distance option sets the distance a selected object moves when you use the arrow keys to "nudge" an object. See "Nudge Keys" in "What's New in FreeHand 3?" for more on moving objects using the arrow keys.

Guides Color. Click on the color swatch. The Select guideline color dialog box appears (I call this dialog box the Apple Color picker dialog box). Click on the color in the color wheel you want to use for the nonprinting guides in your publication and press Return to close the dialog box (see Figure 1-29).

FIGURE 1-29
Apple Color picker
dialog box

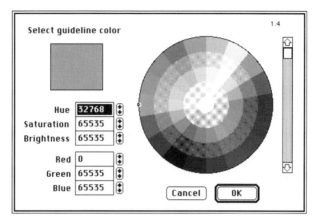

This dialog box appears in several different situations in FreeHand. I call it the Apple Color Picker dialog box.

Grid Color. Click on the color swatch to display the Select grid color dialog box. Click on a color in the color wheel for your grid marks, and then press Return to close the dialog box.

Changing Elements Changes Defaults If you check the Changing elements changes defaults option, any changes you make to a selected object's attributes (colors, type specifications, fills, and lines) are carried over to the next object you create. For example, if you've created a line and set its line width to 6 points and its color to 20-percent gray, the next line you create has the same line width and color.

When this option's unchecked, you set defaults for the entire document by making changes to object attributes (colors, fills, lines, type specifications, and so on) without having any object selected. In this case, each new object picks up the publication's default attributes regardless of what changes have been made to selected objects created or modified previously.

Save Palette Positions. Check the Save palette positions option if you want FreeHand to remember the positions of the toolbox, and of the Layers, Colors, and Styles palettes. The next time you open the publication, these items will be where you left them.

Customizing Your Color Display. If you press the Colors... button in the Preferences dialog box, the Display color setup dialog box appears (see Figure 1-30).

Use this dialog box to adjust FreeHand's color display. Click on the Cyan, Magenta, and Yellow buttons to select the colors you want from the Apple Color picker dialog box. Which colors are correct? I use the settings shown in Table 1-3. You might want to use something else, depending on your monitor and viewing environment.

You can also adjust the colors by holding a color monitor adjustment card next to your screen and modifying your display colors until they match the printed card. Ideally, you'd use printed process color swatches from the commercial printer and press you intend to use to produce the publication, printed on the paper stock you've chosen for the job. In practical terms, the monitor adjustment card works pretty well.

You don't need to adjust the other colors—once you've set Cyan, Yellow, and Magenta, FreeHand will adjust the other colors accord-

FIGURE 1-30
Display color setup
dialog box

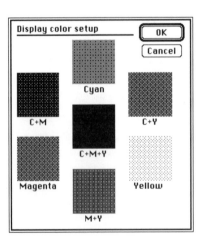

Click on one of the color swatches to change the way FreeHand displays that color.

TABLE 1-3 HSB and HLS color settings for process colors	Color	H	L	S	R	G	B
	Cyan	32768	65535	65535	0	65535	65535
	Magenta	54614	65535	65535	65535	0	65535
	Yellow	10922	65535	65535	65535	65535	0
	Black	65535	65535	65535	65535	65535	65535

ingly (though you won't see a difference in the dialog box display until you close and reopen the dialog box).

These adjustments are for screen display only and have nothing to do with the percentages of process colors FreeHand will print. Specify your colors by referring to printed samples of the spot or process colors you want to use. For more on specifying colors, refer to Chapter 6, "Color."

Setting FreeHand's Defaults

If you want to keep FreeHand's original defaults, but just want to add a couple of things, open the file named ALDUS FREEHAND DEFAULTS that's in the same folder as your copy of FreeHand, make the changes you want, and save the file as a template. If you want to make more drastic changes to FreeHand's defaults, just create a publication with the defaults you want, then save it as a template named ALDUS FREEHAND DEFAULTS in the same folder as your copy of FreeHand.

Tip:
Reverting to
FreeHand's
Original Defaults

If you've gotten hopelessly away from FreeHand's original defaults and want to go back to them, just copy the backup you made of the original default file into your FreeHand folder, overwriting the one you've been mucking about with. What? You didn't back it up? I never do either. To get it back (and, incidentally, to expand—decompress—any one file from the original FreeHand disks without having to go back through the installation process), locate the file on the original Disk 1. This is the compressed FreeHand defaults file. Double-click the file. This will probably launch the Aldus Installer Utility, which is hiding somewhere on your drive. If it doesn't launch the Installer, you'll have to copy the Installer from the original Disk 1 and try again.

The Installer expands the file and copies it into your FreeHand folder, replacing the modified FreeHand defaults file.

Using FreeHand's Toolbox

Some of the following descriptions of the tool functions aren't going to make any sense unless you understand how FreeHand's points and paths work, and that discussion falls in "Points and Paths," later in this chapter. You can flip ahead and read that section, or you can plow through this section, get momentarily confused (remember that confusion is a great state for learning), and then become enlightened when you reach the descriptions of points and paths. Or you can flip ahead to Chapter 2, "Drawing" for even more on points and paths. It's your choice, and either method works. This is precisely the sort of non-linear information gathering which hypertext gurus say can't be done in books.

You can break FreeHand's toolbox into four conceptual sections (as shown in Figure 1-31): tools for drawing basic shapes (the square-corner, ellipse, round-corner, and line tools); path-drawing tools (the pen, freehand, corner tool, and curve tools, also known as the freeform drawing tools); transformation tools (the rotate, reflect, skew, and scale tools); and other tools (the pointer, text, knife, trace, and magnifying glass tools).

The basic shape tools draw complete paths containing specific numbers of points in specific positions on the path, while the path-drawing tools draw paths point by point. Both types of drawing tools are useful in different circumstances.

The transformation tools act on objects you've drawn, typed, or imported. Of the "other" tools, the pointer tool is for selecting objects, the text tool is for entering (but not editing) text, the knife tool is for splitting points and paths, and the magnifying glass tool is for changing your view of your publication.

FIGURE 1-31
The FreeHand Toolbox

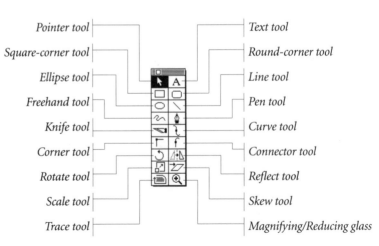

Pointer tool	Text tool
Square-corner tool	Round-corner tool
Ellipse tool	Line tool
Freehand tool	Pen tool
Knife tool	Curve tool
Corner tool	Connector tool
Rotate tool	Reflect tool
Scale tool	Skew tool
Trace tool	Magnifying/Reducing glass

Pointer Tool. You use the pointer tool to select, size, and move objects. You can reach the pointer tool temporarily by holding down Command when any other tool is selected.

Text Tool. You enter text using the text tool. Select the text tool and click on a point in the publication window, and the Text dialog box appears. The Text dialog box is used for both entering and editing text. What can drive you crazy (until you get used to it) is that you can't directly edit text on the page; you've got to go to the Text dialog box. If you're used to PageMaker or MacDraw, you might expect to be able to click the text tool on text on the page and select or edit it. You can't, so get used to double-clicking the text block with the pointer tool and editing the text in the Text dialog box.

Square-corner Tool. Use the square-corner tool to draw rectangles. If you hold down Shift as you're dragging the square-corner tool, you'll draw perfect squares. Note that you can always draw rectangles and squares using the other drawing tools, but that the rectangles drawn using the square-corner tool have their own object info dialog box that offers some special capabilities. Press 1 on the numeric keypad to select the square-corner tool.

Round-corner Tool. Use the round-corner tool to draw rectangles with rounded corners. If you hold down Shift as you're dragging the round-corner tool, you'll draw perfect squares with rounded corners. Note that you could always draw round-corner rectangles using the rectangle tool by setting the rectangle's corner radius in its object info dialog box, or by using any of the other drawing tools. Press 2 on the numeric keypad to select the round-corner tool

Ellipse Tool. Use the ellipse tool to draw ellipses. If you hold down Shift as you're dragging the ellipse tool, you'll draw perfect circles. Note that you can always draw ellipses and circles using the other drawing tools, but that the ellipses drawn using the ellipse tool have their own object info dialog box that offers some special capabilities. Press 3 on the numeric keypad to select the ellipse tool.

Line Tool. Use the line tool to draw lines. The lines drawn with the line tool are exactly the same as lines drawn using the square-corner tool. If you hold down Shift as you drag the line tool, the lines you draw will be constrained to 45-degree angles. Press 4 on the numeric keypad to select the line tool.

Freehand Tool. Select the freehand tool, hold down the mouse button, and scribble. The freehand tool creates a path that follows your mouse movements, adding points as it sees fit. If you double-click the freehand tool, the Freehand dialog box appears. In the Freehand dialog box, you can customize the way your freehand tool works. The Tight option draws more points along the path as you draw, and the Connect the dots option connects the points on your path. With "Connect the dots" turned off, the freehand tool simply places a series of points as you draw and waits until you stop drawing to connect them with paths. Press 5 on the numeric keypad to select the freehand tool.

Pen Tool. Use the pen tool to create paths containing both curves and straight line segments. FreeHand 2 users will recognize the pen tool as the combination tool—for some reason it's gotten a new name and icon. Illustrator users will recognize the pen tool immediately, because it works the same as Illustrator's pen tool. Press 6 on the numeric keypad to select the pen tool.

Knife Tool. The knife tool splits paths or points. Just select a path or point, choose the knife tool, point at a path or point, and click, and FreeHand splits the path or point into separate paths where you clicked. FreeHand 2 users will be happy to note that FreeHand 3's knife tool leaves the paths and points exactly where it found them; the FreeHand 2 knife tool had a bad habit of shifting the positions of curved paths as it split them. Press 7 on the numeric keypad to select the knife tool. For more on splitting paths, see "Splitting Paths" in Chapter 2, "Drawing."

Curve Tool. Use the curve tool to create curve points. Curve points create curved line segments between them and the preceding and following points on a path. Press 8 on the numeric keypad to select the curve tool.

Corner Tool. Use the corner tool to create corner points. Corner points usually create a straight path between the current point and the preceding point on the path. You can always curve line segments between any set of points, however. Press 9 on the numeric keypad to select the corner tool.

Connector Tool. I've been using FreeHand for years, and I still have no idea what you use the connector tool for. The connector tool adds a connector point to the path, and connector points create smooth curved line segments between corner and curve points. I'd probably drag a curve control handle out of the corner point to do this. Press 0 on the numeric keypad to select the connector tool.

Rotation Tool. Use the rotation tool to rotate an object around the object's center, or around some other fixed point.

Reflection Tool. Use the reflection tool to reflect (create a mirror image of) an object around the object's vertical or horizontal axis (or both), around an angled axis, or around a fixed point.

Scaling Tool. Use the scaling tool to scale (or resize) an object around the object's center or around some fixed point. You can scale objects vertically, horizontally, both vertically and horizontally, and both proportionally and nonproportionally.

Skewing Tool. Use the skewing tool to skew an object. Skewing alters the vertical or horizontal axes (or both) of objects, which makes them look as if they're on a plane that's slanted relative to the plane of the publication.

Trace Tool. Use the trace tool to automatically trace objects. If you double-click the autotrace tool, the Trace dialog box appears. The Tight option adds more points to the paths generated by the tracing process. "Trace background elements" and "Trace foreground elements" are pretty straightforward. Choose "Trace background elements" if you want to trace anything on the default layer "Background," and "Trace foreground elements" if you want to trace things in the foreground layer(s).

Magnifying Glass. Use the magnifying glass to change your view of the publication. Holding down Option changes the magnifying glass (which zooms in) into the reducing glass (which zooms out).

Keyboard Shortcuts

You can choose most of the tools in FreeHand's toolbox through keyboard shortcuts. This is usually faster than going back to the toolbox and clicking on the tool. Table 1-4 shows the keyboard shortcuts for choosing tools.

TABLE 1-4
Keyboard shortcuts
for FreeHand's tools

Tool	Key
Pointer tool	Hold down Command and the current tool turns into the pointer tool. Release Command, and the pointer tool turns back into the tool.
Magnifying glass	Hold down Command-Shift and the current tool turns into the magnifying glass. Release Command-Shift and the magnifying glass turns back into the selected tool.
Reducing glass	Hold down Command-Option-Shift and the current tool turns into the reducing glass. Release Command-Shift and the reducing glass turns back into the selected tool.
Square-corner tool	Numeric keypad 1
Round-corner tool	Numeric keypad 2
Ellipse tool	Numeric keypad 3
Line tool	Numeric keypad 4
Freehand tool	Numeric keypad 5
Pen tool	Numeric keypad 6
Knife tool	Numeric keypad 7
Curve tool	Numeric keypad 8
Corner tool	Numeric keypad 9
Connector tool	Numeric keypad 0

Constraining Tools

Most Macintosh drawing programs (beginning with MacPaint) have the concept of constraint; that holding down some key (usually Shift) makes tools behave differently. Usually, constraint limits tool movement to vertical and horizontal relative to the Macintosh screen, though some applications limit movement to 45-degree increments. Table 1-5 shows how Shift-constraining works in FreeHand.

TABLE 1-5

Effects of constraint on tools

Tool	Constraint
Pointer tool	If you're moving an object, holding down Shift limits the movement of the object to 90-degree increments. If you're selecting objects, holding down Shift extends the selection to include the next object or set of objects you click.
Magnifying glass	None
Reducing glass	None
Square-corner tool	Hold down Shift to draw perfect squares
Round-corner tool	Hold down Shift to draw perfect squares with rounded corners
Ellipse tool	Hold down Shift to draw perfect circles
Line tool	Hold down Shift to constrain the line tool to draw lines in 45-degree increments (that is, 0, 45, and 90 degrees, where 0 degrees is horizontal and 90 degrees is vertical, relative to your publication)
Freehand tool	Hold down Option to constrain line segments straight lines (from the point you held down the key); Option-Shift to constrain line segments to 45-degree angles
Pen tool	Shift constrains the next point placed to a 45-degree tangent from the previous point on the path
Knife tool	None
Curve tool	Same as pen tool
Corner tool	Same as pen tool
Connector tool	Same as pen tool

Additionally, you should note that constraint—holding down Shift—is affected by any Angle setting in the Constrain dialog box (see Figure 1-32). All constraint, including drawing, is based on the angle you enter. If you've entered "30" in the Angle text edit box, basic shapes you create will be constrained to 30 and 120 degrees (see Figure 1-33).

FIGURE 1-32
Setting a
constraint angle

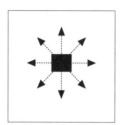

When the constraint angle is 0 (the default), holding down Shift as you drag an object constrains its movement to 45-degree angles.

You can change the constraint angle by choosing "Constrain…" from the Element menu and typing a new angle in the Angle text edit box.

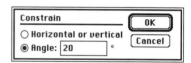

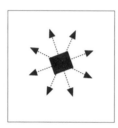

After you've changed the angle, the constraint axes are based on the angle you entered.

FIGURE 1-33
Constraint and
basic shapes

The constraint angle also affects drawing basic shapes.

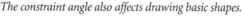

Constraint angle 0

Constraint angle 20

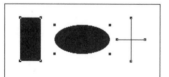
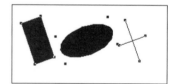

Looking at Things Objectively

FreeHand's world is made up of objects (also called elements)—points, line segments, paths, basic shapes, text blocks, groups, and imported graphics. Each class of object has certain attributes that you can view and edit by selecting the object and choosing "Element info…" from the Element menu (or pressing Command-I). Figure 1-34 shows the different kinds of object info dialog boxes.

FIGURE 1-34
Object info dialog boxes

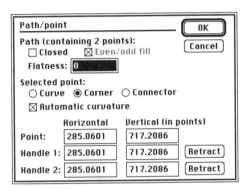

Rectangle dialog box

All of the object info dialog boxes for basic shapes look something like this, showing coordinates and path flatness.

Group

The "Position" shown in the Horizontal and Vertical text edit boxes is that of the center of the group.

Path/point

If you've selected a path, FreeHand displays only the top part of this dialog box. If you've selected a point on a path, FreeHand fills in the information on the specific point.

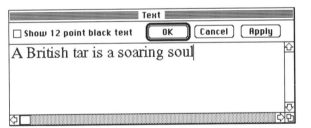

Text block

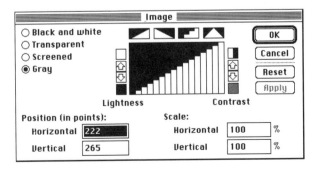

Gray-scale TIFF

If you select a bilevel tiff or paint file, you'll see only two gray level bars in the center of the dialog box.

The object info dialog boxes provide an extremely powerful way of looking at objects in your publication—by the numbers. If you want a rectangle to occupy *exactly* a certain space in your publication, you can always type the numbers right into the dialog box. Can I prove it to you? To position a 6-by-6-pica rectangle 3 picas from the top and 3 picas from the left edge of your publication, follow these steps.

1. Reset the ruler point to the upper-left corner of the publication (see "Rulers," earlier in this chapter).

2. Draw a rectangle with the square-corner tool. Anywhere. I don't care.

3. Without deselecting the rectangle or selecting anything else, press Command-I.

4. In the Top text edit box, type "-3p" (or 3 picas down from the zero point on the vertical ruler). Press Tab. Type "3p" in the Left text edit box (or 3 picas left on the horizontal ruler). Press Tab. Type "-9p" in the Bottom text edit box (which is 3 picas plus 6 picas, our margin plus the height of the rectangle). Press Tab and type "9p" in the Right text edit box (3 picas from the left plus 6 picas to the right edge of our rectangle).

5. Press Return.

The rectangle snaps into the position we specified in the object info dialog box. You could have drawn it, using the shadow cursors, "Snap to guides," or ruler guides, it's true. But, in this case, all you had to do was some simple arithmetic and some typing, and the rectangle is positioned perfectly, exactly where you want it. If you know where something has to go, try using the object info dialog boxes to get it there. It beats dragging, measuring, and waiting for the screen to redraw.

Points and Paths

So much of working with FreeHand depends on understanding the concept of points and paths that I've written about it several times in this book. The following section is an overview of the topic. For more (much more) on points and paths, see "Points and Paths" in Chapter 2, "Drawing."

In FreeHand, continuous lines are called paths. Paths are made up of several points and the line segments drawn between those points. A point can have curve control handles attached to it which control the curve of the line segments associated with the point (see Figure 1-35).

Many people call these handles "control points." I find it confusing talking about two different kinds of "points," so I always call them "control handles" or "curve handles," and use "point" to refer to the point on the path.

FIGURE 1-35
Paths, points, and
control handles

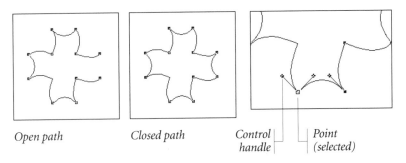

Open path   Closed path   Control   Point
                            handle   (selected)

Types of Points

Points come in several different types, corresponding to the tools introduced earlier in this chapter. Points can appear or be created with or without curve control handles. FreeHand features three kinds of points, each with its own properties.

Curve Points   Curve points add a curved line segment between the preceding and following points along the path. Curve points are shown on screen as small circles, and have curve control handles placed along a straight line from the curve point itself (see Figure 1-36).

The curve handle following the point controls the curve of the line segment following the curve point on the path; the curve handle preceding the point controls the curve of the line segment preceding the curve point on the path. Curve points are typically used for adding smooth curves to a path (see Figure 1-37).

FIGURE 1-36
Curve points

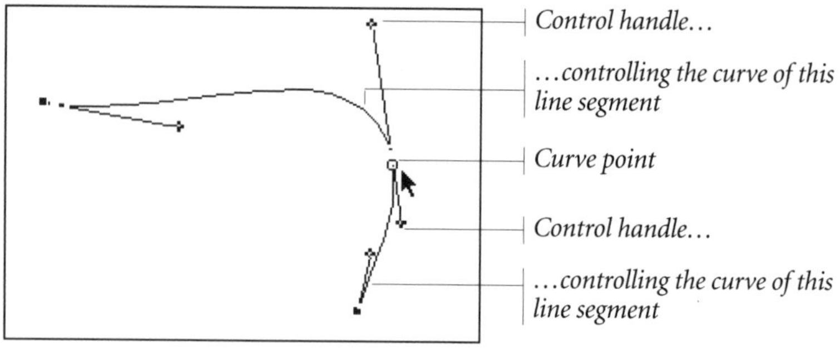

Control handle...

...controlling the curve of this
line segment

Curve point

Control handle...

...controlling the curve of this
line segment

FIGURE 1-37
Adjusting curve handles
on curve points

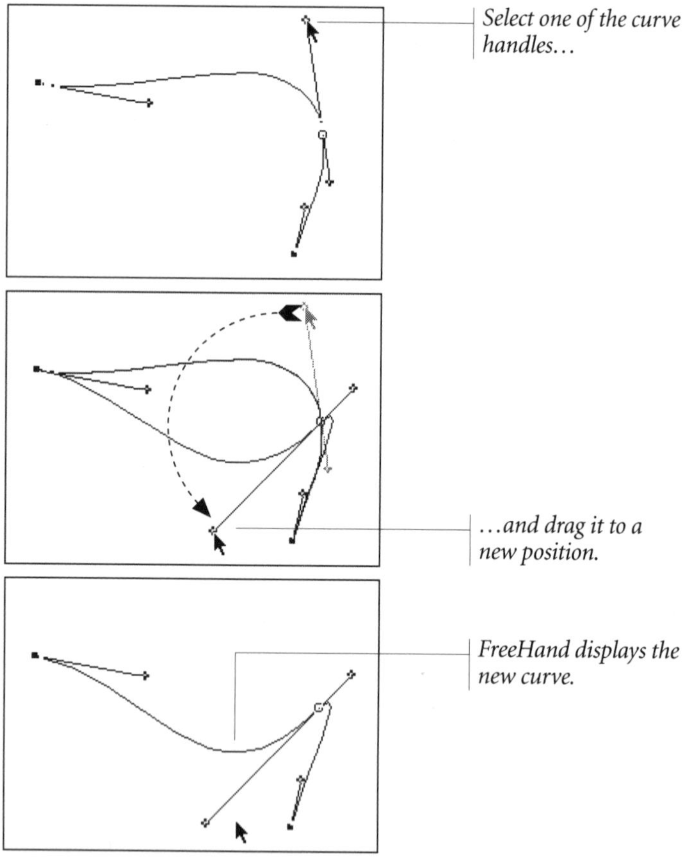

Select one of the curve
handles...

...and drag it to a
new position.

FreeHand displays the
new curve.

Corner Points   Corner points add a straight line segment between the current point
and the preceding point on the path (see Figure 1-38). Corner points
are typically used to create paths containing straight line segments.

You can add curve handles to a corner point by selecting the corner
point, holding down Option, and dragging curve handles out of the

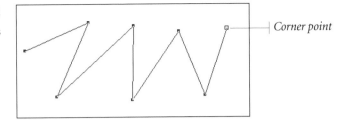

FIGURE 1-38
Corner points

Corner point

corner point. For more on dragging curve handles out of corner points, see "Manipulating Curve Control Handles" in Chapter 2, "Drawing."

Connector Points

A connector point is like a curve or corner point with one curve control handle, and is used to join straight and curved line segments (see Figure 1-39).

You can always drag another curve control handle out of a connector point by selecting the point, holding down Option, and dragging a curve control point out of the connector point. The first curve handle controls the curve of the line segment following the connector point along the path; the second curve handle controls the curve of the line segment preceding the connector point along the path.

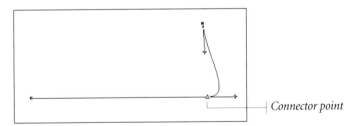

FIGURE 1-39
Connector points

Connector point

What Points Should You Use?

Any type of point can be turned into any other type of point, and anything you can do with one kind of point can be done with any other kind of point. Given these two points (so to speak), you can use the kinds of points and drawing tools you're happiest with and achieve exactly the results you want. There is no "best way" to draw with FreeHand's freeform drawing tools, but it helps to understand how the particular method you choose works.

I always use the corner tool, drawing straight line segments. I add curves later, once I've placed my points where I want them along the path. This seems easiest to me; what you like may be different.

Experiment until you find what method of drawing suits you best. For more on points and paths, see Chapter 2, "Drawing."

Basic Shapes

The square-corner, round-corner, ellipse, and line tools are the tools you use for drawing basic shapes. The line tool draws a straight line segment between two points, which then behaves exactly as if you'd drawn it by placing two corner points. The other three tools all draw paths with specific properties and points in specific places. Objects drawn with the basic shapes tools act like grouped paths, but have certain special properties, as shown in Table 1-6.

If you ungroup any object drawn with the basic shape tools, you won't be able to return to the special object info dialog boxes, and text joined to the path will behave as it would if joined to any path drawn with the freeform drawing tools.

TABLE 1-6 Special properties of basic shapes	Shape	Special properties
	Rectangle	The object info dialog box for these objects contains (drawn with the square-corner tool or the round-corner tool) the x and y (horizontal and vertical) coordinates controlling the width, height, and placement of the rectangle relative to the 0,0 point on the rulers, as well as text edit boxes for specifying its corner radius and flatness. When text is joined to this basic shape, it starts at the upper-left corner of the object.
	Ellipse	The object info dialog box for ellipses contains the x and y coordinates controlling the width, height, and placement of the ellipse relative to the 0,0 point on the rulers, as well as text edit boxes for specifying the object's flatness. When text is joined to this basic shape, it centers across the top of the ellipse.

Text Blocks

FreeHand's text blocks can contain any number of typefaces, colors, and sizes of type. You can also mix FreeHand's text effects inside a text block. FreeHand's text blocks can't handle paragraph formatting, though, so indents, tabs, and paragraph space before and after are out.

You enter text in FreeHand by selecting the text tool and clicking it on the page, typing text in the Text dialog box that appears, then pressing Enter (or clicking OK). A text block appears (see Figure 1-40). PageMaker users will note that FreeHand's text blocks are very similar to PageMaker's.

For more on FreeHand's text-handling capabilities, see Chapter 3, "Text and Type."

FIGURE 1-40
Text blocks

Imported Graphics

FreeHand can import graphics saved in the PICT, EPS, paint-type (MacPaint, SuperPaint, etc.), and TIFF (including color TIFF) formats. PICT graphics are disassembled into their component objects on import (bitmaps inside PICTs are imported as is, though they're sometimes split into strips) and are converted into FreeHand elements you can edit just as if you'd drawn them in FreeHand. EPS graphics you've opened are also converted into FreeHand elements. TIFFs, paint-type, and EPS graphics you've placed are imported and are handled very much like a FreeHand group, except that they cannot be ungrouped. You can use all of FreeHand's transformation tools (for scaling, rotation, reflection, and skewing) to manipulate imported graphics (see Figure 1-41).

For more on working with imported graphics, see Chapter 4, "Importing and Exporting."

FIGURE 1-41
Imported graphics

Selecting and Deselecting Elements

Before you can act on an object, you've got to select it. You select objects by clicking on them, dragging a selection rectangle over them, choosing "Select All" from the Edit menu, or by Shift-selecting (select one object, hold down Shift, and select another object). When you select an object, FreeHand displays the object's selection handles. Free-Hand displays selected objects a little bit differently depending on the method you've used to select them and the type of object you've selected. Figure 1-42 shows you the differences.

To deselect objects, just click on an uninhabited area of the page or pasteboard.

FIGURE 1-42
Selecting objects

Shift-selecting

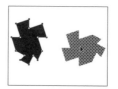

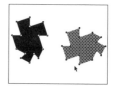

Click on one object to select it.

Hold down Shift, and click on another object.

You've selected both objects.

Selecting objects by dragging a selection rectangle over them

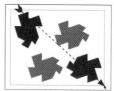

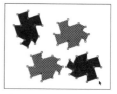

Position the cursor outside the group of objects you want to select...

...and drag a selection rectangle over the objects.

You've selected all of the objects inside the rectangle.

Tip:
Selecting Parts
of Paths

Sometimes, you only want to work on specific points in a path, rather than working on the path as a whole. To do this, drag a selection rectangle over only the points you want to select. If you want to select several points but can't reach them all with one selection rectangle, select some of the points by dragging a selection rectangle, then hold down Shift and drag more selection rectangles until you've selected all of the points you want.

Tip:
Selecting Paths
Instead of Points

If you've selected a path by dragging a selection rectangle over part of it, you've probably got some points specifically selected. While you sometimes want to do this, it can cause problems—when you drag the path, it's likely that the unselected points on the path will stay put while the selected points move. To select the path as a whole when you've got some specific points selected, press the ' (accent grave/tilde) key (see Figure 1-43).

FIGURE 1-43
Selecting paths only

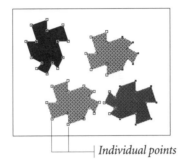

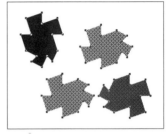

Individual points

Press ` (accent grave/tilde) and FreeHand selects the paths as paths, rather than as individual points.

Tip:
Select Through
Objects

PageMaker users have for years complained that FreeHand offered no simple shortcut for selecting through layers of objects. FreeHand 3 admirably fills this deficit: hold down the Control key and click through the stack of objects until the selection handles of the individual object you want to select appear (see Figure 1-44).

FIGURE 1-44
Selecting through
stacks of objects

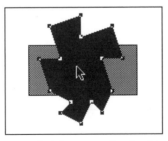

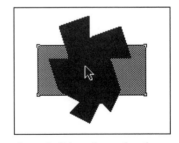

Control-click once to select the object on top of the stack.

Control-click again to select the next object in the stack.

Tip:
Subselecting
Items in a Group

FreeHand 3 offers a great new feature: the ability to subselect items inside groups. Just hold down Option and click on the element that you want to edit inside a group. While it's selected, you can change its attributes, shape, or position. When you deselect the subselected item, it goes back to being part of the group (see Figure 1-45).

If you're trying to select an object in a group that's behind other objects, hold down Option and Control while you're clicking through the stack of elements. You can also select multiple buried objects this way by holding down Control-Option-Shift as you click through the stack of objects.

This is set of features is flexible enough that you can select any number of groups or individual objects through a stack of items containing groups or individual elements.

FIGURE 1-45
Subselecting items
inside groups

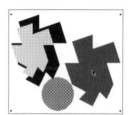 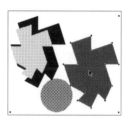 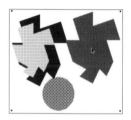

Point at an object inside a group.

Hold down Option and click to select the object.

You can move or edit the object, but it remains inside the group.

Tip:
Deselect All

Pressing Tab deselects all selected objects. This is particularly handy when you're having trouble deselecting an object at a high magnification—you can't see the currently selected object's selection handles because the object is larger than your page view. Pressing Tab is easy, fast, and guaranteed to deselect all objects.

Moving Elements

You can move individual points, selected sets of points, paths, objects, or sets of selected points, paths, or objects. Moving any single object is simple: just position the pointer tool over the object, hold down the mouse button, and drag the object to wherever you want it. To move more than one object at once, hold down Shift and click on the objects you want to move. When you reach the last object you want to select, position the pointer tool over the object, and, while still holding down Shift, press the mouse button and drag all of the selected objects to where you want them (Figure 1-46).

FIGURE 1-46
Moving by dragging

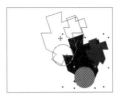
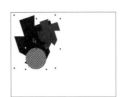

Select the objects you want to move...

...and drag them to a new position. If you wait a second before starting to drag, you'll see the objects' outlines as you drag.

Alternatively, you can move objects using FreeHand's Move elements dialog box. Select an object (or group of objects) and press Command-M. Type the horizontal and vertical distance you want the selection to move in the text edit boxes, and press Return. FreeHand moves the object the distance you specified (see Figure 1-47). For more on moving, see "Moving," in Chapter 5, "Transforming."

FIGURE 1-47
Moving objects using
the Move elements
dialog box

Select the objects you want to move...

...and press Command-M. FreeHand displays the Move elements dialog box. Type the distance you want to move the objects in the text edit boxes, and press Return.

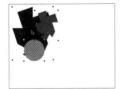

FreeHand moves the objects as you specified.

Working with Palettes

Many authors would save the intricacies of working with the Styles, Layers, and Colors palettes for later in the book. Sorry. The grim and wonderful truth is that these new features are three of the most important things you need to keep in mind when you're creating your publication. They're also three of the most important tools at your disposal for speeding up the process of creating publications with FreeHand.

If you're used to using PageMaker's palettes, you'll find using FreeHand's palettes a snap; they're very similar.

To apply any of the attributes listed in the palettes to elements in your publication, select the elements and click the name for the style, layer, or color in the appropriate palette. This applies the color or style, or sends the object to a specific layer (except the default Guides layer).

The Layers Palette

Like many CAD programs, FreeHand uses the concept of layers—transparent planes on which you create and place elements. Once you've gone beyond creating very simple illustrations, you'll find layers indispensable, because they help you organize and control the elements in your illustration.

Here are some of things you can do using the Layers palette.

- Make the Layers palette visible or invisible

- Create new layers

- Make layers visible or invisible

- Make layers printing or nonprinting

- Change the stacking order of layers

- Copy objects from one layer to another

- Copy the contents of entire layers to other layers

- Remove entire layers (with or without any associated publication elements)

- Make layers active or inactive (objects on inactive layers cannot be selected)

- Rename layers

FreeHand has three default layers—Foreground, Guides, and Background. These default layers are representative of the three major types of layers available in FreeHand.

- Foreground. A printing, visible, and active layer, this is the default layout and drawing layer.

- Guides is a nonprinting layer for placing ruler guides and grids. You cannot edit or remove the default Guides layer (though you can hide it).

- Background. A nonprinting, visible, and active layer, Background is the default layer for placing bitmapped images you want to trace. Objects placed on the default Background layer are screened to 50 percent of their original color (this is intended to make tracing easier).

The dotted line on the Layers palette defines the boundary between all background and foreground layers. Layers above the dotted line are foreground layers; layers below are background layers. You can create or delete any number of background and foreground layers, but you can't create a new, or delete the existing, Guides layer.

Displaying the Layers Palette. If you can't see the Layers palette, you can display it by pressing Command-6. If the palette is up and you want to put it away, press Command-6.

Creating New Layers. To create a new layer choose "New" from the submenu that's off the side of the Layers palette. FreeHand displays the Layers dialog box. Type a name for your new layer and press Return. The name of the layer appears in the Layers palette (see Figure 1-48).

To send objects to this layer, select the objects and click on the layer name in the Layers palette.

FIGURE 1-48   *Select "New…"*
Creating a new layer

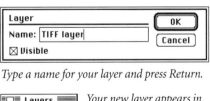

Type a name for your layer and press Return.

    Your new layer appears in the layers palette.

Making Layers Visible or Invisible. If you want to make all of the objects on a layer invisible, click the check mark on the left of the layer's name in the Layers palette. Everything that's on that layer disappears. Don't worry. It's not gone; it's just not visible and can't be selected. To make the layer visible again, click the space to the left of the layer's name. The check mark reappears, and the objects on the layer become visible.

Making Layers Printing or Nonprinting. If you want to print only the visible foreground layers (the layers above the dotted line in the palette with a check mark to the left of their names), click "All visible foreground layers" in the Print options dialog box. If you want to print all foreground layers, whether they're visible or not, click "All foreground layers."

Background layers are nonprinting layers, so dragging a layer below the dotted line in the Layers palette turns it into a nonprinting layer. Alternatively, you can drag background layers above the dotted line in the Layers palette to make them printing layers.

The default Guides layer cannot be printed.

Changing the Stacking Order of Layers. The stacking order of the layers you use is determined by the order in which they appear in the Layers palette. Layers closer to the top of the Layers palette are farther to the front in your publication. If you want to move the contents of a specific layer closer to the front, drag the layer name closer to the top of the Layers palette (see Figure 1-49).

FIGURE 1-49
Changing the stacking
order of layers

 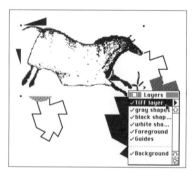

Select the layer and drag it toward the top of the Layers palette.

Objects on the layer move closer to the front.

If you want to make a specific layer a background layer, drag it below the dotted line in the Layers palette (see Figure 1-50). Objects on background layers display as a 50-percent tint of their original colors (the colors don't actually change; only the way the objects are displayed).

FIGURE 1-50
Making layers
background layers

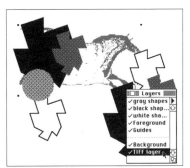

Select the layer and drag it below the dotted line on the Layers palette.

FreeHand moves the objects on the layer to the background.

Tip:
Guides to Back

PageMaker users working with FreeHand used to complain that FreeHand's ruler guides got in the way of selecting and moving objects because there wasn't a way to send the guides to the back, like there is in PageMaker. With FreeHand 3, they'll have to start complaining that PageMaker's guides don't work like FreeHand's.

To send the guides all the way to the back, point at the Guides layer in the Layers palette, press the mouse button, and then drag the Guides layer below the dotted line on the Layers palette. The Guides layer is now behind every foreground layer. If you want the Guides layer to be behind every background layer, as well, drag the Guides layer to the bottom of the list in the Layers palette.

You could also move the Guides layer so that it fell behind one or more foreground layers.

Moving Objects from One Layer to Another. To move objects from one layer to another, select the objects and click on the layer name of the destination layer in the Layers palette.

Removing Layers. When you need to remove a layer, select the layer name in the Layers palette and choose "Remove" from the submenu that pops out of the top of the palette. If there are objects on the layer you're trying to remove, FreeHand asks if you want to remove the objects on that layer. If you do, click OK and all of the objects on that layer will be deleted along with the layer. If you don't want the objects removed, click Cancel, and move the objects to other layers. Then try removing the layer again.

Making Layers Active or Inactive. Visible layers are active; invisible layers are inactive. This differs from FreeHand 2, where layers could be visible and inactive. To make a layer inactive, make it invisible. To make it active again, make it visible. If you want to make a layer visible and inactive, the best you can do is select everything on that layer and lock it.

Renaming Layers. You can rename a layer any time by double-clicking the layer name in the Layers palette. The Layer dialog box appears. Type a new name for the layer and press Return.

Functionally, renaming layers makes no difference to FreeHand, but it might help you remember which layer contains which objects.

The Styles Palette

The styles in the Styles palette contain all of the specifications for a particular line, fill, or line and fill combination, including colors, line weights, and halftone screens. Any attribute you could choose from the Attributes menu can be attached to a specific, named style and applied every time you want to use that particular combination of attributes. It's lots easier than making all of those separate selections every time.

Better still, if you decide that all of the occurrences of a particular style should change, all you have to do is edit the style and every object with that style applied changes to match the new specifications.

Imagine you've spent hours on an illustration, it's only minutes before a deadline, and your client/boss/whatever decides that all of the red lines in the illustration must, simply must, be 3-points wide, rather than the 6-point red lines you've used. Without styles, you'd have to go through the entire illustration, select each 6-point red line, and change it. If you'd used styles, you could simply edit the style definition for the line, perhaps changing the style name from "6-point red line" to "3-point red line" before you send the job to your imagesetter. Using styles saves you time and trouble.

You can display or hide the Styles palette by pressing Command-3. For more on styles and the Styles palette, see "Working with Styles" in Chapter 2, "Drawing."

The Colors Palette

The Colors palette is the color control center of your publication. Command-9 displays or hides the Colors palette. Here are some of the things you can do using the Colors palette.

- Create colors (spot colors, process colors, or tints of either of those)

- Apply colors to objects (including selecting whether the object's fill, stroke, or both fill and stroke should be affected by the color)

- Edit colors

- Rename colors

- Select Pantone colors from a listing

- Copy new colors from external color libraries

- Remove colors

- Choose a color model (RGB, HLS, and CMY for spot colors, CMYK for process colors)

- Change color models (from RGB to CMYK, for example)

For more on using the Colors palette, see Chapter 6, "Color."

FreeHand and the Edit Menu

FreeHand works a little bit differently than other Macintosh applications, particularly in that you don't have to go through the Clipboard to copy items in your publication. Instead, you'll typically use Clone and Duplicate from FreeHand's Edit menu inside a publication (you'll still need to use Cut and Copy to move items from publication to publication). Not only are Clone and Duplicate faster, they use less memory and have some useful features of their own.

Cloning

The Clone command (Command-=) creates a copy of the selected object, in exactly the same position. This can be a little confusing at first, because the cloned object's selection handles look just the same as the selection handles of the original object. New FreeHand users sometimes end up with stacks of identical objects in their publications.

Placing the object in the same position, however, offers distinct advantages. If, for example, you know that you want a copy of a specific object 2 picas right and 2 picas down from that object, just clone the object, then press Command-M to bring up the Move elements dialog box, and move the object numerically. If you hadn't started in exactly the same position as the original object, you'd have to do a bunch of measuring to figure out where the copied object was supposed to go (see Figure 1-51).

FIGURE 1-51
Clone

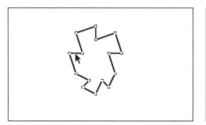 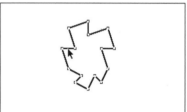

Select an object and press Command-=
to clone the object.

FreeHand places an exact copy of the
object on top of the object. It doesn't
look like a new object, but it's there.

Duplicating

The Duplicate command (Command-D) creates a copy of the object at a slight offset from the selected object (see Figure 1-52), or copies the object and repeats the last series of transformations (uses of the move, scaling, rotation, skewing, or reflection tools). We'll cover more of the complex uses of Duplicate in Chapter 5, "Transforming."

FIGURE 1-52
Duplicate

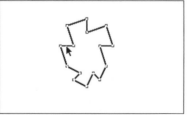 

Select an object and press Command-D
to duplicate the object.

FreeHand places an exact copy on the
page.

The Tao of FreeHand

Here are those rules I promised at the beginning of the chapter.

Keep It Simple. I don't mean don't create complex publications. I mean create publications with an understanding of what's difficult for PostScript printers (especially imagesetters) to do, and do those things sparingly. Understand that you can probably just fill a complex path with a tiled fill, for example, rather than drawing a rectangle, filling it with the tiled fill, and pasting it inside the path. If you've got to use "Paste inside," avoid having more than around 50 (and certainly fewer than 100 in all cases!) points on the containing path. If you don't, you'll get a PostScript error. Understand that adding color TIFFs or "colorizing" gray-scale TIFFs dramatically increases imagesetter processing time and makes it more likely you'll get a VMerror instead of a set of separations.

Use Styles. I think I've stated the advantages of styles earlier in this chapter, but I'll state it again here (for more on styles, see Chapter 2, "Drawing"). (Unless you work for people who never change their minds, and you never change your mind yourself, you need the ability to change things quickly and systematically—and that's where styles really shine. If you work for people who never change their minds, and you never change your mind yourself, please give me a call. (I've never met anyone like you.)

Use Layers. And use them systematically. Not only will you find your publications easier to work with if you've spread the publication elements over several logical layers, but you'll be able to speed up your screen display, as well. Layers speed printing, too.

Use Traps. I can't think of the number of color jobs I've ruined because of failing to think of trapping elements—especially type. See "Trapping" in Chapter 6, "Color."

Use Color Proofs. If you're working with process colors, it's an absolute necessity to make Cromalins (or MatchPrints, or the equivalent) from the same negatives you intend to use to print the publication. They're expensive, but they're cheaper than thousands of publications printed the wrong way because the film was wrong.

Talk to Your Commercial Printer. This can often save you lots of time and money. The thing to remember when you're talking with your printer is that they're the experts. Don't be a jerk. Don't assume you know their job better than they do. If possible, work out a printing contract for your job that spells out in exact terms what you expect of them and what they expect of you.

Talk to Your Imagesetting Service Bureau. First, ask them how to make PostScript dumps from FreeHand. If they don't know, start looking for another service bureau. Once you've found a service bureau that can answer the question, approach them very much the way you'd approach your commercial printer. A good working relationship with an imagesetting service bureau or inhouse imagesetter operator is essential.

Human

beings have always drawn things. The walls of caves inhabited in prehistoric times, the interiors of the tombs of the Pharaohs, and the development of desktop publishing all show that we're a kind of animal that likes to make marks on things. Drawing is at the center of us; it's one of the unique attributes that makes us human.

Drawing is also at the heart of FreeHand. Nine of the 18 tools in the FreeHand toolbox are drawing tools. Using these tools, you can draw almost anything—from simple, straight lines to incredibly complex, twisted shapes.

As I explained in Chapter 1, "FreeHand Basics," the lines you draw in FreeHand are made up of points, and the points are connected by line segments. A FreeHand line is just like a connect-the-dots puzzle. Connect all the dots in the right order, and you've made a picture, or part of a picture. Because points along a line have an order, or winding, we call the lines "paths," and you can think of each point as a milepost along the path. Or as a sign saying, "now go this way."

The drawing tools can be divided into two types: the square-corner, round-corner, ellipse, and line tools are for drawing basic shapes; the freehand, pen, corner, curve, and connector tools draw more complex, or "freeform," paths (see Figure 2-1).

Which tools should you use? Don't worry too much about the distinction. There's no "wrong" tool to use for a particular task. The basic shapes drawn with the basic shapes tools can be converted into freeform paths, and the freeform drawing tools can be used to draw the same basic shapes.

FIGURE 2-1

Drawing tools

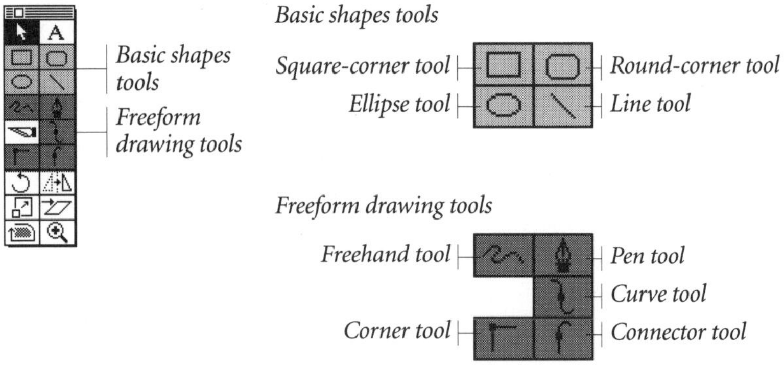

Basic shapes tools

Freeform drawing tools

Basic shapes tools

Square-corner tool ┤ ├ Round-corner tool
Ellipse tool ┤ ├ Line tool

Freeform drawing tools

Freehand tool ┤ ├ Pen tool
├ Curve tool
Corner tool ┤ ├ Connector tool

Still, some tools are better at some tasks, as I'll show you in the next few sections.

Basic Shapes

The square-corner, round-corner, ellipse, and line tools don't draw anything you couldn't draw using the more complex path-drawing tools (which I'll discuss later in this chapter); they just make drawing certain types of paths easier. They're shortcuts.

The operation of the basic shapes tools is very straightforward, but there are a few details you need to know about. FreeHand aces may want to skip the next few paragraphs. It isn't that I'm getting paid by the word to write this (I'm not), but that I'm trying to cover all of the bases. It's amazing, too, what people can miss when they're learning a software product; I've seen FreeHand gurus who could write their own PostScript fills but weren't aware that you could turn a rectangle drawn with the square-corner tool into a round-corner rectangle.

You can think of the paths drawn by the basic shapes tools as grouped paths. The basic shapes have a few other properties, as well, that you can't get by grouping a path you'd drawn with the freeform drawing tools.

- When you join text to a path drawn with the basic shapes tools, it behaves differently than if you join it to a path drawn with the freeform tools. I've added this information to the descriptions of each basic shape, below.

- Basic shapes also have a special constraint key you can use when you resize them, as described in the section, "Resizing Basic Shapes," below.

These magical properties disappear when you convert the paths drawn with the basic shapes tools into freeform paths (see "Converting Basic Shapes into Paths," below), and there's no way to convert the converted path back into a basic shape.

Drawing Rectangles

Use the square-corner and round-corner tools to draw rectangles (including squares) with square and round corners. To draw a rectangle using the square-corner or round-corner tool, follow these steps (see Figure 2-2).

1. Select the square-corner or round-corner tool from the toolbox (press 1 on the numeric keypad for the square-corner tool; press 2 for the round-corner tool). The cursor turns into a cross hair.

2. Position the cross hair where you want one corner of the rectangle to fall. Or position the cross hair where you want the center of the rectangle, and hold down Option. When you use the first method, you draw from one corner of the rectangle. When you use the second method, you draw out from the center of the rectangle.

3. Press down the mouse button and drag the mouse. FreeHand draws a rectangle, starting where you clicked the mouse button. If you hold down Shift as you draw, you draw squares.

4. When the rectangle is the size and shape you want it to be, stop dragging the mouse, and release the mouse button.

The paths created using the square-corner and round-corner tools start with the point at the upper-left corner of the rectangle, and wind clockwise from there (for more on winding, see "Thinking Like a Line" later in this chapter). When you join text to a rectangle (see "Joining Text to a Path" in Chapter 3, "Text and Type"), the first character of the text appears at the upper-left corner of the rectangle, and winds clockwise around the rectangle from there (see Figure 2-3).

FIGURE 2-2
Drawing rectangles

 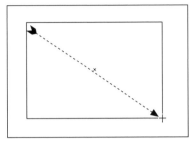

Select the rectangle tool and position the cross hair where you want to position one corner of the rectangle.

Drag the cross hair across the page to draw the rectangle.

FIGURE 2-3
Joining text to a rectangle

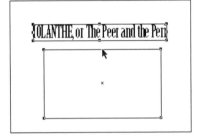 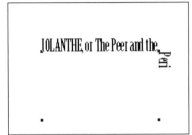

Select the text and the rectangle and press Command-J.

FreeHand joins the text to the rectangle.

Drawing Ellipses

Use the ellipse tool to draw ellipses or circles by following these steps (see Figure 2-4).

1. Select the ellipse tool from the toolbox (or press 3 on the numeric keypad). The cursor turns into a cross hair.

2. Position the cross hair where you want the top and side of the ellipse to fall. Or position the cross hair where you want the center of the ellipse, and hold down Option.

3. Press down the mouse button and drag the mouse. FreeHand draws an ellipse, starting where you clicked the mouse button. If you want to draw a perfect circle, hold down Shift as you drag.

4. When the ellipse is the size and shape you want it to be, stop dragging the mouse, and release the mouse button.

A path you create using the ellipse tool starts with the leftmost point on the ellipse, then winds clockwise from that point. When you

FIGURE 2-4
Drawing ellipses

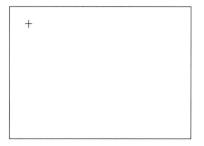

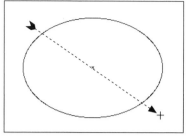

Select the ellipse tool and position the cross hair where you want to position the center of the ellipse.

Hold down Option and drag the cross hair across the page to draw the ellipse.

join text to an ellipse (see "Joining Text to a Path" in Chapter 3, "Text and Type"), the first line of text (up to the first carriage return in the text block) is joined to the upper half of the ellipse. The second line of text in the text block is joined to the bottom half of the ellipse (see Figure 2-5).

FIGURE 2-5
Joining text to an ellipse

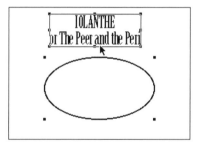

Select the text and the ellipse and press Command-J.

FreeHand joins the text to the ellipse.

Drawing Lines

To draw a line as a single line segment between two corner points, follow these steps (see Figure 2-6).

1. Select the line tool from the toolbox (or press 2 on the numeric keypad). The cursor turns into a cross hair.

2. Position the cross hair where you want one end of the line to fall.

3. Press down the mouse button and drag the mouse. FreeHand draws a line, starting where you clicked the mouse button. If you want to constrain your line to 45-degree increments (based

on the angle you specified in the Constrain dialog box), hold down Shift as you draw the line.

4. When the line is the length you want, stop dragging the mouse, and release the mouse button.

The path created by the line tool starts with the first point you click and ends with the point that's added when you stop dragging. When you join text to a line you've drawn with the line tool (see "Joining Text to a Path" in Chapter 3, "Text and Type"), the text starts at the first point on the path (see Figure 2-7).

FIGURE 2-6
Drawing lines

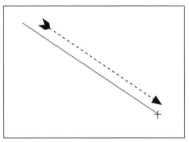

Select the line tool and position the cross hair where you want one end of the line to start.

Drag the cross hair across the page to draw the line. Hold down Shift if you want to constrain the line to 45-degree angles.

FIGURE 2-7
Joining text to a line

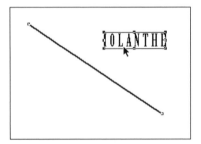

Select the text and the ellipse and press Command-J.

FreeHand joins the text to the ellipse.

Resizing Basic Shapes

To resize any of the basic shapes, use the pointer tool to select the basic shape you want to resize and then drag any corner handle (see Figure 2-8).

If you hold down Option as you resize a basic shape, FreeHand uses a special type of constraint that only works with basic shapes, and resizes the object around its center point (see Figure 2-9). This is a very handy feature when you need to enlarge an object while leaving its center in the same place.

FIGURE 2-8
Resizing basic shapes

 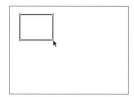

Select a corner handle…   *…and drag to resize a basic shape.*

FIGURE 2-9
Special constraint for
basic shapes

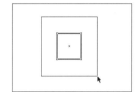 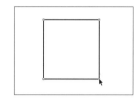

When you hold down Option as you resize a basic shape, FreeHand resizes the basic shape from its center.

Proportionally Resizing Basic Shapes

If you want to resize a basic shape (other than a line) proportionally, you'd expect that you could just hold down Shift and drag a corner handle, but you can't—unless the basic shape is a circle or square—because holding down Shift and clicking a corner handle turns the basic shape into a circle or square.

To resize a basic shape proportionally, use the pointer tool to select the basic shape you want to resize, and then press Command-G to group the basic shape. Position the pointer tool over any corner handle. Hold down Shift and drag the corner handle to resize the basic shape (see Figure 2-10).

FIGURE 2-10
Resizing a basic shape
proportionally

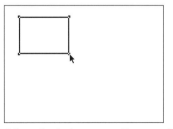 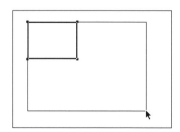

Select a basic shape, press Command-G, hold down Shift…   *…and then drag the corner handle to proportionally resize the basic shape.*

Changing One Kind of Rectangle into Another

A rectangle drawn with the round-corner tool differs from one drawn using the square-corner tool only in that it has a corner radius applied to it. Otherwise, the basic shapes you draw with the two tools are the same. This makes changing one sort of rectangle into another easy.

To change a square-corner rectangle into a round-corner rectangle, use the pointer tool to select the square-corner rectangle you want to change. Press Command-I to display the Rectangle dialog box. When the dialog box appears, enter the corner radius you want in the Corner radius text edit box, and then press Return to close the Rectangle dialog box. FreeHand converts the square-corner rectangle into a round-corner rectangle (see Figure 2-11).

FIGURE 2-11

Rounding corners

Select a square-corner rectangle and press Command-I

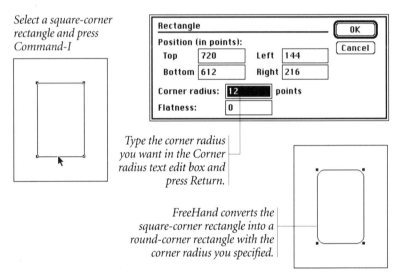

Type the corner radius you want in the Corner radius text edit box and press Return.

FreeHand converts the square-corner rectangle into a round-corner rectangle with the corner radius you specified.

To change a round-corner rectangle into a square-corner rectangle, use the pointer tool to select the round-corner rectangle you want to change, and then press Command-I to display the Rectangle dialog box. Enter "0" in the Corner radius text edit box, and then press Return to close the Rectangle dialog box. FreeHand converts the round-corner rectangle into a square-corner rectangle.

Converting Basic Shapes into Paths

Why would you want to convert basic shapes into freeform paths? Sometimes you want only part of a basic shape to connect to a path. Or you might want to use the unique text-joining attributes of a basic shape, and then attach the basic shape to another, freeform path.

To turn any of the shapes drawn with the basic shapes tools into a path, select the basic shape, and then press Command-U to ungroup the path. The basic shape is now a freeform path, and can be manipulated as you'd manipulate any other freeform path (see Figure 2-12).

FIGURE 2-12
Converting basic shapes into paths

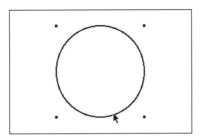

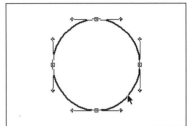

Select a basic shape and press Command-U.

FreeHand converts the basic shape into a freeform path, which you can edit as you would any freeform path.

Tip:
Creating Round Corners on Paths

When you're drawing paths with the freeform path-drawing tools, it can be difficult to get an arc with a specific corner radius. To draw an arc with a specific radius, follow these steps (see Figure 2-13).

1. Draw a round-corner rectangle using the round-corner tool.

2. Press Command-I to display the Rectangle dialog box.

3. Type the corner radius you want in the Corner radius text edit box.

4. Press Return to close the Rectangle dialog box.

5. Without deselecting the round-corner rectangle, press Command-U to ungroup the basic shape and convert it to a path.

6. Select the points on the path on either side of the corner you want to add to your path and choose "Split element" from the Element menu (you could also use the knife tool to split the points).

7. Cut all of the rectangle but the corner you want.

8. Select the corner and move it into the position you want.

9. Join the round corner to the path (for more on joining paths, see "Joining Paths," later in this chapter).

Why don't we draw, ungroup, and split a circle to accomplish this same task? Because there's no way to specify the corner radius of the circle, short of drawing the circle to an exact size. It's far easier to enter a value for the corner radius in a dialog box.

FIGURE 2-13

Adding a round corner to a path

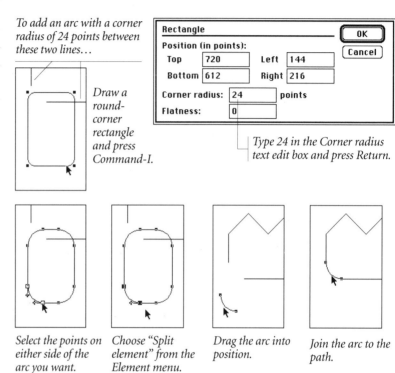

To add an arc with a corner radius of 24 points between these two lines...

Draw a round-corner rectangle and press Command-I.

Type 24 in the Corner radius text edit box and press Return.

Select the points on either side of the arc you want.

Choose "Split element" from the Element menu.

Drag the arc into position.

Join the arc to the path.

Points and Paths

I briefly covered points and paths in Chapter 1, "FreeHand Basics," but there's still more to explain. Why is it that the most important things are often the ones that are the most difficult to learn?

When I first approached FreeHand and Illustrator, drawing by constructing paths, placing points, and manipulating curve handles struck me as alien, as nothing like drawing at all. Then I started to catch on. In many ways, when I used pens and rulers to draw, I was drawing lines from the point of view of everything *but* the line; in FreeHand, I draw lines from the point of view of the line itself. This is neither better nor worse; it's just different and takes time to get used to. If you've just glanced at the toolbox and are feeling confused, I urge you to stick with it. Start thinking like a line.

Thinking Like a Line

Imagine that, through some mysterious potion or errant cosmic ray, you've been reduced in size so that you're a little smaller than one of the dots in the connect-the-dots puzzle I mentioned earlier in this chapter. For detail, imagine the puzzle's in a *Highlights* magazine in a dentist's office.

The only way out is to complete the puzzle. As you walk, a line extends behind you. As you reach each dot in the puzzle, a sign tells you where you are in the puzzle, and how to get to the next dot.

Get the idea? The dots in the puzzle are points. The route you walk from one dot to another, as instructed by the signs at each point, is a line segment. Each series of connected dots is a path. As you walk from one dot to another, you're thinking like a line.

Each point—from the first point in the path to the last—carries with it some specification about the line segments that attach it to the previous and next points along the path.

Paths are made up of two or more points, connected by line segments, as shown in Figure 2-14. Even if the line attribute applied to the path is "None," (and the line doesn't print or show up in Preview mode) there's still a line segment there.

FIGURE 2-14
A path

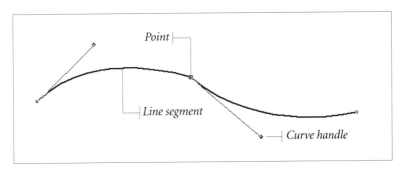

Winding

PostScript paths have a direction, also known as "winding" (as in "winding a clock"—nothing to do with the weather) that generally corresponds to the order and direction in which you place their points as you create the path (see Figure 2-15). In our connect-the-dots puzzle, winding tells us the order in which to connect the dots.

FIGURE 2-15
The direction of a path

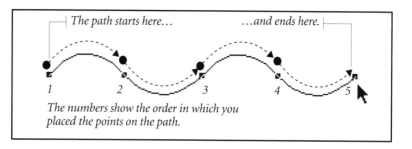

When you create objects using the basic shapes drawing tools, Free-Hand assumes a particular winding (see Figure 2-16). This is a useful thing to know, particularly when you're joining text to a path and want to control where that text begins on the path (FreeHand always positions the first character of the text block at the path's starting point, unless you're joining text to an object you've drawn with the basic shape tools, in which case it behaves differently; see "Joining Text to a Path," in Chapter 3, "Text and Type").

FIGURE 2-16
Winding for
basic shapes

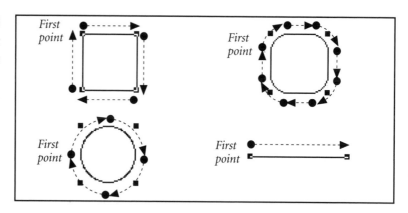

You can use the reflection tool to reverse or change the winding of a path (see Figure 2-17). First, select the object, and then select the reflection tool. Hold down Option and click anywhere to display the Reflection dialog box. In the Axis section of the dialog box, click the Horizontal option, and then, in the Point section, click the Center of selection option. Press Return to close the dialog box.

When you do this, you reflect around the path's horizontal center, which reverses the direction of the path and changes its point of origin. You can also choose to reflect the object around its vertical center, which has about the same result.

FIGURE 2-17
Changing the
direction of a path

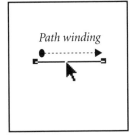 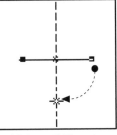 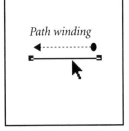

*Select the path, and then
select the reflection tool.*

*Hold down Shift, and
drag vertically to reflect
the path around its
horizontal axis.*

*Reflection reverses the
direction of the path.*

Curve Handles

Curve handles are the way that points control the curvature of the line segments before and after each point. Points can have up to two attached curve handles. Typically, corner points lack curve handles, connector points have one curve handle, and curve points have two curve handles (for more on the different types of points, see "Types of Points" in Chapter 1, "FreeHand Basics").

The first curve handle you pull out of a point controls the curvature of the next line segment in the path along the direction (or winding) of the path. The second curve handle controls the curvature of the line segment before the point (see Figure 2-18).

FIGURE 2-18
Curve handles

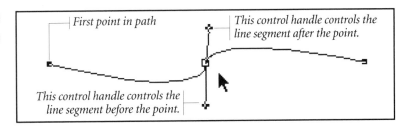

First point in path

*This control handle controls the
line segment after the point.*

*This control handle controls the
line segment before the point.*

Flatness

Besides winding, paths also have another property, flatness, which you'll see if you select a path and press Command-I ("Element info") to display the object info dialog box for the path. Flatness is a PostScript setting controlling the accuracy of the process used to draw the path on your printer or imagesetter. A flatness setting of 0 assures that the path will print at the highest level of accuracy possible, given the printer's resolution.

Lower flatness settings take longer to print and use more of your printer's RAM (which is precious, unless you like PostScript error messages), because the printer has to draw more tiny line segments to render the path's curves.

So it's a tradeoff between printing time and accurate curve rendering. Some publications, in fact, won't print at all unless you increase the flatness of some of their elements.

You can think of flatness this way: a flatness setting of 1 on a 300-dpi printer is equal to an inaccuracy in drawing curves of $\frac{1}{300}$ of an inch, or $\frac{1}{2540}$ of an inch on an L300 at high resolution. The first is acceptable accuracy for proofing; the second is acceptable resolution for most publications. In fact, I've even gone to flatness settings of 3 without any problems when I knew I was going to be printing color separations at 2540 dpi. You can enter flatness values from 0 to 1000. Figure 2-19 shows the effect of increased flatness setting at 1270 dpi.

FIGURE 2-19
Flatness

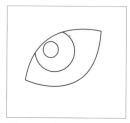
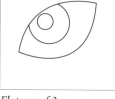
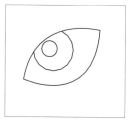

Flatness of 0   *Flatness of 3*   *Flatness of 50*

Path-drawing Tools

You use the freeform drawing tools—the freehand tool, the pen tool, the corner tool, curve tool, and connector tool—to create paths. The following sections discuss each freeform drawing tool. These tools have already been discussed, briefly, in Chapter 1, "FreeHand Basics," but this section gives you more detailed descriptions of their uses.

Freehand Tool

The simplest, quickest way to create a path on a FreeHand publication page is to use the freehand tool. Just select the tool and scribble. As you drag the tool across the page, a path is created that follows your mouse motion (see Figure 2-20).

As you drag, FreeHand places corner and curve points along the path. You have some control over the placement of these points—double-click on the freehand tool to bring up the Freehand dialog box (see Figure 2-21).

FIGURE 2-20
Using the freehand tool

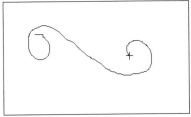

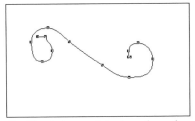

Select the freehand tool and drag it across the page.

FreeHand places points along the path.

FIGURE 2-21
Freehand dialog box

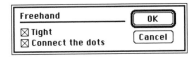

The Tight option controls the number of points FreeHand creates to construct the path. Turn off "Tight" to create a simpler path, but bear in mind that the simplified path follows your mouse movements less accurately.

"Connect the dots" displays a smoother depiction of the path as you drag the freehand tool. Turn "Connect the dots" off to show a simplified representation of the path as you draw it. Why would you want to do this? Drawing's a little faster with "Connect the dots" turned off. I always leave it on. Note that when you've got "Connect the dots" turned off, the path is drawn about the same way as it's drawn in Illustrator.

If you need to back up along the path you've drawn with the freehand tool, hold down Command, hold down the mouse button, and then drag the freehand tool back along the path. To continue drawing the path, let go of Command and continue dragging the tool (see Figure 2-22).

FIGURE 2-22
Erasing part of a
freeform path

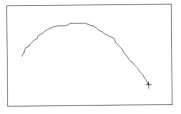

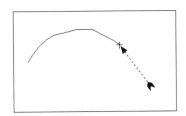

If you don't like what you've drawn with the freehand tool…

…hold down Command and drag back along the path.

If you need to create a straight line segment while you're drawing a path using the freehand tool, hold down Option as you're dragging: each line segment you add forms a straight line from the last point on the path. If you want to constrain the angle of the straight line segment to 45-degree angles (from the angle set in the Constrain dialog box), hold down Option-Shift as you drag the freehand tool (see Figure 2-23).

Though the freehand tool is the easiest way to create paths in FreeHand, I've always found it to be one of the least useful. Why? Mice are wonderful things, and they're probably the best way we currently have of getting positioning information into computers (I've tried trackballs and pens, too), but they're far better at placing points and manipulating curve handles than they are at drawing smooth lines.

FIGURE 2-23
Constraint and the
freehand tool

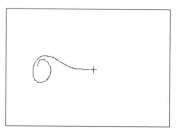

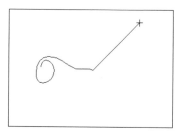

Hold down Option-Shift as you drag the freehand tool…

…and you constrain the lines you draw to 45-degree angles.

Pen Tool When you click the pen tool, you place corner points. If you drag the pen tool, you place a curve point where you first started dragging, and you determine the length of the curve handles (and, therefore, the radius of the curve) by the distance you drag (see Figure 2-24). In essence, the pen tool combines the curve and corner point tools. If you're an Illustrator user, the pen tool works the same way as the pen tool in Illustrator.

To curve the line segment following a corner point, hold down Option as you place a corner point and drag. The curve handle doesn't appear until you place the next point. Once you place the next point, the curve handle appears and can be adjusted as you like (see Figure 2-25).

The trickiest thing about using the pen tool this way is that you often don't see the effect of the curve manipulation until you've placed

FIGURE 2-24
The pen tool

 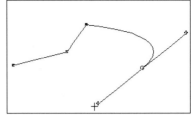

Click to create a corner point.   *Drag to create a curve point.*

FIGURE 2-25
Dragging a curve handle
out of a corner point

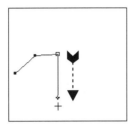 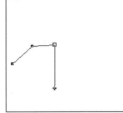 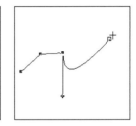

Hold down Option as you drag…   *…and FreeHand creates a corner point with a single curve handle.*   *This curve handle applies to the line segment following the corner point.*

the next point. This makes sense in that you don't need a curve handle for a line segment that doesn't yet exist, but it can be quite a brain-twister.

You can convert a curve point to a corner point as you're drawing with the pen tool by holding down Option after you've finished dragging out the curve handles. Then click on the point. This converts the point into a corner point with one control handle. Just to make life interesting, this control handle applies to the line segment *before* the corner point along the path. Ordinarily, the first curve handle dragged out of a corner point applies to the line segment *after* the point (see Figure 2-26).

If you place a curve point and then, *as you're dragging*, hold down Option, you can adjust the point's curve handles independently. Place a curve point by dragging the pen tool, and then hold down Option and drag. Now place another point. You'll see that the curve point's curve handles aren't equidistant from the curve point, which means that they can be manipulated independently (see Figure 2-27).

You can change the position of points, as you'd expect, by holding down Command (which, as you'll recall, chooses the pointer tool

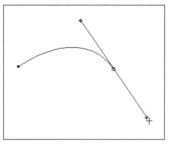
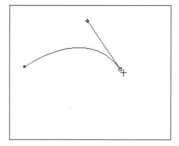

FIGURE 2-26
Converting a curve
point to a corner point

Position a curve point, hold down Option…

…and then click on the point to convert it into a corner point.

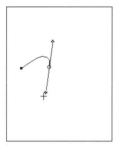
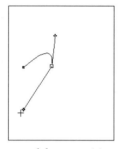
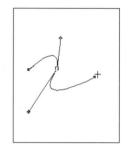

FIGURE 2-27
Creating independent
curve handles with the
pen tool

Place a curve point. As you're dragging, hold down Option…

…and drag to position the curve handles where you want them.

This creates a corner point with two curve handles extended.

without deselecting the current tool), selecting the point, and dragging the point to a new location.

Corner Tool

When you click the corner tool on the page, you're placing corner points—points which have no control handles attached to them. Corner points look like small squares. Because corner points have no curve control handles attached to them, the line segments between corner points are straight (see Figure 2-28).

You can drag curve levers out of corner points: place the corner point as you normally would, then hold down Command and Option, and drag a control handle out of the corner point (see Figure 2-29).

Note that you can also drag a control handle out of a corner point anytime by selecting the point, then holding down Option, and dragging a control handle out of it.

The most significant difference between corner points and curve points is that the angle of control handles pulled out of corner points can be adjusted independently, while changing the angle of one

FIGURE 2-28
Corner points

FIGURE 2-28
Corner points

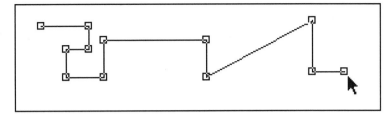

control handle of a curve point changes the angle of the other control handle. This difference, in my opinion, makes corner points much more useful than curve points (see Figure 2-29).

You can turn corner points into curve points by selecting the corner point, pressing Command-I to display the Path/point dialog box, clicking the curve point icon, and pressing Return to close the dialog box. The selected corner point becomes a curve point.

FIGURE 2-29
Dragging curve handles
out of corner points

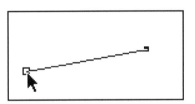

Select a corner point, hold down Option…

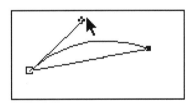

…and drag a curve handle out of the corner point.

Adjusting curve points

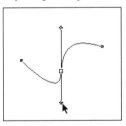

Point at a curve handle…

…and drag.

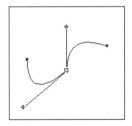

The curve handle moves independently of the other curve handle.

Curve Tool   The curve tool creates curve points—points with two control handles pulled out of them. Curve points look like small circles. When you click to place a curve point, two control handles are extended from the point. How far the control handles are extended depends on the curve point's place in the path (see Figure 2-30).

You can increase or decrease the distance from one control handle to the curve point without moving the other curve point, but both handles move if you change the angle one of them presents to the curve point—they always move along the same axis. This makes them less flexible than corner points (see Figure 2-31).

FIGURE 2-30
Curve points

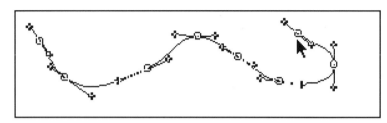

FIGURE 2-31
Manipulating control
handles on curve points

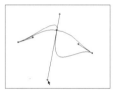
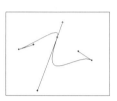

*Select the curve point,
point at a curve
handle…*

*…and drag. Note that
both curve handles move
as you drag.*

*Curve handles always
move along the same
axis.*

Connector Tool

When you click the connector tool, you create connector points—points which may or may not have control handles pulled out of them depending on where they're placed in the path. And, I suspect, depending on their own whim. I never really have figured out connector points. Anyway, they look like little triangles.

If you place a curve point immediately after a connector point, the control handle for the line segment from the connector point to the curve point is extended from the connector point. This control handle is positioned along the axis formed by the connector point and the point preceding the connector point on the path, and is placed at an equal distance from the connector point as the preceding point along this axis. When you drag the control handle, it moves along this axis (see Figure 2-32). If you want to change the curve, you'll have to convert the connector point into another type of point.

What's the use of connector points? They create smooth transitions between straight and curved line segments. I think of them as a sort of "half" curve point. They never seem to give me the curve I'm looking for, but you should experiment with them. In spite of my bias, they might be just what you're looking for.

FIGURE 2-32
Connector points

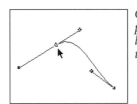

Connector points look like little triangles.

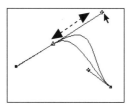

The control handle on a connector point can only move along its original axis.

Manipulating Curve Control Handles

The aspect of drawing in FreeHand that's toughest to understand and master is the care, feeding, and manipulation of curve control handles. These handles are fundamental to drawing curved lines in FreeHand, so you'd better learn how to work with them.

Make sure you have "Display curve levers" turned on in the Preferences dialog box. If you don't turn this option on, you'll have a hard time figuring out which point which curve handle applies to. Turning this option on makes everything about manipulating curve handles easier (see Figure 2-33).

FIGURE 2-33
Display curve
levers option

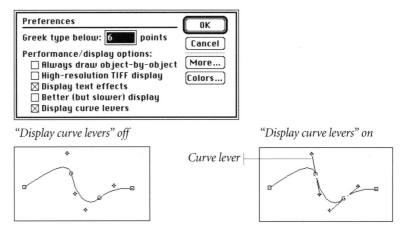

"Display curve levers" off

"Display curve levers" on

Curve lever

To adjust a curve control handle, use the pointer tool to select a point attached to a curved line segment. The curve control points associated with that point appear. Position the cursor over one of the control handles and drag. The curve of the line segment associated with that control handle changes as you drag the handle. When the curve looks the way you want, stop dragging (see Figure 2-34).

You add curve handles to corner points by selecting the point with the pointer tool, holding down Option, and dragging a curve handle out of the corner point, as shown in "Curve points," earlier in this chapter. The first control point you drag out controls the line segment going *out* of the point (along the winding of the path); the second control point you drag out controls the line segment before the point (along the winding of the path).

FIGURE 2-34
Manipulating a
curve handle

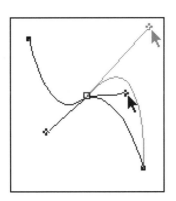 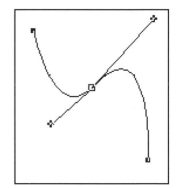

You can add another control handle to a connector point to change the curve of the line segment preceding the connector point. Hold down Option to drag another control handle out of a connector point (see Figure 2-35).

FIGURE 2-35
Manipulating
control handles on
connector points

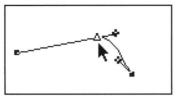 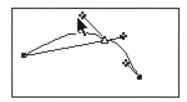

*Normally, there's only one curve
handle attached to a connector point.*

*Hold down Option to drag another
curve handle out of the connector point.*

Tip:
Selecting
Multiple Points

You can select several points at once by dragging a selection marquee over them. Once you have selected the points, their curve control handles appear. You can adjust any of the curve control handles without deselecting the other control handles, which means you can adjust curve control points on a path while looking at the position of the other curve control handles (see Figure 2-36).

FIGURE 2-36
Selecting multiple
points and adjusting
curve control handles

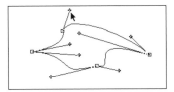

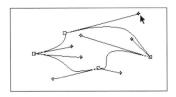

Drag a selection rectangle over a path to select all of the points on the path.

Now you can adjust curve handles while looking at the positions of all of the curve handles on the path.

Automatic Curvature. As you place curve or connector points along a path, FreeHand adds and adjusts curve control points where it thinks you'd like them. It's actually quite good at guessing. This is FreeHand's automatic curvature feature.

When you adjust a curve control handle, automatic curvature is turned off for that point. If you decide you've made an error, and would like to return to FreeHand's automatic curvature, you can open the Path/point dialog box and turn on the Automatic curvature option (see Figure 2-37).

FIGURE 2-37
Automatic curvature

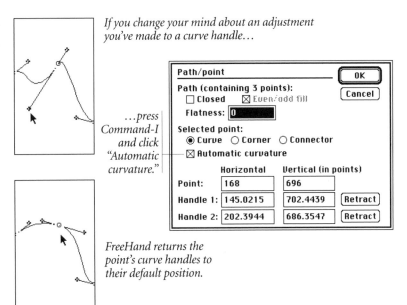

If you change your mind about an adjustment you've made to a curve handle…

…press Command-I and click "Automatic curvature."

FreeHand returns the point's curve handles to their default position.

Retracting Curve Handles. Click one of the new Retract buttons in the Path/point dialog box and the associated handle is pulled back into the point. No more not quite being sure if you'd dragged the handle inside the point! Anything you'd ordinarily do by dragging a curve control handle inside a point, you can do using the Retract buttons (see Figure 2-38).

FIGURE 2-38
Retracting handles

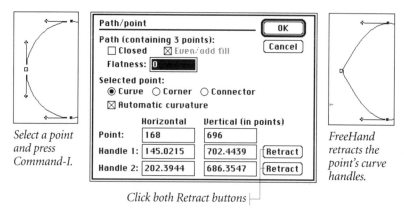

Select a point and press Command-I.

FreeHand retracts the point's curve handles.

Click both Retract buttons

Numeric Positioning of Handles. It seems like a cool new feature to be able to see the numeric position of the curve control points, but it's really hard to figure out what to do with it. I haven't yet thought of anything.

Drawing Techniques

Now that you know all about the elements that make up paths, let's talk about how you actually use them.

Ways to Draw Paths

When you're drawing paths, never forget that you can always change the path after you've drawn it. I've often seen people delete whole paths and start over because they misplaced the last point on the path. Go ahead and place points in the wrong places; you can always change the position of any point on the path. Also, keep these facts in mind:

- You can always split the path (one of the biggest improvements in FreeHand 3 is that the knife tool no longer shifts line segments when you use it to split the path).

- You can always add points to or subtract points from the path.

- You can always change tools while drawing a path.

It's also best to create paths using as few points as you can—but it's not required. Create paths however you find works best for you—there's no "right" way to do it. I've talked with several different FreeHand users, and each one used a different method for putting points on a page.

The Classical Method. Use the curve, corner, and connector tools, and place points one at a time. I call this the "classical" method, because it's how people were taught to place points in FreeHand 1.0. To construct a path using this method, you change tools between placing points (see Figure 2-39), picking the appropriate tool to place the appropriate type of point for the next point you want in a path.

People who use this method of constructing paths tend to keep one hand on the mouse and one hand hovering around the numeric keypad, because they'll change tools by pressing keys on the keypad (9 for the corner tool, 8 for the curve tool, and 0 for the connector tool). These people also use the connector tool and place connector points.

FIGURE 2-39
The classical method

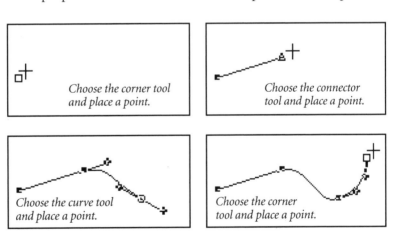

Choose the corner tool
and place a point.

Choose the connector
tool and place a point.

Choose the curve tool
and place a point.

Choose the corner
tool and place a point.

The "Illustrator" Method. Use the pen tool only. I call this method the "Illustrator" method, because I've found that this set of users generally learned to use Illustrator before they started using FreeHand. In this method, you click and drag the pen tool to create paths containing only curve and corner points (see Figure 2-40).

FIGURE 2-40
The Illustrator method

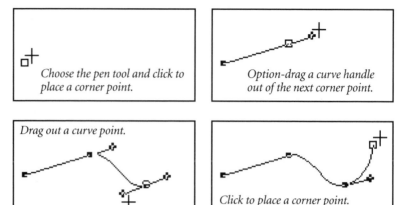

Choose the pen tool and click to place a corner point.

Option-drag a curve handle out of the next corner point.

Drag out a curve point.

Click to place a corner point.

Drawing Paths My Way. Place corner points only, then pull curve handles out of the points. I call this method "my way," because it's how I do it. In this method, you click corner points along the path you want to create, then select points and Option-drag curve handles out of them to create the curves you want (see Figure 2-41).

I like this method because I can place points quickly where I know I want them to go, then work on the fine details of the curves when I can actually see the path changing as I drag—unlike using the pen tool, where you're dragging curve handles controlling a line segment you haven't yet placed. The disadvantage of this method is that you need to know where you're going to place points ahead of time, a skill you acquire by using the program a lot (see also "Keeping Paths Simple," below).

FIGURE 2-41
My way

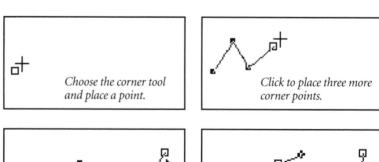

Choose the corner tool and place a point.

Click to place three more corner points.

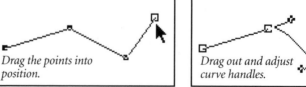

Drag the points into position.

Drag out and adjust curve handles.

All three of these methods work well, and there's no reason not to mix and match methods in different situations. There's also no reason not to mix these methods with the use of the freehand tool, the basic shapes tools, autotracing, or blending.

Keeping Paths Simple

People who've just started working with FreeHand tend to use more points than they need to describe paths. Over time, they learn one of FreeHand's basic rules: Any curve can be described by two points and their associated curve handles. No more, no less (see Figure 2-42).

FIGURE 2-42
Any curve can be described by two points

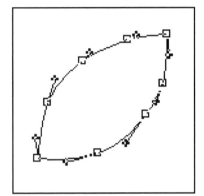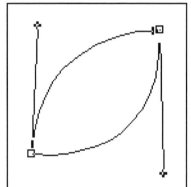

Selecting and Moving Points

If you've gotten this far, you probably know how to select points, but here are a few rules to keep in mind.

- You select a point by clicking on the point with the pointer tool.

- You can select more than one point at a time by holding down Shift as you click on each point with the pointer tool, or you can drag a marquee across a number of points to select them all.

- When you move a point, the control handles associated with that point also move, maintaining their same position relative to the point . Note that this means that the curves of the line segments attached to the point change, unless you're also moving the points on the other end of the incoming and outgoing line segments (see Figure 2-43).

FIGURE 2-43
Effect of moving a
point on its attached
line segments

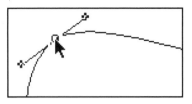 

When you select and move a point...   *...the point's attached control handles move with the point.*

Flipping and Flopping

I hate drawing objects from scratch when I don't have to, so I use flipping and flopping to create most of the objects I use in a FreeHand publication. What's flipping and flopping? The process of cloning one object to create another object with which the original object shares a border. Look at Figure 2-44.

Flipping and flopping comes in especially handy when you need to create two objects—even objects of different shapes—which share a common boundary. Redrawing the boundary between two objects is not just boring, but can be quite difficult, if the boundary is complex enough. I'm not averse to tackling difficult tasks; I just hate to make something more difficult than it has to be, so I use flipping and flopping even when the shapes sharing a boundary are very different (see Figure 2-45).

FIGURE 2-44
Basic flipping and
flopping

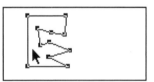 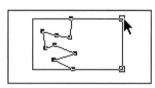

Clone the original object.   *Drag points on the clone to a new location.*

FIGURE 2-45
Flipping and flopping to
create different shapes

 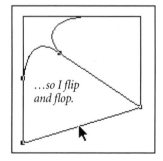

I don't want to draw these curves again...   *...so I flip and flop.*

Open and Closed Paths

You can think of an open path as a line and a closed path as a shape. Open paths can't be filled, have objects pasted inside them, or be added to other paths to create a composite path. You can, however, join the points on either end of an open path to another open path.

First, you can always drag one end point on an open path over another end point. When you do this, FreeHand closes the path.

To use FreeHand's Path/point dialog box to change an open path into a closed path, select the path, press Command-I to display the Path/point dialog box, and then check the Closed option in the Path/point dialog box. Press Return to close the dialog box, and FreeHand creates a straight line segment which joins the first point in the path to the last point in the path (see Figure 2-46).

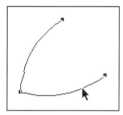

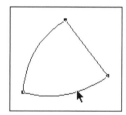

Select the path you want to close and press Command-I.

Click "Closed" and press Return. FreeHand closes the path.

Similarly, you can use the Path/point dialog box to change a closed path into an open path by following the above procedure but deselecting the Closed option.

FreeHand removes the line segment which joins the first point in the path to the last point in the path. When you convert a closed path into an open path, any clipped (pasted-inside) objects or fills disappear. If you then convert the open path into a closed path, the clipped objects and/or fills reappear.

Closing a path using the Path/point dialog box is great, but what if you've got a curved path you want to close but don't want to close with a straight line (see Figure 2-47)?

1. Select the path.

2. Press Command-= to clone the path. A copy of the path appears on top of the path.

3. Drag a marquee over two of the end points (they'll be right on top of each other, so it won't look like anything's selected).

4. Press Command-J to join the end points. FreeHand joins the two points into one point.

5. Press Command-I to display the Path/point dialog box.

6. Click "Closed" and press Return. FreeHand closes the path.

At this point, you've got a closed path that's the same shape as the original, open path. Now you can join it to other closed paths to create compound paths. Beware, however, that adjustments made to the curve handles of points on the top of the path will not be reflected in the position of the curve handles of the points on the bottom of the path (see Figure 2-48).

FIGURE 2-47
Closing an
irregular path

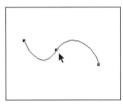

Select the path you want to make a closed path and clone it.

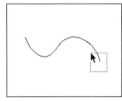

Drag a selection rectangle over the end points and press Command-J.

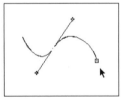

Open the Path dialog box and click "Closed." FreeHand closes the path.

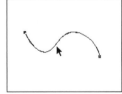

Now you can work with the path as you would with any closed path.

FIGURE 2-48
Adjusting closed
irregular paths

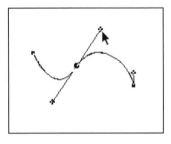

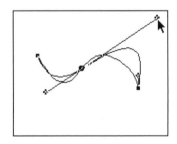

When you adjust the curve handles on a closed path created with the above technique…

…you're only changing the curve of the lines on top. This may or may not be what you want.

Splitting and Joining Paths

You can always add to or subtract from a path in FreeHand. You can split an open or closed path into separate paths, and you can join paths to each other or make a single path a closed path by joining them.

Splitting Paths

You can split a path in one of two ways.

- Select a point (or points) on the path with the pointer tool, and then choose "Split element" from the Element menu.

- Select the path with the pointer tool, select the knife tool, and then click on the path (or on a selected point on the path).

When you split a path by splitting a point, FreeHand creates a new point on top of the point you selected. This new point is connected to the line segment going to the next point along the path's winding (see Figure 2-49).

When you split a path by clicking on a line segment with the knife tool (that is, not on any existing point), two new points are created—one on the end of each line segment (see Figure 2-50).

FIGURE 2-49
Splitting a path by
splitting points

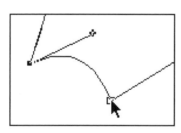 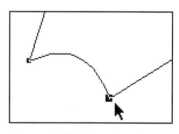

Select a point and choose "Split element" from the Element menu.   *FreeHand splits the path at the point you selected.*

FIGURE 2-50
Splitting a path by
splitting a line segment

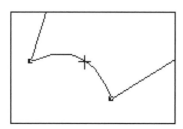 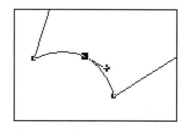

Select a path, select the knife tool, and then click on the path.   *FreeHand splits the path where you clicked.*

To select one or the other of the two paths you've created by split-ting the path, press Tab (to deselect everything), and then select the path you want, or press ' (to select both paths), and Shift-click the path you don't want selected.

When you split a path and create two new points, it can be very difficult figuring out which end point belongs to which path. It's simple, actually. The point closest to the start of the path (following the path's winding) is farthest to the back, and the point farthest from the start of the path is on top of it (see Figure 2-51).

You can use the Split element command to split any number of points. Drag a marquee over all of the points you want to split, choose "Split element" from the Element menu, and FreeHand splits all of the points (see Figure 2-52).

FIGURE 2-51
Which point is on top?

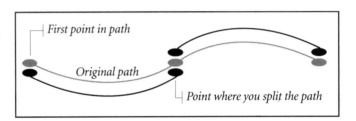

First point in path

Original path

Point where you split the path

FIGURE 2-52
Splitting several
points at once

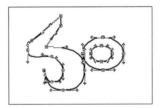

Drag a selection rectangle over the points you want to split.

Choose "Split element" from the Element menu. FreeHand splits all of the selected points.

You can't drag the knife tool over a number of paths and have it split them along the path you specified by dragging. It would be great if it did work like a real knife, but it doesn't.

Joining Paths

You can join two open paths to create a single path, or you can join two closed paths to create a composite path. In this section, I'll talk about joining open paths. For more on joining closed paths to create composite paths, see "Composite Paths," later in this chapter.

To join points on two open paths and create a single path, drag the end points of the two open paths over each other. It's easier to do this when "Snap to point" (on the View menu) is active. Once you've positioned the paths, drag a marquee over the two points and choose "Join elements" from the Element menu (see Figure 2-53).

FIGURE 2-53
Joining two open paths

 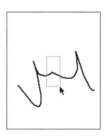 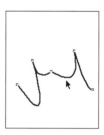

Drag the end points of two open paths over each other and join them to create a single, open path.

Tip:
If "Join
elements" is
Grayed out

One or both of the paths containing the points you've selected is probably a closed path, or both paths are open paths and you haven't selected a pair of points. Check by opening the Path/point dialog boxes for both paths, one at a time.

Tip:
If "Join
elements"
Doesn't Do
Anything

You can't join open paths without having two overlapping (or nearly overlapping) points selected. Move the paths or points so that two end points overlap, then drag a marquee over the two points, and choose "Join elements" from the Element menu to join the paths..

Sizing Paths

You can size paths in a variety of ways. The methods that first come to mind are sizing the path numerically, sizing the path by eye using the scale tool, and stretching the path.

To size the path numerically, follow these steps (see Figure 2-54).

1. Select the scale tool in the toolbox.

2. Hold down Command to turn the scale tool into the pointer tool, and select the path.

3. Release Command, press Option, and click to display the Scale dialog box.

4. Specify how you want the path scaled—including whether the path's attributes (fill, contents, and line weight) are scaled—and press Return.

FreeHand scales the object according to the specifications you entered in the Scale dialog box.

FIGURE 2-54
Numerically
sizing a path

Select the object you want to scale and choose the Scale tool from the toolbox. Hold down Option and click anywhere on the page.

FreeHand displays the Scale dialog box.

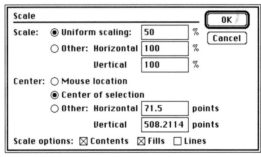

In the Scale dialog box, specify the reduction or enlargement and the scaling options you want and press Return.

FreeHand scales the selected object.

You can also use the scale tool to scale the object by eye (see Figure 2-55). Follow these steps.

1. Select the scale tool from the toolbox.

2. Hold down Command to turn the scale tool into the pointer tool and select the path you want to scale.

3. Release Command, press Option, and click to display the Scale dialog box.

4. Check (or uncheck) the scaling options you want (or don't want) in the Scaling options section of the dialog box.

5. Press Return.

6. Drag the scale tool to size the selected path. Hold down Shift if you want to scale the object proportionally. When the object is the size and shape you want, stop dragging.

FreeHand sizes the object, using the scale options you specified in the Scale dialog box.

FIGURE 2-55
Scaling a path by eye
with the scale tool

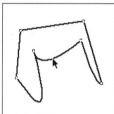

Select the object, switch back to the scale tool...

...and then drag to size the object. Drag up to enlarge the object; down to reduce the object.

Here's another way to stretch the path by eye (see Figure 2-56).

1. Select the path and press Command-G to group the path. If you want to scale the path's attributes (fill, contents, and line weights), press Command-I to display the Group dialog box, check the Group transforms as a unit option, and press Return.

2. Size the path as you would any other grouped object, holding down Shift if you want to size the path proportionally.

FIGURE 2-56
Stretching a path by eye

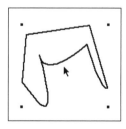
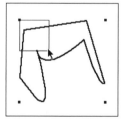

Select the path and press Command-G to group the path.

Drag a corner handle to resize the path. Hold down Shift to scale the object proportionally.

Composite Paths

In the old days, not only did I have to walk miles school in freezing weather, but I also had to create holes in closed paths with complex, voodoo ceremony-like maneuvers, usually including "Paste inside."

These days, creating holes in paths is easier—just make them into composite paths. Composite paths are made of two or more paths (which must be unlocked, ungrouped, and closed) which have been joined with "Join elements." Areas between the two paths, or areas where the paths overlap, are transparent (see Figure 2-57).

1. Select the ellipse tool from the toolbox.

2. Draw two ellipses, one on top of the other.

3. Fill the ellipses with some basic fill.

4. Select both ellipses.

5. Press Command-U to ungroup both ellipses.

6. Press Command-J to join the two ellipses.

FIGURE 2-57
Creating
composite paths

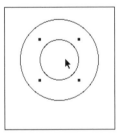

Create two ellipses using the ellipse tool.

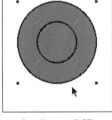

Apply a line and fill.

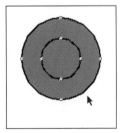

Press Command-U to ungroup the ellipses, and then press Command-J to join the ellipses.

You've just created a composite path. The inside of the shape is transparent.

What if you don't want transparent areas where the paths overlap? Press Command-I to display the Composite path dialog box and uncheck the Even/odd fill option. This fills all of the objects in the composite path with the same fill (see Figure 2-58).

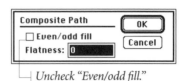

Uncheck "Even/odd fill."

*Select a composite path
and press Command-I.*

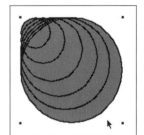

*FreeHand applies
the current fill
and line to all of
the paths inside
the composite
path.*

You make composite paths into normal paths by splitting them. If you decide you don't want the paths to be composite paths anymore, you can change them back into individual paths by selecting the composite path and choosing "Split element" from the Element menu.

Composite paths can be transformed just as you'd transform any other path.

When you join new paths to the composite path, each new path is added to the path in order. When you split the composite path, the first time you choose "Split element" removes the most recently appended subpath; the next "Split element" removes the next most recently appended subpath; and so on.

**Editing
Composite Paths**

You can subselect the individual subpaths that make up a composite path in the same way that you subselect objects inside a group. Once the object's selected, you can alter the position of the path's points, move or otherwise transform the path, delete points, delete the entire path, or clone the path (see Figure 2-59).

You can subselect multiple subpaths inside a composite path by holding down Shift as you select the subpaths. You can also select through any overlapping subpaths or objects by holding down Control and Option as you click on the subpaths, just as you can Control-click your way through stacks of objects. You can apply any of FreeHand's transformations to the subselected subpath.

FIGURE 2-59
Subselecting
individual paths inside
composite paths

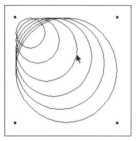

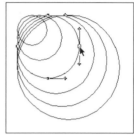

For clarity, these two illustrations are shown in Keyline view.

Select a composite path.

Hold down Option and click to select a subpath.

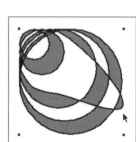

Modify the subpath.

Press Tab to deselect the subpath. The subpath remains part of the composite path.

When you convert characters to paths, FreeHand automatically converts the characters as composite paths. This is great, because you can paste things inside composite paths (see Figure 2-60).

FIGURE 2-60
Characters converted
to paths are
composite paths

Applying Lines and Fills to Composite Paths

When you join paths with different lines and fills, the composite path takes on the line and fill attributes of the path that's the farthest to the back.

To apply a line or fill to a composite path, select the path and click on the style you want (or create a new one through the Styles dialog box, check the Apply check box, and press Return).

Blending

Blending is a way of creating a number of paths, automatically, between two existing paths. Blending is one of FreeHand's most useful tools, especially for creating shaded objects. When Illustrator first introduced the world to blending, all of the marketing materials stressed this great new feature's ability to turn an "S" into a swan, or a "V" into a violin. That's pretty cool, *but how often do you actually need to do that?* Blending's actually a much less glamorous, much more useful tool (see Figure 2-61).

FIGURE 2-61
Blends

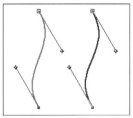

Select two points on two paths and choose "Blend…" from the Element menu.

Type in how many blend steps you want and press Return.

FreeHand fills in the intermediate blend objects.

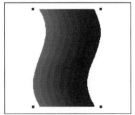

Shading with blends　*Keyline view of blends*

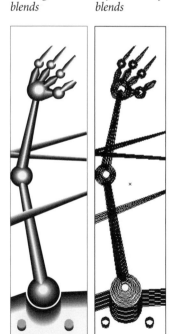

Blending: The Rules of the Road

FreeHand doesn't impose too many limitations on what, when, and how you can blend FreeHand objects. But there are a few things you've got to keep in mind.

You Can Blend Any Two Ungrouped Paths Having Like Attributes. What do I mean by "like attributes?" I mean that you can blend a path containing a radial fill into a path containing another radial fill, but you can't blend a path containing a radial fill into a path containing a graduated fill.

You can blend paths containing process colors or tints of a single spot color, but you can't blend paths containing two different spot colors. You can join two open paths, or two closed paths, but you can't join an open path to a closed path.

When you try and blend paths having different line patterns, or patterned fills, the shapes of the objects blend, but the lines or fills will flip from one to the other at the halfway point of the blend (see Figure 2-62).

FIGURE 2-62
Blending paths with
differing dashed lines

Blending and Reference Points. When you're blending, you have the option of selecting a "reference point" when you're working with open paths, and you *must* select a "reference point" on the starting and ending paths in the blend when you're blending closed paths. What's a "reference point?" It's a way of telling FreeHand, "Blend these two objects; from this point to that point" (see Figure 2-63).

FIGURE 2-63
Reference points

Select two reference points—one on either end of two similar paths—and blend. The position of the reference points has a great effect on the blend.

How Many Steps Do You Need? After picking reference points, the next most important part of creating a blend is the settings you enter in the Blend dialog box (see Figure 2-64).

The number you enter in the Number of steps text edit box is the number of steps you want in your blend, not including the original, selected objects. The number you enter in the First blend text edit box is the percentage of the distance between the original paths where you want to place the first blended path.

The number you enter in the Last blend text edit box is the percentage of the distance between the original paths where you want to place the last blended path.

Most of the time, you'll just type a number in the Number of steps text edit box and press Return. You can enter numbers in the other text edit boxes to create special blend effects (see Figure 2-65).

FIGURE 2-64
Blend dialog box

This text edit box controls where the blend starts.

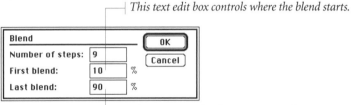

This one controls where it stops. Both percentages are relative to the distance between the reference points.

FIGURE 2-65
Special blend effects

Normal blend: 19 blend steps; first blend step 5%; last blend step 95%.

Special blend: 19 blend steps; first blend step 20%; last blend step 80%.

Now that you know the rules, let's create a blend (see Figure 2-66).

1. Select two ungrouped paths (with matching or compatible attributes).

2. Choose "Blend..." from the Element menu (this is another good command to make up a macro or keyboard shortcut for).

Is "Blend…" grayed out? If it is, at least one of the paths you've selected is a closed path. If both of the paths are closed, you have to select a "reference point." If one of the paths is closed, you have to make it an open path, or make the other path closed.

The Blend dialog box appears.

3. In the Blend dialog box, enter the values you want for your blend.

4. Press Return.

FreeHand creates the paths for the blend you've specified. The original objects and the newly created paths are grouped together following the blend.

FIGURE 2-66
Creating a blend

Select two reference points and choose "Blend…" from the Element menu.

Type the number of steps you want for your blend and press Return.

FreeHand creates your blend.

The blended objects are grouped.

Okay, this example's no more typical of the uses of blending than the swan or violin I mentioned earlier.

But it sure is fun!

If the attributes of the paths you're trying to blend are incompatible, FreeHand displays an alert (shown in Figure 2-67). Sorry, no blend. You'll have to track down what's different between the two paths, make changes, and try again.

You can enter negative numbers (to -100%) in the First blend and Last blend text edit boxes. You can use this to extend the blend past the original objects by up to the distance between them. Of what possible use is this? I haven't yet found one.

FIGURE 2-67
What happens when
you try to blend
incompatible objects

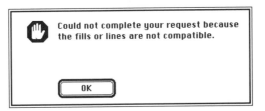

Could not complete your request because the fills or lines are not compatible.

OK

Editing Blends

This part—changing the blend after you've made it—almost scares me. If you want to change the number of steps in your blend, select the blended objects and press Command-I to bring up the Blend dialog box (it's a special object info dialog box for blends). Change the blend by entering new values in the Number of steps, First blend, or Last blend text edit boxes and press Return. FreeHand creates a new blend from the original objects (see Figure 2-68).

FIGURE 2-68
Editing blends

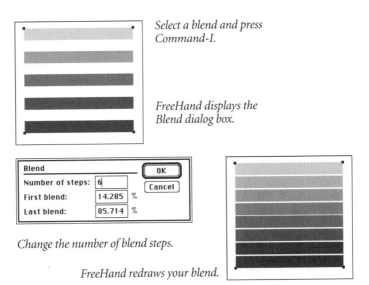

Select a blend and press Command-I.

FreeHand displays the Blend dialog box.

Change the number of blend steps.

FreeHand redraws your blend.

Changing the Shape of the Entire Blend

You can change the shape and attributes of blended objects to a certain extent by changing the shape and attributes of the original shapes in the blend. Subselect the original path (or both original paths) by holding down Option as you click on the path (you are subselecting an element in a group). Next, change the path's attributes and/or shape. As you change the path's shape and attributes, FreeHand recreates the blend based on the current shape and/or attributes (see Figure 2-69).

FIGURE 2-69
Changing the shape and attributes of blended objects

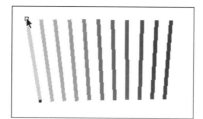 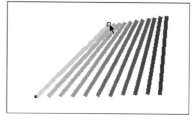

Hold down Option and click on the first or last object in the blend to subselect it.

Reshape the object. FreeHand alters the blend based on the new shape.

Editing an Intermediate Path in a Blend

To edit one or more of the intermediate paths in the blend, ungroup the blend, select the path, and edit away. There's no way to get the changes you make to this intermediate point to ripple through the blend, however. If you want to do that, consider reblending between intermediate objects (see Figure 2-70).

FIGURE 2-70
Editing intermediate paths in a blend

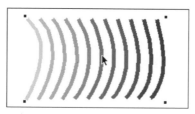 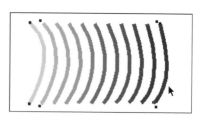

Select the blend you want to edit...

...and press Command-U to ungroup.

 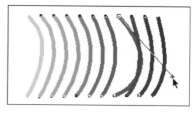

Press Command-U to ungroup the intermediate blend objects.

Now you can edit the intermediate blend objects.

Creating Colors Based on Blend Steps

When you create a blend, the colors applied to the intermediate paths in the blend are not automatically added to FreeHand's Colors palette or the Colors dialog box. If you want to add one or more of the colors created by the blend to your Colors palette, this is the procedure (see Figure 2-71).

1. Select the path.

2. Press Command-E to bring up the Fill and line dialog box.

3. In the Fill and line dialog box, click the color swatch that appears on the Fill or Line pop-up menu. A new Colors dialog box appears.

4. Name your color and press Return to close the Colors dialog box.

5. Press Return to close the Fill and line dialog box.

FIGURE 2-71
Adding colors based on blended elements

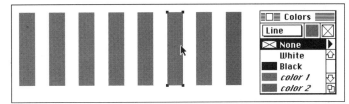

Select the blend step that has the color you want and press Command-E.

Click on the color swatch in the Fill and line dialog box to pop-up the Color menu. Choose a color model from the pop-up menu.

Type a name for your new color and press Return twice to close the Colors dialog box and the Fill and line dialog box.

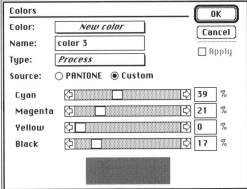

FreeHand adds your new color to the Colors palette.

Using "Blend" to Create Graduated and Radial Fills

If you want total control over the creation of graduated or radial fills in FreeHand, use "Blend," rather than the Graduated or Radial fill types. If you use "Blend," you accrue several significant advantages.

- Control over the graduation. FreeHand's Graduation fill type offers you the choice between "Linear" and "Logarithmic" fill progressions. By blending objects, you can make the blend go as rapidly or slowly from color to color as you choose.

- Control over trapping. See Chapter 7, "Printing," for more information on trapping graduated and radial fills.

- Optimization of your fill for printing on your final output device (printer or imagesetter).

- Superior screen display of fills.

The only disadvantage I can think of is that you've got many more objects on a page to worry about. Still, you can always make them one object with "Group," so it's not a big deal.

Blends also produce very different-looking results. I find that I mix blends and graduated fills inside a publication to get the effects I want. If I want a graduated fill that doesn't follow the shape of an object, I'll often use a graduated fill. But if I want a graduated fill that does follow the shape of an object, I'll use a blend. Figure 2-72 shows the difference.

FIGURE 2-72
Blends and
graduated fills

Graduated fills don't follow the shape of the object.

Blends follow the shape of the object.

It can be difficult getting the center of a radial fill to fall where you want it.

It's easy to get the center of a blend to fall where you want it.

To create a graduated fill using "Blend," follow these steps.

1. Create a path that has the fill attributes you want for one end of the graduation.

2. Create a path that has the fill attributes you want for the other end of the graduation.

3. Select one point from the first object, and then select a point from the second path.

4. Choose "Blend…" from the Element menu.

5. Type a number in the Number of steps text edit box and press Return.

When you're working with blends, you can determine the best number of blend steps to use, based on the length of the blend and the properties of your printer, by solving the following equation.

$$\text{number of steps} = (\text{dpi/lpi})^2 * \% \text{ change in color}$$

In this equation, *dpi* is the resolution of your final output device in dots per inch; *lpi* is the screen frequency you'll be using, in lines per inch. The value *% change in color* is just that, and it's easy to figure out if you're using spot colors.

If you're using process colors, figure out which component process color goes through the largest percentage change from one end of the blend to the other, and use that value for the "% change in color" part of the equation.

The purpose of this equation is to tell you the minimum number of steps you should use. Below this number of steps, you'll start losing gray levels and bands of gray (or color) will appear in your blend. You can always use more blend steps than this, but remember that each blend step is another object for your printer to render. Each additional blend step increases the complexity of your publication, and therefore increases the time your publication takes to print.

What if using the optimum number of blend steps means that gaps appear in your blend? This happens when your original blend objects aren't big enough to cover the distance from one blend step to the next. When this happens, you can either increase the number of blend steps you're using, or you can figure out how much larger you'll have to make your blend objects using the following equation.

distance blend has to cover/number of steps = size of original object

Okay smart guy, you're saying, these equations work great for blending simple rectangles which happen to be running vertically or horizontally, but what about a diagonal blend between two like paths shaped like a camel's back? Huh? Huh?

I am not the son of a high-school Algebra teacher for nothing. I know that in a right triangle, the square of the hypotenuse is equal to the sum of the other two squares (thanks, Dad!). The right triangle I'm talking about is the one we can derive from the horizontal and vertical positions of the points, plus a line drawn straight between them. Here are the steps involved.

1. Select the endpoint of one of the paths and press Command-I to bring up the Path/point dialog box.

2. Write down the numbers in the Point: Horizontal and Point: Vertical text edit boxes and press Return.

3. Select the endpoint of the other of the paths and press Command-I to bring up the Path/point dialog box.

4. Write down the numbers in the Point: Horizontal and Point: Vertical text edit boxes and press Return.

5. Take the larger of the two numbers for horizontal position and subtract the smaller horizontal position from it to give you the width of the horizontal leg of our imaginary right triangle. Let's call the number we get from this subtraction x. Then, subtract the smaller of the two vertical positions from the larger vertical position and call the result, the height of the vertical leg of our imaginary right triangle, y.

6. Now solve this:

distance^2 = x^2+y^2

(square the two values, add them, then take the square root of that number.)

That wasn't that hard, was it? Now you can use that number in the steps above to figure out how wide your lines or paths will have to be to fill the distance without leaving unsightly gaps. If you have a snazzy calculator, you can just press the square root button to derive the squares of x and y.

Note that this is just not going to work for a blend going between unlike paths, because the distances from one point in the path to another aren't the same for all of the points in the paths. The camel's hump blend appears in Figure 2-73.

FIGURE 2-73

Camel's hump blend

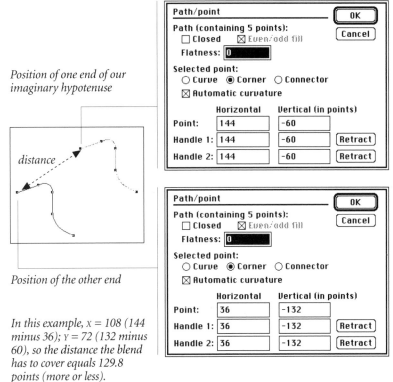

Position of one end of our imaginary hypotenuse

distance

Position of the other end

In this example, x = 108 (144 minus 36); y = 72 (132 minus 60), so the distance the blend has to cover equals 129.8 points (more or less).

Now that you've gone through all of that, remember that you could've drawn a line from one point to another and read the distance from the info bar. I like doing the math, myself. It makes me feel less senile.

You can also blend between intermediate objects to obtain an even higher degree of control over your graduated or radial fills.

**Blends and
Spot Colors**

If you've tried printing a 2-color publication containing a blend from your spot color to white, you've probably encountered one of Free-Hand 3's rare problems. If you create a blend going from your spot color to FreeHand's default color "White," the intermediate blend objects are colored with process colors. This means that they don't print on the same separation as everything else tagged with your spot color.

To get around this bug, create a new color that's a zero percent tint of your spot color and replace the white object with an object colored this color. When you blend using this color, the intermediate blend objects are colored with tints of your spot color, and print on the same overlay as everything else that's tagged with that spot color.

You can't blend between two spot-colored objects. Does this mean you're out of luck if you want to use blends between the two colors? You're not. Use one of the process colors (cyan, magenta, yellow, or black) as a substitute for each spot color in your publication, and blend away.

You can do lots more with spot colors if you substitute one of the process colors for a spot color. For more on how to do this, see "Substituting Process Colors for Spot Colors" in Chapter 6, "Color."

Tracing

When Illustrator 1.0 first appeared, tracing scanned artwork or MacPaint images was seen as the major use for the product. People just couldn't imagine creating entire pieces of artwork using a point-and-path drawing program. While times have changed—I think more people now use FreeHand and Illustrator to create illustrations without tracing—manual tracing is still a powerful option you can use in creating your FreeHand publication (see Figure 2-74).

1. Import an image. Make sure you've got "High-resolution TIFF display" turned on in the Preferences dialog box; this way, you'll see the high-resolution display of your imported image rather than a 72-dpi rendition (this is one of those small but revolutionary new features in FreeHand 3).

2. Click the Background layer in the Layers palette to send the image to the background. This grays the image and makes it easier to trace. You can also color the image some color (I like coloring it cyan, because I'm used to tracing things drawn in nonreproducing blue pen) and send it to some other layer—just make sure you're doing the tracing on a layer that's in front of the layer you send the image to.

3. Zoom in on some portion of the image and start placing points.

4. When you're through tracing the image, delete the image from your illustration or send it to some nonprinting layer.

Why not use the tracing tool? The tracing tool is great, but you're smarter than it is. Often, you can trace an image more quickly than you can autotrace it, given the amount of time it can take to clean up an autotraced image. Still, autotracing is a very handy feature for certain types of images.

FIGURE 2-74
Manually tracing an
imported image

Import the image you want to trace.

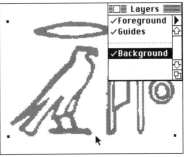

Send the image to a background layer.

Place points and paths until...

...you've traced as much of the image as you want.

Lines

Once you've created a path, you'll probably want to give the path some specific weight, color, or other property. The process of applying a line to a path is often called "stroking."

To apply a line to a path, you can choose one of FreeHand's default line styles from the Attributes menu, or you can specify your line using either the Fill and line dialog box or the Styles dialog box. All of these options are available through the Attributes menu (see Figure 2-75).

Note that you can choose a number of prespecified line weights from the bottom half of the menu. These are great, as far as they go, but you'll be doing most of your serious work through the Fill and line dialog box.

When you choose "Fill and line..." from the Attributes menu (or press Command-E), the Fill and line dialog box appears. Don't be concerned that the dialog box includes specifications for fills, as well as for lines. We'll work with fills later. Concentrate on the "Line" section, the left half of the dialog box.

Use the Line pop-up menu to pick the type of line you want to use. If you select "Basic," the dialog shows you the basic line attributes.

FIGURE 2-75
Attributes menu,
Fill and line dialog box

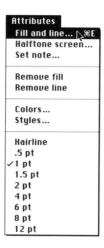

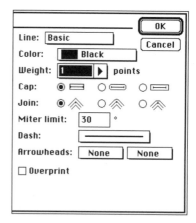

To save space, I'll show only half of the enormous Fill and line dialog box.

Basic Lines   Most of the lines you'll use will be basic lines. Though they're not flashy, there are a few interesting tricks to using them, and a couple of things to look out for.

Color. Choose a color on the Color pop-up menu, or choose "Spot color," "Process color," or "Tint" to create a new color for your line.

Weight. Type a number or choose a line width from the Weight text edit box/pop-up menu for the width of your line. Don't type zero, even if it works to produce the finest line available on your 300-dpi printer, because a line weight of zero on an imagesetter produces an almost invisible line.

Cap. Select one of the Cap options to determine the shape of the end of the line (see Figure 2-76).

FIGURE 2-76
Line caps

Join. The Join option determines the way FreeHand renders corners— the place where two line segments meet in a point (see Figure 2-77).

FIGURE 2-77
Line joins

Miter Limit. The number you enter in the Miter limit text edit box (from 2 to 180 degrees) sets the smallest angle for which FreeHand will use a mitered join. If the angle of the line join exceeds the number you enter in the Miter limit text edit box, FreeHand renders the corner as a beveled line join (see Figure 2-78).

FIGURE 2-78
Miter limit

Miter limit of 2   *Miter limit of 30*

Dash. If you want a dashed line, choose one of the dash patterns from the Dash pop-up menu (see Figure 2-79).

If you've looked at the Dash pop-up menu for a while and still don't see the dash pattern you're looking for, hold down Option as you click the cursor on the pop-up menu. The Line pattern dialog box appears. In the Line pattern dialog box, you can create a wide variety of dashed line patterns (see Figure 2-80).

If you still can't find the dashed line style you want, you can create one using FreeHand's PostScript external resource files. See Chapter 8, "PostScript" for more on creating external resource files.

FIGURE 2-79
Dashed lines

FIGURE 2-80
Setting custom
dashed lines

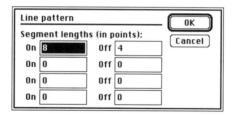

Arrowheads. You can add arrowheads or (I guess) tail feathers to any line you want by choosing an arrowhead style from the pop-up menus. The leftmost pop-up menu applies to the first point in the path (according to the direction of the path); the rightmost pop-up menu applies to the last point in the path. You don't have to make choices from both of the pop-up menus (see Figure 81).

FIGURE 2-81
Arrowheads

Overprint. Clicking on this option makes the line overprint, rather than knock out, whatever's behind it. This setting overrides any ink-level overprinting settings in the Print options dialog box (see Figure 2-82). This might not seem like much, but it's one of the most important features in FreeHand (see Chapter 6, "Color," for more about trapping).

FIGURE 2-82
Overprinting lines

Color 2
Color 1

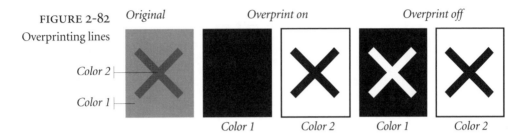

Original   Overprint on   Overprint off

Color 1   Color 2   Color 1   Color 2

Patterned Lines

If you select "Patterned," the dialog box fills in with a variety of patterns you can apply to your line (see Figure 2-83).The color, line weight, line cap, line join, and miter limit settings for patterned lines all work exactly as described above.

If you want to edit the pattern you've chosen, just click inside the cell defining the pattern. It's like a miniature paint program—click on a black pixel and it turns white; click on a white pixel and it turns black. If you want to create a pattern entirely from scratch, click the Clear button to set all of the pixels in the cell to white. Click on the Invert button to invert the pattern shown in the cell.

Patterned lines have several significant limitations.

- The pattern in a patterned line is always the same size, regardless of the width of the line.

- Patterned lines won't color separate into process colors

- Patterned lines can take a long time to print

- Patterned lines have an opaque background, so the pattern won't knock out of whatever's behind them. The entire line will, instead.

- You can't apply a halftone screen to patterned lines.

- Patterned lines are kinda ugly

FIGURE 2-83
Patterned Lines

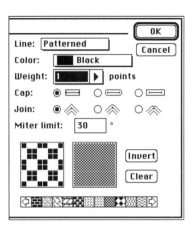

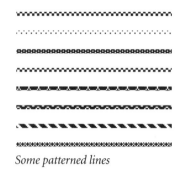

Some patterned lines

Choose a line pattern from the scrolling display at the bottom of the dialog box, or click "Clear" to clear the current pattern and draw your own. Click "Invert" to invert the current pattern.

Patterned lines are really intended to provide compatibility for imported PICTs drawn in MacDraw II. Some people feel more comfortable working with the patterned lines than with the PostScript or custom line types, which is unfortunate. Use tiled fills instead, whenever possible.

PostScript Lines

If you choose "PostScript," a large text edit box appears at the bottom of the line section of the Fill and line dialog box. Enter up to 255 characters of PostScript code in the large text edit box. Don't press a Return to break lines—it'll close the dialog box. Separate your entries with spaces instead; PostScript doesn't need carriage returns to understand the code (see Figure 2-84).

FIGURE 2-84
PostScript lines

Don't type "%" in this text edit box—"%" means that this is a comment, and your effect won't print.

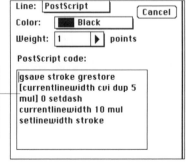

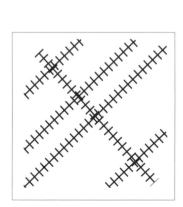

PostScript lines display on screen as a basic line of the weight and color you specify. Remember that the settings for weight and color affect only the display of the line—the actual line width and color are set by the PostScript code you enter.

While you can enter complete descriptions of PostScript lines in this dialog box, you'll usually use it to call PostScript routines in external resource files. See Chapter 8, "PostScript," for more on passing values to external routines through this dialog box.

Custom Lines

If you choose "Custom" from the Line pop-up menu, the Effect pop-up menu appears. The line style names on the pop-up menu are the custom line styles that were previously part of FreeHand's UserPrep file (see Figure 2-85). In FreeHand 2, you'd invoke these line styles by typing parameters in the PostScript dialog box. These days it's a bit easier.

FIGURE 2-85
Custom lines

Here's an example of FreeHand's stock custom lines. I printed each line using a pattern length of 10, a pattern width of 6, and a spacing of zero (except for "Rectangle," which I printed using a spacing of 3).

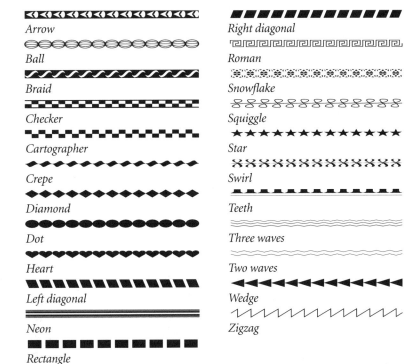

Arrow

Ball

Braid

Checker

Cartographer

Crepe

Diamond

Dot

Heart

Left diagonal

Neon

Rectangle

Right diagonal

Roman

Snowflake

Squiggle

Star

Swirl

Teeth

Three waves

Two waves

Wedge

Zigzag

Most of these custom line styles are variable. Once you've selected a custom line style, a dialog box appears. Use pop-up menus and text edit boxes in the dialog box to specify the custom line's appearance. Except for the Neon line style, all of these dialog boxes look alike (see Figure 2-86).

Using these dialog boxes, you can vary your custom lines tremendously (see Figure 2-87).

FIGURE 2-86
Custom lines dialog box

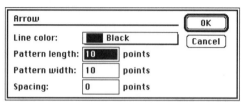

Most of the custom lines dialog boxes look like this one. You can choose a color, and enter values for the pattern length, width, and spacing.

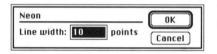

"Neon" is the only custom line effect with a different dialog box.

FIGURE 2-87
Changing variables for
custom lines

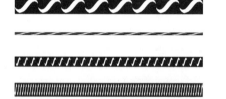

Length 30, width 20, spacing 0

Length 20, width 3, spacing 0

Length 6, width 12, spacing 3

Length 3, width 16, spacing 0

Example settings for the "Braid" custom line effect

Editing Lines

If you've applied a line to a particular path, you can change the line by selecting the path using either of several methods.

- Press Command-E to display the Fill and line dialog box.

- Choose one of the preset lines from the Attributes menu.

- Click on a color in the Colors palette.

- Click on another style name in the Styles palette.

Removing Lines

To quickly remove a line from a path, choose "Remove line" from the Attributes menu while the path is selected, or click "None" in the Colors palette when the "Line" selected.

Fills

Any closed (or composite) path you create can be filled.

Basic Fills. Choose "Basic" to fill an object with a specific color. The color can be a spot color, a tint, or a process color (see Figure 2-88).

Check the Overprint check box to specify that this fill overprints any underlying objects. If you don't check "Overprint," the object will be knocked out of any underlying objects unless its ink color has been set to overprint. Depending on the colors you're using in your publication and the printing process you intend to use, this might not be what you want (see Figure 2-89).

FIGURE 2-88
Basic fills

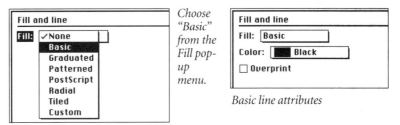

Choose "Basic" from the Fill pop-up menu.

Basic line attributes

Once again, I'm saving space by showing only part of the enormous Fill and line dialog box.

FIGURE 2-89
Overprinting fills

Original *Overprint on* *Overprint off*

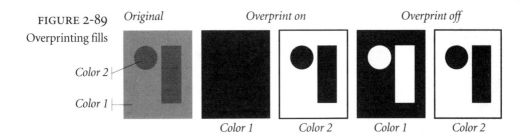

Color 2

Color 1

Color 1   Color 2   Color 1   Color 2

Graduated Fills. Choose "Graduated" to fill an object with a linear or logarithmic graduation from one color to another. You can set the beginning and ending colors, and you can specify the type of the graduation (linear or logarithmic) and the angle the graduation is to follow (see Figure 2-90).

Note that you cannot specify graduations between two spot colors (though you can specify graduations between two tints of the same

FIGURE 2-90
Graduated fills

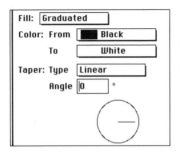

Set up the specifications for your graduated fill in the Fill and line dialog box and press Return.

Graduated fill produced by the settings shown at left.

spot color, or between a spot color and the default color "White"). There's a way around this limitation, however, as shown in "Substituting Process Colors for Spot Colors" in Chapter 6, "Color."

A far more serious problem is that you can't set graduated fills to overprint, which makes it harder (maybe harder than it should be) to trap abutting graduated fills. To see how to do that, see "Trapping," in Chapter 6, "Color."

Finally, if you're considering using a graduated fill, you should take a look at "Blending" earlier in this chapter.

Patterned Fills. Patterned fills have the same problems and limitations as patterned lines, discussed in "Patterned Lines," earlier in this chapter.

PostScript Fills. When you choose "PostScript" from the Fill menu, a large text edit box appears at the bottom of the Fill section of the Fill and line dialog box (see Figure 2-91). PostScript fills work just like PostScript lines, described earlier in this chapter.

PostScript fills display on screen as a pattern of little PSs.

FIGURE 2-91
PostScript fills

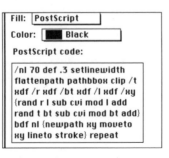

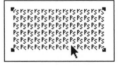

On your screen, PostScript fills look like this…

…but they print like this.

Radial Fills. A radial fill creates a concentric graduated fill from the center of an object to the outside of the object. The center of a radial fill is placed at the center of the two most distant points in the object (see Figure 2-92). This means that the center of the fill can fall in unexpected places.

The From pop-up menu sets the color of the outside of a radial fill. The To pop-up menu sets the color of the center.

FIGURE 2-92
Radial fills

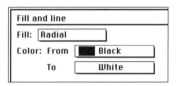

The "From" pop-up menu sets the color of the center of the radial fill.

Tip:
Controlling the
Center Point of a
Radial Fill

Radial fills are great, but how do you get the center of the radial fill to fall just where you want it? I've seen it suggested elsewhere that you create your radial fill, then paste it inside some other object. Don't, because objects pasted inside other objects take longer to print.

Instead, use FreeHand's literal-mindedness and new composite paths feature as follows to position the fill exactly where you want it. (see Figure 2-93).

1. Draw a circle with the ellipse tool.

2. Press Command-E to bring up the Fill and line dialog box and select a radial fill in the Fill section of the dialog box. This trick works best if the paths have no stroke, so choose a line of "None" in the Lines section of the dialog box. Press Return to close the dialog box.

   Note that the center of the radial fill is exactly in the center of the circle. You'll be changing this.

3. Select the line tool and draw a line outside the circle.

4. Press Command-I to display the Path/point dialog box for the line you just drew.

FIGURE 2-93

Controlling the center
point of a radial fill

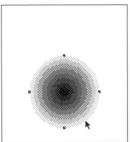

Draw an ellipse, ungroup it, and apply a radial fill to it. Set the line to "None."

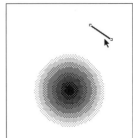

Draw a line outside the or press
ellipse and to un
press Com- then
mand-I.

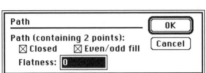

Close the path by clicking "Closed."

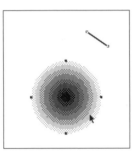

Select both objects and press Command-J to turn them into a composite path.

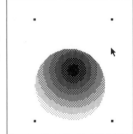

FreeHand centers the radial fill based on the bounding box of the path.

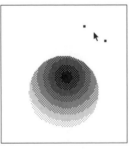

Hold down Option and subselect the line. If you have trouble selecting the line, try Option-dragging over it.

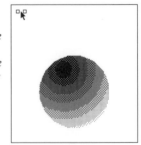

Drag the line until the center of the radial fill is where you want it.

5. Click the Closed option.

6. Without deselecting the point, hold down Shift and select the circle you drew earlier.

7. Press Command-U to make sure that the circle is ungrouped.

8. Press Command-J to join the elements. This joins the point and the circle as one composite path.

Note that the center of the radial fill is no longer in the center of the circle. This is because FreeHand is placing the center of the radial fill in the center of a line drawn between the two most distant points in the object—and the two most distant points in the object are now determined by the distance from the point you placed outside the circle and a point on the circle that's as far from that point as possible.

9. Hold down Option and select the line (you might have to go to the Keyline view to see it) to subselect the line. Drag the line around and watch how the center point of the radial fill moves to follow it. Think of the line outside the circle as a control point for determining the center point of the radial fill.

When you've positioned the center of the radial fill where you want it, you can shorten the line to the width of one point. You want to do this because, otherwise, some of the fill seems to leak through the line and prints where you don't want it.

Tiled Fills. Tiled fills repeat a pattern of FreeHand objects inside a path; they're like the tiles you see in your kitchen or bathroom. Here's how to create a tiled fill (see Figure 2-94).

1. Create the objects you want to have repeated inside a path. You're creating one of the tiles you'll have in your tiled fill.

2. Copy the FreeHand objects to the Clipboard.

3. Select the path you want to apply the tiled fill to.

4. Press Command-E to open the Fill and line dialog box. Choose "Tiled" from the Fill pop-up menu. The tiled fill attributes appear in the Fill section of the dialog box.

5. Click the Paste in button. This pastes the objects you copied to the Clipboard into the window next to the button.

6. Adjust the scale, angle, and offset of the tiles. If you want the fill to be rotated, skewed, scaled, or otherwise transformed when you transform the path, check the Transformed by tools option.

7. Press Return to close the dialog box.

FIGURE 2-94
Creating a tiled fill

Create the objects you want to use in your tiled fill and copy them to the Clipboard by pressing Command-C.

Select the object you want to apply the tiled fill to and press Command-E.

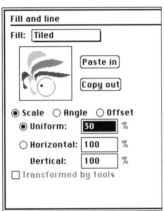

Click "Paste in," and change the scale, angle, and offset as you want, and Press Return.

FreeHand applies the tiled fill to the selected object.

Custom Fills. Choose "Custom" from the Fill menu to use one of FreeHand's special fills, such as "Denim," "Burlap," or "Coquille." The custom fills are the same as those included in FreeHand 2's User Prep PostScript dictionary. These fills are PostScript, so you shouldn't expect them to print on a non-PostScript printer.

To apply a custom fill, follow these steps (see Figure 2-95).

1. Select the path you want to apply the custom fill to.

2. Press Command-E to open the Fill and line dialog box. Choose "Custom" from the Fill pop-up menu. The Effect pop-up menu appears.

3. Choose a fill from the Effect pop-up menu. A dialog box for controlling the parameters of the custom fill you've chosen appears. The number of parameters you can specify varies from fill to fill.

4. Specify the way you want the fill to appear and press Return twice to close both dialog boxes.

Custom fills appear as patterns of little PSs (see Figure 2-96).

While you can only specify the color of the textured fills, you can vary the appearance of the other custom fills to a tremendous degree. For the "Bricks" fill, for example, you can specify the color, width, height, and angle of the "bricks" in the fill, as well as setting the color of the "mortar." Figure 2-97 shows how different variables can make the same fill look very different.

FIGURE 2-95

Custom fills

Select the path you want to fill, press Command-E, and then choose "Custom" from the Fill pop-up menu in the Fill and line dialog box.

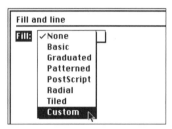

Choose a custom fill from the Effect pop-up menu.

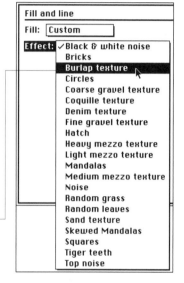

After you've chosen a custom fill, FreeHand displays a specific dialog box for that fill.

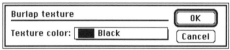

Pick a color (or make other specifications) and press Return twice to close both dialog boxes.

FIGURE 2-96

Custom fills

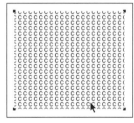

FreeHand displays custom fills like this…

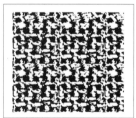

…but prints them like this.

FIGURE 2-97

Changing variables for custom fills

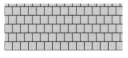  

Variations on "Bricks"

Editing Fills   If you need to change a fill you've applied, just select the object containing the fill, press Command-E, and make changes in the Fill and line dialog box. Or select the object, click the fill icon in the Colors palette, and apply a basic fill of any color by clicking on that color in the Colors palette.

Tip:
Editing
Custom Fills

If you want to edit the same custom fill as you've currently got applied, rather than changing to some other fill or fill type, choose that fill name again from the pop-up menu. The dialog box controlling the fill's specifications will appear.

Removing Fills   To remove a fill from an object, select the object and choose "Remove fill" from the Attributes menu. Or you could select the object, click the fill icon in the Colors palette, and click "None" in the colors palette.

Working with Styles

Styles are named collections of graphic formatting attributes. If you're using a 2-point line that's colored 60 percent gray, you can create a style with those attributes (you can even name it "2-point 60% gray line") and apply it to every path you want to have those attributes, rather than going to the Fill and line dialog box or the Colors palette every time.

When you format a path using the line selections from the Attributes menu, or by choosing colors from the Colors palette, or by making changes in the Fill and line dialog box or the Halftone screen dialog box, you're formatting the path locally. We call this local formatting because the formatting applies to the selected path only, and is not explicitly shared with any other paths in your publication.

If you worked with FreeHand 2, you probably worked with styles and didn't even know it. Any time you named one of your fills or lines in FreeHand 2, you were creating a fill or line style. FreeHand 2 didn't scare people, though, because it didn't call those names "styles." In my experience, as soon as you mention the word "styles," people start to panic.

There's no need to be scared—you're already thinking of the elements in your FreeHand publications as having styles. You think of each path as having a particular set of formatting attributes, and you think of groups of paths as having the same set of attributes ("these are all 12-point gray lines"). FreeHand's graphic styles give you the ability to work with FreeHand the way you already think about your publications.

Use styles. Any time you find yourself choosing the same formatting attributes over and over again, you can create a style and dramatically speed up the process of creating your publication. More importantly, you can use more of your brain for doing your creative work, rather than trying to remember that this sort of path has this sort of a line, this sort of a fill, this color, this line width, and this halftone screen. Forget that! Set up a style and let the style do that kind of thinking for you.

While styles encourage you to think ahead, they're also flexible; you can change all of the paths tagged with a particular style at any time by simply editing the style's definition.

The Styles palette (see Figure 2-98) is the key to working with and applying styles. If the Styles palette is not visible on your screen, press Command-3 to display it. If the Styles palette is visible and you want to put it away, press Command-3.

FIGURE 2-98
Styles palette

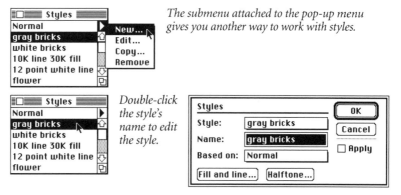

The submenu attached to the pop-up menu gives you another way to work with styles.

Double-click the style's name to edit the style.

After you double-click, FreeHand displays the Styles dialog box. Press "Fill and line..." or "Halftone..." to edit the style.

Creating Styles   To create a style, choose "Styles..." from the Attributes menu. The Styles dialog box appears. Type a name for your style, then choose the attributes you want in the Fill and line dialog box and the Halftone screen dialog box. Press Return to close the Styles dialog box. The name of the style you just created appears in the Styles palette (see Figure 2-99).

If you want to create and apply a style at the same time, select the path you want to apply the style to, then go through the process above and check the Apply option in the Styles dialog box at some point before you press Return to close the Styles dialog box.

FIGURE 2-99

Creating a style

Choose "Styles…" from the Attributes menu. FreeHand displays the Styles dialog box. Type a name for your style, and then press "Fill and line…" or "Halftone" to change your style's appearance.

When you click "Fill and line…," the enormous Fill and line dialog box appears. This is where you define what the style looks like.

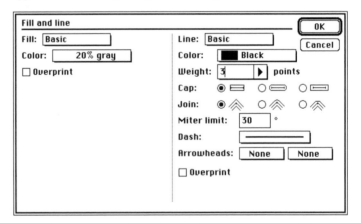

When you click "Halftone…," the Halftone screen dialog box appears. This is where you define what screen type, angle, and ruling FreeHand uses to print your style.

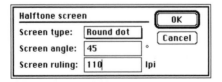

After you press Return to close the Styles dialog box, the name of your new style appears in the Styles palette.

Tip:
Create a QuicKey
for "Styles…"

You'll be choosing "Styles…" from the Attributes menu often, so why not make a QuicKey that'll do it for you? Note that choosing "Styles…" from the Attributes menu is far easier to program in QuicKeys than choosing "New" from the pop-up menu off the side of the Styles palette to get to the Styles dialog box.

Once you've created a style, you can apply it to an element by simply selecting the element and then clicking on the style name in the Styles palette. The element takes on the attributes associated with that style. Change the style, and the element's attributes change.

Creating Styles
by Example

Creating styles by example is the easiest way to create styles. Once you've applied a set of attributes to a path using local formatting, you can turn that formatting into a style, which you can then apply to any other paths (see Figure 2-100).

1. Select the path with the attributes you want the new style to have.

2. Choose "Styles" from the Attributes menu, or choose "New" from the pop-up menu off the edge of the Styles palette (if the Styles palette isn't currently visible, press Command-3 to display it). This brings up the Styles dialog box.

FIGURE 2-100
Defining a style by
example

Select an object that has the attributes you want to turn into a style.

Choose "New" from the submenu attached to the Styles palette.

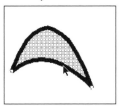

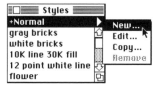

Type a name for your style and press Return.

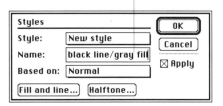

Your new style appears in the Styles palette.

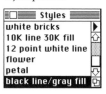

3. Type a name for the new style in the Styles dialog box and press Return. If you want to apply the style to the currently selected path, check the Apply option before you press Return.

That's all there is to it. You've just created a style with the fill, line, color, and halftone attributes of the path you selected.

Basing One Style on Another

Styles can inherit attributes from other styles. You can create a style that's just like an existing style except for some small difference, or create a style that's linked to any changes you make to an original style (color is a good example). To do this, you create a new style that's based on the existing style. Here's how.

1. Select a path tagged with the style you want to base the new style on.

2. Choose "Styles" from the Attributes menu, or choose "New" from the pop-up menu off the edge of the Styles palette. This brings up the Styles dialog box.

3. The Styles dialog box comes up with "New style" displayed in the Style pop-up menu and the name of the style of the path you selected in the Based on pop-up menu.

4. Type the name of the new style in the Name text edit field.

5. Make any changes you want to the fill, line, and halftone attributes.

6. Press Return to close the dialog box.

I call the original style the "parent" style and the inheriting styles "child" styles. When you change the properties of the parent style, the changes you make ripple through the child styles. Child styles inherit changes only in the properties they share with their parent style. The attributes which differ between the parent and child styles stay the same (see Figure 2-101).

People often have difficulty understanding the use and worth of parent and child styles—even to the point of calling attribute inheritance a bug. It's not a bug, it's a feature.

FIGURE 2-101

Changes to parent styles
change child styles

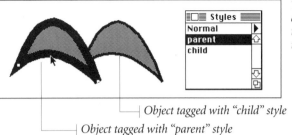

*The only
difference between
the two styles is
the line width.*

—| *Object tagged with "child" style*

—| *Object tagged with "parent" style*

*Double-click "parent" to edit the style. FreeHand
displays the Styles dialog box.*

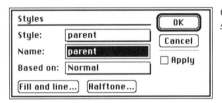

*Click "Fill and line…" to edit the
style's attributes.*

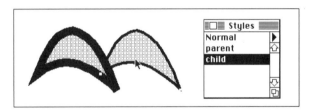

Change the fill of the parent style.

*Because the child
style gets its fill
definition from
the parent style,
the change affects
the object tagged
with the child
style.*

If you know what you're doing, you can use attribute inheritance to experiment—to try out new ideas quickly and easily. What would happen if all of those red lines (of whatever line width and pattern) were blue? What would happen if all of the paths you've filled with this tiled fill were filled with that graduated fill? The ripple-through effect of attribute inheritance from parent to child styles lets me ask "what if" questions quickly and easily (see Figure 2-102).

Attribute inheritance also makes it easier for me to make last-minute production changes almost painlessly (there are no totally painless last-minute production changes). These are usually color changes. (Does anyone have a client/boss/whatever who never changes their mind about color after seeing the chromes? If so, could you please loan them to me?).

FIGURE 2-102
Using attribute
inheritance

In this example, "white fill" is the parent style.

Edit the parent style to change the line.

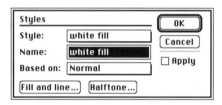 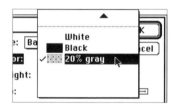

The changes ripple through all of the styles based on "white fill."

Applying Styles   To apply a style, select the path you want to tag with the style, and then click on the style in the Styles palette. The path takes on all of the formatting attributes of the style (see Figure 2-103).

You can also apply a style from the Styles dialog box by checking the Apply option before you close the dialog box.

FIGURE 2-103
Applying a style

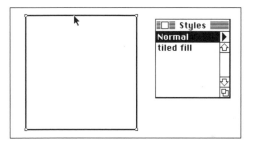

Select the object or objects you want to apply a style to...

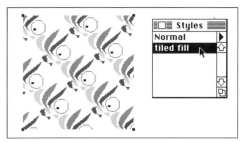

...and click the style name in the Styles palette. FreeHand applies the style to the selection.

Editing Styles

To edit a style, double-click on the style name in the Styles palette. The Styles dialog box appears. Make any changes you want in the Fill and lines dialog box and the Halftone dialog box, and then press Return to close the Styles dialog box. All of the paths formatted using that style change to reflect the changes you've just made.

Copying Styles

If you want to base one style on another but don't want to create a parent/child link between the two styles, use the "Copy" command on the Styles palette pop-up menu (see Figure 2-104).

1. Select the style whose formatting you want to copy.

2. Choose "Copy" from the Styles palette pop-up menu. The Styles dialog box appears. The associated Fill and line dialog box and Halftone dialog box fill in with the attributes specified in the style you had selected when you chose "Copy," but the Based on text edit box in the Styles dialog box indicates that the style will be based on "No style."

3. Type a name for your new style and make any changes you want in the Fill and line dialog box and the Halftone dialog box. When you close the Styles dialog box, your new style appears in the Styles palette.

FIGURE 2-104

Copying style
definitions

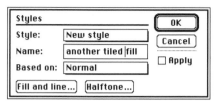

*Select a style in the Styles
palette and choose "Copy…"*

*Type a name for your new style, make any
changes you want in the Fill and line and
Halftone dialog boxes, and then press Return to
create your new style.*

Styles and Local Formatting

You can always override the formatting for a styled path by selecting the path and making changes locally using the selections on the Attributes menu. When you've changed a styled path locally, the style name in the Styles palette appears with a "+" before it when you have the path selected. The "+" indicates that the path's style has been overridden by some sort of local formatting (see Figure 2-105).

Attribute inheritance for paths which are both styled and have local formatting works like this: child styles still inherit changes in the properties they share with their parent style; the attributes which differ between the parent and child styles (including local formatting) stay the same when you change the parent style.

FIGURE 2-105

Local formatting
overrides styles

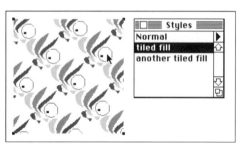

*Select a styled object and make
some local changes (in this
example, I increased the size of
the tiled objects using the Fill
and line dialog box)…*

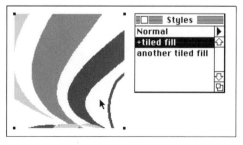

*…and the local changes
override the style. FreeHand
adds a "+" to the left of the
style name in the Styles palette
when the selected object has a
local override.*

If you've overridden the formatting of a styled path with local formatting, and you want to reassert the path's original style, select the path and click on the style name in the Styles palette. The style overrides (wipes out) the local formatting, and the "+" disappears from the style name in the Styles palette (see Figure 2-106).

FIGURE 2-106
Clearing local
formatting

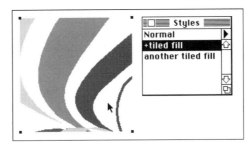

Select an object with a local override…

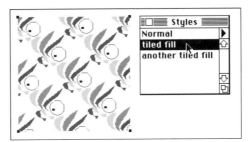

…and click the style name in the Styles palette (sometimes you've got to hold the mouse button down for a bit longer). FreeHand reapplies the style, and removes the local override.

You can select more than one path with more than one sort of local formatting override and reassert the original style—just select the paths and click on the style name in the Styles palette.

If you've locally formatted several paths with the same local formatting attributes and want to clear the formatting for each of the paths without having to select each one and reassert the style, try this.

1. Select one of the locally formatted paths and press Command-E to examine its line and fill settings. Then choose "Halftone screen…" to have a look at its halftone settings. Note any differences between these settings and the settings specified by the style the path is tagged with.

2. Without having any of the paths selected (press Tab to deselect all), double-click the style name to edit the style.

3. Using the Fill and line dialog box and the Halftone dialog box, make the style's definition match the definition of the locally formatted paths you examined in Step 1. When you're through, press Return to close the dialog box. When you select one of the locally formatted paths, note that the "+" no longer displays before the style name in the Styles palette. This is because the style now has the same formatting as the local overrides.

4. Without having any of the paths selected (press Tab to deselect all), double-click the style name to edit the style.

5. Restore the style's attributes to their original state and close the dialog box.

After you close the dialog box, all of the paths—even those that had local overrides before you started this process—change back to the formatting specified by the style.

Note that you might have to go through this process several times if you have paths with different local formatting overrides.

Moving Styles from One Publication to Another

When you need to move styles from one publication to another, follow these steps.

1. Open the publication containing the style you want to move.

2. Select a path that's tagged with the style and press Command-C to copy the path to the Clipboard.

3. Open the publication you want to copy the style into.

4. Press Command-V to paste the path into the current publication. After you paste, the style name appears in the Styles palette and you can press Delete to get rid of the path you just pasted in.

If a style with the same name already exists in the target publication, it'll override the incoming style (the "home team" wins). The path you've pasted will be marked as if it had local formatting overriding the style.

Merging Styles

We can use FreeHand's "home team wins" rule to merge two styles into one style. Why would you want to merge two styles? If your publication needs to change from color to black and white, or from process color to spot color, you might want to change all of the paths tagged with one style into another style.

If you have two styles you'd like to combine into one style, follow these steps.

1. Select a path that's tagged with the style ("style 1") you want to end up with and copy it into another publication.

2. Without deselecting the path, choose "Styles…" from the Attributes menu and use the Styles dialog box to change the name of the style to the name of the style you want to merge it with ("style 2").

3. Return to the original publication. Press Command-A to select everything in the publication.

4. Press Command-C to copy everything in the publication to the Clipboard.

5. Go to the second publication and press Command-V. FreeHand pastes all of the objects on the Clipboard into the current publication, changing the definition of "style 2" as it does so.

Adding Styles to Your Defaults File

You can add styles to your Aldus FreeHand defaults template by opening the template, copying in elements having the styles you want, and then saving the file. This way, the styles you've added will appear in every new publication you create.

Converting Styles from FreeHand 2

When you open a FreeHand 2 file with FreeHand 3, the previous versions of the styles (yes, there were styles in FreeHand 2) are converted into FreeHand 3 styles. Line styles are converted to FreeHand 3 styles having only line attributes, and the style names are preceded by "(L)" in the Styles palette. Fill styles are converted to FreeHand 3 styles having only fill attributes, and the style names are preceded by "(F)" in the Styles palette.

FreeHand 3 tags converted elements which have both a line and a fill style with the fill style and applies the original line style as a local formatting override (see Figure 2-107).

FIGURE 2-107

Converted styles

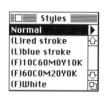

Attaching Notes to Objects

If you want to write a note to someone else who'll be working on your publication, or if you want to add a note to an object that'll be passed along to a PostScript file you create (either when you print, print to disk, or export a publication as EPS), you can use FreeHand's ability to attach a note to an object. You can attach up to 255 characters worth of commentary or abuse to any FreeHand element.

To attach a note to an object, select the object and choose "Set note…" from the Attributes menu. FreeHand displays the Set note dialog box. Type the note you want to attach and press Return to close the dialog box.

You can apply the same note to several objects by selecting them and choosing "Set note…" from the edit menu.

To read a note attached to an object, select the object and choose "Set note…" from the Attributes menu. FreeHand displays the Set note dialog box. Press Return to close the dialog box when you're through reading or editing the note.

Tip:

Read Me Notes

If you're working with other people on your publication, you might want to leave them a note about some part of the publication that needs their particular attention. The only question is: what element will you attach the note to? Consider standardizing on a text block you've placed outside the page (including the bleed area) that says "Read Me." This makes it hard to miss.

When your co-worker opens the publication, they can select the "Read Me" text block and choose "Set note…" from the Attributes menu to read your note.

You can put a PostScript comment line between all of the elements in a PostScript file by pressing Command-A to select all of the elements in your publication, choosing "Set note…" from the Attributes menu, and then typing your note in the Set note dialog box. This way, every element will be preceded by a PostScript comment line in the PostScript that FreeHand generates when it prints (either to a printer or to disk) or exports the file as EPS. This can make reading a PostScript file a bit easier (see Figure 2-108).

FIGURE 2-108

Adding a comment to all elements

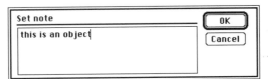

Select all of the objects in your publication, and then choose "Set note…" from the Attributes menu. Type a note in the Set note dialog box.

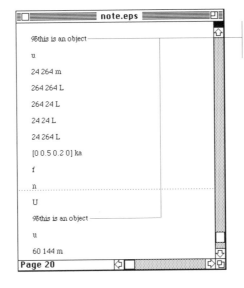

FreeHand sends the note along when you print or create an EPS file.

Charting and Graphing

Because FreeHand works "by the numbers," it's easy to create good-looking charts and graphs. I've always hated the dang things myself.

It might seem that the easiest way to get a chart or graph into your FreeHand publication would be to create one in Excel or Persuasion, then paste or place the chart into FreeHand. Because the chart is an object-PICT, FreeHand will convert it into FreeHand elements as it's pasted or placed.

The trouble with this method is that you often end up spending more time cleaning up the chart than you would if you were creating it from scratch. PICT-generating applications have weird ideas about how to draw things, generally using about three times as many elements as are necessary to draw any given image. For more on importing object-PICT graphics, see "Importing PICTs" in Chapter 4, "Importing and Exporting."

The best method—though it's somewhat embarrassing to die-hard FreeHand fans—is to create the chart in Adobe Illustrator 3, which includes a set of charting tools. Illustrator charts open perfectly in FreeHand, and avoid all of the problems of PICT charts. For more on importing Adobe Illustrator 3 files, see "Importing Illustrator EPS" in Chapter 4, "Importing and Exporting."

Chart creation is best shown by example. Here are the basic steps.

- Choose a scale. For bar, column, and line charts, you set up the vertical and horizontal axes of the chart according to some scale—years, thousands of tons, or dollars—mapped into units of vertical and horizontal distance.

- Choose an equivalent unit of measure to represent the scale you've chosen. Once you know what the scale of your chart is, you can translate that scale into units of your measurement system. If the vertical axis of your chart is marked off in 10-year increments, pick some unit of measure as being equal to that scale. It doesn't matter what unit you choose as long as you're comfortable with the working size of the chart (remember, you can always scale the chart later, after you've got all of the data points plotted). For a chart with a horizontal axis spanning 100 years in 1-year increments, you'd better choose something small—like a point or .001 inch—to represent each year. If the same vertical axis were marked in 10-year increments, you'd do just as well choosing a larger unit of measure—a pica, or .5 inches.

- Set a zero point. If you're new to charts, this is where the horizontal and vertical axes of your chart meet.

- Draw the horizontal and vertical axes of your chart and mark them off in the increments you want with tick marks.

- Plot your data onto the chart using FreeHand's numeric movement features.

- Add labels, and enhance the chart.

Bar and Column Charts

The only difference between bar charts and column charts is that column charts plot their data vertically and bar charts plot their date horizontally. You can use the same techniques to create either type of chart.

Imagine that you want to create a column chart showing how a particular organization's budget has grown over five years. You want to mark off the vertical axis in increments representing thousands of dollars; the horizontal axis in years. We have only a single data point for each year: $12,000 for 1985; $16,000 for 1986; $23,245 for 1987; $1,011 for 1988; $24,600 for 1989.

To create the chart, follow these steps (see Figure 2-109).

1. Choose a scale. For this example, each pica represents $1,000. Two picas represent each year on the horizontal scale. You could set the publication's Snap-to grid to picas to make the task of creating the chart a little easier.

2. Draw horizontal and vertical axes and set the zero point at their intersection.

3. Draw a box 2 picas wide by 1 pica tall using the square-corner tool. Position the box to represent the budget amount for the first year.

4. Ungroup the box, select the two points along its top, and move the points down 1 pica. This positions the top two points of the box on the horizontal axis of the chart.

5. Press Command-M to display the Move elements dialog box. In the Move elements dialog box, type "12" in the Vertical text edit box to move the top of the box up 12 picas, a distance representing the $12,000 budget amount for 1985. The top of the box moves to the point on the chart representing $12,000.

6. Clone the box from the first year across the other years, changing the position of the top of each box so that it matches the

budget for that year. What about the data points that can't be expressed in even units of our measurement system, such as $23,245 for 1987? Simple. When you move those points vertically, we type "23.245p" in the Vertical text edit box in the Move elements dialog box.

7. Add labels and figures to the chart.

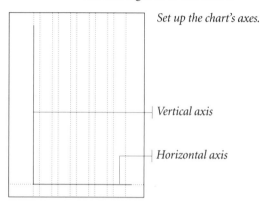

Set up the chart's axes.

Vertical axis

Horizontal axis

Draw a box for the first column, ungroup the box, and select the two top points. Press Command-M. Use the Move elements dialog box to move the two points on top of the box down...

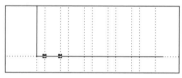

...so that they rest on the horizontal axis of the chart. Without deselecting the two points, use the Move elements dialog box again to move to the top of the bar into position.

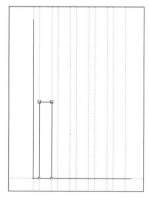

Once you've finished the first bar, use the same techniques to finish the other bars.

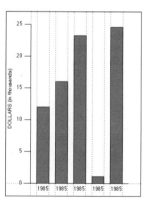

Finish the chart by adding labels and coloring the bars.

Stacked Bar and Stacked Column Charts

Stacked bar and stacked column charts break larger bodies of data into smaller parts, plotting those parts inside the area covered by the total. If you want to break down the budget amounts shown for the non-profit organization from the previous example to show contributions from city, state, federal, corporate, and individual sources, you'd use a stacked column chart.

For the 1985 budget, the amounts contributed were

$2,000 from the city

$1,600 from the state

$4,400 from the federal government

$4,400 from individuals

You'd go through the same Steps 1 through 3 as described in the previous scenario, and then create individual areas for each of the contributing sources to make up the column representing our $12,000 budget total. To do this, you'd follow these steps (see Figure 2-110).

1. Create a column representing the amount contributed by the city using the technique shown in Step 4 in the previous scenario. In this example, create a column representing the city's contribution of $2,000 moving the top of the column up 2 picas.

2. Clone the column by pressing Command-=. Select the bottom two points on the cloned column and press Command-M to display the Move elements dialog box. The dialog box should appear with the same distance as you just moved the top of the column representing the city's contribution entered in the Vertical text edit box, so you can probably just press Return to move the bottom of the cloned column to the same position as the top of the original column (if it doesn't, type "2" again in the Vertical text edit box in the dialog box and press Return).

3. Without deselecting the points you just moved, press Command-M again and enter distance representing the amount contributed by the state government (1.6p). The bottom points you selected earlier now become the top point of a new column whose base rests precisely on the top of the column representing the amount contributed by the city.

4. Clone the column representing the state's contribution, and repeat the process of moving the bottom points on the cloned

FIGURE 2-110
Creating a stacked
column chart

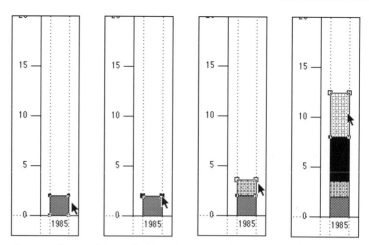

Create each part of the stacked bar chart using the moving and scaling techniques shown in Figure 2-109

column twice to create the column representing the federal government's contribution.

5. Clone the column representing the federal contribution, and repeat the process of moving the bottom points on the cloned column twice to create the column representing contributions made by individuals in 1985.

6. Repeat this process for all of the other years in the chart.

7. Add labels, figures, and a key to the chart.

Line and Area Charts

Line charts and area charts work about the same way a bar chart works—they plot data points along a horizontal axis. A line chart plots its data along a line, rather than on a bar or column. I still think of an area chart as being a line chart with fills, rather than listening to any of the people who've tried to convince me that the two types of charts are different. All I know is that you make them the same way in FreeHand.

Imagine you want to use a line chart to plot the budget of the same nonprofit organization used as an example in the two procedures above; over the same 5-year period. Once again, you want to mark off vertical axis in increments representing thousands of dollars, and mark off the horizontal axis in years. You have a single data point for each year: $12,000 for 1985; $16,000 for 1986; $23,245 for 1987; $1,011 for 1988; $24,600 for 1989.

Set up your chart's scale by following Steps 1 through 3 in "Bar and Column Charts," and then follow these steps (see Figure 2-111).

1. Draw a path along the horizontal axis of the chart using the corner tool, placing a point along the horizontal axis every 2 picas (starting with a point placed at the zero point).

2. Select the first point in the path.

3. Press Command-M to display the Move elements dialog box. In the Move elements dialog box, type "12" in the Vertical text edit box to move the point up 12 picas, a distance representing the $12,000 budget amount for 1985. The point moves to the vertical position on the chart representing $12,000.

FIGURE 2-111

Creating a line chart

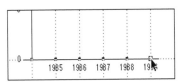

Set up the axes of your chart, select the corner tool and, draw a line with a point at each horizontal increment. Then select the first point and press Command-M.

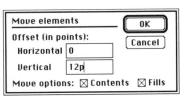

Move the point into position using the Move elements dialog box.

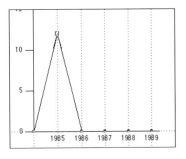

Repeat the process for each point on the line, and then finish the chart by adding labels or changing the line style or color.

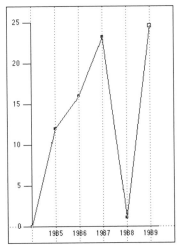

Sherry L. Klepper
10233 Mission Gorge Rd., I110
Santee, CA 92071

4. Repeat the process for the four remaining points.

5. Add labels and figures to the chart.

If you wanted to make this line chart into an area chart, you'd make the line plotting the data points into the top edge of a filled path, as shown in Figure 2-112.

If you wanted to show the amounts contributed by various sources, as we did using the stacked column chart, you'd use an area chart filled with different colors or tints, as shown in Figure 2-113.

FIGURE 2-112
Area chart

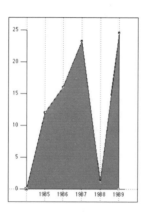

FIGURE 2-113
Area chart showing
individual totals

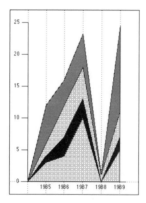

Pie Charts   Pie charts use degrees around a circle as their measurement system, rather than horizontal and vertical axes. Pie charts typically show parts of some total amount or percentage.

Getting there's half the fun.

If you wanted to show the contributions to our example nonprofit agency's budget from 1985 as percentages in a pie chart, you'd first have to convert the raw numbers to percentages. This isn't hard: just divide the amounts by the total ($2,000 divided by $12,000 would give us 16 percent for the city's contribution). The other contributors would be 13 percent from the state, 36 percent from the federal government, and 36 percent from individual contributors. These figures have been rounded a bit, and they do total a little over 100 percent. Don't worry about it.

Now turn these percentages into degrees by multiplying each number by 3.6 (because 360 degrees is equal, in this case, to 100 percent). This multiplication produces 57 degrees from the city, 46 degrees from the state, 129 degrees from the federal government, and 129 degrees from individuals.

To plot this data as a pie chart, follow these steps (see Figure 2-114).

1. Set a zero point on your page.

2. Draw a horizontal line using the line tool, starting at the zero point. Press Command-E and choose "None" from the Line pop-up menu. Switch to Keyline mode by pressing Command-K so that you can see the path.

3. Clone the line (Command-=).

4. Select the rotate tool, hold down Option, and click. The Rotate dialog box appears. In the Angle text edit box, type "57." Press Tab to move to the Horizontal text edit box and type "0." Press Tab again to move to the Vertical text edit box and type "0." This tells FreeHand to rotate the line around the zero point you set. Press Return to close the dialog box and rotate the line.

5. Select the two end points that overlap at the zero point and press Command-J to join the points. Press Command-I to display the Path/point dialog box. Click the Closed option in the Path/point dialog box and press Return to close the dialog box. FreeHand closes the path by drawing a line between the two points farthest from the zero point.

6. Clone the triangle. Select the point on the cloned triangle that's the farthest clockwise, considering the zero point as the center of a clock's face. Select the rotation tool, if it's not already selected, hold down Option, and click. The Rotate dialog box

FIGURE 2-114

Creating a pie chart

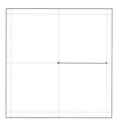 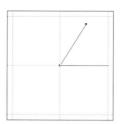 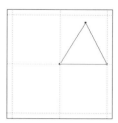

Set the zero point where you want the center of your pie chart, then draw a line out from the zero point.

Clone the line, and select the point on the cloned line that's away from the zero point. Rotate the line around the zero point by 57 degrees.

Join the two lines to make a path. Clone the triangle.

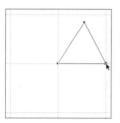 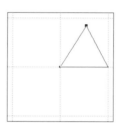 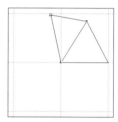

Select the point on the corner of the triangle that's in the same position as the end point of the original line.

Press Command-, to repeat the rotation you used earlier.

Without deselecting the point, use the Rotate dialog box to rotate the point 46 degrees.

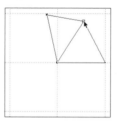 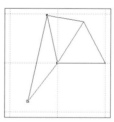 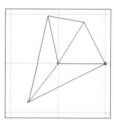

Repeat the process of cloning and rotating the triangles until you've plotted all of your data.

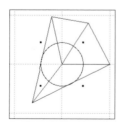 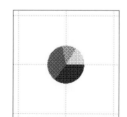 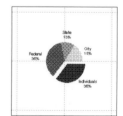

Draw a circle over the triangles. Color each triangle, and then paste each one into a clone of the circle. Add labels, and you've got a pie chart.

appears, with 57 still entered in the Angle text edit box. Type "0" in both the Horizontal and Vertical text edit boxes. This tells FreeHand to rotate the point around the zero point. Press Return to close the dialog box and rotate the line. Hold down Option and click again. The Rotate dialog box appears. Type the number of degrees for the next segment in the Angle text edit box. In this example, this is the percentage contributed by the state government, 13 percent, or 46 degrees. Make sure that the center of rotation is still the zero point, and press return. Repeat this process for the other two contributors.

7. Select the ellipse tool, position the cross hair over the zero point (look at the status bar to make sure you're on the zero point), hold down Option and Shift, and draw as large a circle as you can (without the edge of the circle extending past the outside edges of any of the triangles) at the center of the four triangles.

8. Fill the inside of each triangle with some fill, then cut all of the triangles to the Clipboard. Select the circle and choose "Paste inside" from the Edit menu.

I admit that this isn't the most elegant process in the world—but it does work.

Perspective Projection

Perspective rendering (also known as central projection in the smoke-filled back rooms of the technical illustration bars where I used to hang out) is a drawing technology dedicated to rendering an image in space much the same way as our eyes see things. Perspective rendering came into vogue during the renaissance, and we haven't yet found a better way of representing our three-dimensional world on two-dimensional media (such as computer screens and paper).

Perspective rendering relies on models of the physical positions of these items.

•   The eye of the observer

•   The object or objects being viewed

- The plane of projection

- The vanishing point or vanishing points

Scared yet? Don't be—just have a look at Figure 2-115.

The whole point is understanding where objects fall inside a frame (also called the plane of projection) which lies between you and the objects. The objects exist between the plane of projection and one or more vanishing points. When you look at a photograph, you're looking at an exercise in perspective rendering, frozen in time, where the piece of film is roughly equivalent to the plane of projection.

When did this book become a drafting class? About the time I discovered I couldn't explain how to do this stuff in FreeHand without defining some terms.

FIGURE 2-115
How perspective
rendering works

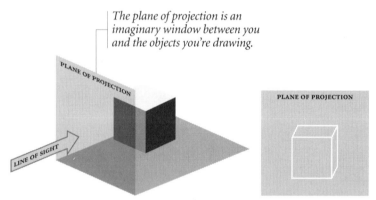

The plane of projection is an imaginary window between you and the objects you're drawing.

Purists will note that this is an isometric view.

What you see through the plane of perspective.

Here's another way of looking at it.

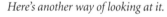

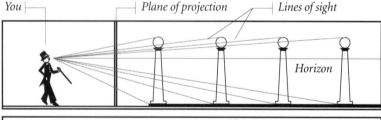

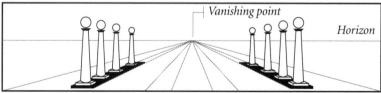

**Single View
Perspective**

Single view perspective relies on a single vanishing point. You rarely see single view perspective in the real world, because there's almost always more than one natural horizon in your field of view. The classic example of single view perspective is that of a highway stretching into the distance on a perfectly flat plain (see Figure 2-116).

FIGURE 2-116
Single view
perspective

WELCOME SPACE FRIENDS

Okay, so I added a few things.

To create guidelines for a single view perspective in FreeHand, follow these steps (see Figure 2-117).

1. Designate a point as your vanishing point. Make this point your zero point. In most cases, this point should be around the vertical and horizontal center of your illustration. If it's not, you've got to ask yourself why you're not using multiview perspective.

2. Use the line tool to draw a horizontal line from the left edge of your publication to the zero point.

3. Press Command-= to clone the line.

4. Select the point on the cloned line that's farthest from the zero point and drag it some distance up or down on the page.

5. Press Command-D to repeat the clone and drag operation you've just performed. Continue pressing Command-D until you've created as many guidelines as you want. You'll probably have to adjust the end point from time to time to get the guidelines where you want them.

6. Select all of the lines you just drew and send them to a Background layer. Now you can use them as drawing guides.

FIGURE 2-117
Creating a
perspective grid

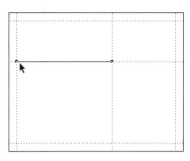

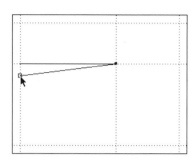

Draw a line.

Clone the line. Select the end point of the cloned line and drag it to a new position.

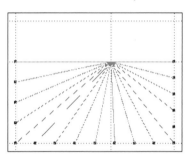

Repeat the clone-and-drag sequence until you have all of the guidelines you want.

Once you've created all of the guides you want, send them to the background to gray them out and make them inactive.

Blending and Single View Perspective

You can use blends as an aid to perspective rendering, particularly if you've got a shape that starts near the plane of perspective and extends toward the vanishing point. You'd draw the nearest and farthest cross-sections of the object, and then blend between the two cross sections, as shown in Figure 2-118.

FIGURE 2-118
Blending and
perspective drawing

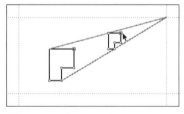

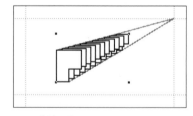

Select two reference points...

...and blend.

Multiview Perspective

Multiview perspective is much more like the way we see the world, because it uses more than one vanishing point. You can use the single view perspective grid building techniques in multiview perspective—you just use more than one grid (see Figure 2-119).

FIGURE 2-119
Multiview perspective

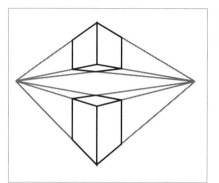

*Multiview perspective
depends on more than
one vanishing point.*

Oblique Projection

Unlike perspective projection, oblique projection is nothing like the way we see objects. It's an abstraction that's good for keeping measurements intact for manufacturing drawings, and it's also a good way to render a 3-D shape quickly.

In oblique projection, one face of an object is always against the plane of projection, and the horizontal lines in that object are always drawn 90 degrees from the vertical (what we normally think of as horizontal). The horizontal lines on the other sides of the object are always drawn at the same angle, rather than at angles that converge on a vanishing point. In oblique projection, 45 degrees, 30 degrees, and 60 degrees are commonly used angles.

The next trick of oblique projection is that the scale of the lines and objects drawn away from the plane of projection isn't foreshortened as they recede from the viewer but are drawn to a single, fixed scale.

Just to add some historical color, oblique projections in which measurements away from the plane of projection are rendered at full scale are called cavalier projections, because they were often used for drawing fortifications in renaissance and medieval times, and half-scale renderings are called cabinet projections because they were used by furniture builders (see Figure 2-120).

If you've been around the Macintosh graphics community for long, you've seen lots of oblique projection—mainly because 45-degree lines offered the least jagged line you could get out of MacPaint. Early Macintosh artists created a style that's stuck with us—even now that we can draw smooth lines at any angle (see Figure 2-121).

FIGURE 2-120
Oblique projection

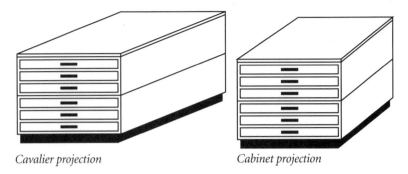

Cavalier projection   *Cabinet projection*

FIGURE 2-121
Macintosh projection

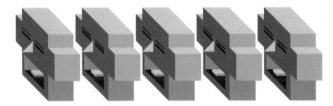

Creating a Grid for Oblique Projection

Creating grids for oblique projection drawing is easy in FreeHand. To create a grid for the most common oblique projection angle—45 degrees—use the Document setup dialog box to set your visible grid and Snap-to grid in the same increment (6 points, for example). When you draw paths, hold down Shift to constrain the angles in your drawing to 45-degree angles, and turn on "Grid" and "Snap to grid" on the View menu. Figure 2-122 shows how it works.

FIGURE 2-122
Grid for 45-degree
oblique projection

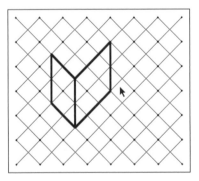

If you want to create a grid for an oblique projection based on 30-degree angles, follow these steps (see Figure 2-123).

1. Create a new publication.

2. Choose "Constrain…" from the Element menu to display the Constrain dialog box. In the Constrain dialog box, enter "30" in the Angle text edit box for the number of degrees, and then press Return to close the dialog box.

3. Draw a series of hairlines (applying a color to them if you want) by choosing the line tool, placing the cross hair at one of the visible grid points, holding down Shift, and drawing a line.

4. Select the grid of 30-degree lines you've drawn and send them to a specific layer. It can be either a foreground or background layer, depending on whether you like having a 50-percent tint applied to your guidelines.

5. Create your paths, using the grid as a reference as you draw.

If you want to create a grid for some other angle of oblique projection, just enter that angle in the Angle text edit box in the Constrain dialog box, and draw a series of guidelines.

FIGURE 2-123
Grid for 30-degree
oblique projection

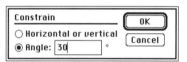

Choose "Constrain…" from the Element menu and type "30" in the Angle text edit box.

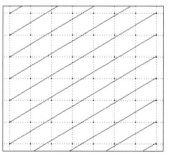

Hold down Shift to constrain lines as you draw them.

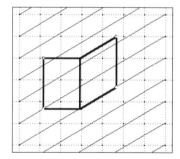

Draw objects, using your grid as a guide.

Axonometric Projection

I'm sure that there are plenty of drafters that'd argue this one with me, but I think of axonometric projection as being about the same as oblique projection. In axonometric projection, the faces of the object are rotated away from the plane of perspective by some pair of different angles.

There are three types of axonometric projection: isometric, dimetric, and trimetric.

Isometric Projection. In isometric projection, the object you're drawing has both of its primary axes rotated away from the plane of projection by the same angle (see Figure 2-124).

You can create grids for isometric projection using the same technique described for creating an oblique projection above, but you'll use only the grid lines—and not the horizontal guides—to draw horizontal lines perpendicular to the major axes of the object. All right, that's pretty abstruse. Figure 2-125 shows what I mean.

Circles in isometric projection are rendered as ellipses, as shown in Figure 2-126.

FIGURE 2-124
Isometric projection

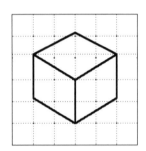

FIGURE 2-125
Horizontal lines in
isometric projection

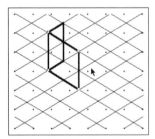

FIGURE 2-126
Circles in isometric
projection

Dimetric Projection. In dimetric projection, the object you're drawing has both of its primary axes rotated away from the plane of projection by different angles (see Figure 2-128). In this case, the grid you create should have one angle going from left to right, and another, different angle going from right to left (see Figure 2-129).

FIGURE 2-128
Dimetric projection

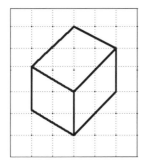

FIGURE 2-129
Grids in dimetric
projection

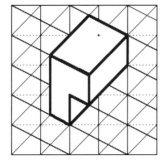

Trimetric Projection. You guessed it, in trimetric projection, the axes of the object you're drawing are rotated at three different angles from the plane of projection. I confess, I never really have figured out how trimetric projection differs from dimetric projection. Once again, you can create a grid that has one angle going from left to right, and another, different angle going from right to left.

Drawing Conclusions

Earlier in this chapter, I noted that I was confused by FreeHand's approach to drawing when I first encountered it. As I worked with the tools, however, I found that the parts of my brain that were used to using rapidographs (an obsolete type of pen used by the ancient Greeks), curves, and rulers quickly adapted to the new drawing environment. Eventually, I realized that this was the easier way to draw.

Then, after reading a related article in a tabloid at the supermarket, it dawned on me that the archaic methods I'd learned were nothing less than an extraterrestrial plot—forced on us in classical antiquity by evil space gods, and to some cosmic purpose which I cannot—as yet—reveal.

Just keep at it.

When you're lying awake with a dismal headache, and repose is taboo'd by anxiety, I conceive you may use any language you choose to indulge in, without any impropriety; for your brain is on fire—the bedclothes conspire of usual slumber to plunder you: first your counterpane goes, and uncovers your toes, and your sheet slips demurely from under you; then the blanket tickles—you feel like mixed pickles—so terribly sharp is the pricking, and you're hot, and you're cross, and you tumble and toss till there's nothing 'twixt you and the ticking.

Then the bedclothes all creep to the ground in a heap, and you pick 'em all up in a tangle; next your pillow resigns and politely declines to remain at its usual angle! Well, you get some repose in the form of a doze, with hot eye-balls and head ever aching, but your slumbering teems with such horrible dreams that you'd very much better be waking; for you dream you are crossing the Channel, and tossing about in a steamer from Harwich—which is something between a large bathing machine and a very small second-class carriage—and you're giving a treat (penny ice and cold meat) to a party of friends and relations—they're a ravenous horde—and they all came on board at Sloane Square and South Kensington Stations.

And bound on that journey you find your attorney (who started that morning from Devon); he's a bit undersized, and you don't feel surprised when he tells you he's only eleven. Well, you're driving like mad with this singular lad (by the by, the ship's now a four-wheeler), and you're playing round games, and he calls you bad names when you tell him that "ties pay the dealer;" but this you can't stand, so you throw up your hand, and you find you're as cold as an icicle, In your shirt and your socks (the black silk with gold clocks), crossing Salisbury Plain on a bicycle: and he and the crew are on bicycles too—which they somehow or other invest in—and he's telling the tars all the particulars of a company he's interested in—it's a scheme of devices, to get at low prices all goods from cough mixtures to cables (which tickled the sailors), by treating retailers as though they were all vegetables—you get a good spadesman to plant a small tradesman (first take off his boots with a boot-tree), and his legs will take root, and his fingers will shoot, and they'll blossom and bud like a fruit-tree—from the greengrocer tree you get grapes and green pea, cauliflower, pineapple, and cranberries, while the pastrycook plant cherry brandy will grant, apple puffs, and three-corners, and Banburys—the shares are a penny, and ever so many are taken by Rothschild and Baring, and just as a few are allotted to you, you awake with a shudder despairing—you're a regular wreck, with a crick in your neck, and no wonder you snore, for your head's on the floor, and you've needles and pins from your soles to your shins, and your flesh is a-creep, for your left leg's asleep, and you've cramp in your toe, and a fly on your nose, and some fluff in your lung, and a feverish tongue, and a thirst that's intense, and a general sense that you haven't been sleeping in clover; but the darkness has passed, and it's daylight at last, and the night has been long—ditto ditto my song—and thank goodness they're both of them over!

Words.

Somehow, we can never quite get away from them. In academic circles, debate continues on whether we're born with the ability to learn and create langauge, or whether it's something we're taught. I don't know the answer, and, most of the time, I don't even know which side of the debate I'm on. It hardly matters—language is the most important technology we humans have yet developed.

As I mentioned at the start of the last chapter, FreeHand serves the language of drawing very well. Does FreeHand neglect text in favor of points and paths, lines and fills? No way—FreeHand gives you almost all of the character formatting tools you could ever ask for. If you consider "Convert to paths" a character format, FreeHand provides more character formatting flexibility than any page-layout program.

Paragraph formatting's another thing though. While you can get any arrangement of text you want by manipulating text blocks, Free-Hand lacks paragraph formatting controls such as indents, tabs, and inter-paragraph spacing.

This chapter is all about working with text and type in FreeHand.

Entering and Editing Text

Entering text in FreeHand is simple. Click the text tool somewhere on the page and the Text dialog box appears (see Figure 3-1). Enter text in the dialog box. Click OK, press Enter, or click the Apply button, and the text appears on the page.

To edit text, select the pointer tool, double-click on a text block, and the Text dialog box appears, containing all of the text in that text block. All text entry and text editing operations are performed in the Text dialog box.

Type specifications, on the other hand, can be applied both inside and outside the Text dialog box; you don't have to enter the Text dialog box to change type specifications.

I've heard lots of people complain because they can't click a text editing cursor in text on the page and edit it there, as they can in MacDraw II, but I find working with the dialog box bearable. In some cases, it's even an advantage—you don't have to zoom in on tiny type to edit it, for example. I didn't find it easy to work with at first, because I didn't know two important things about the Text dialog box.

- Pressing Enter closes the Text dialog box. I kept pressing Return, thinking that would click OK and close the dialog box. Return simply enters more carriage returns in the Text dialog box. I grumbled mightily about having to take my hands off the keyboard to close the dialog box, until, finally, I pressed Enter by mistake. And felt like a fool—it probably *is* documented somewhere, after all.

FIGURE 3-1
Text dialog box

Click to close the dialog box and enter your changes (or press Enter).

Click to close the dialog box without making any changes.

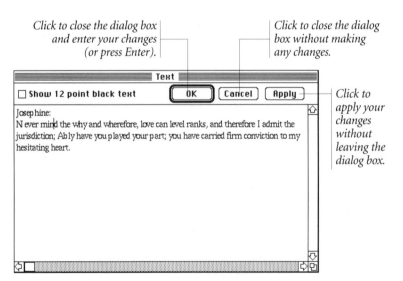

Click to apply your changes without leaving the dialog box.

- Clicking the Apply button applies whatever changes you've made in the Text dialog box to the text in the layout view, so you can drag the Text dialog box out of the way and view kerning and spacing as you adjust them in the Text dialog box.

Now that I know these two things, I'm happy. I urge you to be happy, too.

Tip:
Zooming While
the Text Dialog
Box Is Open

All of FreeHand's keyboard shortcuts (Command-W, Command-8, and so on) for changing the magnification of the publication window work while you've got the Text dialog box open. If you need to zoom in on some text while you've got the Text dialog box open, press the keys for the keyboard shortcut you want. FreeHand zooms in or out, centering the selected text in the publication window.

When you add text to a FreeHand publication, you're creating text blocks (see Figure 3-2). All of the text in a FreeHand publication exists inside text blocks.

A text block can contain any number of different type specifications or colors, and up to 32K (32,767 characters) of text. Each text block is entirely self-contained and is not linked to any other text block. Text blocks can be resized, reshaped, and manipulated in a variety of other ways, and we'll talk more about them in "Working with Text Blocks," later in this chapter.

FIGURE 3-2
Text blocks

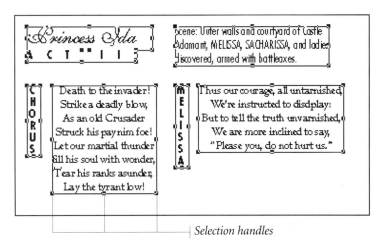

Selection handles

When you select the text tool from the toolbox, the cursor turns into the text insertion point. The text insertion point is also known as the I-beam, because that's what the cursor looks like.

When you click the text insertion point on the page, the baseline of the first line of the text you enter falls wherever you placed the little crossbar on the text insertion point (see Figure 3-3).

When you create a new text block, the alignment option you're using determines where the characters fall horizontally—relative to the place you click the text insertion point (see Figure 3-4).

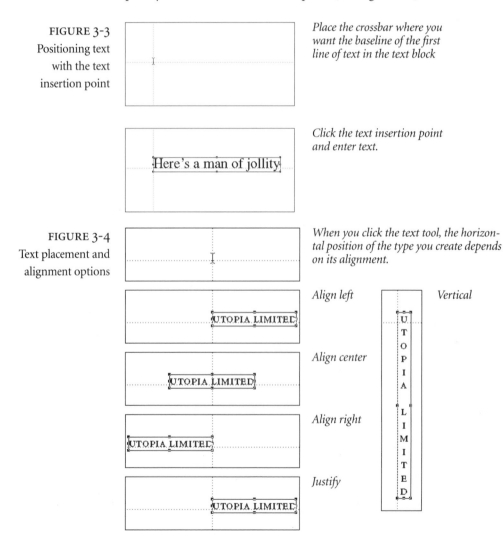

FIGURE 3-3
Positioning text
with the text
insertion point

Place the crossbar where you want the baseline of the first line of text in the text block

Click the text insertion point and enter text.

Here's a man of jollity

FIGURE 3-4
Text placement and
alignment options

When you click the text tool, the horizontal position of the type you create depends on its alignment.

Align left

UTOPIA LIMITED

Vertical

Align center

UTOPIA LIMITED

Align right

UTOPIA LIMITED

Justify

UTOPIA LIMITED

When you drag the text insertion point, FreeHand creates a text block that's as wide as the area you indicated by dragging (see Figure 3-5). I think dragging the text insertion point is the best way to create text blocks in FreeHand, because you can control the size of the text blocks you're creating *before* the text hits the page. This can save time.

FIGURE 3-5
Drag-creating
text blocks

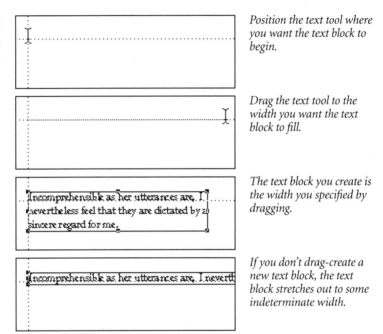

Position the text tool where you want the text block to begin.

Drag the text tool to the width you want the text block to fill.

The text block you create is the width you specified by dragging.

If you don't drag-create a new text block, the text block stretches out to some indeterminate width.

Tip:
Set the Default
Position of the
Text Dialog Box

If you want to set the Text dialog box to appear at a specific point on your screen, simply drag the dialog box to that position and resize it, if you want. Each subsequent time you open the Text dialog box to enter or edit text, it'll pop up in the same position and size. However, this position is not retained when you save the publication, so the next time you open the publication, you'll have to position and size the dialog box again. I like setting mine up so that it's fairly thin and appears at the bottom of the screen.

Tip:
Setting the
Permanent
Position of the
Text Dialog Box

Better yet, use ResEdit to set the position and size of the Text dialog box.

1. Start ResEdit.

2. Locate and open FreeHand with ResEdit (it's a good idea to work on a copy of the file).

3. Select the WIND resource by typing WIND.

4. Select the WIND resource numbered 01005 and open it. You'll see a representation of the Text dialog box's position on the screen. Drag and resize the Text dialog box until it's where you want it.

5. Press Command-S to save your changes to FreeHand, and quit ResEdit.

The next time you open FreeHand, the Text dialog box appears in the position and size you specified in ResEdit (see Figure 3-6).

FIGURE 3-6
New default position
and size for the
Text dialog box

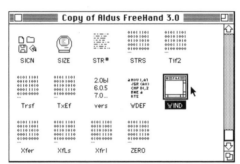

Start ResEdit and open a copy of FreeHand.

Locate and select the WIND resource class. Open the resource class by pressing Return.

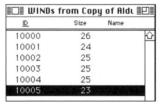

Locate and select WIND resource ID 10005.

Open the resource by pressing Return.

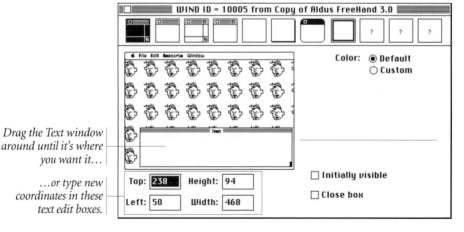

Drag the Text window
around until it's where
you want it...

...or type new
coordinates in these
text edit boxes.

FIGURE 3-6
Continued

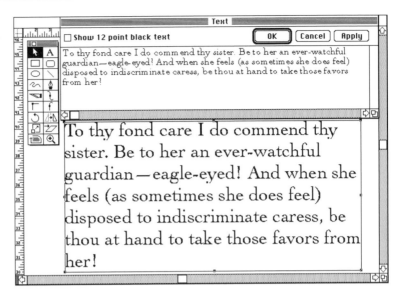

FreeHand's text editing features aren't going to replace your word processor, but they're handy all the same. Drag-selecting and Shift-clicking work exactly as they do in (nearly) any other Macintosh application, as does pressing Command-A to select everything in the text block. Double-clicking selects single words (see Figure 3-7).

The arrow keys move the cursor one character left or right; one line up or down. Watch yourself, though, because the arrow keys are also used for entering kerning increments (see "Kerning" later in this chapter). This is a problem because in virtually every other text-editing

FIGURE 3-7
Editing text

> Oh! a private buffoon is a light-hearted loon,
> If you listen to popular rumor;
> From the morn to the night he's so joyous and bright,
> And he bubbles with wit and good humor.

Use the arrow keys to move around inside the Text dialog box.

> Oh! a private buffoon is a light-hearted loon,
> If you listen to popular rumor;
> From the morn to the night he's so joyous and bright,
> And he bubbles with wit and good humor.

Double-click to select a word.

> Oh! a private buffoon is a light-hearted loon,
> If you listen to popular rumor;
> From the morn to the night he's so joyous and bright,
> And he bubbles with wit and good humor.

Choose "Select all" from the Edit menu or press Command-A to select all of the text in the text block.

application on the Macintosh you can press Command-Shift-Right Arrow to select the next word to the right, Command-Shift-Left Arrow to select the next word to the left. FreeHand does things differently out of, I think, simple perversity.

Cutting, pasting, clearing, and copying function normally inside the Text dialog box and between Text dialog boxes, but you can't switch modes by cutting a text block selected with the pointer tool and pasting it into a text block open in the Text dialog box as you can in, for example, PageMaker.

You can, however, paste text copied to the Clipboard from another application into the Text dialog box. This is the usual way to get large amounts of text into FreeHand, though there are better ways, as described in "Importing Formatted Text from PageMaker" and "Importing Formatted Text from Word" in Chapter 4, "Importing and Exporting."

Tip:
Use "Show as
12-point black"
for Tiny or
Reversed Type

At first glance, the Show as 12-point black check box in the Text dialog box seems a triviality, but it comes in incredibly handy when you need to edit 6-point type or white type. Without the option, the former is unreadable and the latter is invisible in the Text dialog box. So check this option to save your eyesight.

Tip:
Wrapping Text
Around Objects

PageMaker has a great option for wrapping text around objects, that, at first glance, FreeHand seems to lack. But you can, with a little ingenuity, wrap FreeHand text around objects without having to split it into separate text blocks (see Figure 3-8).

1. Position the text block so that it falls over the object you want to wrap.

2. Select the text block and press Command-I to bring up the Text dialog box.

3. Drag the Text dialog box out of the way so that you can see the object you want to wrap.

4. Insert carriage returns and spaces in the text, pressing the Apply button often to update the page view.

FIGURE 3-8
Wrapping text
around objects

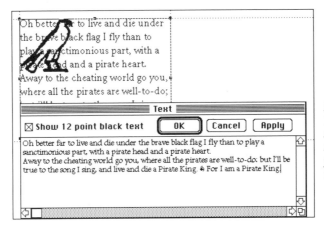

*Position the
Text dialog box
so that you can
see the object
you want to
wrap.*

*Enter spaces to force the
text into position.*

*Enter carriage returns in
your text to break lines.*

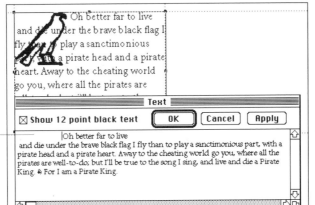

*Press "Apply"
from time to
time to see
what you're
doing.*

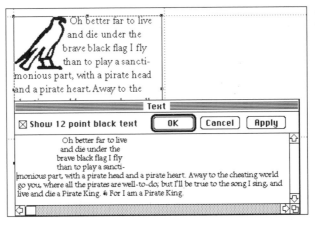

*Completed text
wrap*

Specifying Type

First off, let me say that while there are loads of commands on the Type menu, I only ever make or change type specifications through the Type specifications dialog box. Why? Try selecting a size and leading from the Size and Leading submenus a few times. Now try pressing Command-T, typing the number for the size, pressing Tab, typing a number for the leading, and then pressing Return to close the dialog box.

You're right—it's far simpler to use the latter method. You don't have to follow those little arrows off the side of the menu and then track down the number you want on the submenu that pops out. If you spend much time specifying type, you'll want to use the Type specifications dialog box (select a text block and press Command-T) most of the time.

To format text, you can select as little as one character in a single text block or as much as all of the text blocks in your publication.

FreeHand's Type specifications dialog box has changed—for the better. In FreeHand 2, you had to navigate through two dread pop-up menus to set the size and leading you wanted for a particular piece of type. These pop-ups have been converted to the far more humane combination text edit field/pop-up menu, so, in FreeHand 3, you can set the size and leading of the type you want quickly.

Tip:
Skip Some Fields

FreeHand's Type specifications dialog box does not require that you fill out every field and/or pop-up inside it to close it and apply any changes you've made.

If you've selected a range of text containing mixed type specifications (say, for example, that it contains text that's been baseline shifted) and all you want to do to it is change its horizontal scaling, just open the Type specifications dialog box, make your change in the Horizontal scaling text edit box, and then press Return. FreeHand applies the change to the horizontal scaling of all the selected text without disturbing any of the other specifications.

Font

Choose the font you want from the Type pop-up menu. This is pretty simple, but beware—imagesetters (and multiple-page page-layout programs) can become confused if you specify the specialized screen font for bold, italic, or bold italic versions of a particular font.

How can you tell which of the screen fonts are the specialized versions? This gets very tricky. To specify Times Bold, for example, you want to choose Times, and then make it bold by choosing "Bold" from the Style pop-up menu, rather than choosing the screen font "B-Times-Bold." Stone Serif, on the other hand, contains two bold weights: Semibold and Bold. When you make the roman screen font for Stone Serif ("1StoneSerif") bold, you get Stone Semibold. To get bold, you need to choose the roman screen font for Stone Serif Bold ("B1StoneSerifBold").

There's nothing for it but to experiment with the fonts you've got. If you're getting substituted fonts (usually Courier or Times) when you're trying to print a bold, italic, or bold italic version of a font, you've probably chosen the specialized screen font. Try choosing the roman version of the font, applying the type style you want, and printing again.

Why does this happen? In the dark times before ATM and NFNTs, font vendors provided the specialized screen fonts so that you could get a better rendition of the bold, italic, and bold italic weights on your screen. These days, the specialized screen fonts are still there, but they're displayed on the screen when you choose the roman version of the font and apply the appropriate type style, or they're generated from the PostScript printer (outline) font by ATM. For more on working with fonts, see Appendix A, "System."

Tip:
Grayed-out
Fonts

If a font used in a publication is not currently installed in your System, FreeHand warns you as you're opening the publication (see Figure 3-9). If you press Return (or click "OK"), FreeHand substitutes Courier for all of the text formatted with the missing font.

When you select a piece of type that's been formatted with a font you don't have loaded in your current System, the font name is grayed out in the Type specifications dialog box (see Figure 3-10).

FIGURE 3-9
When FreeHand
can't find a font

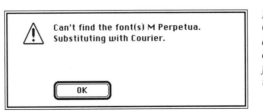

FreeHand substitutes Courier when it can't find a font, which makes it easier to see where text formatted with the missing font is.

FIGURE 3-10

Grayed-out font name

Grayed-out font is not currently loaded into the System

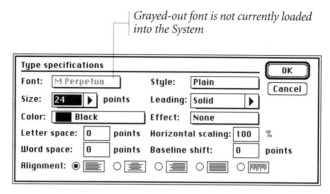

Printing without having all of the fonts used in the publication installed in the System can produce results you don't want (fonts printing as bitmaps or Courier). At this point, you can do one of two things.

- Close the publication, load the font using a suitcase management program like those described in Appendix A, "System," and reopen the publication.

- Search for each occurrence of the font and reformat the text with a font which you do have before you print. Once you've reformatted all of the text that was originally formatted in the missing font, the font disappears from the Font menus.

Obviously, loading the font is the better alternative. If you hadn't wanted that font, you wouldn't have used it in the first place.

Tip:
Programming
QuicKeys to
Select Fonts

I set up QuicKeys to select frequently used fonts (once again, this is to avoid submenus and pop-ups). It's easy to remember that Control-Option-Z changes the font to Zapf Dingbats, or that Control-Option-P selects Perpetua (or Palatino, or whatever you like). Programming QuicKeys to choose fonts from the Type specifications dialog box's Font pop-up menu can be painful, so use the submenus instead. Follow the steps below to set up a font-choosing QuicKey.

1. Invoke QuicKeys (it's usually Command-Option-Return, since that's the default).

2. Choose Menu/DA from the Define menu.

3. Pull down the Font submenu from the FreeHand Type menu and select the font you want.

4. Assign a key to your new Menu/DA QuicKey.

Style

The Style pop-up menu shows you the alternate type styles (other than "Plain," or roman) available for the typeface you've chosen in the Font pop-up menu. If a typeface does not have certain styles, they're grayed out in the Style pop-up menu (see Figure 3-11).

FIGURE 3-11
Style pop-up

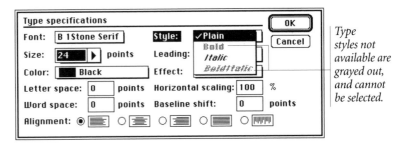

Type styles not available are grayed out, and cannot be selected.

Size

Type the size you want in the Size text edit box, or choose a point size from the pop-up menu. If you're directly entering the size, you can specify it in .0001-point increments. You can also change the size of the type in a text block by stretching the text block (see "Working with Text Blocks," later in this chapter).

Tip:
Greeking

Remember that greeking—whether the type is displayed or drawn as a gray bar—is set in the Preferences dialog box. If you make the type smaller (at the current magnification) than the threshold you set there, it'll appear as a gray bar (see "Preferences" in Chapter 1, "FreeHand Basics."

Leading

Type the leading you want in the Leading text edit box, or choose Solid or Auto leading from the pop-up menu. Solid leading enters the same leading value as you've entered for the point size of your type (12 on 12, for example). "Auto" enters a leading value that's equal to 120 percent of the specified type size. If you're directly entering the leading, you can specify it in .0001-point increments.

You can also change the leading of a text block by manipulating the text block (see "Working with Text Blocks," later in this chapter).

FreeHand's leading measures the lead from baseline to baseline, and it is calculated by measuring *up* from the current baseline to the baseline above (rather than by measuring *down* to the baseline below as in some conventional typesetting systems, as shown in Figure 3-12).

The largest leading in the line predominates to the next line break. If the character containing the larger leading flows to a new line, the leading moves with it (see Figure 3-13).

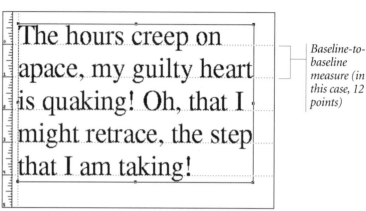

Baseline-to-baseline measure (in this case, 12 points)

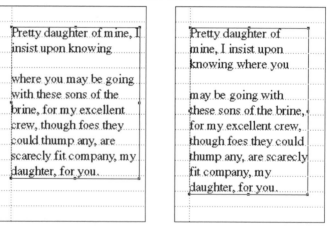

Most of this text is 10/12, but "going" has been set to 10/24.

When the word with the larger leading moves to another line, the larger leading is applied to that line.

Tip:
If Your Leading
Looks Funky

If your leading looks odd inside a text block that should have only one leading setting, select the text block and press Command-T. If the Leading text edit box is blank, you've somehow gotten another leading setting inside the text block. Either reenter the proper leading value, or open the text block and work through the Text dialog box to discover which character is carrying the rogue leading value.

Color

Choose a color for the selected text, or create a new one using any of FreeHand's color models. For more on creating colors, see Chapter 6, "Color."

Tip:
Avoid Fuzzy
Type

Even the most skilled color separators will tell you to avoid applying a process color to fine hairlines and text smaller than about 14 points (12 points for bold). It's difficult, even on the very best presses (let alone the best-maintained imagesetters and film processors) to keep small type and fine lines in register, so it ends up looking fuzzy in your printed publication. So use spot colors for fine lines and type. If you're stuck, try to find a process color which gives you 80 percent of cyan, magenta, or black, and try to apply it to a sans serif face; they're less likely to look fuzzy.

Effect

Text effects are just that—special effects for your type. They're generally for creating eye-catching display type. Choose an effect from the pop-up menu. After you choose an effect, a dialog box for specifying the behavior of the effect appears.

Fill and Stroke. Use "Fill and stroke" to apply a fill to the inside and a stroke to the outside of the selected text (see Figure 3-14). "Fill and stroke" is also the key to trapping text in FreeHand (see Chapter 6, "Color").

Notice that you cannot choose custom lines and fills from this dialog box. If you want to fill your characters with a custom line or a tiled fill, you'll have to convert the characters to paths (see "Converting Characters into Paths," later in this chapter).

FIGURE 3-14
Fill and stroke
dialog box

Fill and stroke effect

Heavy. The Heavy effect applies a stroke to the outline of the text. "Heavy" creates a simulated bold type style if applied to a roman face, or makes a text styled bold appear "bolder" (see Figure 3-15).

FIGURE 3-15
"Heavy"

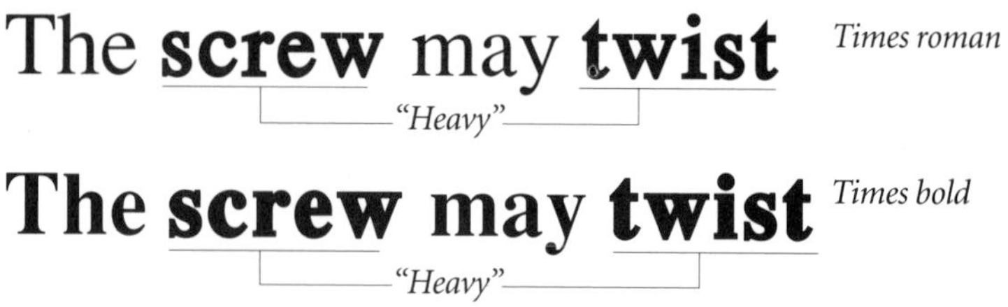

The **screw** may **twist**   *Times roman*
———————"Heavy"———————

The **screw** may **twist**   *Times bold*
———————"Heavy"———————

Inline. Remember "Trace edges" from MacPaint? "Inline" does much the same thing—drawing outlines around solid characters. You set the number and thickness of the outlines in the Inline dialog box (see Figure 3-16).

FIGURE 3-16
"Inline"

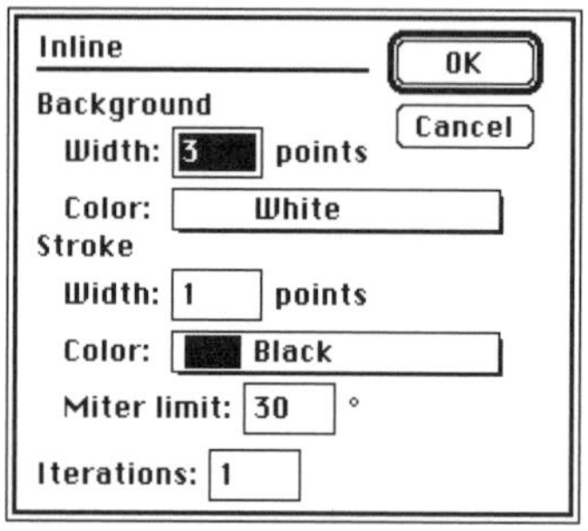

Inline

Background
    Width: **3** points
    Color: White
Stroke
    Width: 1 points
    Color: Black
    Miter limit: 30 °
    Iterations: 1

OK
Cancel

Inline text effect

Oblique. Choose "Oblique" to slant type (by about 21 degrees). If you apply this effect to roman type, FreeHand creates a simulated italic type style (see Figure 3-17). If you apply this effect to italic type, you get something even more oblique. Do not show the result to typographers. They'll get upset.

FIGURE 3-17
"Oblique"

Rose Maybud   *Times Italic*

Rose Maybud   *Times roman with "Oblique" applied*

Rose Maybud   *Times italic with "Oblique" applied*

Outline. Use "Outline" to apply a stroke to the selected characters and set the fill of the character to none (see Figure 3-18). The width of the stroke applied is based on the size of the characters.

FIGURE 3-18
"Outline"

Three little maids from school

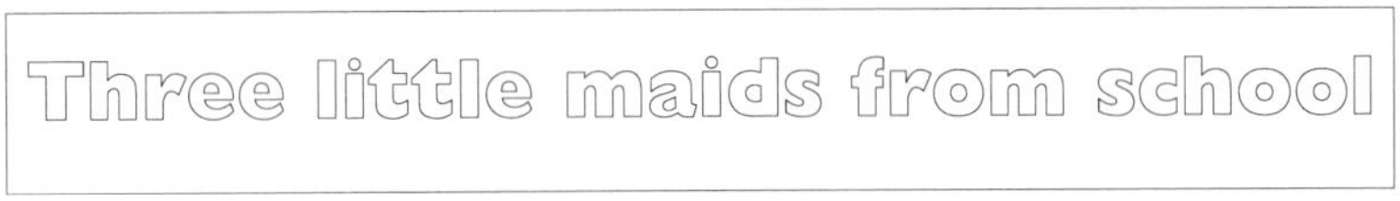

Shadow. Use "Shadow" to apply a drop shadow to the selected text. This drop shadow is offset to the right and below the text it's applied to (see Figure 3-19). The distance that the drop shadow is offset is based on the size of the characters. The drop shadow is set to 50 percent of the color of the selected text.

FIGURE 3-19
"Shadow"

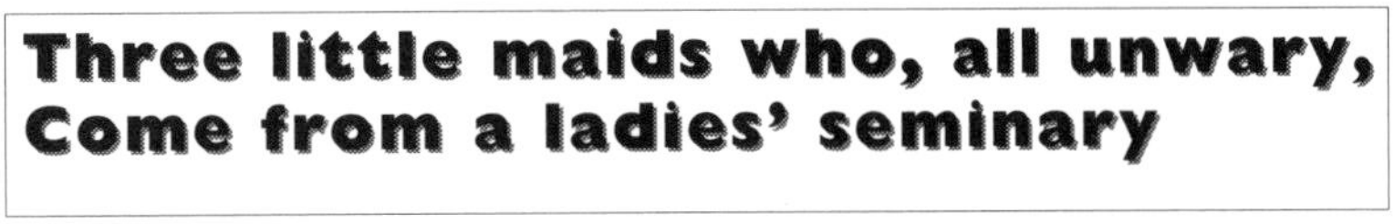

Three little maids who, all unwary,
Come from a ladies' seminary

Zoom Text. You see zoom text all the time in television commercials, usually for furniture and carpet dealers' goin' out of business/liquidation/oncoming recession sales. Right? Use this one with caution, though, and it can be a useful tool. "Zoom text" creates a string of characters that appear to recede toward a vanishing point. You control the size of the farthest character in the zoom, the offset of that character, and the change in color from one end of the zoom to the other (see Figure 3-20). If you're using process colors, or are zooming from one spot color to white or a tint of the same spot color, you can even zoom from one color to another.

FIGURE 3-20
"Zoom text"

Zoom text
OK
Zoom to: 100 %
Cancel
Zoom offset (in points):
Horizontal: 20
Vertical: 20
Color: From: White
To: Black

WSG

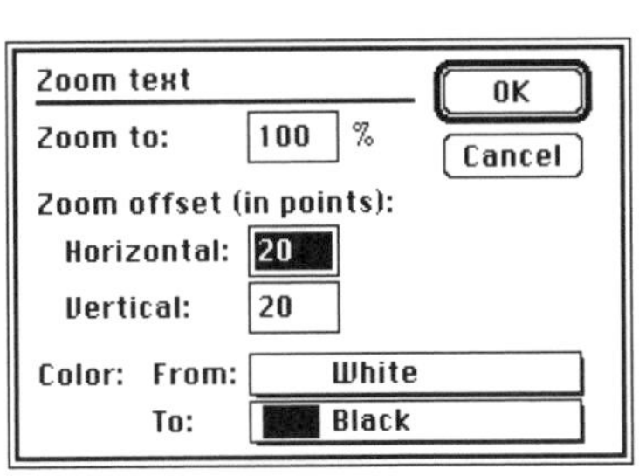

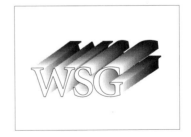

Zoom text effect

Tip:
Bounding Boxes
and "Zoom Text"

If you're exporting text which has the Zoom text effect applied to it, make sure that the bounding box of the EPS is large enough to accommodate the full extent of the zoomed text. The easiest way to do this is to draw a no-line, no-fill box that extends to the edge of the effect around the text.

Letter Space

The value you enter in the Letter space text edit box is added or subtracted between all of the characters in the selection (see Figure 3-21).

You can also add letter spacing by dragging the selection handles of text blocks (see "Working with Text Blocks," later in this chapter).

FIGURE 3-21
Letter spacing

The merry maiden and the tar

The merry maiden and the tar

The merry maiden and the tar

Horizontal Scaling

Use "Horizontal scaling" to create expanded (wider) or condensed (narrower) versions of your type (see Figure 3-22). Before I became too old and tired, I used to argue that these aren't true expanded or condensed fonts, which involve different character shapes and spacings, but never mind. You can also change the horizontal scaling of type by dragging the selection handles of text blocks (see "Working with Text Blocks," later in this chapter).

FIGURE 3-22
Horizontal scaling

The merry cat-o'-nine tails and the tar

The merry cat-o'-nine tails and the tar

The merry cat-o'-nine tails and the tar

XXXXXXX X

Word Space

The amount of space you enter in the Word space text edit box is added between words in the selected text (see Figure 3-23). You can also add word spacing by dragging the selection handles of text blocks (see "Working with Text Blocks," later in this chapter).

FIGURE 3-23
Word spacing

It was the cat!

It was the cat!

It was the cat!

Baseline Shift

Enter an amount in the Baseline shift text edit box to shift the baseline of the selected text by that amount. As you'd guess, positive values move the baseline of the selected text up from the baseline; negative values move the baseline of the selected text down from the baseline (see Figure 3-24).

FIGURE 3-24
"Baseline shift"

ASCENT   12^{144}⁄20736

Tip:
Offsetting the
Baseline of Text
on a Path

You can use "Baseline shift" to offset the baseline of text you've joined to a path from that path (see Figure 3-25).

FIGURE 3-25
Offsetting the baseline
of text on a path

Alignment

FreeHand sports the usual complement of text alignment—Align right (also known as "rag left"), Align left (also known as "rag right"), Center, and Justify—but also throws in the kooky Vertical alignment option (see Figure 3-26).

Tip:
Unjustified
Justification

You may know people who call align right "right justify," or align left "left justify." Feign ignorance until they correct themselves. As you know, justification means to spread a line from one margin to the other, so there can't be anything called "right justify" or "left justify."

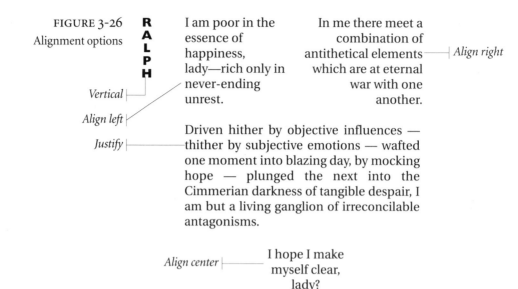

FIGURE 3-26
Alignment options

Tip:
QuicKeys for
Alignment

Because other page-layout programs use keyboard shortcuts Command-Shift-R for right alignment and Command-Shift-L for left alignment, Command-Shift-C for centered text, and Command-Shift-J for justified text, consider adding these keyboard shortcuts with QuicKeys.

Kerning

Kerning brings characters closer together horizontally, or, these days, moves them farther apart (once, kerning meant only *decreasing* the space between characters) by fine increments (see Figure 3-27). FreeHand kerns in coarse increments (.1 em) or fine increments (.01 em). Just as a reminder: an em is equal to the size of the type in the line. An em space in 24-point type is 24 points wide. You can use kerning to add or subtract 2 ems of space.

While some "conventional" (that is, expensive, dedicated, obsolete) typesetting systems kern in absolute increments (fractional points, generally), most typesetting systems (desktop and otherwise), kern in units relative to the size of the type. Practically, this means that you can enlarge the type and retain the same relative amount of kerning.

To kern, select and open open a text block. In the Text edit dialog box, position the text insertion point between two characters and then press key combinations to add or delete space between characters (see Table 3-1).

TABLE 3-1 Kerning keyboard shortcuts	To delete	Press
	.1 em	Command-Delete (or Command-Left arrow)
	.01 em	Command-Option-Delete (or Command+Shift+Left arrow)

To add	Press
.1 em	Command-Shift-Delete (or Command-Right arrow)
.01 em	Command-Option-Shift-Delete (or Command-Shift-Right arrow)

FIGURE 3-27
Kerning

Unkerned text   *Kerned text*

You can achieve effects similar to kerning an entire block of text by dragging the text block's handles (see "Working with Text Blocks," later in this chapter), or by entering positive or negative values in the Letter space text edit box in the Type specifications dialog box (see "Letter Space," earlier in this chapter).

Tip:
QuicKey for
Kerning

It's a bother having to leave the Text dialog box to see the effect of the kerning you enter there. But you don't have to, provided you remember the Apply button in the Text dialog box. Just set up your kerning keys so that they automatically press the Apply button after each kerning increment is entered.

1. Open QuicKeys.

2. Choose "Aldus FreeHand 3.0" to make the keys specific to this application.

3. Create a Button QuicKey for the Apply button.

4. Create a Sequence QuicKey which enters a Literal Option-Left arrow, then presses the Apply button you defined.

5. Assign a key to this Sequence QuicKey—I usually use Option-Delete (which is another shortcut for the same kerning value).

Now, every time you press Option-Delete, QuicKeys will press the Apply button and update your screen display with the kerning increment you've entered. You can make QuicKeys for all of the other kerning values following the same procedure.

Working with Text Blocks

Once you've created a text block, you can work with it and transform it just as you can anything else on the FreeHand page and pasteboard. You can rotate text blocks, scale them, reflect them, skew them, group and ungroup them, and apply colors to them. You cannot, however, paste things inside the characters in a text block without first converting the text to paths (see "Converting Characters into Paths," later in this chapter).

Besides that, however, text blocks have a number of unique features. By dragging the selection handles on a text block (see Figure 3-28), here's what you can do.

• Change the width of the text block and recompose the text inside it

• Scale a text block proportionally or nonproportionally

• Adjust the leading of the text block

• Adjust the word and letter spacing of the text block

• Snap the text block into new positions

The handles on text blocks do different things when you drag them, as shown in Table 3-2.

These shortcuts are interactive versions of several dialog box options and text edit boxes. If you want to repeat a particular spacing, select the text block and check the values in the text edit boxes in the Type specifications dialog box.

FIGURE 3-28

Text block handles

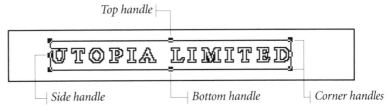

Top handle

Side handle   *Bottom handle*   *Corner handles*

TABLE 3-2

Text block handles

Drag this handle	While holding down	To
Corner	No key	Resize the text block. If you're dragging up and/ or to the left, dragging the corner handle moves the top of the text block to a new position.
Corner	Option	Stretch type inside the text block.
Corner	Shift-Option	Proportionally stretch type inside the text block.
Top and bottom	No key	Increase leading.
Side	No key	Increase letter spacing.
Side	Option	Increase word spacing.

Changing the Width of Text Blocks

While you can always wrap the lines (change line breaks) in a text block by entering carriage returns in the text, you can also change the text composition by dragging a corner handle of the text block (see Figure 3-29).

Note that this change affects only the width, not the height of the text block. As you drag the corner handle, the text inside the text block reflows to fit the new width. Dragging the corner handle to resize a text block is a more flexible way of controlling line breaks than inserting carriage returns, so use this technique when you think you might change your mind about the text block's layout. I change my mind often.

FIGURE 3-29
Changing line breaks
inside a text block

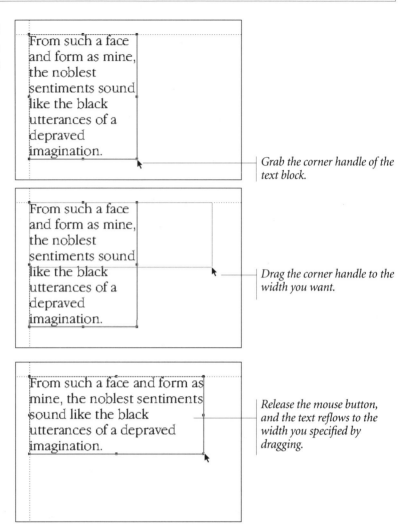

Grab the corner handle of the
text block.

Drag the corner handle to the
width you want.

Release the mouse button,
and the text reflows to the
width you specified by
dragging.

Tip:
Centering
Text Blocks
by Dragging

FreeHand's Center alignment option can be a bit frustrating to work with. Sure, it centers the text inside the text block, but what if you want to center the text block across a certain measurement (say, for example, a column). You could always draw another object the width of the column, then center the text block to the object using the Alignment dialog box, and then cut the object, but that's a bother. Instead, follow the steps below (see Figure 3-30).

1. Place ruler guides at the right and left edges of the area you want to center the text on.

FIGURE 3-30
Centering by dragging

Open the text block containing the text you want to center. Select the text and copy it to the Clipboard. Press Enter to close the Text dialog box.

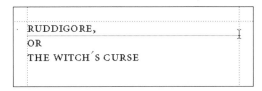

Drag the text tool across the area you want the text centered on. When the Text dialog box appears, paste the text from the Clipboard.

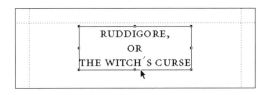

Press Return to close the Text dialog box, and then delete the original text block. Your new text block is centered where you want it.

2. Open the text block containing the text you want to center and copy the text to the Clipboard. Close the Text dialog box.

3. Select the text tool from the toolbox.

4. Drag the text insertion point from one ruler guide to the other. Release the mouse button, and the Text dialog box appears.

5. Press Command-V to paste the text from the Clipboard into the Text dialog box. Make sure that the text is set to Center alignment, and press Enter to close the Text dialog box.

FreeHand centers the text block across the width you defined by dragging the text tool. Now you can delete the original text block, if you want.

Scaling Text Blocks

You can change the size, leading, and horizontal scaling of the text in a text block by dragging the text block's selection handles while holding down Command-Option (see Figure 3-31). Hold down Command-Option-Shift as you drag to scale the text proportionally. If the text block contains a mix of type sizes, all of the size settings inside the block are increased or decreased by the same percentage.

FIGURE 3-31
Scaling text blocks

Hold down Option
and select a corner
handle.

Drag the corner
handle until the box
is about the size you
want the text.

Release the mouse
button. FreeHand
scales the text in the
text block to the size
you've specified by
dragging.

**Adjusting the
Leading of Text
Blocks**

You can adjust the leading of the text in a text block by dragging the
center selection handles on the top or bottom of the text block (see
Figure 3-32). If the text block contains a mix of leading settings, all of
the leading settings inside the block are increased or decreased by the
same percentage.

FIGURE 3-32
Adjusting leading

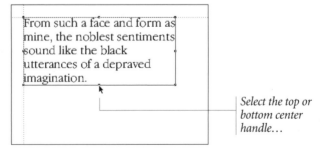

Select the top or
bottom center
handle…

FIGURE 3-32
Continued

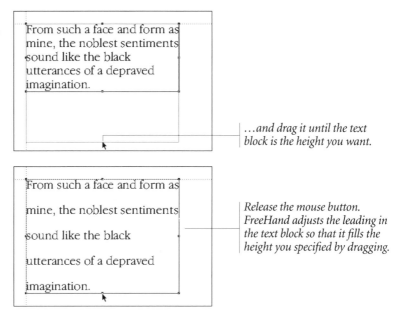

…*and drag it until the text block is the height you want.*

Release the mouse button. FreeHand adjusts the leading in the text block so that it fills the height you specified by dragging.

Adjusting Word and Letter Spacing

You can adjust the letter spacing of the text in a text block by dragging the center selection handle on either side of the text block. Adjust the word spacing of the text in a text block by holding down Option as you drag the side handle on either side of the text block (see Figure 3-33).

FIGURE 3-33
Adjusting word
and letter spacing

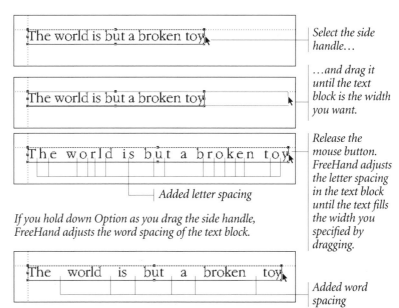

Select the side handle…

…*and drag it until the text block is the width you want.*

Added letter spacing

Release the mouse button. FreeHand adjusts the letter spacing in the text block until the text fills the width you specified by dragging.

If you hold down Option as you drag the side handle, FreeHand adjusts the word spacing of the text block.

Added word spacing

Tip:
Adjusting Both
the Word and
Letter Spacing
for a Text Block

Typically, when you're justifying blocks of type, you want to increase or decrease both the word and the letter spacing of the text. You can always enter both values in the Type specifications dialog box, but you want to change both values by eye (that is, by dragging a handle of the text block). Try this: hold down Option and drag the side handle about one third of the distance you want to go, let go of the side handle (let go of the mouse button), and then drag the side handle the rest of the distance without holding down Option. With some practice, you can get the word and letter spacing values you're looking for by simply dragging the side handles.

**More Text Block
Manipulations**

You can also use a text block's selection handles as a method of moving the text block. Why would you want to do this? It can sometimes be difficult to drag a text block into a precise position. It always seems to snap to the wrong grid mark or ruler guide. You can get around this by simply dragging one of the corner handles to the point you want to move the text block (see Figure 3-34).

With a little practice, you can even do this without changing the shape of the text block (of course, a text block with line breaks forced by carriage returns will retain its shape in most cases, anyway).

FIGURE 3-34
Moving by dragging

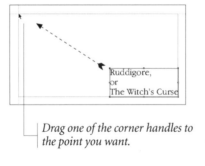

Drag one of the corner handles to the point you want.

The text block moves to the point you specified by dragging.

Joining Text to a Path

One of FreeHand's signature features is the ability to place text along paths of any shape or length. To join text to a path, select some text, press Shift and select a path, and then press Command-J (or choose "Join" from the Element menu). FreeHand joins your text to the path (see Figure 3-35).

FIGURE 3-35
Joining text to a path

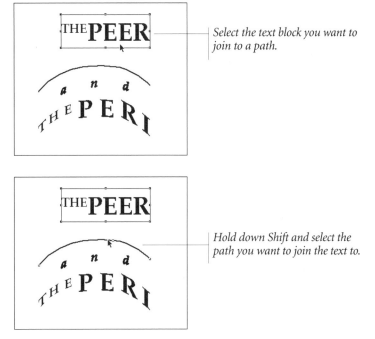

Select the text block you want to
join to a path.

Hold down Shift and select the
path you want to join the text to.

Press Command-J or choose "Join
elements" from the Element menu.
FreeHand wraps the text along the
path, using whatever text alignment
options you've specified for the text
block.

Once you've joined text to a path, you select the text and the path by selecting the path—you can click on the text all day and not select the path. Switching to Keyline view can make it a little easier to see and select the path.

If you want to unjoin, or split, the text from the path, select the path and choose "Split element" from the Element menu. The text and the path become separate objects again.

Joining text to a path is a great—if somewhat overused—feature. It's often confusing, though. People have a hard time understanding why the text they've just joined to a path falls where it does on the path. There are a few simple rules to keep in mind when you're joining text to a path.

- Text joins the path according to the alignment of the text block.

- Only the first line (up to the first carriage return) of the text gets joined to the path. The rest of the text's still there; it's just invisible and won't print.

- If the path is shorter than the first line of text, the excess text gets shoved off the end (or ends) of the path.

Now here are the exceptions to the rules.

- Ellipses drawn with the ellipse tool use the first two lines of text in the text block (up to the second carriage return in the text block). The first line of text gets joined to the top of the ellipse; the second line of text gets joined to the bottom of the ellipse.

- Justified text will bunch up as much as possible when joined to a path that's shorter than the text.

If you're confused, I understand. Take a look at Figure 3-36.

FIGURE 3-36
Joining text and
text alignment

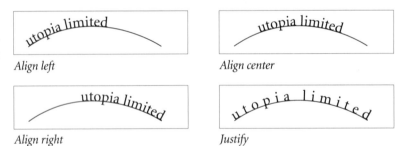

Align left

Align center

Align right

Justify

When you join text to an ellipse, its alignment depends on the settings in the Text on an ellipse dialog box.

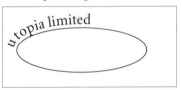

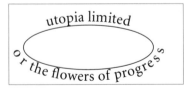

If you leave "Centered" unchecked, and you're using left alignment, a two-line text block joins to the ellipse like this.

When you check "Centered," the same text block looks like this.

One of FreeHand 3's nicest new features is that you don't have to go through the Text along a path dialog box to make changes to the format of the text along the path. These days, just select the path and press Command-T to bring up the Type specifications dialog box. Make changes there, press return, and the new attributes are applied to the text along the path.

There's a lot more to controlling the appearance of the text you've joined to a path than the Type specifications dialog box, however. If you select the path and press Command-I, you'll see an entirely new object info dialog box (see Figure 3-37).

FIGURE 3-37
Text along a path
dialog box

If your text is joined to a freeform path, this dialog box appears.

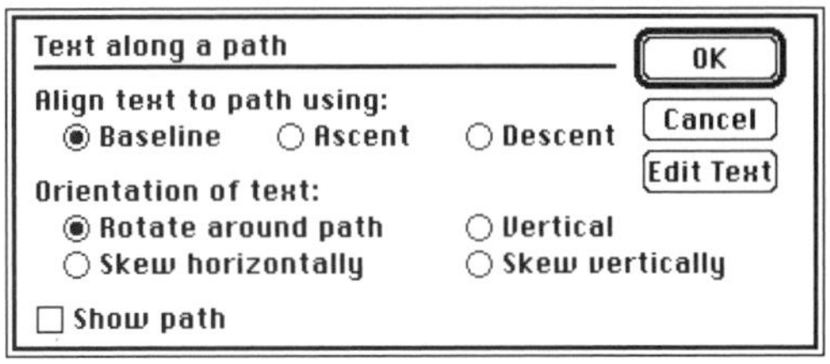

If your text is joined to a basic shape, this dialog box appears.

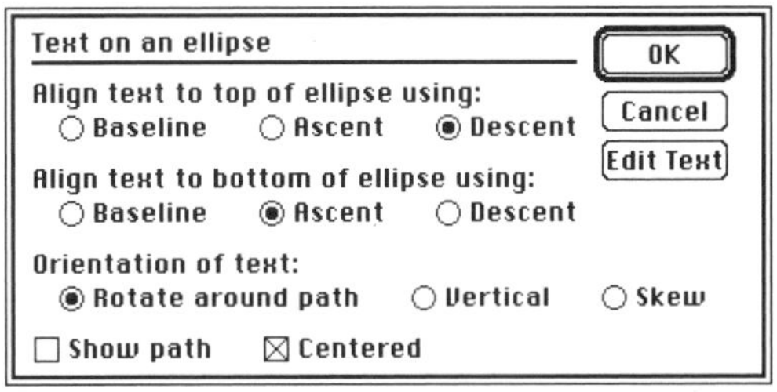

In the Text along a path dialog box, you can set the way that the text you've joined to a path follows that path. Some pretty crazy effects are possible, and, rather than trying to describe them all, I'll just refer you to Figure 3-38.

Beyond these options, the Show path option makes the path a visible and printing path. You can alter the stroke and color of the path as you would any other path.

If you click the Edit text button, the Text dialog box for the text you've joined to the path appears. You can't use the Apply button (which is a shame) so it's grayed out.

FIGURE 3-38
Text along a
path options

Align text to path (using the "Rotate around path" orientation)

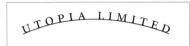

Baseline   *Ascent*

Descent

Orientation of text (aligned to path using "Descent")

"Rotate around path"   *"Vertical"*

"Skew horizontally"   *"Skew vertically"*

More extreme curves produce more extreme text effect.

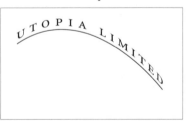

"Skew horizontally"   *"Skew vertically"*

Tip:
Autoskewing
Text

The skew tool is lots of fun, but this trick is even more fun. When you need to make some text appear as if it's on a plane that's rotated away from the plane of the page and pasteboard, follow these steps (see Figure 3-39).

1. Draw a line.

2. Type some text.

FIGURE 3-39

Autoskewing text

Select the text and the line.

Press Command-J to join the text to the line.

Press Command-I to bring up the Text along a path dialog box. Choose "Ascent" and "Skew vertically" for your alignment options.

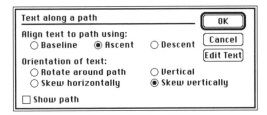

Now you can skew the text by dragging the handles of the path.

Why you want to do stuff like this

3. Select the text and the line.

4. Choose "Join" from the Element menu.

5. Press Command-I.

6. In the Text along a path dialog box, click "Ascent" for your alignment option, then click "Skew vertically" for the text's orientation relative to the path. You might want to set the text's alignment to "Justify," while you're at it.

7. Now you can skew the text by dragging either end of the path anywhere you want.

Converting Characters into Paths

With FreeHand 3, you can convert characters from just about any font (Type 1 and Fontographer Type 3 PostScript fonts) for which you have the printer (outline) font into freeform paths.

Once you've converted the characters into paths, you lose all text-editing capabilities, but you gain the ability to paste things inside the character outline, to apply lines and fills that you can't apply to normal text (including tiled, graduated, radial, or PostScript fills), and to change the shape of the characters themselves.

To convert characters into paths, select the text block or text blocks you want to convert, and then choose "Convert to paths" from the Type menu. FreeHand converts the characters into paths (see Figure 3-40).

FIGURE 3-40
Converting text
into paths

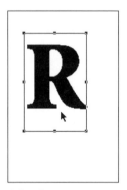  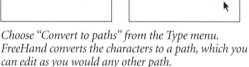

Select the text you want to convert to paths.

Choose "Convert to paths" from the Type menu. FreeHand converts the characters to a path, which you can edit as you would any other path.

Tip:
If That Didn't
Work...

If you weren't able to convert the text into paths, make sure that you have the outline (printer) fonts and that they're somewhere FreeHand can find them. If you don't have the outline fonts, FreeHand won't be able to convert your text into paths.

Generally, your outline fonts should be "loose" (that is, not inside any other folder) inside your system folder. If you use a suitcase management program such as Suitcase II or MasterJuggler, the outline fonts should be in the same folder as the suitcase containing the bitmap (screen) fonts, and the suitcase containing the bitmap fonts must be open.

When you first convert characters into paths, all of the converted characters are joined as a single, composite path. To work with an individual character, just choose "Split element" from the Element menu.

All characters converted into paths are converted as composite paths (see "Composite Paths," in Chapter 2, "Drawing"). This is handy. Not only are multiple part characters (such as i, é, and ü) treated as single paths, but characters with interior paths (such as O, P, A, and D) are transparent where they should be, and fill properly (see Figure 3-41).

You can always make the characters into normal (that is, not composite) paths, if you want, by selecting the character and choosing "Split element" from the Element menu.

FIGURE 3-41
Text converted into
composite paths

When you convert characters to paths, they're converted as a single, composite path.

To work with individual characters, choose "Split element" from the Element menu.

To work with paths inside a single character, select the character and choose "Split element" from the Elements menu.

Tip:
Don't Worry
about Down-
loadable Fonts

If you've exported FreeHand files containing lots of downloadable fonts as EPS, then imported them into other page-layout applications, you've probably had trouble getting the EPS to print. For whatever reason, EPS graphics and downloadable fonts don't mix very well.

So why bother with fonts? Instead, you can convert all of your text to paths (though this might not work for zoom text and other text effects) before you export your publication as an EPS. This way, the application that's printing your EPS doesn't have to worry about getting the downloadable fonts right. Your EPSs will print faster, too.

After Words

A picture might be worth a thousand words, but there are lots of words you'd have a hard time getting across with a thousand pictures ("mellifluous," for example). FreeHand handles both words and pictures beautifully, so you don't have to choose.

Importing and Exporting

Someday,

you'll need something FreeHand's native drawing and typesetting abilities can't give you. You'll need paragraph formatting, or the ability to edit color TIFFs, or 3-D rotation and rendering. Other programs do these things better than FreeHand does. But once you've done the work you need to do using some other application, you can bring the files you create back into your FreeHand publication.

You can open EPS files saved in the Illustrator 1.1 format from other PostScript drawing programs, and you can import any EPS file. You can use word processors and page-layout programs to generate and format text using paragraph indents and tabs, and then bring the formatted text into FreeHand as either an EPS graphic (in which the text isn't editable), or as an assemblage of FreeHand text blocks (in which the text is editable). You can scan an image in either color or gray scale, edit it with an image-editing program, then place it in Free-Hand, and use it as part of your FreeHand publication—including generating color separations of the images when you print. You can also create graphics in other drawing programs, and open or import them into FreeHand.

FreeHand's no slouch at exporting graphics for use in other applications—FreeHand's exported EPS formats can be imported into every major page-layout or illustration program and combined with text and graphics created in those programs. And, if exporting as an EPS doesn't work, there are several ways to export object-PICT graphics (with attached PostScript, so you won't lose any details or PostScript effects) to applications that don't support EPS import (such as Microsoft Word).

About Graphic File Formats

FreeHand can import a wide range of graphic file formats, including Adobe Illustrator 1.1, Adobe Streamline files, gray-scale and color TIFFs, EPS files, paint-type images, and PICT-type graphics. From FreeHand's point of view, there are certain limitations and advantages to each of these file formats.

Just to refresh everybody's memory, here are a few quick definitions, rules, and exceptions regarding graphic file formats.

First, each Macintosh file contains information on the type of file it is (the "File type") and what application was used to create it (the "Creator"). Both the File type and Creator are stored as distinctive, four-letter codes. We don't have to worry too much about the Creator, but the File type code makes an enormous amount of difference in how FreeHand deals with the file.

PNTG and TIFF

File types PNTG and TIFF are bitmap, or image, formats which store their pictures as matrices (rows and columns) of pixels, each pixel having a particular gray or color value (also known as a gray depth or color depth).

PNTG-type graphics are also called paint-type graphics (because they are in the format created by the venerable MacPaint). Each pixel in a paint-type graphic has a value of either one or zero, on or off, black or white. Pixels in gray-scale and color TIFF images, on the other hand, can be represented by up to 32,767 numbers, which means that each pixel in these images can be one of 32,767 possible color (or gray) values. Paint-type graphics and bilevel TIFFs (1-bit TIFFs are called bilevels because each bit is either on or off, black or white) are functionally equivalent.

PICT and EPS

File types PICT and EPS store their pictures as sets of instructions for drawing graphic objects. Because of this, they're often called "object-oriented," which you shouldn't confuse with the "object-oriented programming" you hear so much about these days. The drawing instructions say, "Start this line at this point and draw to that point over there," or "This is a polygon made up of these line segments." The instructions contain values for fills and colors—"This polygon is filled with a specific gray level."

The main difference between these two formats is that the instructions in PICT graphics are expressed in QuickDraw, which is the language your Macintosh uses to draw lines, images, and characters on its screen, and the instructions in EPS graphics are written in Post-Script, the language your PostScript printer uses to make marks on paper. PostScript is a far richer language for describing graphic objects.

Because the EPS graphics aren't written in the Macintosh's display language, they often carry a bitmapped PICT rendition along as a screen preview of their contents. How do they get this image? Remember that FreeHand can convert its internal database into QuickDraw (what you see on the screen) or into PostScript (what FreeHand sends to your PostScript printer). Once the file's exported as an EPS, it's not in FreeHand's native format anymore, so FreeHand can't convert it into QuickDraw commands for your screen display. When you choose to export an EPS as "Macintosh EPS," FreeHand generates and attaches a QuickDraw version of the graphic to the PostScript code.

Here are the exceptions to the above descriptions.

- PICT files can contain PNTG and TIFF images. They don't do it very well, but they can do it.

- EPS files can also contain PNTG and TIFF images. They don't do it very well, but they do it better than PICT does.

FreeHand can also directly open a number of EPS file types. You can open all Adobe Illustrator 1.1 files, most Adobe Illustrator '88 files, most Adobe Illustrator 3.0 files, and all Adobe Streamline files. If you can't open an Illustrator '88 or 3.0 EPS file, open the file with Illustrator and save it in the Illustrator 1.1 format, which FreeHand can always open.

When you open an EPS file (as opposed to placing it), the objects in the file are converted into FreeHand elements and can be edited as you'd edit any FreeHand element.

FreeHand can also open and interpret object-PICT files created by MacDraw, Persuasion, or most CAD programs.

Bitmap-only PICT files are converted to TIFF files and stored inside your FreeHand publication. Note that this is unlike normal TIFF files, which are stored outside your FreeHand publication. If you're saving your scanned images as bitmap PICT files, you can expect your FreeHand files to become huge as you import the images. For best performance (and, probably, better printing of your images), save your scans as TIFF, not as PICT.

Most graphics applications can save their files in more than one file format, and almost every illustration or page-layout application can write at least one file format that FreeHand can read. If you're having trouble placing or opening a file, try opening it again in its original application (or another application that can read its original file type and save it in a file type FreeHand can read) and saving it in one of the file types FreeHand supports (see Table 4-1).

	Application	File formats supported	FreeHand can read
TABLE 4-1 File types and FreeHand	MacDraw II	MDRW, PICT	PICT
	MacPaint	PNTG	PNTG
	PixelPaint	PNTG, EPS, PICT, TIFF	PNTG, PICT*, EPS**, TIFF
	Photoshop	PNTG, EPS, PICT, TIFF	PNTG, PICT*, EPS**, TIFF
	LetraStudio	EPS	EPS
	SuperPaint	PNTG, PICT	PNTG, PICT
	Digital Darkroom	PNTG, PICT, TIFF	PNTG, PICT*, TIFF
	Super 3D	PICT	PICT

* Bitmap PICT   **Bitmap EPS, including DCS

Some programs are real "Swiss army knives," and can open and save files in lots of different formats. Photoshop, for example, can open and save files in a dozen different formats. If you're working in a studio that has to deal with files from MS-DOS systems and/or dedicated computer graphics workstations (such as the Quantel Paintbox), Photoshop is a great program to have around even if you use it for nothing more than file conversions.

Tip:
There's Always
Pasting…

If the application you're trying to get something out of isn't able to save in any format FreeHand can read, try copying elements out of it and pasting them into FreeHand. This will sometimes work when all else fails.

There are several different file-conversion programs on the market that can make it easier to convert an unreadable file into a file type that FreeHand can read.

Studio Convert

StudioConvert is a utility program written by Integrated Systems Design & Consulting, Ltd. (ISDC), a desktop color service bureau and consulting firm in the Midwest.

As I understand it, StudioConvert's main function is to convert LetraStudio 1.0 EPS files to Illustrator 1.1 EPS, but it'll also convert some FreeHand 2 EPS files to Illustrator 1.1 EPS. The conversion is not foolproof or perfect; most of the converted files (when they convert at all) contain only paths and simple fills, and text is not converted.

ISDC doesn't really advertise this software, relying instead on word-of-mouth referrals. I can see why they do this—StudioConvert isn't ready for prime time. Its user interface is clunky, and its results are not all that good—even for FreeHand 2 EPS files. I say this with considerable understanding and sympathy; I happily write and use little utilities that I'd never want to release to the world at large. I couldn't get by without them. If you're desperate, or if you're willing to be understanding, you might want to give ISDC a call (see Appendix B, "Resources," for ISDC's address).

See "Converting FreeHand 3 EPS Files to Illustrator 1.1 EPS Format" later in this chapter for more information.

The Graphics Link Plus

If you're working with graphic files from the MS-DOS/Windows world, you should check out The Graphics Link Plus. The Graphics Link Plus is distributed by PC Quik-Art, and is an MS-DOS utility for converting various DOS graphic file formats to other DOS graphic file formats and to several Macintosh file formats (see Appendix B, "Resources," for PC Quik-Art's address). If you need to convert .PCX files into TIFFs, or Windows Paint files into MacPaint files, The Graphics Link Plus is for you.

Importing PICTs

FreeHand imports PICT-type graphics created by charting programs (such as Aldus Persuasion or Microsoft Excel), PICT-type tables created by Microsoft Word or Aldus Table Editor, and graphics created by PICT drawing programs (such as MacDraw II). Once you've opened or placed these files, each of the elements drawn in the original illustration is converted to a FreeHand element. Often, it'll seem like you've got two or three times as many elements as you need. This is just because PICT has weird ideas about how to draw things (see Figure 4-1).

FIGURE 4-1
"Extra" elements in converted PICT

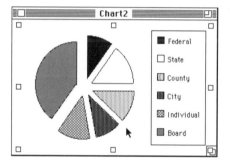

This chart looks fine in Excel...

Each filled object becomes at least two paths (one for the line; one for the fill). In this example, each line segment is a separate path.

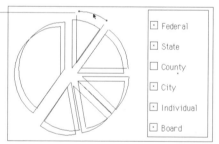

...but when you paste it into FreeHand you see that it has far more objects than you'd think it'd need.

Importing Charts from Microsoft Excel and Aldus Persuasion

Both Excel and Persuasion have good charting features, and you can bring their charts into FreeHand with a minimum of fuss. To save a chart created in Persuasion, go to the slide containing the chart and choose "Export" from the File menu. Choose "Pict" from the Format pop-up menu, type a name for your chart, and press Return to export the chart. Now you can open and convert the chart with FreeHand (see Figure 4-2).

FIGURE 4-2

Exporting a slide
from Persuasion

*In Persuasion, go to the slide you want and choose
"Export…" from the File menu.*

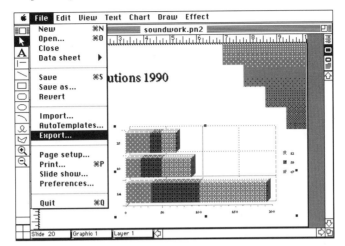

*Type a name for your
chart and choose "PICT."*

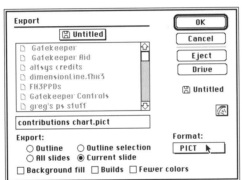

*When you open the
chart, FreeHand converts
the PICT objects into
FreeHand elements.*

*You can edit the
converted objects as you
would any FreeHand
elements.*

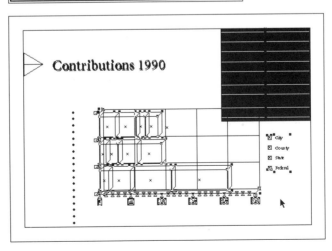

Excel can't export its charts as PICTs, so you'll have to copy them to the Clipboard, and then paste them into FreeHand. As you paste the chart into FreeHand, it's converted into FreeHand elements.

Once you've gotten these charts into FreeHand, you'll have some clean-up to do. Both Persuasion and Excel use patterned fills to fill areas in their charts. Since you want to avoid using patterned fills for all but the simplest publications, you'll probably want to change all of the patterned fills to basic (color or gray) fills (see Figure 4-3).

FIGURE 4-3
Patterned fills
masquerading as grays

*This looks like a
harmless gray fill...*

*...but if you select it and
press Command-E, the
Fill and Line dialog box
shows you that it's a
nasty patterned fill.*

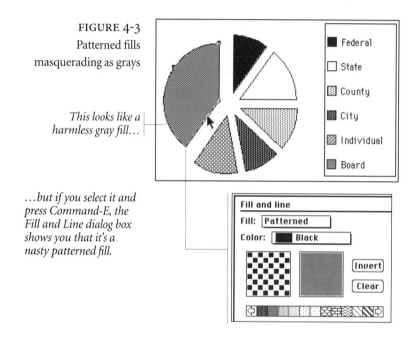

Tip:
Pasting
Excel 3 Charts

As this book is written, Excel 3 charts can't be pasted into FreeHand—or many other applications, for that matter (including Microsoft Word). Microsoft intends to fix this bug by distributing an INIT that changes the way Excel writes PICTs to the Clipboard/Scrapbook. If you're having trouble pasting Excel charts into FreeHand, call Excel technical support at (206) 635-7080 and ask for the INIT.

Tip:
For Fewer
Converted
Objects

Before you export (or copy) your chart from a PICT-type charting program, set the line widths of the filled objects in the chart to "None" (or whatever the equivalent is in the program you're using). When FreeHand converts PICTs, a line means one object, a fill means another object, and so on. Because you always end up deleting all of the lines and then applying a line to the filled object, doesn't it make sense to get rid of the lines before exporting the PICT?

Importing PICTs from CAD Programs

Because most Macintosh CAD programs are capable of saving their drawings in the PICT format, it's easy to bring engineering or architectural drawings into FreeHand. Why would you want to take the drawings out of their native CAD program? Macintosh CAD programs are great at rendering precise views of an object or building, but they're just not that good at making a drawing sexy or handling type in a professional manner. Often, versions of the drawings for marketing and technical illustration need the PostScript drawing features found in FreeHand.

To get objects out of your CAD program and into FreeHand, export or save your drawing as a PICT and then open and interpret the PICT file with FreeHand. If your CAD program can't save as PICT, you can still get the drawing into FreeHand by copying the objects out of the drawing program and pasting them into FreeHand.

There are a few things about converted CAD drawings you need to keep in mind (see Figure 4-4).

- FreeHand converts each line segment into a closed path.

- Arcs and ellipses are often converted into sets of closed paths made up of single straight line segments.

FIGURE 4-4
Imported CAD drawing

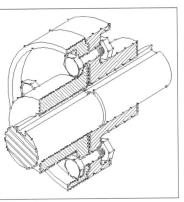

CAD drawing pasted into FreeHand

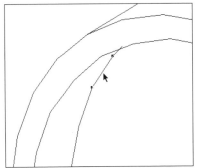

When you zoom in on the imported drawing, you'll see that all of the curves in the drawing are rendered as straight, closed paths.

• Line joins will often miss, particularly where lines meet arcs.

The good news, however, is that you've still got the fundamental shape of the object you want. Once the objects are in a FreeHand publication, you can do as much—or as little—clean-up as you want or have time for.

Importing PICTs from 3-D Drawing Programs

3-D drawing programs are great at producing the snappy multimedia presentation or on-screen animated feature of your dreams, but what happens when it's time to print? You guessed it—72-dpi bitmaps and PICTs with weird fills are the order of the day. You can use FreeHand to spruce up images you've created in 3-D drawing programs like Swivel or Super 3D for publication (see Figure 4-5).

1. Create your 3-D graphics in your 3-D drawing program.

2. Export or save the graphics as object-PICT. Before you export the graphic, you'll probably want to set all of the line widths to "None" (or "No line"—fill in whatever your drawing program uses), and it's best to use hidden line removal if your program has that feature (in Super 3D it's called "Cull Back Faces").

3. Open and convert the object-PICT with FreeHand.

If you can't export or save the graphics as object-PICT, copy the graphics out of the program and paste them into FreeHand.

FIGURE 4-5
Importing 3-D graphics

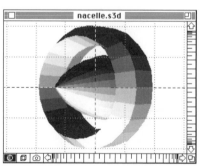

Create an object in your 3-D drawing program. Export or copy the object.

Paste, open, or import the graphic into FreeHand. FreeHand converts the object into FreeHand elements, which you can edit as you would any other.

All of the cautions regarding importing PICTs from CAD programs also apply to importing PICTs from 3-D drawing programs, though some of them, notably Super 3D, write excellent PICTs.

Incredible as it might seem, I've seen magazine tips columns recommend that you import a TIFF of the 3-D image and trace it to bring a 3-D graphic into FreeHand. As you can see, it's easier than that.

What if you want to create a 3-D rendering of something you've drawn in FreeHand using one of the 3-D drawing programs? You can convert FreeHand's EPSs into a Super 3D text file—see "Converting EPS Graphics to Super 3D Display Lists," later in this chapter.

Importing TIFFs

The big news is that FreeHand can now place and separate color TIFF images, and that TIFF printing has been greatly improved from version 2. Printing a gray-scale TIFF you've applied a color to—a major printing performance problem in FreeHand 2—is pleasantly quick.

If you prefer separating your color images before final production, or if you prefer another program's separations, you can preseparate your color images, then save them as EPS graphics and place them in FreeHand. See "Importing EPS Graphics," later in this chapter.

Halftones

Commercial printing equipment can only print one color per printing plate at one time. We can get additional "tints" of that color by filling areas with small dots; at a distance (anything over a foot or so), these dots look like another color. The pattern of dots to represent another color or shade is called a halftone (for more information on color printing, see Chapter 6, "Color").

To print photographic images, we use halftones for the different shades inside the photograph. The eye, silly and arbitrary thing that it is, tells our brain that the printed photograph is made up of shades of gray (or color)—not different patterns of large and small dots.

TIFFs, Line Screens, and Resolution

Let me introduce you to the TIFF balancing act. It goes like this: for any printer resolution there's an ideal screen frequency—a frequency that gives you the highest number of grays available at that printer resolution. If you go below this line screen, you start losing gray levels.

It's natural to assume that by scanning at the highest resolution available from your scanner you can get the sharpest images. This bit of common knowledge, however, doesn't hold true for gray-scale or color images; for these, scan at no more than twice the line frequency you intend to use. Higher scanning resolutions do not add any greater sharpness, but the size of your image files increases dramatically. To determine the size of an image file, use this equation.

file size in kilobytes = (dpi^2*bit depth*width*height)/8192 (bits in a kilobyte)

Ideally, you should scan at the same size as you intend to print the image. Resolution changes when you change the size of the image, so if your scanner won't create an image at the size you want, you can compensate for the effect of resizing the image in FreeHand using this equation.

(original size/printed size)*original (scanning) resolution = resolution

If you'd scanned a 3-by-3-inch image at 300 dpi and reduced it to 2.25 by 3.75 inches (a reduction of 75 percent), the resolution of the image is 400 dpi.

To find the line screen that'll give you the largest number of grays for your printer's resolution, use this equation.

number of grays = (printer resolution in dpi/screen ruling in lpi)^2+1

If the number of grays is greater than 256, the number of grays equals 256. PostScript (at the time of this writing) has a limit of 256 gray shades at any resolution.

So if you want 256 grays, and your printer resolution is 1270 dpi, the optimum screen ruling would be around 80 dpi.

Steve prefers using the following equation instead.

max screen frequency = output resolution/16

Tip:
Scanning
Line Art

If you're scanning line art, save the file as a bilevel TIFF rather than as a gray-scale TIFF. You'll save lots of disk space, and your line art TIFFs will be just as sharp as they'd be if you saved them as gray-scale TIFFs.

Also, scan your line art at the highest resolution you can get out of your scanner. Line art, unlike gray-scale and color images, does benefit from increased resolution, because you're not creating halftones.

Bilevel and Gray-scale TIFFs and Image Control

When you select a paint-type graphic, bilevel TIFF, or gray-scale TIFF file and press Command-I, you'll see the Image dialog box. Color TIFFs have a different object info dialog box. Inside the Image dialog box, you'll find FreeHand's image controls (see Figure 4-6).

FIGURE 4-6
Image dialog box

Gray level presets

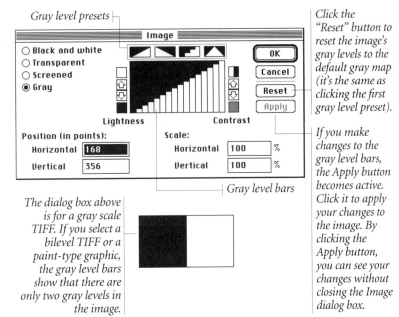

Click the "Reset" button to reset the image's gray levels to the default gray map (it's the same as clicking the first gray level preset).

If you make changes to the gray level bars, the Apply button becomes active. Click it to apply your changes to the image. By clicking the Apply button, you can see your changes without closing the Image dialog box.

Gray level bars

The dialog box above is for a gray scale TIFF. If you select a bilevel TIFF or a paint-type graphic, the gray level bars show that there are only two gray levels in the image.

Black and White. If you open the Image dialog box when you've got a bilevel TIFF or paint-type graphic selected, the Black and white option is selected by default.

If you choose this option when you've got a gray-scale TIFF selected, the TIFF behaves as if it were a bilevel TIFF. Note that the background of the TIFF is an opaque white box the size of the TIFF's selection rectangle. This differs from PageMaker, where bilevel TIFFs are always transparent (unless you choose "Gray" or "Screened" in the Image control dialog box) and gray-scale TIFFs are always opaque (unless you choose "Black and white" in the Image control dialog box).

Transparent. When you choose the Transparent option, the white areas of a TIFF become transparent (see Figure 4-7). If you choose this option when you've got a gray-scale TIFF selected, the TIFF becomes a bilevel TIFF. It'll seem like you've lost some image information, but don't worry—you can always click "Gray" again and all of your gray-scale information will reappear.

FIGURE 4-7
Making the background
of a TIFF transparent

Paint-type graphics set to "Black and white" have an opaque background.

Click "Transparent," and you'll be able to see through the background of the image.

Tip:
Set Bilevels to
"Transparent"
for Faster
Printing

Bilevel TIFFs (and paint files) set to "Transparent" print four times faster than the same images set to "Black and white." Why? To make a long story short, it has to do with conformance to the OPI specifications. If you need an opaque background, why not draw a box with an opaque fill behind the transparent image?

Screened. Click "Screened" to speed up FreeHand's display of grayscale images. If you choose "Screened" in the Image dialog box when you've got a bilevel TIFF or paint-type graphic selected, you can adjust the image's gray levels using the gray level bars, just as you would for a gray-scale TIFF.

Gray. When you open the Image dialog box for a gray-scale TIFF, this option is chosen by default.

If you choose this option when you've got a bilevel TIFF or paint-type graphic selected, you can adjust the gray values of the two gray levels in the image.

Tip:
Altering the
Grays in Bilevel
Images

You can add a different look to bilevel images by altering the gray values used to render them. Select the bilevel image and press Command-I to display the Image dialog box. Click "Gray." Manipulate the gray level bars, clicking the Apply button from time to time to see what effect you're having, until the image looks the way you want it to. Press Return to close the dialog box (see Figure 4-8).

FIGURE 4-8
Changing gray levels
inside bilevel images

*Bilevel image with
default gray levels.*

*Bilevel image with
adjusted gray
levels.*

Lightness and Contrast. The Lightness slider controls the brightness of the entire image. Increase the brightness of the image by clicking the up arrow; decrease the brightness of the image by clicking the down arrow. Note that as you click on the arrow, the slider bars in the window to the right of "Lightness" move (see Figure 4-9).

FIGURE 4-9
Changing lightness

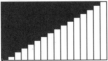
Default lightness

*Image darkened by pressing on the
down arrow in the Lightness control*

If you want to increase the contrast of the image, press the up arrow above "contrast." If you want to decrease the contrast of the image, press the down arrow. As you click on the arrow, the slider bars in the window to the left of "Contrast" move (see Figure 4-10).

FIGURE 4-10
Changing contrast

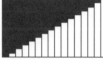

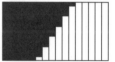

Default contrast   *Increased contrast*

Position. The numbers in the Position text edit boxes ("Horizontal" and "Vertical") show the current position of the upper-left corner of the image relative to the ruler zero point. You can type new values in these text edit boxes to change the position of the image.

Scale. The numbers in the Scale text edit boxes ("Horizontal" and "Vertical") show the current scale of the image relative to the size it was when placed. You can resize the image by typing new values in these text edit boxes.

Gray Level Sliders. Each slider inside the window in the of the Image dialog box applies to one-sixteenth of the gray levels in the image, so each slider in 4-bit TIFF equals one gray level (there are 16 possible gray levels in a 4-bit TIFF); each slider in an 8-bit TIFF represents 16 adjacent gray levels, because there are 256 possible gray levels in an 8-bit TIFF. The gray level bars control gray levels from the darkest to the lightest in your image as they go from left to right. Slide a gray level bar up to increase the lightness of all of the pixels with that group of gray levels; slide it down to decrease their lightness (see Figure 4-11).

FIGURE 4-11
Working with
gray level bars

FIGURE 4-11
Working with
gray level bars

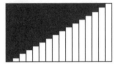
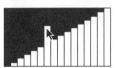

Default gray levels   *You can adjust individual gray bars until you've*
achieved the effect you want.

Gray Level Presets. The Image dialog box contains four default settings for the gray-scale slider bars: Normal, Negative, Posterize, and Solarize. Clicking the Normal icon returns the image control settings for the TIFF to the position they were in when the TIFF was first imported. Clicking the Negative icon reverses all of the gray-scale slider bar settings from their "Normal" setting. Posterize maps all of the gray levels in the TIFF to four gray levels. Solarize maps all of the gray levels to a kind of bell curve. This produces an effect similar to the photographic effect "Solarization," which is produced by exposing photographic film to light before developing the film (see Figure 4-12).

FIGURE 4-12
Gray level bar presets

Normal   *Negative*   *Posterize*   *Solarize*

Reset. Click the Reset button to undo any changes you've made in the Image dialog box since the last time you opened the dialog box.

Apply. Click the Apply button to see what the changes you've made in the Image dialog box look like without closing the Image dialog box.

Color TIFFs   When you select a color TIFF and press Command-I, the Color image dialog box appears (see Figure 4-13). You can use the Color image dialog box to scale and position your color images, but that's about it. If you want to change the contrast, lightness, or color map of color images, try Adobe Photoshop or Letraset Color Studio.

FIGURE 4-13
Color image dialog box

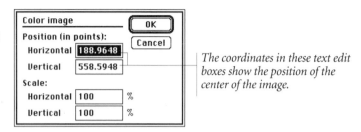

The coordinates in these text edit boxes show the position of the center of the image.

Resizing Images to Your Printer's Resolution

Paint-type images and bilevel TIFFs often use regular patterns of pixels to represent gray areas in the image. You can see these patterns of black and white pixels in the scroll bars in most Macintosh applications. You'll also see them if you're scanning and saving images as halftones from most popular scanner software (see Figure 4-14).

When you print graphics containing these patterns, you'll often get moiré patterns in the patterned areas (see Figure 4-15).

Purists will argue that these aren't true moiré patterns, because moiré patterns are created by the mismatch of two (or more) overlapping screens. While it's true we have only one overlay, we nevertheless have two overlapping, mismatching screens—the resolution of the image and the resolution of the printer. Both are matrices of dots.

When the resolution of the image you're trying to print and the resolution of the printer don't have an integral relationship (that is, when the printer resolution divided by the image resolution equals other than a whole number), some rounding is going to have to occur, because your printer can't render fractional dots. When this happens, parts of pixels get cut off or added to make up the difference (see Figure 4-16).

Instead of figuring out the scaling percentages for each bilevel image you're working with, take advantage of FreeHand's "magic stretch" feature, which resizes images to match the resolution of your target printer.

FIGURE 4-14
Pixel patterns
representing grays

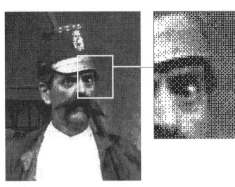

*Paint-type graphics and
bilevel TIFFs often use
patterns of black and white
pixels to represent grays.*

FIGURE 4-15
Moiré patterns

Moiré patterns

*Image not resized to match
printer resolution*

Image resized to match printer resolution

FIGURE 4-16
Integral and non-
integral relationships

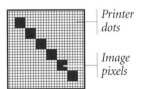

Printer
dots

Image
pixels

*Your printer can't print
fractional dots—they're
either on or off. When your
image pixels and printer
dots have an integral
relationship (4:1 in this
example), the printer can
match your image's pixels.*

*When the image pixels
don't match your
printer's resolution, the
printer has to guess
which printer dots it
should turn on or off…*

*…which distorts
your image.*

Hold down Option as you resize an image and the image snaps to sizes that have an integral relationship with the selected printer resolution. Hold down Shift and Option as you size the graphic both to size the graphic proportionally and to match the printer's resolution (see Figure 4-17).

Where do you set the printer's resolution? Enter a value in the Target printer resolution text edit box in the Document setup dialog box that matches the resolution of the printer you'll be use for the final printing of the publication, not the resolution of your proof printer.

The value you enter in the Target printer resolution text edit box does not affect the actual resolution of your printer; it's just there to give FreeHand a value to use when calculating magic stretch sizes.

Magic stretching doesn't improve the printing of gray-scale or color TIFFs—even though they'll snap to the same sizes—and it doesn't have any effect on object-PICT or EPS graphics.

But what if you've got a bilevel TIFF that contains "gray" dot patterns that has to fit a size that doesn't match any of the magic stretch sizes? The answer is to resize the image in an image-editing application to the correct size, then resample the image so that its resolution has an integral relation to the resolution of your printer (Photoshop's a great place to do this). Then place the image where you want it.

FIGURE 4-17
Magic-stretching
an image

Point at a corner of an image, hold down Option-Shift...

...and drag. The image snaps to possible sizes (based on the resolution of the image and of your printer) as you drag.

When you've reached the size you want, stop dragging.

Extracting Paint-type Graphics

If you need to extract sized paint files from your FreeHand publication so that you can edit them in a paint program, you can't just copy them out of FreeHand and paste them into the paint program. If you do, the graphics will look distorted when you paste them into the paint program. You'd need this trick if the original paint-type graphics had been lost, because FreeHand has to link to an external file to be able to print images.

What you have to do is return them to their original, glorious, 72-dpi state. You can do this using the Image dialog box.

1. Select the graphic you want to extract.

2. Press Command-I.

3. Type "100" in the Horizontal and Vertical scale text edit boxes and press Return. The graphic pops back to its original size.

4. Copy the image to the Clipboard.

5. Paste the image into a paint program.

6. Save the image.

7. Replace the unlinked image in your FreeHand file with the file you've just created. You can use the numeric position and scaling information in the Image dialog box to get the image into the same position as the original.

This trick won't work with images that have an original resolution of other than 72 dpi, because FreeHand constructs a 72-dpi screen image of each image as it's placed. For images with resolutions over 72 dpi, a file you'd create this way would lack some of the information found in the original image.

Cropping TIFF Images

If you're used to PageMaker's cropping tool, and are looking for a similar tool in FreeHand, you're out of luck—there isn't one. Instead, however, you can use FreeHand's Paste inside feature to crop your image. It's better than the cropping tool anyway. When you want to use just part of a TIFF image in your FreeHand publication, try this (see Figure 4-18).

1. Size the TIFF to the size you want.

2. Draw a path around the part of the TIFF you want to use.

3. Select the TIFF and press Command-X to cut it to the Clipboard.

4. Select the path and choose "Paste inside" from the Edit menu. FreeHand pastes the TIFF inside the path.

While I'm telling you about cropping images, I should also mention that it's better to create your images in your scanning or image-editing software so that you don't have to crop. When you crop an image, the parts of the TIFF you can't see don't just go away; FreeHand still has to keep track of the entire TIFF, which means slower printing and slower screen redraw. It also means you've got a larger TIFF than you need stored somewhere. So don't crop in FreeHand unless you have to.

FIGURE 4-18
Cropping a TIFF

Draw a path around the area you want to crop.

Cut the TIFF image to the Clipboard, then select the path and paste the image inside the path.

Changing the Way You've Cropped a TIFF

If you decide that you'd rather see some other part of the TIFF you've cropped, you can take these steps.

1. Select the cropped TIFF.

2. Choose "Cut contents" from the Edit menu. FreeHand cuts the contents of the path out of the path and pastes the TIFF into your publication.

3. Reposition the path where you want it.

4. Select the TIFF.

5. Choose Command-X to cut the TIFF to the Clipboard.

6. Select the path and choose "Paste inside" from the Edit menu. FreeHand pastes the TIFF back inside the path.

Tip:
Adjusting
Cropping

If you just need to make a minor adjustment to the way you've cropped a TIFF, try this.

1. Select the cropped TIFF.

2. Press Command-M to display the Move elements dialog box.

3. Enter the distances you want to move the edges of the path in the Vertical and Horizontal text edit boxes, then uncheck "Contents," and press Return. FreeHand moves the clipping path without changing the position of the TIFF inside the clipping path.

My favorite way to change cropping is to move the path by its component points. As long as you're moving all the points in the path at once *as points*, the TIFF cropped by the path stays in its original position. To do this, select all the points in the path (you can Shift-select all the points, or you can drag a selection marquee over all the points in the path), then drag the path to a new position (see Figure 4-19).

FIGURE 4-19
Changing the way
you've cropped a TIFF

Select the individual points on the clipping path as points (either drag a selection rectangle over them or Command-Shift-click each point).

Drag the clipping path around until you've cropped the image the way you want.

Creating an Outline Mask for a TIFF Image

Something that people often miss when they think about cropping images in FreeHand is that the path you're using to crop the image can be any size or shape. You can paste TIFFs inside ellipses, characters, or totally freeform paths. This comes in handy when you've got to pull a particular object out of a placed TIFF file. Trace the part of the TIFF you want, cut the TIFF to the Clipboard and paste it inside the shape you've just drawn (see Figure 4-20).

Voilà, instant outline mask. Note that you can adjust the cropping by dragging individual points on the clipping path to get it just right, and that you can stroke the path to trap the image if you need to (for more on trapping images, see Chapter 6, "Color"). Just for fun, go ask your local prepress outfit what they'd charge to do this.

FIGURE 4-20
Creating an
outline mask

Draw a path around the parts of the image you want (it helps to send the image to the background before tracing).

Paste the image into the path. You can adjust the points on the path to change the cropping of the image.

Creating a Vignette Mask for a TIFF Image

Here's another photographic effect that used to cost a bundle—creating a vignette. What's a vignette? It's where a photo progressively lightens as it approaches the edge of some shape (traditionally, an ellipse) until the photographic material is entirely white at the point at which it reaches the edges of the shape. Think of the photos of your nineteenth century ancestors—they're probably vignettes.

While this technique is still going to be cheaper than doing the same thing photographically, it's going to take some time to print, especially on an imagesetter. The process is illustrated in Figure 4-21.

FIGURE 4-21
Creating a vignette

Create several paths.   *Create several clones of the image. Paste the images into the paths, pasting the lightest image into the largest path. Choose "Remove line" from the Attributes menu.*

1. Draw a path around the part of the TIFF that you want to leave unchanged. This area is the center of the vignette effect. The TIFF should extend for some distance beyond this area in all directions.

2. Cut the TIFF to the Clipboard and paste it inside the path.

3. Clone the clipped TIFF.

4. Scale the cloned clipping path so that it's larger than the original clipping path (in the example shown below, I scaled each path in the vignette so that it was 105 percent of its original size).

5. Select the cloned clipping path and choose "Cut contents" from the Edit menu. FreeHand places the TIFF on top of the path.

6. Without deselecting the TIFF, color the TIFF so that it's lighter than the original TIFF. In our example, I made each TIFF 10 percent lighter than the previous one.

7. Cut the TIFF to the Clipboard, select the cloned path, and choose "Paste inside" from the Edit menu to paste the TIFF inside the path.

8. Send the path to the back, or to another layer that's behind the original clipping path.

9. Repeat Steps 3 through 8 until all or nearly all of the color values inside the TIFF are white.

When you work through this procedure, you end up with a stack of cropped images, with the TIFFs inside each clipping path getting lighter and lighter as they get farther and farther from the center of the vignette.

It's occurred to me that you could probably produce the same effect using the Lightness control in the Image dialog box instead of coloring each TIFF a lighter shade. I used colors because it's easier to control the amount of a color—there's no numeric way to adjust lightness. Another point is that you can do this technique much faster if you work in Keyline view—you don't have to spend any time redrawing the TIFF. Finally, you can probably do a better job of this in an image-editing program.

Enhancing Images Using Aldus PrePrint

Because FreeHand's got the ability to color separate color images, you don't necessarily need Aldus' color separation application PrePrint. But its image-enhancement controls are worth taking a look at.

To enhance an image with PrePrint, start PrePrint, open a TIFF image, and use the commands on the Image menu to alter the TIFF. Once you've applied the commands you want, save the TIFF and place it in FreeHand.

"Auto enhance," in particular, is a shocker. It actually does a great job of improving images for color printing. It doesn't, and shouldn't replace the manual controls you'll find in image-editing programs, but it's a quick and painless way to get pretty good results when you don't have time, experience, or patience enough to twiddle with more sophisticated systems.

When you're through working with the image in PrePrint, you can save the file as either a color TIFF or as a set of DCS separations (for more on DCS separation, see "Preseparating Color TIFFS" later in this chapter.

Importing EPS Graphics

If you work with other programs that can export files as EPS, or if you write your own PostScript programs, you can import those files into FreeHand and combine them with text and graphics you've created in FreeHand.

If You See an "X" Instead of a Graphic

When you import an EPS graphic (and you're not in Keyline mode), if you see a box with an "X" through it, instead of a screen preview, you've imported a file that doesn't have a screen preview attached. The file contains the dimensions of the graphic, and it'll probably print correctly, but there's nothing for you to look at as you lay out your page. This happens in these scenarios.

- There's too little memory to display the preview. Increase FreeHand's application size if you're running MultiFinder (see "RAM Indicator" in Chapter 1, "FreeHand Basics"), or close some publications.

- There was too little memory available to create the screen preview when FreeHand (or other application) created the EPS file. If you're placing a FreeHand EPS, think again: wouldn't it be better to paste that graphic into the current publication instead of placing it?

- The graphic has no screen preview attached. This happens if the file is a PostScript program written by an application that doesn't support preview images, or if the file is a PostScript program written with a text editor or word processor. This also happens if you've edited a normal EPS with a word processor and have not reattached the screen preview PICT. See "Converting FreeHand 3 EPS Files to Illustrator 1.1 EPS Format" below on editing EPS graphics with a word processor.

If you can't get by without a screen preview, see the section "Creating a Screen Preview for EPS Graphics," later in this chapter.

Importing FreeHand EPS

Think about it—why do you want to import a FreeHand EPS instead of copying the elements out of one publication and pasting them into the current publication? When you import an EPS, there's a whole bunch of information attached to the FreeHand objects that you just don't need. And it takes longer to print—have a look at Figure 4-22.

If you're placing the EPS instead of pasting elements from one publication to another because you want to deal with the objects as a single graphic, why not group them?

FIGURE 4-22
Importing FreeHand
EPS versus pasting
FreeHand objects

FreeHand EPS placed in FreeHand.
Processing time: 34 seconds

FreeHand elements pasted from one
publication to another. Processing
time: 2 seconds

Importing Illustrator EPS

If I had to choose between FreeHand 3 and Illustrator 3.0, I'd take FreeHand. In fact, I don't use Illustrator much, these days, though it's an excellent program. But I do know lots of people who swear by Illustrator, and I know even more people who strongly prefer using both. Luckily, the path from Illustrator to FreeHand is clear. FreeHand can open or place EPS files created by Adobe Illustrator 1.1, or EPS files created in Adobe Illustrator '88 or Adobe Illustrator 3.0 that you've saved in the Illustrator 1.1 format. I've been able to open EPS files created in Illustrator '88 and 3.0 some of the time.

When you open an Illustrator EPS, FreeHand converts the paths and type into FreeHand elements. If you place an Illustrator EPS, FreeHand displays the screen preview image (if there is one) and treats the file as an imported graphic—you can transform it, but you can't edit its contents.

When you open an Illustrator EPS, some of Illustrator's features are converted; some aren't.

Paths. FreeHand imports paths in Illustrator EPSs just as they were drawn in Illustrator. FreeHand converts Illustrator points into curve points whenever possible, though points defining sharp angles or sudden changes of curve direction are converted into corner points. As points are converted, FreeHand adds handles to each converted point so that the path matches the path you drew in Illustrator.

Text. FreeHand converts Illustrator text into FreeHand text blocks. Typically, the Illustrator text is converted one line at a time, though any changes in type style or font will create new text blocks, as will any kerning (including automatic kerning pairs).

Color. Process colors you've defined in Illustrator are imported as you defined them, but the color names don't appear in your Colors palette. You can add the colors to your colors palette as follows.

1. Select one of the objects you've converted from Illustrator that's the color you want to add to your Colors palette.

2. Press Command-E to display the Fill and line dialog box. In the Fill and line dialog box, one of the two Color pop-up menus will display a swatch of the color.

3. Pop up the menu and choose the color type (tint, spot, process, or Pantone) you want the color to be. The Colors dialog box appears.

4. Type a name for your color and press Return.

5. Press Return to close the Fill and line dialog box. FreeHand adds the color to the list of colors in the colors palette.

Blends. Illustrator blends are made up of separate, colored objects, so you can't change the blend once you've imported it except by deleting the intermediate blend steps and blending again.

Complex Paths. Compound paths you've created using Illustrator's Make Compound command are converted to FreeHand's composite paths ("Composite path" and "Compound path" are just two ways of saying the same thing).

Finally, it's a one-way trip—unless you've got EPS Exchange from Altsys (see "EPS Exchange," later in this chapter) or are prepared to edit your EPSs with a text editor (see "Converting FreeHand 3 EPS Files to Illustrator 1.1 EPS Format," later in this chapter). Otherwise, you can't make changes to a converted Illustrator EPS in FreeHand and export the file in a form that Illustrator can open and edit.

Importing EPS Graphics from LetraStudio, TypeStyler, and TypeAlign

While you can accomplish almost any text effect you can imagine using FreeHand by converting text into paths and manipulating the paths, some effects are simply too difficult to accomplish by that method. Perspective rendering of characters and the overall shape of text following a certain shape are two great examples.

Luckily, LetraStudio, TypeStyler, and TypeAlign exist to automate much of the process of creating this warped, distorted type. All three can export files in a format that FreeHand can read, so the next time you need a complex text effect—particularly one involving distortion of characters—try using one of these programs.

LetraStudio is the most capable, the hardest to use, and the most expensive, but TypeStyler's got some good features and costs less. The only thing you can do with TypeAlign that you can't do with FreeHand is create "perspective" text. Figure 4-23 shows an example of the effects you can achieve easily with these products.

FIGURE 4-23
An example EPS file
from TypeStyler

Importing Other EPS Files

You can place EPS files generated by PageMaker, QuarkXPress, DesignStudio, and other applications in FreeHand. It's actually better to paste PageMaker elements into FreeHand, as described later in this chapter, in "Importing Formatted text from PageMaker," because you can edit them, but EPS versions of PageMaker publications work fairly well.

Creating Your Own EPS Graphics

You can create EPS graphics using a word processor or LaserTalk, but you've got to remember two things.

- If it doesn't print when you download it, it won't print after you've placed it in FreeHand. Always test every change you make in your word processor by downloading the text file to the printer and seeing what you get before you place the file in FreeHand, or at least before you take the FreeHand file to a service bureau.

- When you edit an EPS graphic with a word processor and save it in the text-only (ASCII) format, you break the link between the PostScript text part of the EPS and the screen preview PICT resource. You can use ResEdit to rejoin the two parts of the EPS, provided you don't overwrite the original file.

Why would you want to create your own EPS graphics? There are lots of things you can do with PostScript that FreeHand doesn't do (yet). See Chapter 8, "PostScript," for some examples and more on creating your own EPS graphics.

Creating a Screen Preview for EPS Graphics

If you're creating your own PostScript graphics, or if you're working with an application that can't (or won't) add a screen preview to your file, you can add a screen preview using Adobe Systems' SmartArt.

1. Make sure you're connected to a PostScript printer and that the printer is turned on. SmartArt will use the PostScript interpreter inside the printer to generate the screen preview of the file.

2. Start SmartArt (it's a desk accessory).

3. Open your PostScript file.

4. Click the Reimage button. SmartArt sends your PostScript code to the printer, and brings back and displays a 72-dpi screen preview.

5. Choose "Save as…" from the SmartArt menu.

6. Type a name for your EPS file and press Return to save the file. SmartArt attaches the screen preview to the PostScript text file.

Creating Invisible EPS Graphics

This is my trick. I can't believe I'm just giving it away.

I often want to use full-page EPS backgrounds but I can't stand waiting for the background's screen preview to redraw every time I do something. In FreeHand, of course, the easiest thing to do is to set the layer the background's on to be invisible. But if you're creating a FreeHand EPS background to place in some (other) page-layout program, you definitely need this trick (see Figure 4-24).

1. Open the EPS file with ResEdit.

2. Open the PICT resource.

3. Choose Clear from the Edit menu.

4. Press Command-K to create a new PICT resource.

FIGURE 4-24
Creating an invisible
EPS graphic

*Locate and open the
EPS file with ResEdit
and double-click on
the PICT resource
class icon.*

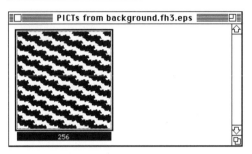

*ResEdit displays the EPS
file's screen preview image.
Select the image and press
Delete.*

*Press Command-K to create
a new PICT resource.*

*Press Command-I to display
the Info dialog box. Type
"256" in the ID text edit
box.*

*Press Command-S to save
your work, and quit ResEdit.*

*When you place the EPS file,
you won't see the screen
preview, but it'll print just as
it did before.*

5. Make sure that the new PICT has a resource ID number of 256 by pressing Command-I and typing 256 in the ID text edit box in the Info window that appears.

6. Press Command-S to save the file, and quit ResEdit.

Now, when you place the EPS file, you'll get a transparent bounding box that's the size of the graphic, but no screen preview will appear, and it won't take any time to redraw the image. The image will print out, though.

Creating Visible, Nonprinting Graphics

This one's my trick, too. I actually learned this one and the preceding trick while visiting Jostens, Inc., the high-school yearbook publishing people. It was a glorious November week in Topeka.

If you want to place a graphic on the page, but don't want it to print, the best thing to do is to move it to some nonprinting layer.

Use this trick when you want to create a FreeHand EPS to import into a page-layout program, and want the contents of the graphic to display but not print.

1. Open a copy of the EPS file with a word processor.

2. Delete everything in the document from the line that begins with "%%BoundingBox:" to the line that says "%%EndDocument" and save the file as text-only.

3. Start ResEdit.

4. Locate and open the text file you just created. When ResEdit asks if you want to add a resource fork to the file, click "OK."

5. Open the original EPS file and select the PICT resource class.

6. Copy the PICT resource class out of the original EPS file and paste it into the resource listing for the text file.

7. Press Command-S to save the file, and quit ResEdit.

Why would anyone want to do this? It's handy to be able to place nonprinting notes ("type headline here") in page-layout programs. Sometimes people want to lay out and proof their publications without having to take the time to print the EPS. You might also consider giving slow-paying clients the screen image only, providing the printing part of the graphic on payment (I disapprove of this sort of thing, myself).

Converting EPS Files to PICT

There are two ways to convert EPS files to PICT files.

- Convert the screen image into a bitmap PICT and throw away the PostScript. What do you get? A 72-dpi bitmap. Yuck.

- Convert the EPS file into a PICT and attach the PostScript to the PICT (the PICT file format has a provision for this). What do you get? A PICT to view on your screen and PostScript that prints exactly the same as the EPS file would have.

Trouble is, it's kind of tricky getting the second method to work. Sure, you can convert the FreeHand elements into a PICT with attached EPS by holding down Option as you copy out of FreeHand, but that doesn't make a file—it just writes it to the Clipboard. How can you turn what's on the Clipboard into a file you can import into another application?

Use CanOpener. CanOpener is a nifty utility written by the folks at Abbott Systems (see Appendix B, "Resources" for their address) which, among other things, can open the Clipboard and save files as TIFF, PICT, and text. CanOpener comes as both a stand-alone application and a DA, but they work about the same way and I always use the DA. Once the converted elements are in the Clipboard, open CanOpener, and press Command-V to paste the contents of the Clipboard into CanOpener. CanOpener's listing updates to show the name of the file ("Clipboard") and its contents. If everything's gone right, it'll say you've just pasted in a PICT. Select the listing that says "PICT," and click the Save button. CanOpener saves your file as a PICT with attached PostScript, since that's what it found on the Clipboard.

What if you've already got an EPS file, don't have the original file, and still need to convert the EPS into a PICT? There are (at least) two things you can do.

One is to use a utility (another DA) called eps->pict written by Altsys and available in the public domain (I got mine from the Adobe forum on CompuServe). eps->pict opens an EPS file and sends the contents to the Clipboard as a PICT with attached PostScript. Once the contents of the file are on the Clipboard, you can save them using CanOpener, as described above.

The other technique is to use SmartArt.

1. Launch SmartArt.

2. Open the EPS file you want to convert.

3. Choose "Export" from the SmartArt menu.

4. Choose "PICT" from the Format pop-up menu, type a name for your file, and press Return to export the file as a PICT.

Preseparating Color TIFFs

If you prefer the color separations of color TIFF images created by some other program—Adobe Photoshop and Aldus PrePrint 1.5 come to mind—to the separations created by FreeHand, you can preseparate color TIFFs and place them in FreeHand as EPS or DCS files.

EPS files created this way contain all of the information the color separation application would have sent to a printer to create color separations of an image. DCS is a variation of EPS, and stores the color separated image as five files (one for each color plus a "header" file that's the part you work with).

When you place the preseparated file (either EPS or DCS) in Free-Hand and print the publication, FreeHand separates the file as the original application would have.

The following steps show how you'd preseparate an image using Adobe Photoshop.

1. In Photoshop, make sure that your separation settings are the way you want them and that the color mode is set to CMYK (choose "CMYK" from the Mode menu).

2. Choose "Save as…" to display the Save as dialog box. In the Save as dialog box, choose "EPS" from the File Format pop-up menu. Click the Save button. The EPS Options… dialog box appears.

3. In the EPS Options… dialog box, pick a screen preview from the list of preview options, choose either ASCII or binary as your encoding scheme (binary files are smaller), check the Include Halftone Screens and Include Transfer Functions options. Check the "Desktop Color Separation" option if you want to use the DCS method of storing the file as five separate files. Press Return to save your image as an EPS file.

Place this file in FreeHand, and it'll be separated like any other EPS graphic.

Importing Text

The basic method for importing large amounts of text from other applications into FreeHand is pretty simple: select the text in the other application, copy the selection to the Clipboard, then paste the text into an open Text dialog box in FreeHand. Any formatting will be lost, but at least all of the text is now in FreeHand and you won't have to rekey it. There are lots of better ways, though.

**Importing
Formatted Text
from PageMaker**

I should have patented this trick long ago. You can copy PageMaker text blocks—complete with their paragraph formatting (indents, tabs, and spaces before and after the paragraph)—straight out of Page-Maker and paste them right into FreeHand (Figure 4-25).

1. Open both FreeHand and PageMaker under MultiFinder.

2. In PageMaker, select all of the text you want to copy into Free-Hand and press Command-M to bring up the Paragraph specifications dialog box. Press the Spacing button. In the Spacing dialog box, uncheck the Auto pair kerning above *n* pixels option. Don't worry about it; FreeHand will apply the pair kerning as you bring the text into FreeHand.

3. Select the text block (or text blocks) with the pointer tool.

4. Press Command-C to copy the text block to the Clipboard.

5. Switch to FreeHand.

6. Paste the text block(s) into FreeHand.

If everything looks right, congratulations; you must live right or something. If, on the other hand, it looks like the text has been spattered all over the page by a pipe bomb (and it often does) don't panic—just follow these steps.

1. Press Command-U to ungroup the interpreted PICT you've just imported.

2. Press Command-T to display the Type specifications dialog box.

3. Type "0" in the Letter space text edit box and press Tab twice to move to the Word space text edit box.

4. Type "0" in the Word space text edit box.

5. Press Return to close the Type specifications dialog box.

6. Redraw your screen by pressing the keyboard shortcut for some screen magnification other than your current one.

At this point, your type should look exactly as it did in PageMaker, except that each line will be (at least) one separate text block.

FIGURE 4-25
Transferring formatted text from PageMaker to FreeHand

Importing Formatted Text from PageMaker

I should have patented this trick long ago. You can copy PageMaker text blocks—complete with their paragraph formatting (indents, tabs, and spaces before and after the paragraph)—straight out of PageMaker and paste them right into FreeHand.

1. Open both FreeHand and PageMaker under MultiFinder.

2. In PageMaker, select all of the text you want to copy into Free-Hand and press Command-M to bring up the Paragraph specifications dialog box. Press the Spacing button. In the Spacing dialog box, uncheck the Auto pair kerning above *n* pixels option. Don't worry about it; FreeHand will apply the pair kerning as you bring the text into FreeHand.

3. Select the text block (or text blocks) with the pointer tool.

4. Press Command-C to copy the text block to the Clipboard.

5. Switch to FreeHand.

6. Paste the text block(s) into FreeHand.

If everything looks right, congratulations; you must live right or something. If, on the other hand, it looks like the text has been spattered all over the page by a pipe bomb (and it usually does, as shown in Figure 4-25), don't panic.

Select the text blocks you want in PageMaker and press Command-C to copy them to the Clipboard.

If your text explodes as you paste it from the Clipboard, ungroup the imported text, press Command-T, and then, in the Type specifications dialog box, set the word and letter spacing to 0.

Importing Formatted Text from PageMaker

I should have patented this trick long ago. You can copy PageMaker text blocks—complete with their paragraph formatting (indents, tabs, and spaces before and after the paragraph)—straight out of PageMaker and paste them right into FreeHand.

1. Open both FreeHand and PageMaker under MultiFinder.

2. In PageMaker, select all of the text you want to copy into Free-Hand and press Command-M to bring up the Paragraph specifications dialog box. Press the Spacing button. In the Spacing dialog box, uncheck the Auto pair kerning above *n* pixels option. Don't worry about it; FreeHand will apply the pair kerning as you bring the text into FreeHand.

3. Select the text block (or text blocks) with the pointer tool.

4. Press Command-C to copy the text block to the Clipboard.

5. Switch to FreeHand.

6. Paste the text block(s) into FreeHand.

If everything looks right, congratulations; you must live right or something. If, on the other hand, it looks like the text has been spattered all over the page by a pipe bomb (and it usually does, as shown in Figure 4-25), don't panic.

Switch to Free-Hand and press Command-V to paste the text from the Clipboard. FreeHand converts the text to FreeHand text blocks.

If you don't turn off PageMaker's automatic kerning, FreeHand splits text blocks at each automatic kerning pair as it imports the text.

FreeHand breaks the text blocks wherever it encounters tabs as it imports the text.

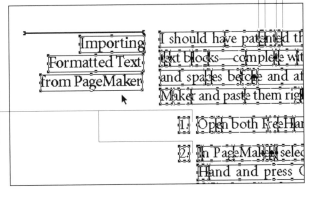

Anywhere there's a tab in the PageMaker text, FreeHand will create a separate text block.

Text blocks will even break between characters that have been kerned, which is why I said you should turn "Auto pair kerning" off before copying out of PageMaker.

One thing that doesn't come across in this method is justification. All of PageMaker's hyphenation and line breaks are still intact, though, so all you have to do is adjust the width of each text block.

What makes this trick work? PageMaker posts a variety of formats to the Clipboard—PICT, TEXT, RTF, and PageMaker's internal Clipboard format. FreeHand picks the one of these it likes best—PICT—and interprets the PICT as it would any other.

Importing Formatted Text from Word

The trick for bringing text from Word into FreeHand is quite a bit like the one for bringing text from PageMaker—you copy text selected in Word to the Clipboard as a PICT. Luckily, Word has a keyboard shortcut for this.

1. In MultiFinder, start both Word and FreeHand.

2. In Word, make sure that "Show ¶" on the Edit menu is turned off. If you don't turn "Show ¶" off, FreeHand will import the characters Word uses to display spaces, carriage returns, line ends, and tabs.

3. Select the text you want to import into FreeHand and press Command-Option-D. This copies the text to the Clipboard as a PICT.

4. Switch to FreeHand and press Command-V (or choose "Paste" from the Edit menu).

The text is pasted into FreeHand as a grouped, interpreted PICT. When you ungroup, you'll see that FreeHand has made at least one separate text block from each line, and that the text blocks break where you've entered tabs.

Importing Text as an EPS Graphic

Besides all of the tricks shown above, you can export text from almost all of these applications as an EPS graphic and place the EPS in FreeHand. This does mean you'll lose the ability to edit the text, but you'll still have all of the formatting you specified in the other program. As far as I can tell, this is the only way to get formatted text from QuarkXPress and LetraSet Design Studio into FreeHand.

Exporting

Actually, exporting EPS graphics is what most people think of when they think of using FreeHand with other applications. It's only because of the twisted orientation of this book (that FreeHand is your main publishing program for short, complex documents) that exporting FreeHand elements appears in this chapter as a kind of afterthought.

All of the tricks shown earlier in this chapter for importing data from other applications make it clear that FreeHand's good at importing. What about exporting? FreeHand supports three EPS export formats (with no screen preview, Macintosh screen preview, and MS-DOS screen preview), and you can Option-Copy FreeHand elements out of FreeHand to create a PICT with attached PostScript that can be pasted into just about anything.

The first half of this chapter covered how to get from there to here. Here's the dope on how to get from here to there.

Creating EPS Graphics

When you choose "Export…" from the File menu (I suggest making a macro or adding a keyboard shortcut for this command, as you'll be using it all of the time), the Export dialog box appears. At the bottom of this dialog box, you'll see a pop-up menu listing three export options (see Figure 4-26).

Tip: Choose the EPS Type First

Choose the EPS type you want to use from the Format pop-up menu in the Export dialog box *before* you type the name of your file in the text edit box. If you type the name first, then choose the EPS export type, FreeHand fills the text edit box with whatever it thinks should be there ("Untitled," usually). This means that you'll have to go back and retype the file name. This is an annoying habit of FreeHand's, but I haven't been able to train my copy of FreeHand to stop doing it. Yet.

FIGURE 4-26
Export dialog box

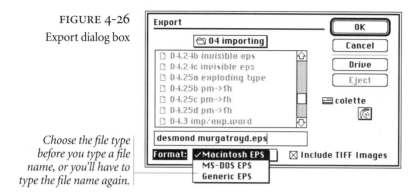

Choose the file type before you type a file name, or you'll have to type the file name again.

Generic EPS. When you need to create an EPS file containing the Post-Script required to print the FreeHand publication you've created, but don't want the file to have a screen preview attached, choose "Generic EPS" from the Format pop-up menu.

If you place a Generic EPS file in FreeHand, you'll see a box with an "X" through it. There's a way to add a screen preview to a Generic EPS file, as described in "Creating a Screen Preview for EPS Graphics" earlier in this 33.

Use "Generic EPS" when you're exporting a FreeHand graphic for use in a non-Macintosh, non-MS-DOS system (if you're preparing a graphic that'll be placed in a FrameMaker publication on a Sun workstation, for example), or if you just don't want to bother with a screen image. The Generic EPS file is a straight text file.

Macintosh EPS. A Macintosh EPS file is a PostScript text file with a PICT resource attached. The PICT is displayed on screen when you place the EPS file in FreeHand or any other Macintosh program that can import EPS.

MS-DOS EPS. Because MS-DOS files are structurally different from Macintosh files in that they're data files only (there's no concept of different forks for data and resources in the MS-DOS world) MS-DOS EPS files have a TIFF image of the graphic embedded in the file as hexadecimal data.

If you're exporting a FreeHand file as MS-DOS EPS, don't forget to use a file name your MS-DOS system can understand (generally, the name must be eight or fewer characters long), and add the extension

.EPS to the file name. Most MS-DOS applications have no way of knowing what file type a file is without the extension.

EPS Exchange

EPS Exchange gives FreeHand the ability to export files as Illustrator '88 and Illustrator 3.0 EPS formats, and is the first of a series of Free-Hand add-ons from Altsys (see Appendix B, "Resources," for Altsys' address). EPS Exchange is a FreeHand external resource file—not a separate utility. Like other FreeHand external resource files, it's loaded into FreeHand when FreeHand starts up. For more on external resource files, see "Creating External Resource Files" in Chapter 8, "PostScript."

Once FreeHand's loaded EPS Exchange, the pop-up menu at the bottom of the Export dialog box includes the two new formats, as shown in Figure 4-27.

FIGURE 4-27
EPS Exchange

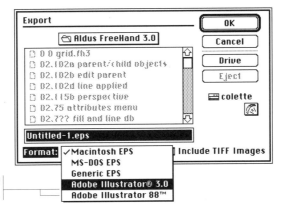

EPS Exchange adds two
more export formats.

Option-copying: Another Way to Export

There's another way to get objects out of FreeHand, and this one doesn't involve the Export dialog box. Use this technique when you want to use a FreeHand graphic in an application that can't import EPS files (Microsoft Word, for instance).

1. Select the FreeHand objects you want to export.

2. Press Command-Option-C or hold down Option as you choose Copy from the Edit menu. FreeHand displays a message saying it's converting the Clipboard. What this means is that FreeHand is converting the selected elements into a PICT with attached PostScript.

3. Go to another application and press Command-V to paste the graphic. You can also paste the graphic into the Scrapbook for future use.

Note some points about Option-Copying.

• The screen image that results when you Option-Copy a graphic is not as good as the image FreeHand adds to an EPS file when you're exporting a file as EPS.

• Graphics that you Option-Copy do not include any downloadable fonts, and it's often difficult to get the fonts to download from whatever application you've pasted the graphics into; so be prepared to manually download fonts if you're using these graphics.

• Graphics that you Option-Copy and paste *seem* to print much faster than placed EPS files.

• These graphics rely somewhat on the Apple printer driver, so you can expect weirdness when you change printer drivers.

Placing FreeHand Graphics in Page-layout Programs

If you need to produce documents longer than a few pages, you're going to have to look to a page layout program. Luckily, you can take your FreeHand illustrations with you. There are a few tricks and twists to this process.

Bounding Boxes. You'll note that FreeHand's bounding boxes are sometimes just a little bit larger than the edges of the graphic, or that the graphic is not positioned inside the bounding box the way you'd like it. You can create a bounding box that's precisely the size you want by using the cropping tool, and you can slide an image around inside its bounding box.

Working with Downloadable Fonts. You've probably heard that EPS graphics include any downloadable fonts used in the file. It's not quite true; they do contain a list of the fonts used in the file.

When your page layout program's printing, it creates the image of the page in your printer's memory by starting with the objects on the page that are the farthest to the back (actually, I'm only certain of this for PageMaker). When the application starts to print an EPS graphic, it reads the fonts listed in the EPS and downloads any needed fonts to your printer.

This does not, however, guarantee that the fonts will still be in the printer's memory when they're called for inside the EPS, because a lot can happen between the start of the file (when your page layout program downloads the font) and whenever the font is needed.

Your page layout application cannot manage the printer's memory once you're inside the EPS—only before and after you're in the EPS. By contrast, you're printing objects you've created using your page layout program's tools, it manages font downloading and printer memory on an object-by-object level, and can always download another copy of the font if necessary.

If you've got an older printer with 1MB of RAM, like a LaserWriter or LaserWriter Plus, it's much more likely that this will be a problem, because it's much more likely that your page layout program will have to flush the downloadable font out of the printer's RAM to make room to print something else. It's also something you'll sometimes run into when you're printing to an imagesetter, because the higher resolution of imagesetters also means that these printers will run short of RAM.

Converting FreeHand 3 EPS Files to Illustrator 1.1 EPS Format

It's going to happen to you someday. You'll need to edit a FreeHand graphic and will have only an EPS version of the file—not the original file (first, try opening the EPS with FreeHand—it can open some simple EPSs). Or you'll want to open a FreeHand publication with Illustrator (in this case, you could buy Altsys' Illustrator export filter). You'll just have to give up and start recreating the illustration—unless you know how to translate FreeHand's EPS file into an Illustrator 1.1 format EPS file. If you could do that, you'd be able to open the file in either Illustrator or FreeHand.

The best way to learn about the differences between the two formats is to take a look at the EPS files written in them.

1. Create a file in Illustrator and save it as Illustrator 1.1 EPS.

2. Open it with FreeHand and export it as "Generic EPS."

3. Open both files with a word processor (if you're using Microsoft Word, hold down Shift as you pull down the File menu or press Shift-F6 to open any file, regardless of its file type) and compare them. You'll start seeing similarities and differences almost at once.

Focus on the parts of the files between the "%%EndSetup" comment and the "%%PageTrailer" comment. These are the parts that describe points, paths, and other objects. Table 4-2 shows the significant part of two EPS files describing the same path. Note that these lines show the same object, but that the line on the right does not necessarily match the line on the left.

TABLE 4-2
Illustrator and
FreeHand syntax
compared

Illustrator 1.1 version	FreeHand version
0 i 0 J 0 j 1 w 4 M [ ]0 d[ ]	0 d
%%Note:	3.863708 M
192 1044 m	1 w
192 -252 L	0 j
N	0 J
-342 480 m	0 O
954 480 L	0 R
N	0 i
-342 336 m	false eomode
954 336 L	[0 0 0 1] Ka
N	[0 0 0 1] ka
336 1044 m	vms
336 -252 L	u
N	234 468 m
0 G	234 324 L
192 480 m	378 324 L
192 336 l	378 324 378 406 327 382 C

TABLE 4-2 *Continued*

Illustrator 1.1 version	FreeHand version
336 336 l	276 358 285 362 285 362 C
336 418 285 394 v	278 400 L
234 370 243 374 y	378 413 L
236 412 l	378 468 L
336 425 l	234 468 L
336 480 l	4 M
192 480 l	s
s	U
	vmr

First of all, note that the coordinate systems differ slightly. In this case the Illustrator coordinate system starts 42 points farther along the horizontal axis and 12 points earlier along the vertical axis than the FreeHand coordinate system. Differences in coordinate systems will vary between publications. In this case, "192 480 m" ("m" is for *moveto*) in the Illustrator file equals "234 468 m" in the FreeHand EPS. In general, don't worry about differences in coordinate systems; the point is to get the objects into one program or the other. You can always adjust their positions once you've opened the file.

The first thing you need to do to convert a FreeHand EPS file into an Illustrator 1.1 format EPS file is to edit the file's header.

1. Open the file with your word processor. If you're using Microsoft Word, hold down Shift as you choose "Open…" from the File menu, or press Shift-F6. The first six lines of the file should look like this (the words shown in italics will vary—don't worry about them).

   %!PS-Adobe-2.0 EPSF-1.2
   %%Creator: FreeHand
   %%Title: *filename*
   %%CreationDate: *date and time*
   %%BoundingBox: *x1 y1 x2 y2*
   %%DocumentProcSets: FreeHand_header 3 0

2. Change the line beginning with "%%DocumentProcSets" to look like this:

%%DocumentProcSets: Adobe_Illustrator_1.1 0 0

3. Delete the line beginning with "%%DocumentSuppliedProcSets:".

4. Leave the line beginning with "%%ColorUsage:" as it is.

5. Delete the line beginning with "%%FHPathName:".

6. Leave the line "%%EndComments" as it is.

7. Select from the line beginning with "%%BeginProcSet:" to the end of the line "%%EndProcSet" and delete the selection. Leave the two lines following ("%%EndProlog" and "%%BeginSetup").

8. Select from the beginning of the line "FHIODict begin" to the start of the line "%%EndSetup" and delete the selection. Type two lines between "%%BeginSetup" and "%%EndSetup" as follows.

Adobe_Illustrator_1.1 begin
n

The text you see between the line "%%EndSetup" and the line "%%Trailer" is the body of your FreeHand EPS file. Table 4-3 shows you how to convert paths, while Table 4-4 covers converting text objects.

Text is tricky. You'll usually have to guess for *alignment* and *kerning*, and you'll have to derive *horizontalScale* from the *size* specified in Free-Hand, because FreeHand's already done all of the positioning and scaling before exporting the file as EPS. Still, I've had good luck moving text back and forth.

Once you've reached the line "%%Trailer" you've finished converting the body of the file. Select through the line "%%Trailer" to the end of the file and delete the selection. Type in the Illustrator 1.1 codes for the end of the file as shown below.

%%PageTrailer
%%Trailer
_E end
%%EOF

	When you see this in a FreeHand EPS	Convert it to this	What it does
TABLE 4-3 Converting from FreeHand to Illustrator syntax	[]0d	[]0d	The numbers between the brackets set the dash pattern, if any, of the path. In this example, the line's not dashed, so the array inside the brackets is empty. For a dashed line, the code would look something like "[2 1]0d" for a 2-unit-on, 1-unit-off dashed pattern. This code is the same as PostScript's *setdash* operator.
	x M	x M	The number before this code sets the miter limit of the path. This code is the same as the PostScript *setmiterlimit* operator.
	x w	x w	The number before this code sets the width of the path, in points. This code is the same as the PostScript operator *setlinewidth*.
	x i	x i	The number before this code sets the flatness of the path. "i" is the same as the PostScript operator *setflat*.
	x j	x j	The number before this code sets the line join of points inside the path. 0 = miter joins; 1 = round joins; 2 = beveled joins. This code is the same as the PostScript operator *setlinejoin*.

TABLE 4-3 *Continued*	When you see this in a FreeHand EPS	Convert it to this	What it does
	x J	*x* J	The number before this code sets the line cap style. 0 = butt caps; 1 = round caps; 2 = projecting caps. This code is equivalent to the PostScript operator *setlinecap*.
	x1 y1 m	*x1 y1* m	Moves to the specified point. This code is the same as the PostScript operator *moveto*.
	x1 y1 L	*x1 y1* l	Draws a line to the specified point and places a curve point (a "smooth" point in Illustrator parlance) with no curve control handles extended at that point. If you want to place a corner point, use "L" instead of "l." This code is the same as the PostScript operator *lineto*.
	x1 y1 x2 y2 x3 y3 C	*x2 y2 x3 y3* v or *x1 y1 x3 y3* y	Sets a curve point and curve control handles. If *x1 y1* in the FreeHand version equals the previous point (usually *x1 y1* L), then convert it to a "v"; otherwise, convert the curve point to a "y."*

*An example of when to use "v":

FreeHand	Illustrator
336 336 L	336 336 l
336 336 336 418 285 394 C	336 418 285 394 v

See facing page

TABLE 4-3 *Continued*	When you see this in a FreeHand EPS	Convert it to this	What it does
	s	s	Close and stroke the current path with the predefined line weight, miter specifications, and color. Exactly the same as the PostScript operator *stroke*.
	b	b	Close the current path, and then fill and stroke the path with the predefined line weight, miter specifications, and colors.
	[*c m y k*] Ka	*c m y k* K	Sets the fill color. 80C0M10Y10K would be written as .8 0 .1 .1 K.
	[*c m y k*] ka	*c m y k* k	Sets the stroke color. 20C5M0Y0K would be written as .2 .5 0 0 k.
	x O	Delete this line	
	x R	Delete this line	
	Vms	Delete this line	
	Vmr	Delete this line	
	Vmrs	Delete this line	
	U and u	U and u	"u" indicates the start of a group, "U" indicates the end of a group. You can delete these if you want.

An example of when to use "y":

FreeHand	Illustrator
285 394 L	285 394 l
276 358 285 362 285 362 C	276 358 285 362 y

If you want to attach your curve control handles to a corner point, use "V" for "v" and "Y" for "y."

	FreeHand	Illustrator
TABLE 4-4 Converting text	%%IncludeFont: *fontName*	/_*fontName size leading kerning*
	MacVec 256 array copy	*alignment* z
	/*fontNumber* /I_____*fontName* dup RF findfont def	[*horizontalScale* 0 0 1 *x y*]e*
	{	(*textString*)t
	fontNumber [*size* 0 0 *leading* 0 0] makesetfont	T
	x y m	
	0 0 32 0 0 (*textString*) ts	
	}	
	[*c m y k*]	
	sts	

* use "e" for text that's filled but not stroked, "o" for text that's both
filled and stroked, and "r" for text that you want stroked but not filled.
These options use the current stroke and fill settings—see Table 4-2,
above, for more information on setting strokes, fills, and colors.
Table 4-5 shows an example of converting FreeHand text to Illustrator
1.1 format.

	FreeHand	Illustrator
TABLE 4-5 Text conversion example	%%IncludeFont: /_Utopia-Regular	.8 0 .2 0 K
	MacVec 256 array copy	/_Utopia-Regular 14 16 0 0 z
	/f2 /I_____Utopia-Regular dup RF findfont def	[.8 0 0 1 200 200]e*
	{	(Pinafore)t
	f2 [11.2 0 0 16 0 0] makesetfont	T
	200 200 m	
	0 0 32 0 0 (Pinafore) ts	
	}	
	[.8 0 .2 0]	
	sts	

Save the file as text only. Try opening it with Illustrator. If you've made a mistake, Illustrator displays a dialog box containing a hint (see Figure 4-28).

Make a note of what Illustrator thinks is wrong with the file, return to the file, and try to fix it.

FIGURE 4-28
Illustrator's hint

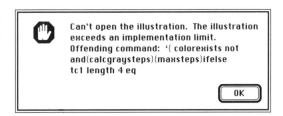

Can't open the illustration. The illustration exceeds an implementation limit.
Offending command: '{ colorexists not and{calcgraysteps}{maxsteps}ifelse tc1 length 4 eq

OK

Converting EPS Graphics to Super 3D Display Lists

If you've slogged through all of the 3-D drawing stuff in Chapter 2, "Drawing," you already know that I'm keen on 3-D drawing. We've talked about drawing in 3-D in FreeHand and about importing objects from 3-D drawing programs, but what about exporting FreeHand objects to 3-D programs?

Super 3D can import and export text descriptions of 3-D objects. These text files are called display lists. It's not too tricky to turn a Free-Hand EPS into a Super 3D display list, because they're both text descriptions of lines and polygons drawn in some coordinate system. The main difference is that the position of objects in Super 3D display lists are specified in x, y, and z coordinates, while object positions in FreeHand's EPS are specified in x and y. Table 4-6 shows a short list of Super 3D display list functions, and Table 4-7 shows the differences between FreeHand's EPS representation of objects and the same objects represented in a Super 3D display list.

If you want to draw an object in FreeHand, then import the object into Super 3D for 3-D manipulation, you can export the object as EPS, edit the EPS file with a text editor to convert it into a Super 3D display list, and then open the display list using Super 3D. The only catch is that everything in the object has to be rendered in straight lines. Super 3D can't draw curves. You could even bring the modified object back into FreeHand after altering it in Super 3D by exporting it from Super 3D as a PICT.

If you think this sounds like fun, draw something in FreeHand (keep it simple, to start with, and work your way up to more complex

TABLE 4-6	Function	What it does
Super 3D text format	start X Y Z	move to location X, Y, Z
	line X Y Z	next point along a path at location X, Y, Z
	normal X Y Z	start polygon at location X, Y, Z
	polygon X Y Z	next point in polygon, at location X, Y, Z
	return 0 0 0	end of display list

TABLE 4-7	Path in a FreeHand EPS	Polygon in a Super 3D display list
FreeHand EPS and Super 3D text format compared	100 100 M	normal 100 100 0
	100 200 L	polygon 100 200 0
	200 200 L	polygon 200 200 0
	200 100 L	polygon 200 200 0
	100 100 L	polygon 100 100 0
	n	return 0 0 0

objects), export it as a Generic EPS file, and open the EPS with your word processor. Then follow these steps.

1. Delete everything in the file except the drawing instructions (the lines that end with "m," an "L," or a "C."

2. Delete the first four numbers in the lines ending with a "C."

3. Convert each line to a Super 3D line, and convert each polygon to a Super 3D polygon.

4. Save the file as text-only.

5. Open Super 3D and open the display list you just saved. If the object's not visible, try zooming out to see if you can find it. It's probably there, somewhere.

6. Manipulate the object as you would any other Super 3D object.

Why not just draw the object in Super 3D to begin with? You try it. Super 3D's a great 3-D rendering program, but its drawing capabilities are barely removed from those of MacDraw. I find this procedure, baroque as it seems, far easier than trying to draw a complex path in Super 3D.

The Best of All Possible Worlds

All of your programs (desktop-publishing and otherwise) should be capable of importing and exporting anything from/to any other program. Today, we must measure the flexibility of a program more by what it can do with data from other programs, rather than solely on the basis of what you can do inside the program.

Only software developers have the blindness required to think that their program is the only program you'll need to use. We, on the other hand, know that our needs are complex and varied enough that no one program can handle all of the tasks we need to do.

How does FreeHand measure up? Pretty well, actually. It'd be great to be able to open all FreeHand EPS files as editable FreeHand elements. Ideally, we should be able to exchange page layouts with PageMaker (or Illustrator, at least). I expect all of this capability will show up with the coming page-description and page-instruction specifications—notably editable PostScript from Adobe Systems.

Until then, keep dreaming.

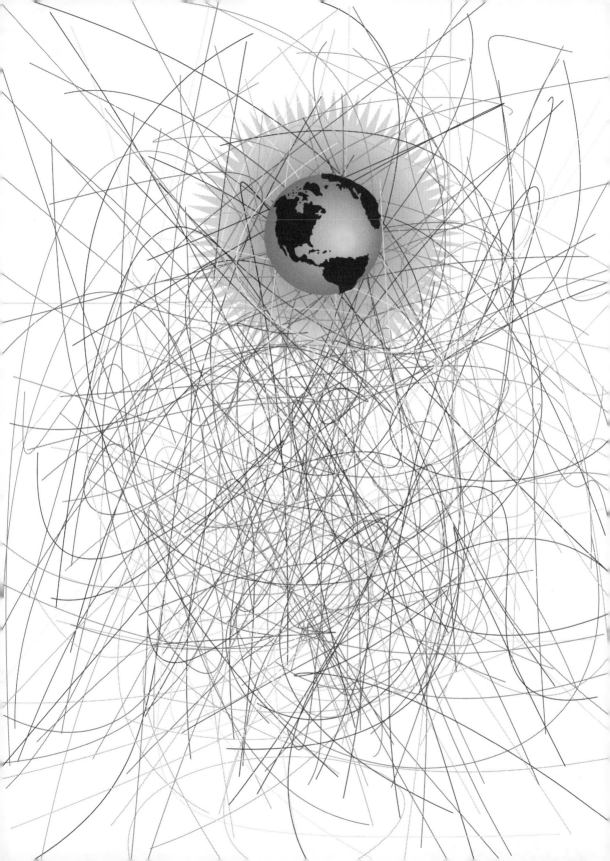

In the previous chapters, I've covered the process of creating FreeHand elements. This chapter talks about what you can do with those elements once you've drawn, typed, or imported them. I call the process of rotating, reflecting, skewing, scaling, cloning, or moving objects "transformation."

Many of the topics in this chapter have been touched on in some of the preceding chapters—mainly because everything in FreeHand is interconnected. In the old days, software was entirely linear: one had to proceed from this screen to that screen following a particular set of steps. These days, software is extremely nonlinear (that is, you can do things many different ways in many different orders), and, therefore much harder to write about. Your purchase of this book will make my time at Looney Farm that much more pleasant. Thank you.

Most of FreeHand's transformations can be controlled by moving the mouse or by typing values into dialog boxes. Try out the different ways of doing things and see which methods you like best.

Transformations are really the key to using FreeHand efficiently. I don't know how many times I've seen people laboriously drawing and redrawing repetitive shapes when they could have been using Free-Hand's clone, rotate, and reflect commands to accomplish the same end faster and with far less trouble. Any time you can see a similarity between shapes on one side of an object and another, you should be thinking about reflection. Any time you see an object that's made up of the same shape rotated about a center point, you should be thinking about rotation. Start looking at things as patterns of clones and transformations, and you'll be a long way toward becoming a FreeHand wizard.

It all works through the magic of two FreeHand keyboard short-cuts: Command-, and Command-D.

Command-, means "Transform it again," and performs the last transformation you used (see Figure 5-1). You don't have to have the same object selected as the one you originally transformed—you can transform, select another object, transform that object using the same settings, and so on.

Command-, is great for experimentation, because just by pressing the keyboard shortcut you can ask, What if I moved it a little bit more? or What if I skewed it a little bit more? If you don't like what you've done, press Command-Z to undo it.

Command-D means "Clone it and transform it again," and per-forms the most recent transformation while cloning the currently selected object. You can use Command-D to do all kinds of things (see Figure 5-2).

Note that the transformation (whatever it was) persists until the next transformation. That is, if you rotate something, drag out some ruler guides, copy something to the Scrapbook, then select an object and press Command-, FreeHand rotates the object as you specified in the earlier transformation.

FIGURE 5-1
Transform again

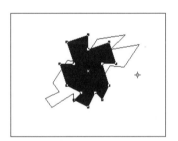 

Skew an object by dragging the skewing tool.

Press Command-,

FreeHand skews the object again, by the same amount.

FIGURE 5-2
Clone and
transform again

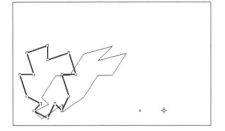

*Clone an object, then skew
it using the skewing tool.*

*Press Command-D, and
FreeHand clones the selected
object and applies the skew to it.*

Moving

FreeHand provides several ways to move objects.

- Dragging

- Entering numbers in the Move elements dialog box

- Pressing the arrow, or "nudge" keys

**Moving
by Dragging**

Moving by dragging is the most obvious way to move an object. Just grab the object and drag it to a new position. And, often, moving by dragging is the best way to move an object.

Dragging Things Quickly Versus Dragging Things Slowly. If you select something and immediately start dragging, you'll see only a box the shape of the object's selection rectangle. If, on the other hand, you hold down the mouse button for a second before dragging, you'll see the object as you drag it.

Dragging quickly is great for snapping objects into position by their outlines; waiting a second before dragging is best for seeing things inside a selection as you position them on the page.

Smooth Dragging. Smooth dragging is one of FreeHand 3's best new features. In FreeHand 2, a selection dragged on the screen produced a noticeable flicker. If you have enough memory, FreeHand 3's dragging and drawing is flicker-free.

I have always felt that smooth drawing and dragging are one of Illustrator's strongest points, because they make the program feel smooth and solid. Now FreeHand die-hards can enjoy the same feeling of stability.

If smooth dragging doesn't seem to be working, see "RAM Indicator" in Chapter 1, "FreeHand Basics."

Moving by Specifying Coordinates

When I need precision, I always move objects by entering numbers in the Move elements dialog box (see Figure 5-3), and it's not just because I'm a closet rocket scientist. It's because I don't trust a 72-dpi screen, even at 800%. You shouldn't either, when it comes to fine adjustments of elements in your FreeHand publication.

The Move elements dialog box is simple: type positive numbers to move objects up (toward the top of the screen) or right; type negative numbers to move them down or left.

FIGURE 5-3
Move elements
dialog box

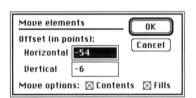

Moving elements numerically also gives you two very interesting options in the Move elements dialog box: "Contents" and "Fills." Ordinarily, you'll probably want to leave both options checked, but when you need to adjust the position of a tiled fill inside an object, or when you want to change your view of a clipping path's contents, these options really come in handy.

Moving by Pressing Arrow Keys

As if dragging by eye and specifying coordinates weren't enough movement options, FreeHand also sports "nudge" keys. Select an element and press one of the arrow keys, and the element moves in that direction in the increments you set in the More preferences dialog box.

Constraining Movement

Holding down Shift as you drag elements constrains their movement to 45-degree angles (just as in almost every other Macintosh graphics application), which makes it easy to drag objects only horizontally or vertically. FreeHand adds another wrinkle, however: the axis from which those 45-degree increments are derived can be set to present any angle (see "Constraining Tools" in Chapter 1, "FreeHand Basics").

Grouping and Ungrouping

While grouping doesn't make too much of a difference in terms of the appearance of your publication, it makes a huge difference in how you work with your publication. Grouping is a way to lock the relationships (distance, stacking order) between objects while leaving those objects free to be moved, resized, or otherwise transformed as a unit. When you select a group and press Command-I, the Group dialog box appears (see Figure 5-4).

When you transform objects, grouped or not, FreeHand transforms all of the lines and fills inside the group proportionally, unless you've checked "Group transforms as a unit." This option transforms the line weights and fills inside the group nonproportionally, resulting in an effect that resembles perspective drawing (see Figure 5-5).

FIGURE 5-4
Group dialog box

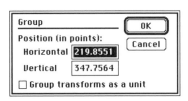

FIGURE 5-5
The effect of "Group transforms as a unit"

Original group

"Group transforms as a unit" on   *"Group transforms as a unit" off*

When you group objects that occupy different layers, all of the objects in the group move to the layer of the topmost object in the group. The stacking order of the objects is retained, even though they're all on the same layer. When you ungroup, the objects don't return to their original layers. Watch out for this.

Text on a Path and Grouped Transformations

When you transform text on a path, FreeHand transforms only the path unless you group the text on a path and check "Group transforms as a unit." At that point, you can transform the text on a path as you would any other object. If you ungroup or split the text from the path, it'll revert to its original type specifications. It's best, therefore, to join text to a path after transforming that path (see Figure 5-6).

FIGURE 5-6
Transforming text
on a path

When you scale text that's been joined to a path…

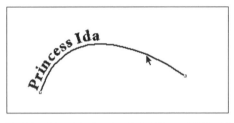

…FreeHand resizes the path, but leaves the type the same size.

If you group the text on a path before you scale it…

…FreeHand scales both the text and the path.

Aligning and Distributing

For most people, MacDraw ushered in the era of object alignment. You could align the left, right, top, bottom, or center of selected objects. It was the greatest. I spent whole afternoons just aligning things. You couldn't do that in MacPaint.

FreeHand, which counts MacDraw as one of its forebears, also features object alignment. FreeHand aligns objects based on the rectangular area each object takes up, which I'll call the object's bounding box. You can see what an object's bounding box looks like by selecting the object and pressing Command-G to group it (it it's already grouped, you don't need to group it again). The selection handles of the object show you the object's bounding box. Note that imported EPS graphics and TIFF files can have bounding boxes that have nothing to do with the actual content of the graphic (see Figure 5-7).

FIGURE 5-7
Object bounding boxes

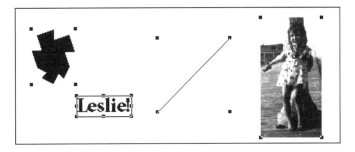

FreeHand's object alignment capabilities include both "Align," which does exactly what it says, and "Distribute," which is explained in "Distributing objects," later in this chapter. "Align" and "Distribute" can be used at the same time: you can, for example, vertically align objects while horizontally distributing them.

Aligning Objects

You align objects based on the top, bottom, side, and center of their selection rectangle or text block, rather than somehow being aligned based on their contents.

When you've selected the objects you want to align, press Command-/ to bring up the Alignment dialog box, pick an alignment, and then press Return. FreeHand aligns the selected objects as you've specified (see Figure 5-8).

FIGURE 5-8
Aligning objects

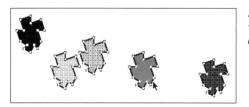

Select all of the objects you want to align and distribute, and press Command-/.

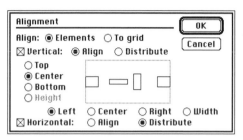

Pick an alignment and press Return to close the dialog box.

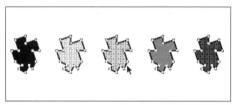

FreeHand aligns (and distributes) the objects.

Tip:
Locking as an
Adjunct to
Alignment

If any of the selected objects is locked, FreeHand aligns objects based on that object's position (see Figure 5-9). If more than one of the selected objects is locked, FreeHand bases alignment on the object nearest the alignment specified (that is, the topmost locked object for Top alignments, the leftmost locked object in Left alignments, etc.).

If you set up a keyboard shortcut for lock and unlock, you can fly through your publication locking things and aligning things, then unlocking the objects, and so on.

FIGURE 5-9
Locking and alignment

This object is locked.

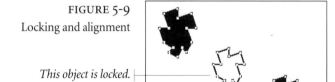

Align the tops of these objects, and they'll align to the top of the locked object—even if it's not the topmost object selected.

Tip:
Centering Text
Vertically

When you want to center text vertically inside an object, simply choosing to align by object centers doesn't usually work. Why? Because the alignment is based on the size of the text block—not on the size of the text. If you're trying to center text that has no descenders, try aligning the text based on the center of the text block and the object, and then shift the block down an amount equal to from one-sixth to one-third of the leading. It's just something you'll have to tweak by eye (see Figure 5-10).

Alternatively, you might convert the text to a path. The bottom of the path will truly be the bottom of the character and the character will align properly to the center of the object (see Figure 5-11).

FIGURE 5-10
Aligning text to objects

Alignment is based on the top and bottom of the text block, so you can end up with extra space below the text.

FIGURE 5-11
Converting text to paths
aids object alignment

If you convert the text to paths, it'll be aligned based on the actual height of the characters.

Align to Grid
Option

When you choose "Align to grid" in the Alignment dialog box, you direct FreeHand to align a specified part (top, bottom, left side, right side, or center) of an object to the "Snap-to" grid you specified in the Document setup dialog box. FreeHand aligns the specified part of the object with the grid intersection nearest that part of the object (see Figure 5-12).

FIGURE 5-12
Align to grid option

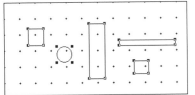 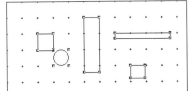

In this example, the visible grid is the same as the "Snap-to" grid. I used the Alignment dialog box to align the top left of each object to the grid.

Distributing Objects

Have you ever wanted to align a bunch of objects at even distances from each other (from each other's centers, at any rate) across a particular horizontal measurement? If you have, FreeHand's Distribute feature should make your day.

"Distribute" moves objects around relative to the part of the object you've specified in the Alignment dialog box. If you choose to distribute objects vertically and click "Top," FreeHand places the tops of the objects an even vertical distance apart, based on the current position of the tops of topmost and bottommost objects in the selection.

To distribute several objects along a horizontal area, select the objects you want to distribute, press Command-/ to display the Alignment dialog box, select the alignment and distribution options you want, and then press Return. FreeHand aligns and distributes the objects as you've specified (see Figure 5-13).

When you choose "Align to grid" while you're distributing objects, FreeHand snaps the objects to the nearest grid intersection as it distributes them.

FIGURE 5-13
Distributing objects

Select the objects you want to distribute and press Command-/.

Select the distribution and alignment you want.

This window shows you a preview of the distribution or alignment you've specified.

Press Return when you like the way it looks.

FreeHand distributes the objects as you've specified.

Scaling

If you want to make a selected object (or objects) larger or smaller, you can scale (or size) them either by eye or numerically.

To scale an object by eye, select the object you want to scale, and then select the scaling tool from the toolbox. The cursor turns into a cross hair. Position the cross hair at the point you want to scale from. Drag the cross hair to scale the selected object (see Figure 5-14).

If you drag horizontally, the object will be scaled along its width only. If you drag vertically, only the object's height will be scaled. If you drag the cross hair diagonally, both the object's height and width will be scaled. Hold down Shift to scale the object proportionally.

FIGURE 5-14
Scaling an object by eye

Select the object you want to scale, select the scale tool from the toolbox...

...and then drag to scale the object. Drag up to enlarge the object; drag down to reduce the size of the object.

When you stop dragging, FreeHand scales the object as you've specified.

Note that if the selected object is a paint-type graphic or a bilevel TIFF, you can hold down Option and Shift to scale the object both proportionally and to the printer's resolution (which you specify in the Document setup dialog box).

Scale an object numerically by following the steps below (see Figure 5-15).

1. Select the object you want to scale.

2. Select the scaling tool from the toolbox. The cursor turns into a cross hair.

3. Position the cross hair on the page, hold down Option, and click the mouse button. The Scale dialog box appears.

4. Enter the scaling values you want and set the options for where you want the scaled object's center to fall.

5. Press Return to close the dialog box.

FreeHand scales the object.

FIGURE 5-15
Scaling an object
numerically

Select the object you want to scale. Select the scale tool from the toolbox, hold down Option, and then click anywhere on the page.

Scale			OK
Scale:	● Uniform scaling:	50 %	Cancel
	○ Other: Horizontal	100 %	
	Vertical	100 %	
Center:	○ Mouse location		
	● Center of selection		
	○ Other: Horizontal	288.8813 points	
	Vertical	390.8204 points	
Scale options: ⊠ Contents ⊠ Fills ⊠ Lines			

The Scale dialog box appears. Enter the scaling values and options you want and press Return.

FreeHand scales the object as you specified.

In the Scale dialog box, the Center options give you the ability to place the center of the scaled object at the point you clicked the mouse button, at the center of the selected object, or at a numerically specified position. This last position is specified relative to the current zero point, so it's a good idea to know where that is before you enter any coordinates.

Whether you scale an object numerically or by eye, scaling options in the Scale dialog box affect the contents, lines, or fills in the object (see Figure 5-16).

FIGURE 5-16
Scaling options

Original object

Scaled with "Lines" unchecked

Scaled with "Lines" checked

Tip:
Positioning
Things
Numerically by
Setting the Zero
Point

You can control the point at which the center of your scaled object is placed by positioning the zero point where you want the center of the scaled object to fall, and then entering "0" in the Horizontal and Vertical text edit boxes in the Center options section of the Scale dialog box.

Tip:
Scaling Text
on a Path

When you scale text that's been joined to a path, FreeHand scales only the path—the text stays the same size. If you want to scale text as you scale the path, either group the path before scaling or scale the text and the path as separate objects, and then join the text to a path (see "Text on a Path and Grouped Transformations," earlier in this chapter).

After you've scaled an object, you can repeat the scaling by pressing Command-, ("Transform again"). If you cloned the object before you scaled it, you can repeat that, too, by pressing Command-D ("Clone and transform again"), as shown in Figure 5-17.

FIGURE 5-17
Scale it again

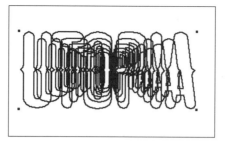

Rotating

In FreeHand, you can rotate things either by eye or numerically, and you can combine the two techniques. Follow these steps to rotate a FreeHand object by eye (see Figure 5-18).

1. Select the object you want to rotate.

2. Select the rotation tool from the toolbox. The cursor turns into a kind of cross hair.

FIGURE 5-18
Rotating an object
by eye

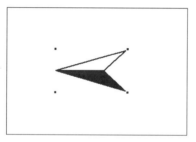

Select the object you want to rotate.

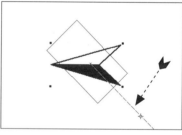

Select the rotation tool from the toolbox and start dragging where you want to place the center of rotation.

| ch:310.5 | cv:397 | angle:62 |

As you drag, the Info bar shows you the center of rotation and the angle of rotation.

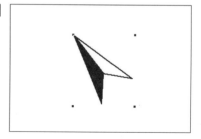

Stop dragging when the object's rotated the way you want it.

3. Position the cross hair at the point at which you want the center of rotation and hold down the mouse button. Handles appear along the selected object's axis of rotation.

4. Drag the object clockwise or counterclockwise around the center of rotation. If you want to constrain the rotation of the object to 45-degree increments, hold down Shift as you drag. The amount of rotation is displayed in the status bar.

5. When you're through rotating the object, release the mouse button.

Sometimes, you know just the angle of rotation you want. Follow these steps to rotate a FreeHand object numerically (see Figure 5-19).

1. Select the object you want to rotate.

2. Select the rotation tool from the toolbox. The cursor turns into a cross hair. Position the cross hair at the point you want to use

FIGURE 5-19
Rotating objects
numerically

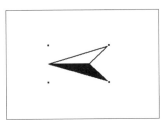

Select the object you want to rotate.

Select the rotation tool from the toolbox, hold down Option, and then click anywhere on the page.

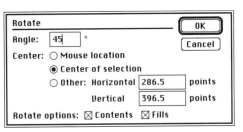

Enter the rotation angle and any rotation options you want in the Rotate dialog box and press Return.

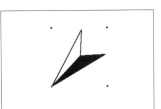

FreeHand rotates the object as you specified.

for the axis of rotation (this is optional), hold down Option, and click the mouse button. The Rotate dialog box appears.

3. Type the values you want in the Rotate dialog box.

4. Press Return to close the Rotate dialog box.

FreeHand rotates the object as you specified.

The Angle text edit box does exactly what you think it would, though you should know that positive values entered here rotate the selected object counterclockwise, while negative values rotate the object clockwise.

The Center options give you the choice of rotating the selected object from the location of the cross hairs cursor when you held down Option and clicked the mouse button, from the center of the selected object, or from a specific location (the coordinates are relative to your current zero point; it's good to know where that is if you want to use this option).

You can use the Rotate options check boxes to rotate the object without rotating its contents or fills, or to rotate the object and its contents or fills (see Figure 5-20).

FIGURE 5-20
Rotate options

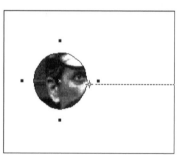 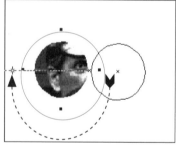

Uncheck "Contents" in the Rotate dialog box...

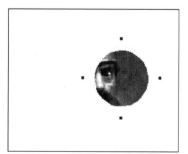

...and you can rotate an object without moving or rotating the objects pasted inside it.

Once you've rotated something, you can repeat the rotation by pressing Command-, ("Transform again").

If you clone an object, and then rotate it, you can repeat the rotation and cloning by pressing Command-D ("Clone and transform again"), as shown in Figure 5-21.

While you're rotating things, remember that the winding of rotated paths does not change (for more on PostScript path winding, see "Thinking Like a Line" in Chapter 2, "Drawing")—it still starts from the same point as it did before you rotated it. Rotation, therefore, can be another method to change the apparent winding of a path (see Figure 5-22).

FIGURE 5-21
Clone and rotate again

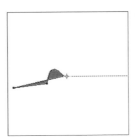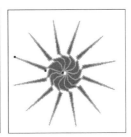

FIGURE 5-22
Rotation and
path winding

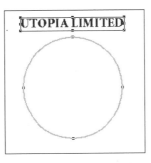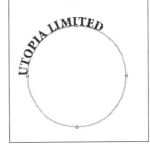

Path winding starts at the leftmost point on the path and winds clockwise from there.

When you join these two objects… *…you get this…*

…unless you've rotated the circle…

…in which case, you'll get something like this.

After rotation, path winding still starts at the original leftmost point on the path and winds clockwise.

Reflecting

Reflection flips a selected object or objects along a specified axis. You can reflect selected objects by eye or, once again, numerically.

To reflect an object by eye, follow these steps (see Figure 5-23).

1. Select the object you want to reflect.

2. Select the reflection tool from the toolbox. The cursor turns into a kind of cross hair.

3. Position the cross hair at the point at which you want the axis of reflection and hold down the mouse button. Handles appear along the axis of reflection of the selected object.

4. Drag the object across the axis of reflection. The angle of reflection is displayed in the status bar.

5. When you're through reflecting the object, release the mouse button. FreeHand reflects the object as you've specified.

FIGURE 5-23
Reflecting an
object by eye

Select the objects you want to reflect. Choose the reflect tool from the toolbox and start dragging to where you want to position the axis of reflection. As you drag, FreeHand shows you a preveiw of your reflected object.

Stop dragging when the preview image looks the way you want it. FreeHand reflects the selected objects as you specified.

To reflect a FreeHand object numerically, follow these steps (see Figure 5-24).

1. Select the object you want to reflect.

2. Select the reflection tool from the toolbox. The cursor turns into a cross hair. Position the cross hair at the point you want to use for the axis of reflection (this is optional), hold down Option, and click the mouse button. The Reflect dialog box appears.

3. Type the values you want in the Reflect dialog box.

4. Press Return to close the dialog box. FreeHand reflects the object as you specified.

FIGURE 5-24
Reflecting objects
numerically

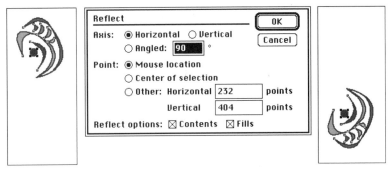

Select the object you want to reflect, choose the reflect tool from the toolbox, and then hold down Option and click anywhere on the page. In the Reflect dialog box, specify the reflection you want and press Return.

Positive values entered in the Angle text edit box reflect the selected object counterclockwise; negative values reflect the object clockwise.

When we're drawing, we very often work with paths which are mirror images of each other around some center point. FreeHand's reflection tool makes it possible for us to work the way we think. Any time you want to create some element that's the same as some other element, but reflected across some axis, use the reflection tool.

Reflection changes the winding of the reflected paths (for more on PostScript path winding, see "Thinking Like a Line" in Chapter 2, "Drawing"). The path still starts from the same point as it did before you reflected it, but the path's winding now goes around the path in the opposite direction (see Figure 5-25).

FIGURE 5-25
Reflection and path
winding

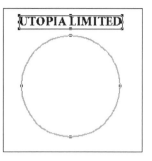

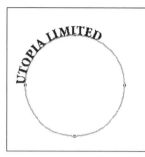

*Path winding
starts at the
leftmost
point on the
path and
goes
clockwise
from there.*

When you join these two objects...   *...you get this...*

*...unless you've reflected the circle
around its vertical center...*

...in which case, you'll get this.

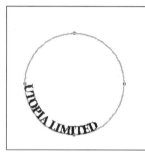

*Path winding
starts at the
leftmost
point on the
path and
goes counter-
clockwise
from there.*

Like all of the other transformations, you can repeat reflection by pressing Command-, ("Transform again"), or repeat cloning plus reflection by pressing Command-D ("Clone and transform again"). There's not too much point to this, however, as the reflected objects usually just stack up on top of each other.

Rotation and Perspective Drawing

You can use rotation and scaling to create isometric projections of 3-D objects in FreeHand (for more on perspective drawing, see "Perspective Projection" in Chapter 2, "Drawing"). The following steps show you how (see Figure 5-26).

1. Create an orthographic view of the object (also called a plan view: front, top, and side views of the object).

2. Choose the Rotate tool from the toolbox. Hold down Command and select the top view of the object. Hold down Option and click anywhere to display the Rotate dialog box. Type "90" in the Rotate dialog box and press Return to rotate the top view of the object 90 degrees.

FIGURE 5-26
Rotating and scaling
create an isometric
projection

Draw the front, side,
and top of an object.

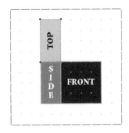

Rotate the top of the
object 90 degrees.

Rotate all three objects
-45 degrees.

Scale the top and front
vertically by 57.735
percent.

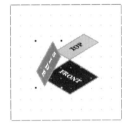

Scale the side horizon-
tally by 57.735 percent.

Rotate the front 60
degrees.

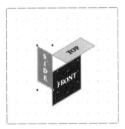

Rotate the side 30
degrees.

Snap all the pieces
together.

3. Hold down Command and select all three views of the object. Hold down Option and click anywhere to display the Rotate dialog box. Type "-45" in the Rotate dialog box and press Return to rotate all views of the object 45 degrees clockwise.

4. Without deselecting the objects, choose the scale tool from the toolbox. Hold down Command and Shift and click on the side view to deselect it (the top and front view should stay selected). Hold down Option and click anywhere to display the Scale

dialog box. Type "57.735" in the Scale text edit box and press Return to close the dialog box.

5. Hold down Command and select the side view (now the side view should be selected; the top and front views should be deselected). Hold down Option and click anywhere to display the Scale dialog box. Type "57.735" in the Scale text edit box. Press Return to close the Scale dialog box.

6. Select the rotate tool from the toolbox. Hold down Command and select the front view of the object. Hold down Option and click anywhere to display the Rotate dialog box. Type "60" in the Rotate text edit box and press Return to close the dialog box.

7. Hold down Command and select the side view. Hold down Option and click anywhere to display the Rotate dialog box. Type "30" in the Rotate text edit box and press Return to close the dialog box.

8. Snap the three pieces of the object together, and you've got an isometric projection of the object. You can enhance the 3-D effect of the projection by shading the sides of the object, if you want.

Skewing Objects

Skewing an object makes it appear the plane that the object's resting on has been rotated. It's good for creating perspective effects.

Skewing is hard to get used to at first, because vertical skewing seems to affect the horizontal lines in an object, while horizontal skewing affects the vertical lines in an object. It's just something you'll have to get used to (see Figure 5-27).

Follow these steps to skew an object by eye (see Figure 5-28).

1. Select the object you want to skew.

2. Choose the skewing tool from the toolbox. The cursor turns into a cross hair.

FIGURE 5-27
Horizontal and
vertical skewing

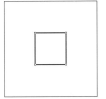

Original object

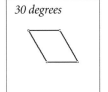

30 degrees

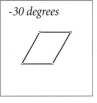

-30 degrees

Horizontal skewing

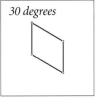

30 degrees

-30 degrees

Vertical skewing

FIGURE 5-28
Skewing an object
by eye

*Select the object you
want to skew.*

*Position the cross hair to
define the center point
you're skewing around,
and drag.*

*Hold down Shift before
you drag to constrain the
skewing to either vertical
or horizontal.*

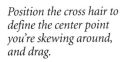

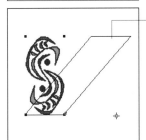

*FreeHand displays a rectangular preview of the
skewed object as you drag.*

*As you're dragging, the Info bar
shows you what's going on.*

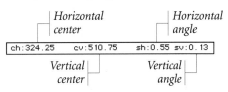

*Horizontal
center*   *Horizontal
angle*

`ch:324.25    cv:510.75    sh:0.55 sv:0.13`

*Vertical
center*   *Vertical
angle*

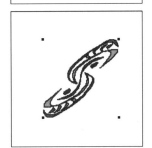

*When you stop
dragging, FreeHand
skews the object.*

3. Position the cross hair where you want the skew to start.

4. Drag the cross hair to skew the object. If you hold down Shift while dragging the cross hair horizontally, the object is constrained to horizontal skewing. If you hold down Shift while dragging the cross hair vertically, the object is constrained to vertical skewing. If you drag the cursor diagonally, the object is skewed both horizontally and vertically. As you drag the cursor, the skewing angles display on the status bar.

Here's how to skew an object numerically (see Figure 5-29).

1. Select the object you want to skew.

2. Choose the skewing tool from the toolbox. The cursor turns into a cross hair.

3. Position the cross hair where you want to position the center of the skew (this is optional).

4. Hold down Option and click the mouse button. The Skew dialog box appears.

FIGURE 5-29
Skewing numerically

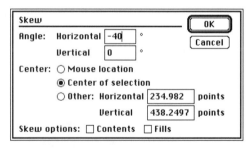

Select the object you want to skew. Choose the skew tool from the toolbox, hold down Option, and then click anywhere on the page.

Type the skewing angle (or angles) you want, pick any skewing options you want, and then press Return.

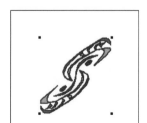

FreeHand skews the object as you specified.

5. Enter angles for skewing in the Horizontal and Vertical text edit boxes in the Angle section of the dialog box, and then choose an option for the placement of the center of the skewed object. Click the Mouse location option if you clicked where you wanted the center of the skewed object to fall; click "Center of selection" to skew around the selected object's center; click "Other" and enter a numerical position for the center of the skewed object. If you use this last option, the horizontal and vertical coordinates are based on the current location of the zero point on your rulers.

Once you've skewed an object, you can repeat the skewing for that object or for another selected object by pressing Command-,.

If you clone the object before skewing it, you can repeat the skewing and cloning by pressing Command-D ("Clone and transform again"), as shown in Figure 5-30.

FIGURE 5-30
Clone and skew again

Skewing and Perspective Drawing

If you survived the parts of Chapter 2, "Drawing," covering perspective, oblique, and axonometric projections, here's your reward: skewing is a fantastic way to automate drawing oblique and axonometric projections. In many cases, these simple projections can substitute for (much more complicated) perspective rendering. The following steps show you how to create an oblique projection of an object (see Figure 5-31).

1. Draw the orthographic views (top, side, and front) of an object.

2. Select the skewing tool from the toolbox.

3. Hold down Command and select the side view of the object.

4. Hold down Option and click the pointer tool anywhere.

FIGURE 5-31

Skewing to create an oblique projection

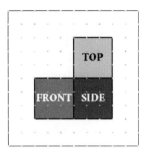

Draw the top, front, and side of the object.

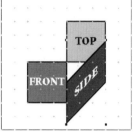

Select the side view and skew it 45 degrees vertically.

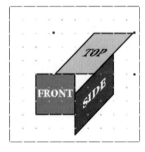

Select the top view and skew it -45 degrees horizontally.

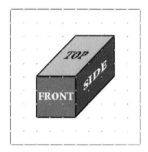

Snap the three views together.

5. Type "45" in the Vertical text edit box and press Return to close the dialog box. FreeHand skews the front of the object as you specified.

6. Hold down Command and select the top view of the object.

7. Hold down Option and click the pointer tool anywhere.

8. Type "-45" in the Horizontal text edit box and press Return to close the dialog box. FreeHand skews the front of the object as you specified.

9. Snap all of the objects together, and, voilà, you've got an oblique projection.

Skewing is also a great help in creating axonometric views of an object. Axonometric views differ from oblique views in that they're both skewed and scaled, and that the front view is skewed away from the plane of perspective.

Creating Clipping Paths

Another of FreeHand's basic transformations is "Paste inside"—the ability to use any path as a clipping path for any object or objects. "Paste inside" has already gotten some coverage in Chapter 2, "Drawing," but here's more. Clipping paths are the key to three.

- Trapping objects which cross color boundaries (this technique is covered in depth in Chapter 6, "Color").

- Cropping imported graphics (this technique is covered in Chapter 4, "Importing and Exporting").

- Transparency and translucency effects.

Clipping paths are also just plain fun. Be aware, however, that clipping paths increase the complexity of your publication by an order of magnitude as far as the PostScript interpreters in printers and imagesetters are concerned. This doesn't mean they should be avoided! Just remember that publications containing clipping paths will take longer to print, and may produce overtime charges at your imagesetting service bureau. In other words, make sure that the effect you hope to achieve by using clipping paths is worth the added expense and time.

Tip:
Illustrator
Users Beware

In Illustrator, most graduated and radial fills are accomplished by using blending, and then pasting the blended objects inside another shape. While you can create blends the same way in FreeHand, you'd usually create an object and fill it with a graduated or radial fill. I frequently see Illustrator users working in FreeHand by blending and using "Paste inside" where they could simply use a fill.

Use the following steps to create a clipping path (see Figure 5-32).

1. Draw, type, or import an object.

2. Draw a path on top of the initial object.

3. Select the path and press Command-X to cut it to the Clipboard.

4. Select the first object and choose "Paste inside" from the Edit menu. The parts of the second object which fell within the first object's area appear inside the first object.

If you need to edit the objects you've pasted inside a path, or if you want to remove them, select the object that contains them and choose "Cut contents" from the Edit menu. The objects which had been pasted inside the path you selected are pasted on top of the path you cut them from (see Figure 5-33).

FIGURE 5-32
Creating a clipping path

Draw, type, or import something...

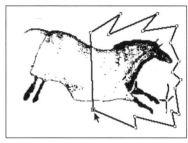

...and draw a path on top of it. Select the original object and cut it to the Clipboard.

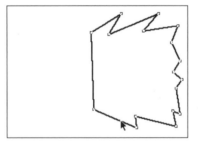

Select the path...

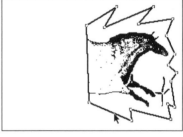

...and choose "Paste inside" from the Edit menu. FreeHand pastes the object on the Clipboard inside the path.

FIGURE 5-33
Removing objects from inside a clipping path

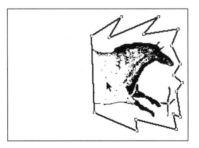

Select the clipping path...

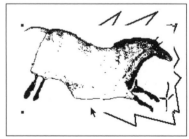

...and choose "Cut contents" from the Edit menu. FreeHand pastes the contents of the object on top of the clipping path.

What happens when you use "Paste inside" more than once for the same clipping path? Each successive "Paste inside" places the contents of the Clipboard on top of any objects already inside the clipping path. You'll still be able to see any objects not obscured by opaque lines or fills (see Figure 5-34).

When you select a clipping path and choose "Cut contents" from the Edit menu, all of the objects inside the clipping path are cut out of the clipping path, retaining the stacking order they had inside the path (the last object pasted inside it on top).

FIGURE 5-34
Multiple "Paste-insides"

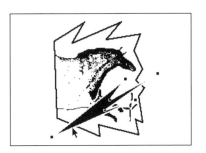
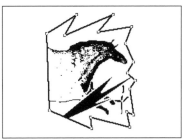

When you paste a new object inside a clipping path that already contains other objects...

...the new object is pasted on top of the other objects inside the path.

Using "Paste Inside" to Crop Imported Images

FreeHand lacks a tool analogous to PageMaker's cropping tool, but you can simulate the behavior of the cropping tool using FreeHand's "Paste inside" feature. Actually, the ability to create clipping paths of any shape in FreeHand is more powerful and flexible than the PageMaker's cropping tool (which crops only in rectangles).

For more on cropping images, see "Cropping TIFF Images" in Chapter 4, "Importing and Exporting."

Creating a Color Change Where an Object Crosses a Color Boundary

Here's an effect that we used to sweat over in the dark days when everything was done with a copy camera, wax, and a knife. Suppose you have some black text that crosses from a white background onto a black background. If the edge of the black background is a straight line, the effect is pretty easy to create. But if the edge of the black background is a curved or jagged line, it's nearly impossible to create this effect using a copy camera. With FreeHand, it's so easy that a number of power users I know have missed it (see Figure 5-35).

FIGURE 5-35
Changing colors as you
cross a color boundary

Create two paths. Fill one with black; fill the other with white. Create a text block that crosses both paths. Color the text block black.

Clone the text block and cut the clone to the Clipboard. Select the white shape and choose "Paste inside" from the Edit menu.

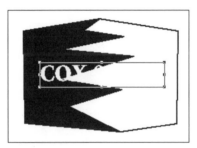 

Select the text block and color it white.

Cut the white text block. Select the black shape and choose "Paste inside" from the Edit menu.

1. Create your type.

2. Create the black background object.

3. Position the type and the black background object in the alignment you want.

4. Clone the text block.

5. Color the clone of the text block white and press Command-X to cut it to the Clipboard.

6. Select the black object and choose "Paste inside" from the Edit menu. FreeHand pastes the white text block inside the black object. Can't see it? Select the black text block and send it to the back.

Note that this same trick works just as well for colored text and a colored background, and that, by extension, it works for multiple adjacent color fields which have multiple overlapping objects which change color as they pass through the different color fields. For an example of this trick, refer to the color section of this book. And don't forget to trap!

Creating the Illusion of Transparency Using Clipping Paths

Have you ever wondered why you can't just select a FreeHand element and click an option that makes the object transparent? (You can, of course, for placed images, but that's not what I'm talking about.) When PostScript fills an object, it assumes that the fill is opaque. FreeHand, being a child of PostScript, adheres to this assumption, but also gives you a number of ways to fool PostScript into rendering objects that look transparent.

When an object passes behind some transparent or translucent plane, it changes color. Sometimes very subtly. To simulate this effect in FreeHand, clone the partially obscured object and change the colors of the cloned objects from their original colors. Then paste those objects inside the transparent or translucent object. You can use this optical illusion to simulate the effect of looking through a number of simple transparent/translucent planar surfaces. The main difficulty of rendering transparency and translucency in two-dimensional work is that you walk a fine line. If the color shift is too great, it'll look like you've created another object; if the color shift is too slight, it won't look like an object's transparent. Overall, transparency is harder to simulate than translucency.

I'll demonstrate this technique using an example, because I really can't think of how to boil the rules down into a step-by-step technique you can apply to any situation (see Figure 5-36).

FIGURE 5-36
Creating transparent objects

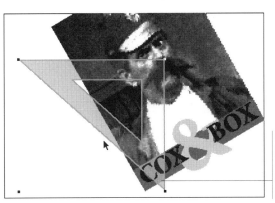

This object is colored 20 percent gray, and has lightened copies of the background objects pasted inside it.

Creating three-dimensional transparency is simultaneously easier and more difficult. It's easier because color shifts and perspective shifts around three-dimensional objects provide more cues to the eye and so are more easily simulated; it's more difficult because you've got to figure out what those shifts are to be able to simulate them.

Once again, you'll have to look at my example and figure out how the techniques I use work with the publication and effect you're creating (see Figure 5-37).

FIGURE 5-37
Creating three-
dimensional
transparent and
translucent effects

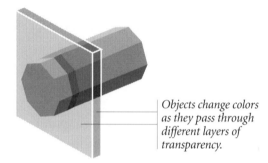

Objects change colors
as they pass through
different layers of
transparency.

Creating Transparent Text

An effect you see very often, especially in television video advertising, is that of a character or word superimposed above an image where the characters are wholly or partially transparent. Here's how you can you achieve this effect in FreeHand (see Figure 5-38).

1. Place an image.

2. Create some type and position it over the image. Without deselecting the type, choose "Convert to paths" from the Type menu. FreeHand converts the characters to a composite path.

3. Select the image and press Command-= to clone the image. Without deselecting the cloned image, press Command-I to display the Image dialog box. Inside the Image dialog box, change the image's gray levels so that it's about half as dark as the original image. When you're through changing the gray levels, press Return to close the Image dialog box.

4. Press Command-X to cut the altered image to the Clipboard.

5. Select the text (which is now a composite path) and choose "Paste inside" from the Edit menu.

FreeHand pastes the altered image inside the characters. This produces the illusion that you're looking through transparent text. You can enhance this illusion by cloning the type and offsetting the clone slightly from the original text to create a drop shadow, and then pasting another clone of the original image inside the drop shadow.

FIGURE 5-38
Transparent text
above an image

Place an image.

Create some type above the image.

Clone the image and color it with a lighter shade of gray (I use 80 percent—it comes out lighter than you'd think).

Convert the text to paths.

Paste the lightened clone of the image inside the characters.

My Life Was Transformed

All around you, every day, things are changing from one thing into another. Fuzzy caterpillars turn into moths. Clark Kent jumps into a phone booth and emerges as Superman. Werewolves stalk the moors under the full moon. The bat shown on page 98 is, by day, a harmless graphic designer with prominent canines. These changes are all every-day, natural, phenomena.

I didn't understand this when I first approached FreeHand's trans-formation tools. The tools seemed alien, awkward, and I didn't use them very much. Then, one day, I saw them as extensions of the way I already thought about drawing. Now, I use them more than I use the drawing tools.

Make FreeHand's tranformation tools an integral part of how you work with the program, and you'll have their powerful, almost magical forces on your side. And that means you'll have more time for other things. Like howling at the moon.

REAL WORLD FREEHAND 3

nthe.poster.fh3 2:50 am 6/30/91

PMS 327

iolanthe.poster.fh3 2:54 am 6/30/91

REAL WORLD FREEHAND 3

CHAPTER

Color

6

I remember

drawing things when I was a kid. I enjoyed drawing with a pen or pencil, but I didn't really get excited until someone got out the crayons. Or the finger-paints. Or the watercolors and brushes. Drawing black lines on paper was fun, but that color stuff was *what it was all about.*

Color communicates, telling us things about the object bearing the color. Without color cues, we'd have a hard time guessing the ripeness of a fruit or distinguishing a poisonous mushroom from an edible one. And many animals would have a hard time figuring out when to mate, or with whom.

We associate colors with human emotions: we are green with envy; we've got the blues; we see red. Colors affect our emotions, as well. Various studies suggest that we think best in a room of one color, or relax best in a room of another color.

What does all of this mean? Color's important. A rule of thumb in advertising is that a color advertisement gets ten times the response of a black-and-white ad.

Since version 1.0, FreeHand's been one of the best desktop-publishing tools for creating color publications. FreeHand 3 adds:

- The ability to separate color images (saved as color TIFF files).

- Automatic trapping.

- Optimized screen printing angles (through the use of PPDs and PDXs) to decrease the likelihood of obvious moiré patterns.

- Support for color film recorders for printing color slides.

- Open PrePress Interface (OPI) support.

In addition, all aspects of color printing performance have been improved. In particular, printing of gray-scale TIFFs that have colors applied to them is dramatically faster.

Color TIFF Separations. Place a color TIFF in FreeHand 3 and print separations, and FreeHand will separate the TIFF. The quality of the separation is actually pretty good, as you can see from the side-by-side PrePrint, Photoshop, and FreeHand separations of the same color TIFF file in the color section of this book.

Automatic Trapping. FreeHand's automatic trapping is a global parameter activated by choosing "Spread size" in the Print options dialog box. It doesn't work for type, but it does work for all elements having basic fills and lines, spreading them by the amount you type in this dialog box.

Optimized Screen Angles. FreeHand uses PPD and PDX files, while continuing to support the APDs that FreeHand 2 used. What's the difference? Mainly that PPDs and PDXs contain sets of optimized screen angles for color printing for specific screen frequencies at specific printer resolutions. If you choose a Linotronic L300 PPD ("L300_493.PPD") and choose 1270 dots per inch (dpi) and 128 lines per inch (lpi), the stock screen angles are 70.0169 for cyan, 19.9831 for magenta, 0 for yellow, and 45 for black. These angles and line frequencies were determined by Adobe through extensive testing. I wouldn't mess with them unless I had a really good reason to do so (and this is me, Ole "Mess with Everything" Kvern, right?).

Why can't you just use any screen angle you want? First, because of how color printing works (see "Color Printing," later in this chapter), and second, because of how PostScript works. In this case, I should say, how PostScript doesn't work. Without getting too technical, I'll say that the screen angle you ask for might not be the one you get, and if you don't get the screen angle you asked for in a four-color printing job, you'll probably get an obvious moiré pattern in your image.

PostScript level two is supposed to offer at least a partial remedy to this, but, until then, I'll refer you to Steve Roth's definitive work on

PostScript halftoning in *Real World PostScript* for a full examination of the topic.

Color Slides. FreeHand 3 does a pretty good job of printing slides on film recorders. You'll get the best results using an Agfa ChromaScript RIP—the ChromaScript uses PostScript. Most other film recorder RIPs are QuickDraw devices, and, as such, have a hard time with fonts, graduated fills, etc.

Open Prepress Interface Support. Open Prepress Interface (OPI) is a standard for links between desktop systems and dedicated color prepress systems, such as those manufactured by Scitex, Hell, and Crosfield. OPI concerns imported images (TIFFs and paint-type graphics) only.

When you export an EPS from FreeHand, the EPS contains the OPI structuring comments (they're just a set of PostScript comments) that these systems need to be able to work with the file. OPI comments are most important if you're going to do something like drop a Scitex-separated color image into a FreeHand publication.

To be entirely frank, I'm not sure it's worth it. As I write this (November, 1990), it's definitely not—but I expect that the links between the systems will improve as time passes (and remember that time passes very quickly in the desktop-publishing world). The cost of time on the color prepress systems should decline, as well.

For my purposes, however, the separations FreeHand, Photoshop, and/or PrePrint, and an L300 can produce give me excellent quality in the 150-lpi-and-under range. If you want better than 150 lpi, you should contact a prepress house to do the separation for you, then direct your commercial printer to strip their separation into your FreeHand film. Expect imagesetters and desktop systems to catch up with color prepress systems within the next five years.

Desktop Color Separations, or DCS, is another approach to color image separation (see "Separating Color Images," later in this chapter). OPI and DCS are often presented as competing standards for desktop color separation, and they're not. OPI provides a link to color prepress systems; DCS provides a way of separating color images using desktop applications and imagesetters. In FreeHand, you can use either image separation method, or both.

Color Printing

It's almost impossible to discuss creating and using colors in FreeHand without talking a little bit about printing. If you already know about color printing, feel free to skip ahead, though you'll miss all the jokes if you do. Everyone else should note that this is a very simple explanation of a very bizarre and complex process.

After you've printed your FreeHand publication to film and delivered your film to your commercial printer (I like to walk in through the loading dock), your printer takes your film and uses it to expose (or "burn") a photosensitive printing plate. The surface of the plate has been chemically treated to repel ink. When the printing plate is exposed, the image areas from your film become able to accept ink. Once the plate's been exposed, your printer attaches the printing plate to the cylinder of a printing press.

As the cylinder containing the plate turns, the parts of it bearing your image become coated with ink, which is transferred (via another, rubber covered cylinder—the offset cylinder) to the paper. This transfer is where we get the term "offset," as in "offset printing," because the plate itself does not touch your paper.

Printing presses put ink on paper one ink color at a time. Some presses have more than one printing cylinder (also called a printing "head," or "tower") and can print several colors of ink on a sheet of paper in one pass through the press, but each printing cylinder carries only one color of ink. We can make it look like we've gotten more than one color of ink on a printing plate by using screens—patterns of dots that, from a distance, fool the eye into thinking it sees a separate color (see Figure 6-1).

FIGURE 6-1
Black and...gray?

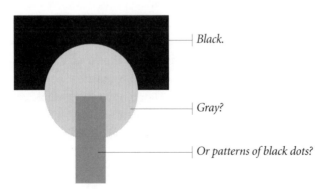

Black.

Gray?

Or patterns of black dots?

Spot color printing is simple: we just mix inks to get exactly the color we want, then we load our press with that color of ink. In process color printing, we use different screens of four inks (cyan, magenta, yellow, and black) to simulate a large part of the visible color spectrum by printing screens of the different colors so that they overlap. If everything's gone well, the dots of the different colored inks are placed near each other in a pattern called a rosette (see the color pages in this book for an example of a rosette).

Process color printing can't simulate all of the colors our eyes can see (notably metallic and fluorescent colors), but it can print color photographic images. Spot colors can print any color you can see, but can't be used to print color photographic images.

Recently, some companies have been experimenting with color separation methods that do not produce rosettes. Instead, they print all process inks at the same screen angle and line screen, producing a grid of color dots. Once again, the eye reads these juxtaposed dots of the four process inks as any number of colors. While this method can produce good-looking images that lack moiré patterns at fairly low line screens, higher line screens often show severe color shifting from one part of the image to another. In effect, it's a huge moiré pattern. While I expect this technology to improve, I've found that the optimized screen angles in PPDs/PDXs work well enough for my purposes. And Adobe's PostScript Level 2 promises considerable improvement to PostScript's halftoning capabilities.

Color in FreeHand

Now that you know all about color printing, it's time to get down to specifying colors in your FreeHand publication.

How you specify colors affects what you can do with objects you apply the colors to. You can blend between objects with different process colors applied, or create graduated or radial fills from one process color to another. You can't do that with spot colors—though you can go from one spot color to white, black, or another tint of that same spot color.

When it comes to printing, your ink list (in the Print options dialog box) displays the four process inks and any spot colors you've defined in your publication. If you need to convert any of your spot colors to process colors, or vice versa, you'll have to leave the Print options dialog box and change the color's definition. You can't, as in Adobe Separator or PrePrint, select an ink and convert it to a process color from the Print options dialog box.

Spot Color or Process Color or Both?

Whether you use spot colors, process colors, or both depends on the needs of your specific publication—which has to do with your printing budget, your communications goals, and, most importantly, your mood. If you're printing a bunch of color photographs, you're going to have to use at least the four process inks. If you're printing on a tight budget, you'll probably want to use one or two inks.

When you're creating a color, you're offered a variety of choices: is the color a spot color or a process color or a tint? If you don't yet know how your publication will be printed, don't worry too much about whether a color is defined as a spot or process color—you can always change it later.

Is What You See Anything Like What You'll Get?

Any time you're working with colors, refer to printed samples of the colors, rather than looking at the colors on your screen. Remember that, unlike the paper you'll be printing on, your screen is backlit.

If you're using uncoated paper, look at samples of the ink (spot color) or ink mix (process color) printed on uncoated stock. If you're using coated paper, look at examples printed on coated paper. If you're using a colored paper, try to find an example of the ink printed on a colored paper—though these examples are much harder to find.

If you're working with Pantone (or PMS) colors, Pantone makes a line of books showing their colors printed as spot colors and books of process color conversions of their colors; they're printed on both coated and uncoated stocks and though they're kind of expensive, they're not as expensive as pulling a job off of a press because you didn't like the press check.

Though I know everybody does it, I'd never use a Pantone color to specify a process color. Pantone is a spot color specifying system, and the colors don't convert to process colors particularly well (this is because of the process color method's inability to simulate the entire color spectrum, as discussed earlier in this chapter).

Next, don't rely on a color PostScript printer to give you an accurate version of what your colors are going to look like. They can't do it, because they simply lack the resolution to produce good process colors (and bear in mind that, because color PostScript printers print using the process color method, your spot colors will be converted to process colors during printing).

When you need to create a color proof of your publication, but aren't yet ready to have your commercial printer set up their press to print a sample for you, use one of the color proofing processes (such as Chromalin or Matchprint) to create your proofs from the film you've gotten out of your imagesetter. More imagesetting service bureaus are offering color proofing as part of their business. Some of these proofing processes can give you a proof on the paper you're intending to use, or can give you transparent overlays that you can place on top of your selected paper to get an idea of what your publication will look like when printed.

Controlling Your Color Viewing Environment

If it's important to you that what you see on your screen looks as much like what the printed version of your publication as possible, there are a few rules you need to follow.

- Use a monitor and video card capable of displaying 24-bit color. Eight-bit color, as built into the Macintosh IIci, IIsi, and LC, is simply not going to do the trick.

- Calibrate your monitor. Radius, SuperMac, and Tektronix all make color monitor calibrators that work with FreeHand's on-screen display of colors. Find the one that works with your monitor and use it.

- Control the lighting around your monitor and keep it consistent when you're working. Just about everyone agrees that the fluorescent lighting used in most of our office buildings is the worst possible lighting for viewing colors. Turn it off, if you can, and rely on incandescent lighting (desk lamps with one sort of bulb or another) to light your work area. If you can't turn it off, try getting some "full spectrum" (or "amber") fluorescent tubes to install above your monitor. These also reduce eye strain.

- Control the lighting of the area where you'll be viewing your color proofs. Ideally, you'd have a room or small booth equipped with "daylight" (or 5000-degree Kelvin) lamps—but few of us can afford the money or space required.

These rules have been passed on to me by people who are serious about color, and whose opinions I respect. But, this being a "real world" book, I have to point out that these conditions are difficult to achieve. My Macintoshes run in 8-bit color 98 percent of the time, and their monitors have never been anywhere near a calibration system. The lights above my desk are fluorescent tubes—and white ones, at that. Even my desk lamps use fluorescent tubes. And as for having a special booth or room for viewing color proofs—hah!

To compensate, I design based on printed examples of spot and process colors and pay little attention to what's on the screen except to remind me of what colors I've put where. When I get a color proof, I look at it in several different lighting environments: outdoors, indoors under typical fluorescent lighting, and indoors under typical incandescent lighting. These are, after all, the conditions it'll be seen in by the people it's intended for.

Color Models

Which color model should you use? It's pretty simple:

- If you're working with spot colors, it doesn't matter what color model you choose, and it really doesn't matter what the color looks like on the screen, as long as you let your commercial printer know what color of ink they need to use to print your publication. How do you know what color of ink to use? If you use Pantone colors, you can tell them the PMS color number. If you don't, it's trickier, but your printer can probably help you match the color you want to an ink they can mix.

- If you're working with process colors, you must specify your color using the CMYK color model, or be ready for some nasty surprises when your publication gets printed. Once again, be looking at a printed sample of the process color and enter the values given in the sample book for the color. It might seem too obvious to state, but don't enter other CMYK values unless you want a different color!

• Use "Tint" to create a tint of an existing color. You can base your tint on a spot color, a process color, or another tint. Don't base your tints on other tints unless you want to lose your mind. What's a 20 percent tint of a 67 percent tint of a 45 percent tint of PMS 327?

Tip:
If You
Can't Get the
CMYK Model

If you can only see a "CMY" option under the list of available color models, you've probably still got "Spot" chosen in the Type pop-up menu of the Colors dialog box. Choose "Process" from the Type pop-up menu, and the "CMYK" Model option will appear. Why can't you specify a spot color by entering CMYK values? Beats me, actually.

Tip:
Setting Color
Defaults

If you find you're always using one specific color type, source, and model, why not make it your default? Open your Aldus FreeHand defaults file (it's in your FreeHand folder), choose "Colors" from the Attributes menu, and make the changes you want in the Colors dialog box. Then save the file (using the same file name) as a template and close the file. The changes you made in the Colors dialog box will now appear in every new publication you create.

Creating Colors

You create colors using the Colors dialog box. You can reach the Colors dialog box by choosing "Colors…" from the Attributes menu, or by choosing "New" in the submenu attached to the Colors palette. I prefer choosing "Colors" from the Attributes menu, because I can make a QuicKey for it.

From the Colors dialog box, follow these steps (see Figure 6-2).

1. Type a name for your new color.

2. Pick a color type ("Process," "Spot," or "Tint") from the Type pop-up menu.

3. Pick a color source. If you're using PMS colors, click the PANTONE option; otherwise, click "Custom."

4. Choose a color model. The options displayed depend on what color type and source you've selected, but you'll see one of the following models: Pantone, Tint, HLS, RGB, CMY, or CMYK.

5. Type percentages into the text edit boxes or drag the slider bars to enter specific amounts of each part of the color model (for example, Red, Green, and Blue for the RGB model) until the color looks the way you want it or until you've matched the percentages shown in your printed color sample book. If you've chosen "PANTONE" as your color source, pick a Pantone color from the list of colors that appears, or type the PMS number of the color you want in the text edit box. If you type the number, FreeHand scrolls to and selects the nearest Pantone color to the PMS number you typed. Not all PMS numbers are available in the Pantone color library included with FreeHand.

6. Press Return to close the dialog box. The color you've just created appears in the Colors palette.

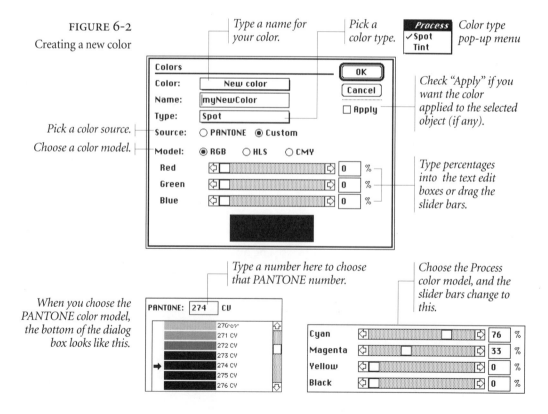

FIGURE 6-2

Creating a new color

Type a name for your color.

Pick a color type.

Color type pop-up menu

Check "Apply" if you want the color applied to the selected object (if any).

Pick a color source.

Choose a color model.

Type percentages into the text edit boxes or drag the slider bars.

When you choose the PANTONE color model, the bottom of the dialog box looks like this.

Type a number here to choose that PANTONE number.

Choose the Process color model, and the slider bars change to this.

Tip:
Leave the
Name Alone

If you're working with Pantone spot colors, don't rename the color unless you're working with one of the applications that names PMS colors differently from FreeHand (see "Keep Your Color Names Straight," below). Just stick with the color name that's entered in the Name text edit box when you select the PMS color. This way, when you print, you can turn on the Separation names option in the Print options dialog box and the color name will print on the correct color overlay. Your commercial printer has a pretty good idea what "PMS 327 CV" means, but might go mad trying to guess what you meant by naming a color "angry spam."

Tip:
Use the Correct
Color Guide (If
You Can Find It)

The PMS colors used by FreeHand are supposed to be the same as the colors in the *PANTONE Color Formula Guide 747XR*. I don't know, because I've never seen a copy of this book, which is also rumored to contain the process color equivalents for all of the PMS colors used by FreeHand. The stores I've gone to always have several different Pantone color sample books, but never seem to have this one.

Keep Your Color
Names Straight

If you're using FreeHand to create EPS graphics containing spot colors that'll be placed in a publication created by another application, and you want to color-separate that publication, make sure that your spot color names match between FreeHand and the other application. Color separation programs are as literal-minded as every other piece of software, so when you're separating a file containing the spot colors "OceanBlue" and "Ocean_Blue" you can expect to get two overlays. Since you only want to pay your imagesetting service bureau for one overlay, keep your color names consistent between documents. Make sure they're identical—down to capitalization and punctuation.

This is especially true when you're working with Pantone colors, because different applications use different names for the same Pantone colors.

Note that all of this makes no difference whatever if you're converting these colors to process colors as you separate the file. If you're doing that, read the next section.

Keep Your Color
Definitions
Straight

If you're using FreeHand to create EPS graphics containing process colors that'll be placed in a publication created by another application, and you want to color-separate that publication, make sure that your process color specifications match between FreeHand and the other application for colors that are supposed to print as the same color.

Once again, you can't rely on your screen display, because different applications display colors differently. Make the CMYK settings for your process colors identical, though, and you can count on their printing identically when you separate the publication.

Adding Colors from Color Libraries

FreeHand is shipped with a color library, the file CRAYONLIBRARY.CLIB (if you've followed a standard installation, it'll be inside your FreeHand folder). CRAYONLIBRARY.CLIB contains a set of 64 color definitions that correspond to the 64 colors in the Crayola set I used to have (in around 1964). I don't know if anyone's been watching, but today's crayon sets have very different colors. They're brighter and somehow shallower than the ones I remember chewing on.

Follow these steps to add a color or colors from a color library (see Figure 6-3).

1. Choose "Library" from the submenu that's attached to the Colors palette.

FIGURE 6-3
Adding colors from a color library

Choose "Library…" from the Colors palette submenu.

Locate and open the color library you want.

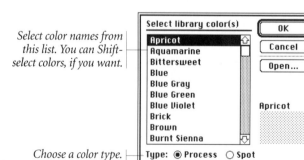

Select color names from this list. You can Shift-select colors, if you want.

Choose a color type.

Press OK when you've selected all of the colors you want.

This swatch shows a preview of any one selected color.

2. Locate the library file "CRAYONLIBRARY.CLIB" in the dialog box that appears.

3. Double-click on the file name or click Open to open the library. The Select library colors dialog box appears, showing a list of the colors in the color library.

4. Select "Process" or "Spot" from the Type options at the bottom of the dialog box.

5. Select a color in the listing (or hold down Shift and select several colors) and press Return to add that color to your current publication's list of colors.

Creating a Color Library

You can create a color library or edit the existing color library (CRAYONLIBRARY.CLIB) using any word processor that can save files as text-only (ASCII). If you're working from a process color sample book, here's your chance to enter lots of colors at once.

Color library files begin with "ColorLibrary 1.0" followed by "BeginColorDefs." Following this header, enter your color definitions as shown below, where *colorname* is the name you give the color and *cyan*, *magenta*, etc. are the color percentages for the color model being used (where 1.0 = 100 percent).

name=(*colorname*) cmyk=(*C, M, Y, K*) rgb=(*red, green, blue*)

When you're through adding colors to your color library, end the file with "EndColorDefs" followed by "EndColorLibrary." Save the file as text-only, giving the file the file extension ".CLIB." An example of a very short color library is shown in Figure 6-4.

FIGURE 6-4
A very short
color library

```
ColorLibrary 1.0
BeginColorDefs
name=(purple_haze) cmyk=(0.90, 0.67, 0.00, 0.00)
name=(husky_gold) cmyk=(0.00, 0.20, 1.00, 0.05)
name=(rose_bowl) cmyk=(0.00, 0.50, 0.00, 0.00)
name=(cougar_maroon) cmyk=(0.20, 0.60, 0.00, 0.20)
EndColorDefs
EndColorLibrary
```

Importing Colors from PageMaker

Because it's so important to have your spot color names match or your process color specifications match, it's great to be able to import objects from PageMaker into FreeHand and have FreeHand's Colors dialog box fill in with the color names and specifications used in Page-Maker. Here's how you do it.

1. Create your colors in PageMaker.

2. Print one page containing objects with the colors you want to bring into FreeHand to disk as EPS. (In PageMaker, press Command-P to display the Print dialog box, type the page you want to print in the Range text edit boxes, click the PostScript button, click the EPS option, click the "File name..." button, type a file name in the Print PostScript to disk dialog box, and then press Return three times to close all of the dialog boxes and print the page to disk as EPS.)

3. In FreeHand, choose "Place" from the File menu.

4. Locate and select the EPS file you just printed to disk and press Return. FreeHand displays a loaded EPS place gun. Click the gun to place the PageMaker EPS. Your Colors palette fills in with the color names defined in the PageMaker EPS.

PageMaker-defined colors are always imported as spot colors, regardless of how they've been specified in PageMaker. If they should be process colors, double-click on the color name in the Colors palette and choose "Process" from the Type pop-up menu in the Colors dialog box.

You can't, unfortunately, take color names and definitions created in FreeHand back to PageMaker—PageMaker's Colors palette doesn't update with colors inside imported EPS graphics.

If you're pasting objects from PageMaker to FreeHand, the Page-Maker color definitions are imported into FreeHand, but the color names don't appear in the Colors palette. You can, however, easily add them to your list of colors (see Figure 6-5).

1. Select the colored object you've pasted from PageMaker.

2. Press Command-E. The Fill and line dialog box appears. In the Fill section of the Fill and line dialog box, a swatch of the

FIGURE 6-5
Adding a color copied
from PageMaker

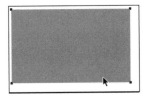

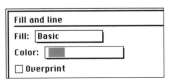

*Select a colored object you've pasted
from PageMaker.*

*Press Command-E to display the Fill and
line dialog box.*

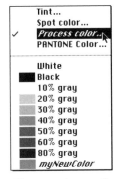

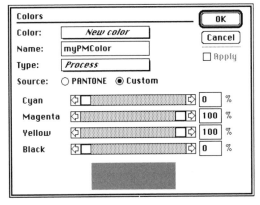

*Choose a color type from
the Colors pop-up menu.*

*Type a name for the color in the Colors dialog box and
press Return twice (once to close the Colors dialog box;
once to close the Fill and line dialog box.*

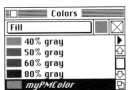

*FreeHand adds
your color to the
Colors palette.*

selected color appears in the Color pop-up menu. Choose a
color type ("Process," "Spot," or "Tint," depending on how you
want the color specified) from the Color pop-up menu. The
Colors dialog box appears with the color specifications of the
selected color filled in.

3. Type a name for the color and press Return twice to close both
the Colors dialog box and the Fill and line dialog box. The new
color name appears on your Colors palette.

Adding Colors from Illustrator 3.0

You can't name colors (other than spot and PMS colors) in Illustrator, so when you open or place EPS files created in Illustrator, your colors palette doesn't update with any custom process colors you've used in the Illustrator file.

If you've placed the EPS file, there's not much you can do to get the color specifications from the Illustrator file into FreeHand and you'll have to recreate the colors from scratch. Remember that you've got to make the color definitions identical to have the colors match when you separate the publication.

If you've opened and converted the EPS file, you can add the colors to your Colors palette (this process is identical to the one shown in Figure 6-5, above).

1. Select a colored object in the converted graphic.

2. Press Command-E. The Fill and line dialog box appears. In the Fill section of the Fill and line dialog box, a swatch of the selected color appears in the Color pop-up menu. Choose a color type ("Process," "Spot," or "Tint," depending on how you want the color specified) from the Color pop-up menu. The Colors dialog box appears with the color specifications of the selected color filled in.

3. Type a name for the color and press Return twice to close both the Colors dialog box and the Fill and line dialog box. The new color name appears on your Colors palette.

Importing Colors from Other Applications

In general, you can import color definitions from other applications that support named colors by creating an EPS file containing the colors you want in the original application and placing the EPS in FreeHand. The named colors in the EPS file appear in the Colors palette. At that point, you can delete the EPS graphic, if you want.

If you edit the properties of the color you've imported with an EPS graphic, don't expect the changes you've made to affect the color definitions inside the EPS—they won't. The colors inside the EPS are, in effect, locked.

If you imported the EPS only to get the color definitions and have deleted the EPS, there's no problem. If you've imported an EPS, edited the colors that are imported with the EPS, and applied the edited colors to FreeHand objects, you can expect the colors inside the EPS and the colors of the FreeHand objects to separate differently. If they're spot colors, you'll end up with (at least) an extra overlay. If they're process colors, colors that should look the same will look different.

If you want to match a color that occurs in a scanned color photograph you're using in your publication (the perfect shade of green in the leaves of a tree, or the bright red of a classic sports car, for example) so that you can color type or other graphic elements to match part of the photographic image, and you have PrePrint, Color Studio, or Photoshop (or some other program that can open a color TIFF and derive a CMYK value from a pixel), try this (I'll use Photoshop in my example, as shown in Figure 6-6).

1. Open Photoshop.

2. Locate and open the TIFF file.

   If the you haven't adjusted the color of the TIFF, and you want to adjust it, do it now. It won't do you any good to derive a color from part of an image if you're going to change the colors in the TIFF later.

   Different programs have different ways of converting RGB (all color TIFFs are RGB, at present) to CMYK. PrePrint's values, for example, differ from those of Photoshop. Get your CMYK values from the application you're going to use to separate your TIFF image, if possible. If you're separating using FreeHand's built-in separations, the values displayed by PrePrint will be very close, if not exactly the same.

3. Select the eyedropper tool.

4. Click the eyedropper tool on the area in the image that contains the color you want to match.

5. Read the CMYK values for the color. In Photoshop, you double-click the foreground color swatch in the toolbox, and the Color Picker dialog box would appear.

FIGURE 6-6

Deriving colors from
photographic images

*Click the eyedropper tool
on an area of the color
you want to match.*

*If this icon appears
next to the color
swatch, the color
you've chosen
cannot be
simulated by a
process color.*

*Click on the foreground
color in Photoshop's
toolbox, and Photoshop
displays the Color Picker
dialog box.*

*Read the color values out
of the text edit boxes at
the right of the Color
Picker dialog box.*

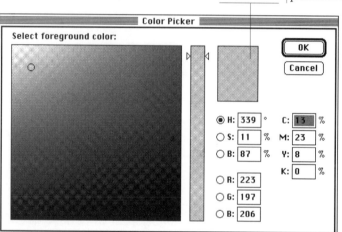

Photoshop tip: If the color you've chosen cannot be simulated
with CMYK process color, Photoshop displays an alert marker
next to the color swatch in the Color Picker dialog box. If you
click the marker, Photoshop adjusts the color swatch and the
color's CMYK values to be as close to the color as process color
can get.

6. Return to FreeHand and define the color using the CMYK values you captured from the photographic image.

Now you can apply the color to any graphic element you want.

Editing Colors

To edit a color, double-click on the color name in the Colors palette. The Colors dialog box appears, filled in with the name and specifications of the color you selected. Make any changes you want to the color and press Return to close the dialog box (see Figure 6-7).

FIGURE 6-7
Editing colors

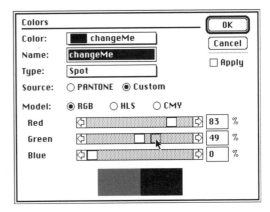

Double-click the name of the color you want to edit. FreeHand displays the Colors dialog box.

Make the changes you want in the Colors dialog box and press Return.

Converting Spot Colors to Process Colors

Sometimes you need to change a color you've specified as a spot color into a process color. Your budget's expanded, you've got a sweetheart deal from your commercial printer, your client/boss/whatever just *has* to have a color photograph—something happens so that you need to change your publication's color printing method from spot color to process color. Here's what you do (see Figure 6-8).

1. Double-click the name of the spot color in the Colors palette. If the Colors palette isn't visible, you can display it by pressing Command-6. The Colors dialog box appears.

2. Choose "Process" from the Type pop-up menu.

FreeHand converts your spot color to a process color. The process colors will not always match the spot color—this is partly because the conversion process isn't perfect, but it's mostly because process color can't simulate the range of colors you can print with spot colors (especially, as I've noted elsewhere, Pantone inks). Tweak the new process

FIGURE 6-8
Converting a Spot Color
to a Process Color

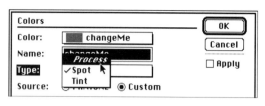

*Double-click the name of
the color you want to
edit. FreeHand displays
the Colors dialog box.*

Choose "Process" from the Type pop-up menu.

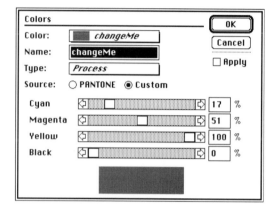

FreeHand converts your spot color to a process color.

color until it looks the way you want, or until it matches the specs in
your process color swatch book.

Converting Pantone Colors to Process

If you suddenly find that you've got to change your Pantone spot colors to process colors, you can have FreeHand convert your Pantone
colors into process colors for you. Note that you can use Pantone colors to specify process colors (horrors!) by choosing "Process" from the
Type pop-up menu after you choose your Pantone color.

1. Double-click the name of the Pantone color in the Colors palette. If the Colors palette isn't visible, you can display it by
   pressing Command-6. The Colors dialog box appears.

2. Choose "Process" from the Type pop-up menu. FreeHand converts the Pantone color to a process color.

If you want to change the CMYK values of the new process color,
click the Custom option. The CMYK values for the process color
appear. Alter the values until the color swatch looks the way you want
(or until you've matched the values in a printed color reference book).

Applying Colors

Really, there's not much to applying colors to objects—just select the object you want to apply a color to and click the color name in the Colors palette. Well… I guess it's a little more involved than that.

First, note that the pop-up menu at the top of the Colors palette always tells you whether you're applying the color to the selected object's line, or fill, or to both line and fill. You can select the line or fill by clicking on the icon for the line or fill, or you can select both line and fill by holding down Shift and clicking on the line and fill icons until the pop-up menu shows "Both." You can also choose "Line," "Fill," or "Both" from the pop-up menu (see Figure 6-9).

FIGURE 6-9
Selecting lines,
fills, or both

Whether you're applying a color to a fill or a line (or both) depends on what's showing in the Colors palette.

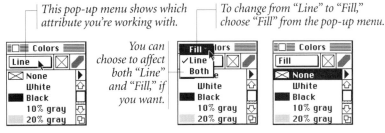

This pop-up menu shows which attribute you're working with.

You can choose to affect both "Line" and "Fill," if you want.

To change from "Line" to "Fill," choose "Fill" from the pop-up menu.

You can also click the Line and Fill icons.

Fill icon

Line icon

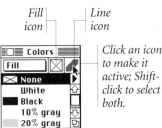

Click an icon to make it active; Shift-click to select both.

To apply a color, select an object…

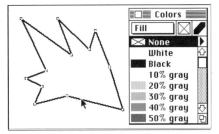

…and click the color in the Colors palette.

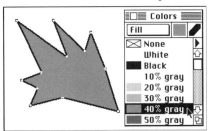

Changing the Order of the Colors in the Colors Palette

To change the order in which colors appear in the Colors palette, point at a color name in the Colors palette, and then drag the color name up or down in the Colors palette. Once you've got the color where you want it, release the mouse button (see Figure 6-10). This can be handy when you've got a long list of colors and want to position the most-used colors near the top of the palette.

FIGURE 6-10
Moving colors inside the Colors palette

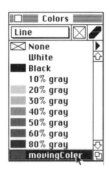 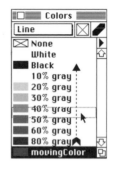 

Applying Colors to Groups

You can apply a color to all of the lines or fills inside a group. There are some odd wrinkles to this.

- Objects inside the group with any basic fill or a fill of "None" will be filled with a basic fill of the color you apply.

- Patterned fills are colored with the color you apply, but remain patterned fills (you shouldn't be using these anyway, as explained in "Fills" in Chapter 2, "Drawing").

- Graduated and radial fills change so that the color you've applied to the group is their starting color.

- Tiled and PostScript fills are unaffected.

You can still subselect objects inside the group and change their color and fill specifications, regardless of any color you've applied to the group.

Applying Colors to Imported Graphics

FreeHand separates imported EPS graphics according to the color definitions inside the EPS, so applying a color to an EPS image has no effect.

You can apply colors to paint-type graphics, bilevel TIFFs, and gray-scale TIFFs. FreeHand will remap the gray levels inside the image based on the color you apply, and separate the image when you print. Applying a color to a color TIFF has no effect on the way that TIFF is separated by FreeHand.

Creating Duotones

Contrary to what you may have heard elsewhere, a single gray-scale TIFF with two process colors applied to it does not a duotone make. It doesn't even make a "fake" duotone—which you create by printing a gray-scale image on top of a tint of some color.

The trouble is, I haven't found two people who agree on what a real duotone is. Some people change the screen frequency of the image for one color. Some people enhance the highlights in the image that prints on the overlay for the more dominant color and enhance the shadows in the image that prints on the overlay for the subordinate color. Some people do both. And so on.

Inside this book, I'm the absolute dictator (Right, Steve? *Right, Ole*), and I say that a duotone is created by printing two slightly different TIFFs on top of each other. The TIFF for the more dominant color in the color scheme has had its shadows enhanced; the TIFF for the subordinate color has had its highlights enhanced. By "enhanced," I mean that the darkest 5 percent (or so) of the pixels in the image become black and that the lightest 5 percent become white. The darkest—or lightest—areas in the image seem to spread out slightly.

The screen frequencies and screen angles are the same for the two TIFFs. Here's how to do it (see Figure 6-11 and Color Figure 4).

1. Open your original gray-scale TIFF with PrePrint (or Photoshop, or Color Studio).

2. Enhance the shadows in the image. In PrePrint, you'd choose "Shadows" from the Enhance submenu on the Image menu (in other programs, you'd change the map of the lowest gray levels so that more of them became black). Save this version of the TIFF under a different name.

3. Open the original gray-scale TIFF again. Enhance the highlights in the image. In PrePrint, you'd choose "Highlights" from the Enhance submenu on the Image menu (in other programs, you'd change the map of the highest gray levels so that more of them became white).

FIGURE 6-11

Creating duotones

Create two copies of the image using Aldus PrePrint or Adobe Photoshop. Enhance the shadows in one image, and enhance the highlights in the other.

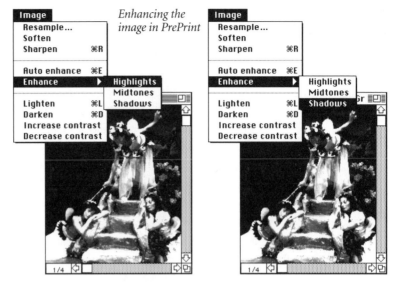

Enhancing the image in PrePrint

Place the two images on top of each other in FreeHand, color them different colors, and print them so that they overprint each other.

4. Place the two TIFFs into your FreeHand publication, making sure that one is exactly on top of the other. Color the one with its shadows enhanced with the dominant color you intend to use to create the duotone. Color the TIFF with enhanced highlights with the subordinate color you intend to use to create the duotone.

5. When you print the publication, print the ink colors you've applied to the TIFFs one color at a time, starting with the color of whichever TIFF is on top. Once that overlay's printed, bring the other TIFF to the top of the stack (remember that you can Control-click through the stacked objects to select it) and print the other color used to create the duotone. When plates are made from the two overlays, the TIFFs will overprint each other, producing a real duotone.

Why couldn't you just stack up the TIFFs and use ink-level overprinting commands to make them overprint? You can, if you modify your copy of FreeHand as instructed in "Overprinting TIFFs" in Chapter 8, "PostScript." To see what this effect looks like, see Color Figure 5 in the color pages in this chapter.

Removing Colors

To remove a color, select the color name in the Colors palette and choose "Remove" from the submenu attached to the Colors palette. If there are other colors in the publication based on the selected color (tints, mostly), or if there are objects with that color applied to them, FreeHand complains that that color is in use somewhere in the publication and cannot be removed. Locate the objects or colors containing the color you want to remove and (for objects) change their colors or (for tints) remove them.

This is something of a bother. FreeHand should make it easier to merge or change all of one color to another color. Until that feature's added, it's something you've got to be aware of, and plan for.

Copying Colors

If you need to copy a color or set of colors from another FreeHand publication into the current publication, just open the source publication, select some objects with those colors applied, copy them out of the source publication and into the target publication. Remember FreeHand's "home team wins" rule—any colors in the target publication with names the same as those of the incoming colors override the incoming color definitions.

Creating Tint Builds

When you're working with spot color publications, you often want to create tint builds (also known as stacked screens) of the colors you're working with to broaden the range of colors in your publication. Since you can't create a color containing percentages of two or more spot colors (20 percent black and 60 percent PMS 327, for example), it'd seem, at first glance, that you're stuck. You're not, though, as the following exercise demonstrates.

1. Open a new publication and create a spot color. If one doesn't already exist, create a 20 percent tint of black.

2. Draw a rectangle.

3. Without deselecting the rectangle, fill it with the spot color you created in Step 1 and choose "Remove line" from the Attributes menu.

4. Clone the rectangle by pressing Command-=.

5. Fill the clone with the 20 percent tint of black.

6. Press Command-E to display the Fill and line dialog box. Click the Overprint check box on the Fill side of the dialog box to make the tinted rectangle overprint.

That's all there is to it. When you print, the gray rectangle overprints the spot color rectangle, creating a combination of the two spot colors. The next section shows another, more flexible, means to this same end.

Using Blending to Create Process Color Tint Builds

Here's a trick I use to create a palette of tint builds for my publications (see Figure 6-12).

1. Draw a rectangle, fill it with 100 percent of cyan, magenta, or yellow, and choose "Remove line" from the Attributes menu.

2. Clone the rectangle, move it away from the original rectangle, and fill it with 100 percent black.

3. Select both rectangles, press Command-U to ungroup them, and select a blend reference point on each rectangle. Choose "Blend" from the Element menu. The Blend dialog box appears. Type the number of tint builds you'd like to create in the Number of steps text edit box and press Return to blend the two objects. FreeHand creates a blend between the two objects, filling each intermediate blend object with a tint. These new colors do not appear in your Colors palette.

4. Ungroup the blended objects.

5. Select an object filled with one of the colors you want and press Command-E to display the Fill and line dialog box.

FIGURE 6-12

Creating a palette
of tint builds

Draw a rectangle and
fill it with 100 percent
black. Ungroup the
rectangle.

Clone the rectangle
and drag the clone
away from the
original rectangle.
Color the clone 100
percent of some
process color.

Blend the rectangles.

Ungroup the blended
objects (press
Command-U twice)
and select a rectangle
that's colored a color
you like.

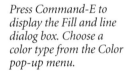

Press Command-E to
display the Fill and line
dialog box. Choose a
color type from the Color
pop-up menu.

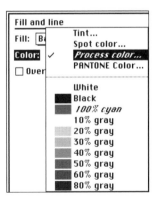

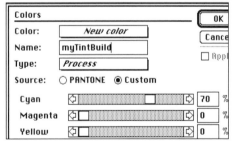

The Colors dialog box appears. Type a name for
your color and press Return twice to close both
dialog boxes.

FreeHand adds your color
to the Colors palette. Now
you can apply it to any
other object in your
publication.

6. In the Fill section of the Fill and line dialog box, a swatch the color of the object you've selected appears in the Color pop-up menu. Choose "Process color" from the Color pop-up menu. The Colors dialog box appears, filled in with the specifications for the color applied to the selected blend object.

7. Type a name for your color and press Return twice to close the Colors and Fill and line dialog boxes. The new color appears in your Colors palette.

8. Repeat Steps 5 through 7 until you've defined all of the colors you want.

Substituting Process Colors for Spot Colors

Blending's a great way to create a set of tint builds, but you can't blend one spot color into another, even if one of the two colors is Black. This makes it tough to quickly create a set of tint builds in FreeHand. What to do? Substitute process colors for your spot colors. But what if you want to see something like the spot color you're working with on screen, instead of looking at cyan, magenta, or yellow?

The following procedure shows you how to change the on-screen display of a process color to match that of a spot color.

1. Choose a Pantone color in the Colors dialog box.

2. Click the Custom button to convert the Pantone color into an editable color.

3. Click the RGB button.

4. Write down the Red, Green, and Blue percentages for your spot color. Multiply each percentage by 65535 and write the numbers down. Close the dialog box.

   Example PMS 299 CV = r15 g56 b75 or r9830.25 g36699.6 b49151.25

5. Choose "Preferences…" from the File menu. The Preferences dialog box appears.

6. Click the Colors… button. The Display color setup dialog box appears.

7. Click the swatch of process color you're using to substitute for your spot color. The Apple Color picker dialog box appears.

8. Type the numbers you derived in the Red, Green, and Blue text edit boxes and press Return three times to close all of the dialog boxes.

Your process color now matches (or comes close to matching) your spot color.

When you change the color display options via the Preferences dialog box, the changes remain in effect until you change them again. They're not stored in the individual publications. This means you'll have to change the color display options again when you want to display a normal process color publication. You can make a QuicKey to reset your color display options. Create a QuicKey sequence containing the QuicKeys shown in Table 6-1.

	QuicKey type	QuicKey contents	What it does
TABLE 6-1 Reset color display to normal QuicKey	Menu/DA	"Preferences…"	Selects "Preferences…" from the File menu.
	Button	Colors…	Clicks the Colors… button in the Preferences dialog box.
	Click	120, 54*	Clicks the Cyan color swatch in the Display color setup dialog box.
	Text	ΔΔΔ0Δ65535Δ65535**	Enters the correct (in my opinion; you might want to enter something else) values for screen display of cyan.
	Literal	Enter	Closes the Color picker dialog box.
	Click	37, 202*	Clicks the Magenta color swatch in the Display color setup dialog box.

	QuicKey type	QuicKey contents	What it does
TABLE 6-1 *Continued*	Text	ΔΔΔ65535Δ0Δ65535**	Enters the correct values for screen display of magenta.
	Literal	Enter	Closes the Color picker dialog box.
	Click	204, 201*	Clicks the Yellow color swatch in the Display color setup dialog box.
	Text	ΔΔΔ65535Δ0Δ65535**	Enters the correct values for screen display of yellow.
	Literal	Enter	Closes the Color picker dialog box.
	Literal	Enter	Closes the Display color setup dialog box.
	Literal	Enter	Closes the Preferences dialog box.

* These coordinates might be slightly different on your system. You'll have to create these QuicKeys outside of the Sequence and then import them, because you can't create clicks inside sequences. Open the Display color setup dialog box, invoke QuicKeys, choose "Clicks" from the Define menu, and click on the cyan, magenta, and yellow color swatches.

** Δ indicates a tab in the QuicKeys Text dialog box. Where you see a Δ, just press Tab.

Now that you've got on-screen correspondence, you can create stacked screens to your heart's content using individual process colors as substitutes for individual spot colors.

Trapping

A trap is a method of overlapping abutting colored objects to compensate for the imperfect registration of printing presses. Because registration, even on good presses with good operators, can be off by as much as .5 point, abutting elements in your publication may not end up abutting perfectly when the publication is printed by your commercial printer. What happens then? The paper stock shows through where you don't want it to show through (see Figure 6-13).

FIGURE 6-13
Why you need to trap

Color 1
Color 2

When you don't trap, you can end up with paper showing through where it shouldn't.

When you trap, you enlarge (or shrink) the objects so that they'll overlap a little bit when they print—regardless of the paper stretching or shifting on the press.

Do I need to tell you what happens if you take your work to a less skilled printer? Or to a press that's badly out of register or run by turkeys? Disaster. Also, some printing processes, notably silk-screening, require larger traps than others. In any case, talk with your commercial printer regarding the tolerances of their presses and/or operators.

If you've been using FreeHand to produce artwork containing spot or process colors, you've probably encountered publications containing elements that need trapping.

FreeHand 3 has four approaches to trapping, which can be used in combination.

- Object-level overprinting, which you specify in the Info dialog box for each object.

- Ink-level overprinting, which you specify in the Print options dialog box.

- Automatic trapping via the Spread size option in the Print options dialog box.

- Manual trapping via the Fill and line dialog box (for paths) and the Fill and stroke dialog box (for text), combined with "Paste inside."

Object-level Overprinting

The key to trapping, in FreeHand and elsewhere, is in controlling what objects—or what parts of objects—print on top of other objects as the printing press prints your publication. While choosing to overprint entire inks can be handy (especially overprinting black), you really need to control the overprinting characteristics of individual objects to make trapping work (see Color Figure 1).

Luckily, you can. Any object you create in FreeHand can be specified as an overprinting object (that is, it won't knock a hole in any objects behind it when you print), regardless of the object's color. The controls for object-level overprinting are found in different places for different types of objects (see Figure 6-14).

FIGURE 6-14
Object-level
overprinting controls

The Overprint settings for fills and lines are in the Fill and line dialog box. Check these, and your fills and lines will print over anything that's behind them.

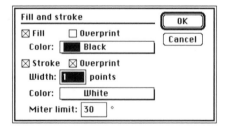

For text, the overprinting settings are found in the Fill and stroke dialog box (open the Type specifications dialog box and choose "Fill and stroke..." from the Effects menu).

Ink-level Overprinting

In FreeHand's Print options dialog box, you can choose to overprint an entire ink color (see Figure 6-15). While this can be useful in some limited circumstances, most of your trapping will, of necessity, apply to individual objects.

FIGURE 6-15

Ink-level overprinting

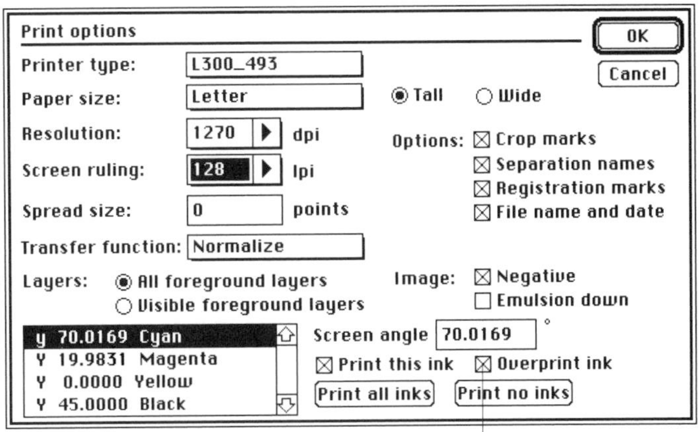

```
┌─────────────────────────────────────────────────────────────┐
│ Print options ──────────────────────────────────┐  ┌──────┐ │
│                                                     │  OK  │ │
│ Printer type:    L300_493                           └──────┘ │
│                                                   ┌────────┐ │
│ Paper size:      Letter          ● Tall  ○ Wide   │ Cancel │ │
│                                                   └────────┘ │
│ Resolution:      1270  ▶  dpi    Options: ⊠ Crop marks      │
│                                           ⊠ Separation names │
│ Screen ruling:   128   ▶  lpi             ⊠ Registration marks│
│                                           ⊠ File name and date│
│ Spread size:     0       points                              │
│                                                              │
│ Transfer function: Normalize                                 │
│                                                              │
│ Layers:  ● All foreground layers    Image:  ⊠ Negative       │
│          ○ Visible foreground layers        □ Emulsion down  │
│  ┌──────────────────────────────┬─┐                          │
│  │ y 70.0169  Cyan              │⬆│  Screen angle 70.0169  ° │
│  │ Y 19.9831  Magenta           ├─┤                          │
│  │ Y 0.0000   Yellow            │ │  ⊠ Print this ink ⊠ Overprint ink│
│  │ Y 45.0000  Black             ├─┤  ┌────────────┐ ┌──────────────┐│
│  └──────────────────────────────┴─┘  │Print all inks│ │Print no inks││
│                                       └────────────┘ └──────────────┘│
└─────────────────────────────────────────────────────────────┘
```

Select an ink from the ink list
and check "Overprint."

Automatic Trapping

FreeHand 3 improves on FreeHand 2's trapping by offering the Spread size option in the Print options dialog box. The value that you enter in this text edit field will be applied to all FreeHand-drawn objects with simple fills or lines in your publication. It won't, however, apply to the following FreeHand objects.

- Objects with custom PostScript lines and fills

- Objects with graduated, tiled, or radial fills

- Text

FreeHand's automatic trapping spreads the overlapping object entirely over the object beneath, even if only part of the object overlaps a background object.

Automatic trapping specified in FreeHand using the Spread size setting is included in EPS files you export for use in other page-layout software. EPS files exported from FreeHand and placed in FreeHand publications are affected by the current publication's Spread size setting. Basic fills inside placed EPS graphics from other applications are not affected by the value you enter in the Spread size text edit box.

Unless you're doing very simple illustrations, I urge you to do all your trapping yourself, and leave a zero in the Spread size text edit box. Another way to approach it is to do all the trapping for everything other than basic elements, then enter something in this text edit box to take care of trapping the basic elements.

Manual Trapping

The key to trapping in FreeHand lies in the Fill and line dialog box for nontext elements, and in the Fill and stroke dialog box for text. These controls, plus FreeHand's Paste inside command, provide incredible manual trapping flexibility.

When you're working with FreeHand's trapping features, you'll be creating *spreads* (outlines of objects, in the same color as the object, that are slightly larger than the object itself) and *chokes* (outlines of the object that are the same color as the underlying object's color). Spreads make the object larger so that the edges of the object print over the underlying object; chokes make the area knocked out of the underlying object smaller than the outline of the foreground object.

In general, you use chokes when the foreground object is a darker color than the background object, and you use spreads when the color of the foreground object is lighter. In other words, trap from light colors into darker colors. Sound subjective? It is. I tend to use chokes, especially when I'm trapping type, because I feel they're less likely to give the impression that the shape of the foreground object has been distorted.

Spot Color Trapping

In most cases, it's more important to trap abutting color fields in spot color publications than it is in process color publications. Why? Because when you're working with process colors, you've almost always got some kind of dot between objects (cyan, magenta, yellow, or black), so you're less likely to see the tell-tale lines showing a poor trap (see Figure 6-16).

FIGURE 6-16
Spot color trapping and
process color trapping

In process color trapping, there's almost always some color value—dots—on one of the other plates...

...while in spot color trapping, there's usually not.

The easiest way to demonstrate how spot color trapping works is to show you some examples. As you work through these examples, you'll trap an ellipse into a rectangle by manipulating the color, width, and overprinting specifications of the path that surrounds the ellipse. First, draw the colored objects.

1. Create a rectangle. Fill the rectangle with a spot color (in these instructions, I'll call this color "Color 1") and choose "Remove line" from the Attributes menu.

2. Draw an ellipse on top of the rectangle. Make sure that the ellipse is entirely inside the rectangle. Fill the ellipse with a different color from that of the rectangle (I'll call this color "Color 2") and choose "Remove line" from the Attributes menu.

3. Save the file.

The ellipse needs to be trapped, or you'll run the risk of having paper-colored lines showing up around the ellipse when the publication is printed. You can either spread or choke the ellipse, or both.

To spread the ellipse, follow these steps (see Color Figure 3).

1. Select the ellipse.

2. Press Command-E to display the Fill and line dialog box.

3. In the Fill and line dialog box, choose Basic from the Line pop-up menu, set the line color to Color 2 (the color of the ellipse), choose a line weight for your trap from the Weight pop-up menu (or type the weight you want in the Weight text edit box). Finally, check the Overprint check box (on the "line" side of the dialog box) and press Return (or click OK).

The line weight you enter in the Weight text edit box should be equal to twice the trap amount—if you enter 2, you'll get a stroke of 1 point on either side of the path defining the ellipse, because PostScript lines grow out from the line's center. If your commercial printer has asked you for a trap of .5 points, enter 1 in the Weight text edit box.

When you print, the ellipse is larger than the hole that's knocked out of the background rectangle, which means that the outside of the ellipse slightly overprints the background rectangle. You've just created a spread.

After you're through looking at the objects, or printing, choose "Revert" from the File menu and revert to the version of the file you saved earlier. This way, you're ready for the next procedure.

To choke the ellipse, follow these steps.

1. Select the ellipse.

2. Press Command-E to display the Fill and line dialog box.

3. In the Fill and line dialog box, choose "Basic" from the Line pop-up menu, set the line color to Color 1 (the color of the background rectangle), choose a line weight for your trap from the Weight pop-up menu (or type the weight you want in the Weight text edit box). Finally, check the Overprint check box (on the line section of the dialog box) and press Return (or click OK).

When you print, the hole that's knocked out of the background rectangle is slightly smaller than the ellipse. This way, the outside of the ellipse slightly overprints the background rectangle. You've just created a choke.

Choose "Revert" from the File menu again to get the file ready for the next procedure.

To both spread and choke the ellipse, follow these steps.

1. Select the ellipse and press Command-= to clone the ellipse.

2. Press Command-E to display the Fill and line dialog box.

3. In the Fill and line dialog box, choose "Basic" from the Line pop-up menu, set the line color to Color 2 (the color of the ellipse), choose a line weight for your trap from the Weight pop-up menu (or type the weight you want in the Weight text edit box). Finally, check the Overprint check box (on the line section of the dialog box) and press Return (or click OK).

4. Press Command-B to send the ellipse to the back. Press Tab to deselect the ellipse.

5. Select the ellipse that's on top of the rectangle and press Command-E to bring up the Fill and line dialog box.

6. In the Fill and line dialog box, choose "None" from the Fill pop-up menu, choose "Basic" from the Line pop-up menu, set the line color to Color 1 (the color of the background rectangle), choose a line weight for your trap from the Weight pop-up menu (or type the weight you want in the Weight text edit box). Finally, check the Overprint check box for the line and press Return (or click OK).

7. Select the background rectangle and press Command-B to send it to the back.

The ellipse prints a little bit larger than it appears on screen, and the hole that's knocked out of the background rectangle is smaller than the ellipse so that the outside of the ellipse overprints the background rectangle. There aren't, actually, too many cases where you'll want to use both a spread and a choke, but this is how you do it.

Choose "Revert" from the File menu to get your demo file ready for the next example.

The techniques described above work well as long as you're working with objects that don't cross color boundaries. If the objects cross color boundaries (especially going from a color background to a white background), it's too obvious that you've changed the shapes of the objects. What do you do?

1. Drag the ellipse so that it's partially outside of the rectangle.

2. Clone the ellipse by pressing Command-=.

3. Without deselecting the cloned ellipse, press Command-E to display the Fill and line dialog box.

4. In the Fill and line dialog box, choose "Basic" from the Line pop-up menu, set the line color to Color 1 (the color of the background rectangle), choose a line weight for your trap from the Weight pop-up menu (or type the weight you want in the Weight text edit box). Finally, check the Overprint check box (on the line section of the dialog box) and press Return (or click OK).

5. Press Command-X to cut the ellipse to the Clipboard.

6. Select the background rectangle and choose "Paste inside" from the Edit menu.

7. Select the original ellipse and press Command-B to send it to the back.

At this point, the ellipse you pasted inside the rectangle spreads slightly, while the part of the ellipse outside of the rectangle remains the same size and shape (see Color Figure 3).

Choose "Revert" from the File menu to get ready for the next trapping example.

What happens if the object you need to trap overlaps more than one other, differently colored object? In this case, you can run into trouble. The trap you use for one background color might not be the trap you want to use for the other. You might want to spread one and choke the other, depending on the colors you're using.

In these cases, you use the same basic techniques described above for all of the overlapping objects. Try it (see Color Figure 3).

1. Draw another new rectangle (I'll call it "Rectangle 2") so that it partially overlaps the original rectangle (which I'll call "Rectangle 1"). Create a third spot color ("Color 3") and apply it to the rectangle's fill. Choose "Remove line" from the Attributes menu. Drag the ellipse so that it partially overlaps both rectangles.

2. Select Rectangle 2 and press Command-= to clone it. Without deselecting the clone, press Command-E to display the Fill and line dialog box.

3. In the Fill and line dialog box, choose "Basic" from the Line pop-up menu, set the line color to Color 1 (the color of the background rectangle), choose a line weight for your trap from the Weight pop-up menu (or type the weight you want in the Weight text edit box). Finally, check the Overprint check box for the line and press Return (or click OK).

4. Select the ellipse and repeat Step 3. Select both of the clones you've just created and press Command-X to cut them to the Clipboard. Make sure that the clone of the ellipse is in front of the clone of the rectangle.

5. Select Rectangle 1 and choose "Paste inside" from the Edit menu. You've just created chokes for the ellipse and Rectangle 2 at the points they overlap Rectangle 1.

6. Select the Ellipse and press Command-= to clone it. Change the stroke of the cloned ellipse as directed in Step 3. Press Command-X to cut the new clone to the Clipboard. Select Rectangle 2 and choose "Paste inside" from the Edit menu. The ellipse is now choked at the points it overlaps Rectangle 2.

Trapping Lines

The trapping techniques above work well for filled paths, but what about lines? After all, you can't apply two different line properties to a single line. Instead, you clone the line and make the width of the cloned line larger or smaller to achieve the spread or choke you want. One of the lines overprints; the other line knocks out. Follow these steps to spread a line (see Color Figure 2).

1. Draw a rectangle. Create a spot color and fill the rectangle with it.

2. Draw a line inside the rectangle. Create another spot color and apply it to the line. Do not set this line to overprint.

3. Select the line and press Command-= to clone the line.

4. Press Command-E to display the Fill and line dialog box. Increase the width of the line by twice the amount of spread you need (remember, PostScript lines grow out from their centers) and set the line to overprint.

That's all there is to it. The original line knocks a hole in the background rectangle, and the clone of the line spreads to just a little bit beyond the edges of the knockout.

If you need to choke the line, follow these steps (see Color Figure 2).

1. Draw a rectangle. Create a spot color and fill the rectangle with it.

2. Draw a line inside the rectangle. Create another spot color and apply it to the line. Set this line to overprint.

3. Select the line and press Command-= to clone the line.

4. Press Command-E to display the Fill and line dialog box. Decrease the width of the line by twice the amount of choke you need. Do not set the line to overprint.

5. Hold down Control and select the original line. Press Command-F to bring it to the front.

This time, the cloned line is narrower than the original line, and knocks out an area that's slightly smaller than the original line, creating a choke.

If the line you need to trap crosses a color boundary, follow the same steps described above for trapping paths: clone the line, edit the line, cut the line, select the background object, choose "Paste inside," and send the original line to the back.

Trapping Text   Text is probably the trickiest FreeHand element to trap, and it's usually the element that needs trapping the most. For whatever reason, it's easier to notice poor trapping around text than around other elements. At the same time, traps that are too large distort the shapes of the characters you're trapping.

Trapping text works a little bit differently from trapping objects. There's no Fill and line dialog box for text. Instead, you use "Fill and stroke" from the Effect pop-up menu in the Type specifications dialog box and set up your traps in the Fill and stroke dialog box. Here's how to create a spread for text (see Color Figure 3).

1. Draw a rectangle, create a spot color ("Color 1"), and apply it to the rectangle.

2. Type a text block. Create a second spot color ("Color 2") and apply it to the text block. Position the text block on top of the rectangle so that it's entirely within the area occupied by the rectangle.

3. Press Command-T to bring up the Type specifications dialog box for the text block. Choose "Fill and stroke" from the Text effects pop-up menu. Set the color of the text to Color 2, and then set the stroke to Color 2. Set the line width of the stroke to twice the amount of spread you need, and set the stroke to over-

print by checking the Overprint check box. Do not set the fill to overprint. Press Return twice to close the dialog boxes.

The next example shows how to choke text by making the shape the characters knock out of the background a little bit smaller than the characters themselves.

1. Draw a rectangle, create a spot color ("Color 1"), and apply it to the rectangle.

2. Type a text block. Create a second spot color ("Color 2") and apply it to the text block. Position the text block on top of the rectangle so that it's entirely within the area occupied by the rectangle.

3. Press Command-T to bring up the Type specifications dialog box for the text block. Choose "Fill and stroke" from the Text effects pop-up menu. Set the color of the text to Color 2, and then set the stroke to Color 1. Set the line width of the stroke to twice the amount of spread you need, and set the stroke to overprint by checking the Overprint check box. Do not set the fill to overprint. Press Return twice to close both dialog boxes.

If text crosses color boundaries, use the techniques described earlier for trapping overlapping paths.

Tip:
Type and
Black Ink

Type that's specified as 100 percent black always overprints, regardless of the settings you've made in the Fill and stroke dialog box or in the ink list in the Print options dialog box. You probably want 100 percent black text to overprint most of the time, but what if you don't? Create a color that's specified as 99 percent black, and apply it to the text you want to knock out of whatever is behind it. 99 percent black works just like every other color, and it can be set to knock out or overprint as you want, and it'll look just like 100 percent black.

**Advanced Spot
Color Trapping**

All of the trapping techniques demonstrated above assume that you're working with solid (that is, 100 percent) spot colors. What happens when you're working with tints of spot colors, and what happens when you're working with graduated or radial fills?

When you're working with tints, you simply use the above procedures, substituting the tints for the colors specified for the overprinting strokes that create your traps. When you're trapping graduated and radial fills, on the other hand, things get complex.

Trapping Spot Color Graduated Fills

When graduated fills abut in your spot color publications, you need to provide for some sort of trapping between the two fills, or you'll end up with your paper color showing through between the fills. The simplest thing to do is to set one or both spot colors to overprint, and then overlap the graduated fills by some small amount (something less than 1 point).

If you can't, or don't want to, overprint the spot colors you've used in your graduated fills, life gets harder. You'll have to create a pair of blends—one in each spot color—that mimic your graduated fills and position them where the graduated fills abut. Why create blends? Remember that each intermediate object in a blend is a solid color, or tint, and can be set to overprint.

Once again, I'll show you how to do this by leading you thorough a series of steps. You'll probably run into more complex examples of abutting graduated fills than the one shown in this example, but you can use these techniques for all situations in which spot color graduated fills abut (see Color Figure 4).

1. Draw two abutting rectangles.

2. Create two spot colors ("Color 1" and "Color 2").

3. Fill one of the rectangles with a graduated fill going from Color 1 to white. Fill the other rectangle with a graduated fill going from white to Color 2.

Next, you'll set up the objects for the blend.

1. Create two squares that are the width of the trap you want to use. Position one rectangle at either end of the point where the two graduated fills abut.

2. Fill one of the squares with Color 1, and fill the other one with a 0 percent tint of Color 1.

3. Set both squares to overprint using the Fill and line dialog box.

4. Select the same point on each of the small squares you've just created. It's probably easier to do this in Keyline view. If you can't select a point, ungroup the squares and try again.

5. Choose "Blend" from the Element menu. The Blend dialog box appears. Type some number in the Number of steps text edit field and press Return (or click OK) to close the dialog box. Does the blend fill the distance from one of the objects to the other without any gaps? If not, return to the Blend dialog box, increase the number of blend steps, and press Return to close the dialog box and apply the new blend. Keep increasing the number of steps until there are no gaps in the blend.

6. Clone the original squares. Repeat the process substituting Color 2 for Color 1 in the blend.

When you print, the blended objects print over the area where the graduated fills abut, spreading the two graduations into each other. This technique brings up a point—if you can trap blends, and can't trap graduated fills, why not just use blends for all of the graduated fills you need to trap? Why not, indeed. See "The Golden Rules" in Chapter 7, "Printing," for more on why you should use blends instead of graduated fills.

Trapping Spot Color Radial Fills

After all of the trouble we had to go through to create a trap for adjacent spot color graduated fills, you'd think radial fills using spot colors would be more difficult. Luckily, that's not the case all of the time. When you create a radial fill inside an object, you can simply add an overprinting stroke to the object containing the radial fill that's the color of the background object, thereby creating a choke.

Where things get ugly is in those cases where two radial fills abut each other. When that happens, try this trick.

1. Select one of the objects containing a radial fill and clone it.

2. Set the fill of the clone to "None," and stroke it with a 1-point line that's the color of the outermost value of the radial fill (if you went from White to Color 1, as we did in our example, you'd set the line's color to Color 1). Set the line to overprint.

3. Select the other object containing a radial fill and clone it.

4. Set the fill of the clone to "None," and stroke it with a 1-point line that's the color of the outermost value of the radial fill (if you went from White to Color 2, as we did in our example, you'd set the line's color to Color 2). Set the line to overprint.

5. Cut the clone of the second object.

6. Select the first object you created and choose "Paste inside" from the Edit menu.

7. Select the object you created in Step 2 and cut it to the Clipboard.

8. Select the second object and choose "Paste inside" from the Edit menu.

Process Color Trapping

Process color trapping is a bit simpler than spot color trapping, because it's usually less critical that process-colored elements have traps, but it can be far harder to figure out exactly what color to make the stroke for a process-colored object. And when you're talking about trapping two process-colored graduated fills, watch out!

Simple Process Color Trapping

In process color trapping, you've got to make your overprinting strokes different colors from either the background or foreground objects. Why? Because process colors have a way of creating new colors when you print them over each other. It's what they do best.

As in the spot color trapping section above, I'll demonstrate process color trapping techniques by example. First, create a couple of objects.

1. Create a rectangle that's filled with Color 1, which is specified as 20C 100M 0Y 10K.

2. On top of this rectangle, draw an ellipse and fill it with Color 2, which is specified as 0C 100M 50Y 0K.

3. Select both objects and choose "Remove line" from the Attributes menu.

4. Save the file.

COLOR FIGURE 1
Overprinting

Objects colored with spot color 1 not set to overprint

Spot color 1 overlay

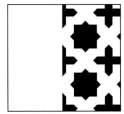

Spot color 2 overlay

Color 1 knocks out color 2

Objects colored with spot color 1 set to overprint

Spot color 1 overlay

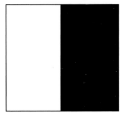

Spot color 2 overlay

Color 1 prints over color 2

COLOR FIGURE 2
Trapping a line

This line needs to be trapped.

To create a spread, clone the line, and then increase the width of the cloned line. Set the cloned line to overprint.

The thinner line knocks out objects behind it.

The thicker line overprints objects behind it.

To create a choke, clone the line, and then decrease the width of the cloned line. Set the original line to overprint.

Trapped line

The cloned line knocks out the background objects, while the original line overprints.

COLOR FIGURE 3
Trapping fills
and text

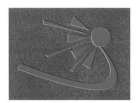

Unless I've been very lucky, you'll see the paper showing through around the blue shape in this example. To prevent the paper from showing, trap the object.

Select the object you want to trap and press Command-E to display the Fill and line dialog box. There, add a line to the object by choosing "Basic" from the Line pop-up menu.

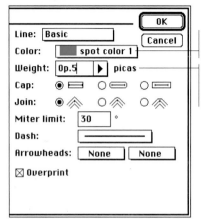

Make the line the same color as the fill.

Enter a value in the Weight text edit box that's twice the spread you want.

When you print, the outline of the shape overprints the background, creating a trap.

UTOPIA

Again, unless I've been lucky, you'll see the paper showing through around these characters. That means that this text needs to be trapped.

Check "Overprint."

Enter a number that's twice the amount of spread you want.

Select the text, then press Command-T to display the Type specifications dialog box. Choose "Fill and stroke" from the Effect menu. Give the text an overprinting stroke that's the same color as the text to spread the text.

UTOPIA

The stroke overprints the background objects, creating a spread. Once again, unless I've been very unlucky, you won't see the paper showing around the edges of these characters.

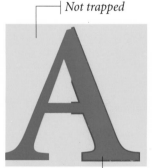

Not trapped

Trapped (trap exaggerated to illustrate point)

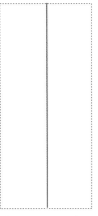

When two graduated fills abut, you run the risk of having the paper show through between the fills.

Create a new shape that's twice the width of the trap you want. Position it where the two fills abut, and fill it with a graduated fill based on both of the graduated fills of the original objects. When you print, the new fill traps the graduated fills.

A "fake" duotone created by printing an image over a colored background

A duotone created by printing two slightly different versions of the same image, one on top of the other. I enhanced the shadows in the black image; the highlights in the blue image.

COLOR FIGURE 6

Separating
color images

*Color TIFF placed in
FreeHand and
separated by
FreeHand*

*Color TIFF separated
using Aldus PrePrint
1.5 (saved as a DCS
file, placed in
FreeHand, and
printed from
FreeHand)*

*Color TIFF separated
using Adobe
Photoshop 1.0.7
(saved as a DCS file,
placed in FreeHand,
and printed from
FreeHand)*

The ellipse needs to be trapped, or you run the risk of having cyan-colored lines showing up around the ellipse when the publication is printed—which could happen if the cyan and yellow plates slipped. Whether you spread or choke the ellipse depends on its color. If the ellipse is darker than the background rectangle, choke the ellipse. If the ellipse is a lighter color than the background rectangle, spread the ellipse. In this case, the ellipse is a lighter color, so you'll spread it. To spread the ellipse, follow these steps.

1. Create a new process color containing only those colors in Color 2 having higher values than Color 1. Quick quiz: what component colors in Color 2 have higher values than their counterparts in Color 1? If you said 50Y, you're the lucky winner. Specify a new process color as 0C 0M 50Y 0K.

2. Select the ellipse.

3. Press Command-E to display the Fill and line dialog box.

4. In the Fill and line dialog box, choose "Basic" from the Line pop-up menu.

5. Choose Color 3 from the Color pop-up menu.

6. Choose a line weight for your trap from the Weight pop-up menu (or type the weight you want in the Weight text edit box). It should be twice the width of your desired trap. Finally, check the Overprint check box in the line section of the dialog box and press Return (or click OK).

When you print, all of the areas around the ellipse have some dot value inside them, and the new colors created where the objects abut won't be too obvious.

Choose "Revert" from the File menu to get ready for the next example.

What if the ellipse were the darker color? If it were, we'd have to choke it. To choke the ellipse, follow these steps.

1. Select the ellipse and fill it with Color 1. Select the rectangle and fill it with Color 2.

2. Create a new color ("Color 3") that contains only the largest color component in Color 1. That's 100M, so Color 3 should be specified as 0C 100M 0Y 0K.

3. In the Fill and line dialog box, choose "Basic" from the Line pop-up menu, set the line color to Color 3, choose a line weight for your trap from the Weight pop-up menu (or type the weight you want in the Weight text edit box). Finally, check the Overprint check box in the line section of the dialog box and press Return (or click OK).

When you print, the stroke you applied to the ellipse guarantees that there's no gap around the ellipse, even if you run into registration problems when you print the publication.

Complex Process Color Trapping

What if the ellipse in the examples given above was not completely contained by the underlying rectangle? What if, in fact, only half of the ellipse passed into the rectangle?

You don't want to make the entire ellipse larger, so limit the spread and choke of the ellipse to the area inside the underlying rectangle by using the "Paste inside" techniques shown in the section on spot color trapping earlier in this chapter.

Advanced Process Color Trapping

Because you can place color TIFF images in FreeHand 3, you can run into some truly hairy trapping situations. What happens when you need to cut out part of a color TIFF and place it on a process color background? This isn't actually as scary as it sounds. Just follow the instructions in the section "Cropping TIFF Images" in Chapter 4, "Importing and Exporting," to construct a clipping path for the TIFF, and then stroke the path with an overprinting line that's the same color as the background colors. In this case, if the object passes over several color boundaries, avoid pasting both the TIFF and the path it contains into the underlying objects—it'll never print. Instead, clone the path, choose "Cut contents" from the Edit menu and delete the extra TIFF. Then fill the new object with White, stroke it with your overprinting line (choke), and paste it inside the underlying object. Then place the original clipped TIFF above the area you've just choked.

Trapping Process Color Graduated and Radial Fills

If you've gotten this far, call me the next time you're in Seattle and I'll buy you a beer at The Trolleyman. You've mastered the basic trapping techniques for spot and process colors, and you're ready to trap abutting process color graduated and radial fills.

Create an object which covers the area where two process color graduated fills abut and we fill this object with a graduated fill. The colors in this graduated fill are derived from the colors used in the abutting graduated fills underneath it. Once again, I'll demonstrate the technique by having you work through an example, and once again we'll start by creating some objects.

1. Create two side-by-side, abutting rectangles.

2. Fill one rectangle with a graduated fill that goes from Color 1 (25C 30M 0Y 20K) to Color 2 (70C 20M 0Y 0K) at 90 degrees. Fill the other rectangle with a graduated fill that goes from Color 3 (0C 80M 45Y 0K) to Color 4 (0C 20M 60Y 0K) at 270 degrees.

3. Select both rectangles and choose "Remove line" from the Attributes menu.

4. Draw a new rectangle over the abutting edges of the rectangles. Make the new rectangle the height of the existing rectangles, and make it twice as wide as the trapping amount you want. Center it horizontally over the line where the two rectangles abut.

5. Create two new process colors ("Color 5" and "Color 6"). Color 5 should contain the highest color components from Color 1 and Color 3 (the two colors at the tops of the original rectangles): 25C 80M 45Y 20K. Color 6 contains the largest color components from Color 2 and Color 4: 70C 20M 60Y 0K.

6. Fill the new rectangle with a new graduated fill going from Color 5 to Color 6 at 270 degrees.

It's harder to come up with a precise way to trap radial fills containing process colors, because, unless the object with the radial fill is a perfect circle and the center of the fill is in the center of the circle, it's hard to know what color is at the edge of the radial fill. And it's almost never the same color all the way around the outside of the path.

So here's the sleazy way. Stroke the radial fill with an overprinting line containing about 20 percent of the background color. This way, there are at least some dots in any out-of-register areas. If you come up with a better way to trap process color radial fills, please let me know.

Trapping: Who's on First

With all of these different trapping options available, you need to know which ones take precedence. It's pretty simple. Both "Spread size" and object-level overprinting settings override ink-level overprinting, and object-level overprinting settings override any "Spread size" you've specified. As you'd expect, the more specific, object-level commands take precedence over the more general, publication-level settings.

Tip: Blends and Trapping

Use blends, not FreeHand's Graduated and Radial fill commands, to create graduated or radial fills you need to trap. Heck, use them even when you don't need to trap (see "Using Blend to Create Graduated and Radial Fills" in Chapter 2, "Drawing" for the reasons why). You can't specify an object filled with a graduated or radial fill to overprint, but you can easily make such an adjustment to an individual, blended object.

Separating Color Images

FreeHand can separate color TIFFs you've placed, and can also separate DCS and EPS preseparated images. You can also place a color TIFF inside a FreeHand publication, export the page as an EPS graphic, and separate the EPS file using PrePrint. In my opinion, the fastest and best method is to use a color separation program such as Photoshop or PrePrint to create an EPS or DCS separation file and place the file in FreeHand.

The color separation programs have controls for correcting color images and for improving them for color separation and printing. FreeHand really has very few tools for working with the content of color images. Like none, now that I think of it.

Preseparating Color Images

If you want to separate your color images with Photoshop (or Color Studio, or PrePrint, or any other program capable of saving color separations in the EPS/DCS format) and then place the preseparated image in FreeHand, you can save the file as either a single EPS file or as DCS (five linked files). If you saved the image as a single EPS, place the entire EPS in FreeHand. If you saved the image as DCS, place the DCS header file (it's the one without a C, M, Y, or K extension on its file name). In either case, when you separate the image with FreeHand, the separations will be the same as if you'd printed the separations directly from Photoshop. You might like FreeHand's separations better, though. Take a look at the side-by-side FreeHand, Photoshop, and Pre-Print separations in the color section of this book (see Color Figure 6).

Which EPS preseparation method should you use? Saving the file as a single EPS makes a large EPS file, but saving as DCS creates five files you've got to look after. The four DCS separation files (the ones with C, M, Y, or K in their file names) have to be in the same folder as the DCS header file, or FreeHand won't be able to find them to print.

Color Me Gone

When you're working with color, take it easy. Always remember that you're at the mercy of a series of photochemical and mechanical processes—from your imagesetter through your commercial printer's press—that, in many ways, haven't changed since the turn of the century (if that recently). Temperature, humidity, and ambient static electricity play a large role, and the people who operate these systems are at least skilled craftspeople; at best, artists. Ask them as many questions as they'll answer, set your job up the way they want it, and then sit back and watch your job come off the press. If it's not perfect, there's always next time.

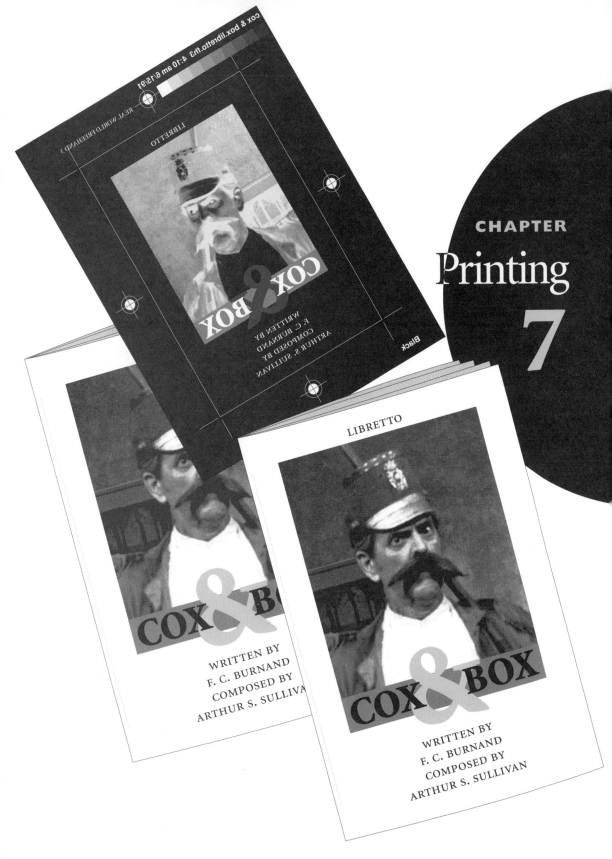

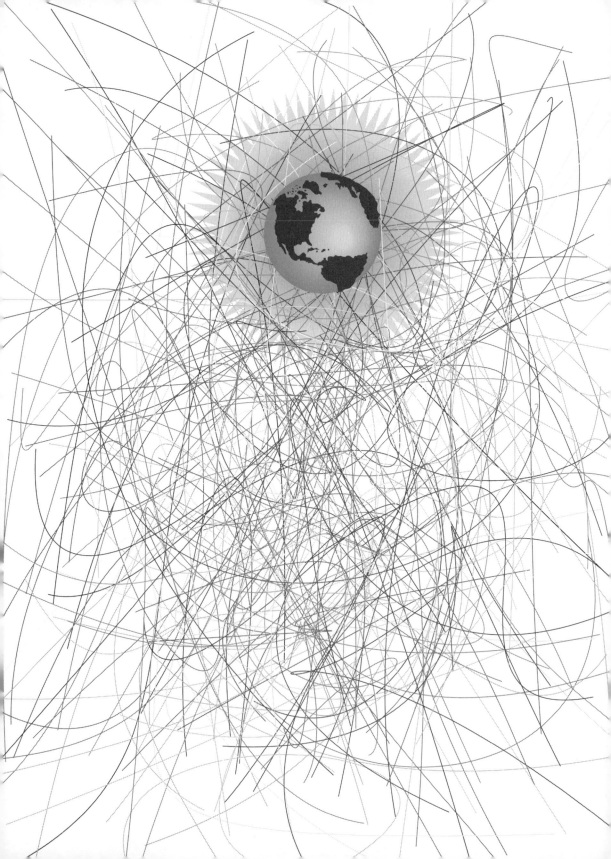

Clay.

Roll a carved cylinder of stone, or hardened clay, over a flat sheet of wet clay. The carvings on the cylinder are transferred—in reverse—to the surface of the clay. Once the clay hardens, the marks are there to stay.

The ancient Mesopotamians noticed this. They figured that by carving characters on the cylinders in reverse they could transfer them to the clay tablets. Roll the cylinders over several tablets, and you've made several copies of the symbols on the cylinders. They were a bureaucratic bunch, and covered their tablets with bills of lading, legal contracts, nondisclosure agreements, and other rules and regulations.

They invented printing.

We've improved on this process a little bit since then.

We found that, by smearing ink over the surface of the cylinder (or over the tablets, for that matter), we could transfer the images on the cylinder to that new stuff—the white sheets of beaten, bleached papyrus reeds the Egyptians made. It was easier to carry than the tablets.

Later, somebody came up with moveable type, and scribes the world over lamented the decline in the quality of written materials. The romance novel followed closely on the heels of this technological advance. Printing—the ability to make dozens, hundreds, thousands, millions of copies of the same image—flourished.

Printing, ultimately, is what FreeHand is all about. Everything you do in FreeHand is directed toward the production of a mechanical (whether an illustration or a publication) for printing. If you're using FreeHand to create on-screen (rather than printed) artwork, you might want to invest in some other (pixel-based) illustration program.

339

If you're a seasoned FreeHand 2 user, there are a few things about printing with the new version of FreeHand that you need to keep in mind as you print.

- FreeHand 3 automatically splits paths if they're too complex.

- FreeHand 3 uses PPDs and PDXs to optimize printing of color separations.

- FreeHand 3 features limited automatic trapping through the Spread size text edit box in the Print options dialog box.

Automatic Path Splitting. FreeHand 3, like version 2, will increase the flatness of a path which fails to print (usually because your printer has run out of working memory) until it does print. In addition, Free-Hand 3 splits unstroked (that is, those with a line of "None") paths during printing (or export) if it thinks that the printer would have trouble printing the path (based on the value in the Resolution text edit box in the Print options dialog box). You can turn off automatic path splitting by holding down Command and Option as you press Return (or click OK) in the Print dialog box.

Why would you want to turn off automatic path splitting? You should turn it off when you're working with complex paths with TIFFs pasted inside them. In this case, automatic path splitting can force FreeHand to download the TIFF several times, greatly lengthening the time it'll take to print your publication.

PPDs and PDXs. FreeHand 3 continues to support APDs (Aldus Printer Description files), but primarily uses PPDs (PostScript Printer Description files) and PDXs (Printer Description Extension files— these are extensions of PPDs) to optimize printing to specific models of printers. PPDs contain sets of screen angles created by Adobe Systems to minimize moiré patterns in color separations printed by PostScript printers.

Automatic Trapping. Objects filled with basic fills or stroked with basic lines will be enlarged, or spread, by the value you enter in the Spread text edit box in the Print options dialog box. For more on automatic trapping, see Chapter 6, "Color."

The FreeHand Print Dialog Box

When you press Command-P, FreeHand displays the Print dialog box (see Figure 7-1). Never mind that it says "LaserWriter '*printername*'" instead of "Print." It's the Print dialog box and everybody knows it. Here's a rundown of the options in the Print dialog box, and how to use them.

FIGURE 7-1
FreeHand's Print
dialog box

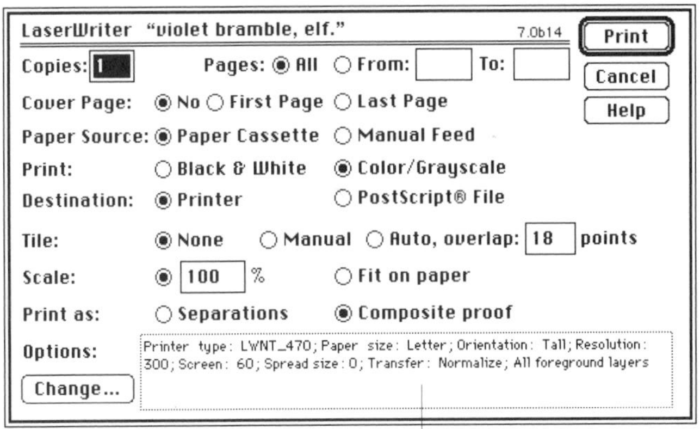

The options you've chosen in the Print options dialog box are listed here.

Copies

Enter the number of copies of the page you want to print here. You can print up to 999 copies of your publication.

Tip: Printing More Than 999 Copies

Honest, I get asked about this, so here it is. If you need to print more than 999 copies of your publication, print your publication to disk as PostScript, open the file with a text editor, and search for "#copies." Once you've found this string, just type the number of copies you want after it and save the file as text-only. Then download the PostScript file to your (long-suffering) printer.

Pages

Only kidding. Whenever I see this, my heart leaps up. Can you imagine a multipage FreeHand? Wouldn't that be great? Are you ready to start calling Aldus and Altsys?

Cover Page

When you check "Cover Page," FreeHand prints a cover page for you. It's not very pretty, but it does have your name, the date, and the title of the publication on it, and might keep your co-workers from taking your print job back to their offices, where they'll misplace it forever. "First Page" prints a cover page before the publication; "Last Page" prints a cover page after the publication.

Before you go crazy with cover pages, remember that trees died for this feature. This book was printed on recycled paper.

Paper Source Where's the paper coming from? Some printers have multiple paper bins. You choose the one you want here. If you're feeding the printer a piece of paper by hand, check "Manual."

Tile Use "Tile" when your publication is larger than the maximum page size of your printer. Automatic tiling splits your publication into as many parts as FreeHand thinks are necessary; manual tiling lets you tell FreeHand what the individual tiles should be.

When you choose automatic tiling, FreeHand bases the tile on the current page size, and starts tiling from the lower-left corner of the page. Note that this is different from PageMaker, which measures down and to the right from the zero point when tiling.

When you choose automatic tiling, the measurement you specify in the text edit box is the amount of the image that's duplicated between adjacent tiles. This feature comes in handy when you're printing using a printer that won't run the image out to the edge of the paper.

Manual tiling is generally better than automatic tiling, because FreeHand's automatic tiling has no idea what's in your illustration, and can't, therefore, make decisions about where the seams between the tiles should fall. When you tile manually, you can make sure that the edges of the tiles don't fall across any fills (especially graduated and radial fills). When the edge of a tile falls across anything with a halftone screen, it's difficult to piece the two tiles together. It's much easier to join lines and solid fills, and you should do your manual tiling with that in mind. Even if you have to make more tiles, it's best to tile across simple lines and solid fills.

Scale Enter a scaling value from 10 percent to 1000 percent of the publication's original size (in 1 percent increments). The Fit on paper option scales your page automatically to the largest size that'll fit on your currently selected paper size.

Print as Options

Click the Separations option when you want to print color separations of your publication (which inks print depends on the specifications you've entered in the Print Options dialog box), and click the Composite proof option when you want to print all of your colors as black and shades of gray, or when you want to print a color proof of your work on a color PostScript printer.

Printing and Page Setup

Because you're creating a publication that'll be printed on an existing PostScript printer, you've got to pay attention to the page sizes that are available. It might be too obvious to state, but if you can't print it, it's of no use to you.

You could tile your publication, but tiling only works in a few cases. Can you imagine grafting a bunch of halftoned images together? Or graduated fills? On negative film? You get the idea: it's impossible. Don't even try tiling unless you can set it up so that the edges of the tiles don't bisect anything containing a halftone screen.

That brings us back to paper sizes.

Page Size and Paper Size

When I talk about page size, I'm talking about the page size you've defined for your publication using the Document setup dialog box. This page size should be the same as the page size of the printed piece you intend to produce. "Paper size" means the size of the paper as it comes out of your printer or imagesetter. There can be a big difference between these two sizes. Try to print your publication on a paper size that is no larger than the publication's page size, unless you need printer marks (crop marks and registration marks). For more on page size and paper size, see "Paper Size" later in this chapter.

Tip:
Paper Size and
Printer Marks

If you need printer marks, print your publication on a paper size that is the size of your publication's page size plus about 60 points in either dimension.

Page Orientation and Paper Orientation

You set the orientation of the page in the Document setup dialog box by clicking either the Tall or Wide radio button. You set the orientation of the paper you're printing to by clicking either the Tall or Wide radio button in the Print options dialog box. What do these two orientation settings have to do with each other? Lots.

If you create a tall page and print it to a normal orientation, wide paper size, expect the top and bottom of your publication to get clipped off. Ditto for a wide page size printed to a normal orientation, tall paper size.

Always print tall pages to tall paper sizes, and wide pages to wide paper sizes—even when you're printing to a transverse page size (see Figure 7-2).

- If you need to print a wide publication down the length of an imagesetter's paper roll (because it's too wide for the width of the imagesetter's paper roll), use a wide, transverse orientation paper size.

- If you want to save paper on the imagesetter's roll and speed up printing time, print tall page sizes to transverse paper sizes (provided that the page size isn't taller than the width of the imagesetter's paper roll).

FIGURE 7-2

Page orientation and paper orientation

Don't choose "Tall" in your Document setup dialog box, and then print to a "Wide" paper size, or parts of your publication might get clipped off.

Similarly, don't choose "Wide" in the Document setup dialog box and then try to print to a "Tall" paper size. You'll lose things.

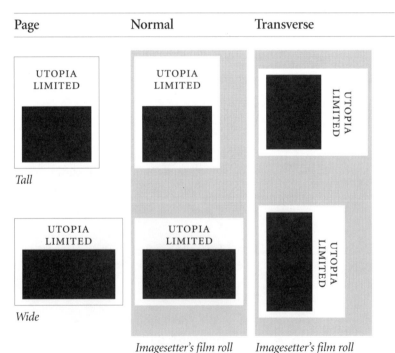

Printing Signatures

FreeHand's 40-by-40-inch maximum page size is large enough that you can arrange whole press sheets for many common presses; laying out and printing multiple pages in a single FreeHand publication (see Figure 7-3). When you print on both the front and back of a press sheet, then fold and cut the sheet, you've created a signature.

Signatures can be a real brain-twister. The object of creating a signature is to get pages onto a press sheet in such a way that your commercial printer can fold and cut the sheet so that it starts on the first page of the signature and ends on the last page. This means you have to position the correct pages in the right places and in the right orientations on both the front and back of the signature. Figure 7-4 shows how it works for a very simple signature.

You should try to leave ¼ inch for trim on each end of the signature and ½ inch on each side of the signature for color bars and for the press' grippers. Also, if your pages have bleeds, make sure you add ⅛ inch to all four sides of the page to accommodate the bleeds.

FIGURE 7-3
Press sheet

Example press sheet—sheet size 19 by 25 inches.

Page size is 9 by 6 ⅛ inches.

⊢ *Pages*

⊢ *Space for press grippers, trim*

⊢ *Press sheet*

FIGURE 7-4
Setting up a
simple signature

After you print, fold, and cut this press sheet, you've got an 8-page signature, with the pages in the correct order.

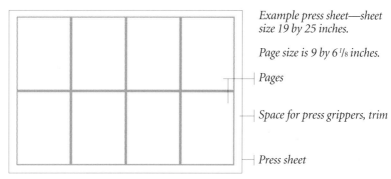

PAGE 8   PAGE 1   PAGE 2   PAGE 7

Allow some space for folding, press grippers, color bars, etc.

PAGE 5   PAGE 4   PAGE 3   PAGE 6

Front of sheet   *Back of sheet*

You'll still have to find some way of printing your signatures—very few imagesetters can handle paper sizes as large as you'll want for signatures (the largest image area I know of right now is the Optronics ColorSetter, which prints on a 36-by-36-inch single sheet). Table 7-1 shows some typical press sheet sizes and typical page sizes you can get out of them. Talk to your commercial printer about the sheet sizes their presses are capable of handling.

Don't despair if no imagesetters in your area can handle these sheet sizes. The most important thing about understanding how many of what size pages make up a press sheet is that you set up your publication to match sizes that don't waste too much paper. This isn't a comment about saving the environment—I've found it's cheaper by far to design for certain press sheet sizes.

In addition, commercial printers do lots of their printing on smaller sheet sizes. Table 7-2 shows some typical paper sizes you can use on smaller presses. You can fit signatures on these paper sizes, as well.

You're probably going to run into resistance from your commercial printer. After all, they make money setting up signatures. Next, you need to be absolutely certain you want to do this and that you know what you're doing before you try it. Make folded dummies of the sig-

TABLE 7-1
Common press sheet sizes and signatures

Sheet size		19 x 25	23 x 29	23 x 35	25 x 38	26 x 40
Image area		18 x 24½	22 x 28½	22 x 34½	24 x 37½	25 x 39½
Pages per sheet	3	18 x 8⅛	22 x 9½	22 x 11½	24 x 12½	25 x 13⅛
	4	18 x 6½	22 x 7⅛	22 x 8⅝	24 x 9⅜	25 x 9⅞
	4	9 x 12¼	11 x 14¼	11 x 17¼	12 x 18¾	12 ½ x 19¾
	6	9 x 8⅛	11 x 9½	11 x 11½	12 x 12½	12½ x 13⅛
	8	9 x 4⅞	11 x 7⅛	11 x 8⅝	12 x 9⅜	12½ x 9⅞
	10	9 x 6⅛	11 x 5¹¹⁄₁₆	11 x 6⅞	12 x 7 ½	12½ x 7⅞
	15	3⁹⁄₁₆ x 8⅛	4⅜ x 11	4 ⅜ x 11	4¾ x 12½	5 x 13⅛
	16	4½ x 6⅛	5½ x 7⅛	5½ x 8⅝	6 x 9⅜	6¼ x 9⅞

All dimensions in inches

TABLE 7-2	Text weights	Cover weights	Bond
Typical sheet sizes for smaller presses	19 x 25	20 x 26	8½ x 11
	23 x 29	23 x 35	17 x 22
	23 x 35	26 x 40	22 x 34
	25 x 38		24 x 38

All dimensions in inches

natures you want to use, and make sure that all of the pages, front and back, fall where you want them to. When in doubt, leave it to the pros at your printer.

FreeHand Printing Options

FreeHand's Print options dialog box is where you control what paper size you're printing to, which (if any) printer marks you want, and which inks you want to print, among other things. You get to the Print options dialog box when you press the Change... button in the Print dialog box (see Figure 7-5).

Because I find that I almost always have to go to the Print options dialog box before I print, I've set up a QuicKey that takes me to the Print options dialog box when I press Command-P.

FIGURE 7-5
Print options dialog box

Ink list

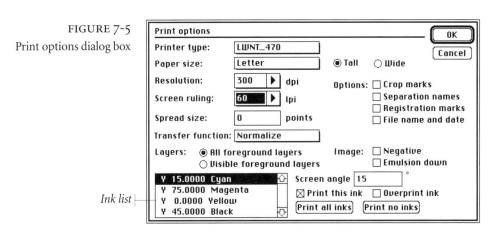

Printer Type

Select the PPD/PDX for your printer. If you don't know which one's the right one for your printer, don't feel too bad. I don't know who decided to name PPDs this way, but I'd very much prefer they'd used the actual product names (like "LaserWriter II NT" instead of "LWNT_470.PPD"). What is this, MS-DOS? In the meantime, see Table 7-3.

Tip:
Renaming Your
PPDs and PDXs

This is trivia, but you can rename your PPDs and PDXs to whatever you want. However, you must remember to update the name of the PPD file listed in the beginning of the PDX to the new name of the PPD. You could, for example, rename the PPD for a LaserWriter II NT to "LaserWriter II NT.PPD" and the related PDX file to "LaserWriter II NT.PDX," provided you change a line in the PDX from "*Include: LWNT_470.PPD" to "*Include: LaserWriter II NT.PPD."

Paper Size

When you choose a PPD, the available paper sizes for your printer appear in this pop-up menu, including any custom paper sizes you've added to the PDX for this PPD (see "Adding Custom Page Sizes to PDXs" later in this chapter).

Always choose a paper size that's at least the size of your publication's pages. If you're printing a publication that needs crop and registration marks (collectively known as printer's marks; see "Crop Marks" and "Registration Marks" later in this chapter) printed off the page, or if parts of your publication bleed (extend beyond the edge of the publication page), you'll need to choose a paper size that's larger than your publication's page size to accommodate the printer's marks and/or the bleed.

If you've chosen an imagesetter PPD, another option, "Other," will appear on the pop-up menu. When you choose "Other," FreeHand displays the Paper size dialog box, in which you can type whatever paper size you want. Remember, however, that the values you enter here need to take the width of the imagesetter's paper roll into account. Enter a width value greater than the width of the imagesetter's paper roll and you'll get a "limitcheck" error when you try to print.

In FreeHand 2, trying to print an "Other" size page with an orientation of "Wide" would result in a PostScript error. This has been fixed, so you can now enter wide-orientation page sizes without fear.

TABLE 7-3	PPD/PDX name	Printer name	PostScript ROM version
PPDs and their printers	APPLE230	Apple LaserWriter	23
	APPLE 380	Apple LaserWriter Plus	38
	APPLE 422	Apple LaserWriter Plus	42.2
	AST__470	AST TurboLaser/PS	47
	CG94_493	Agfa Compugraphic 9400P	49.3
	DATAP462	Dataproducts LZR-2665	46.2
	DP_US470	Dataproducts LZR 1260	47
	IBM20470	IBM 4216-020*	47
	IBM30505	IBM 4216-030*	50.5
	L100_425	Linotronic 100	42.5
	L200_471	Linotronic 200	47.1
	L200_493	Linotronic 200	49.3
	L300_471	Linotronic 300	47.1
	L300_493	Linotronic 300	49.3
	L500_493	Linotronic 500	49.3
	LWNTX470	Apple LaserWriter II NTX	47
	LWNT_470	Apple LaserWriter II NT	47
	NEC_470	NEC LC-890 Silentwriter	47
	QMS81470	QMS-PS 810	47
	QMS8P461	QMS-PS 800 Plus	46.1
	QMS8_461	QMS-PS 800	46.1
	QMSCS494	QMS Colorscript 100	49.3
	QUME_470	Qume ScripTEN	47
	S5232503	Schlumberger 5232	50.3
	TI08_450	TI OmniLaser 2108	45
	TI15_470	TI OmniLaser 2115	47
	VT42P493	Varityper 4200B-P	49.3
	VT43P493	Varityper 4300P	49.3
	VT60P480	Varityper VT-600P	48
	VT60W480	Varityper VT-600W	48

*Don't you just love IBM? These product names are as indecipherable as the PPD/PDX names!

Tip:
Line Screens and
Transverse Page
Orientation

When you choose one of the transverse page sizes/orientations from the Paper size pop-up menu, FreeHand rotates the publication 90 degrees when printing. Halftone screens you've applied to specific objects in your publication are not rotated. If the direction of the halftone screen you've applied is important to your design, you can either add 90 degrees to the screen angles applied in your publication, or you can print to one of the normal-orientation page sizes.

Resolution

The Resolution text edit box works the same way as the Target printer resolution text edit box in the Document setup dialog box. It doesn't change your printer's resolution, but it does give FreeHand a number to work with when calculating image scaling when you're resizing bitmapped graphics using "magic-stretch" (see "Magic-stretching an Image" in Chapter 4, "Importing and Exporting") and when determining whether a path should be split (when "Automatic path splitting" is on).

When you change the number in this text edit box, the number in the Target printer resolution text edit box in the Document setup dialog box changes, as well.

Screen Ruling

Choosing a screen ruling for your publication can be difficult. Higher frequency screens produce smoother-looking grays, but increasing screen ruling also results in a loss of grays which can make your publications print with noticeable banding and posterization. Lower screen frequencies can provide more tints (grays), but also look coarser. What to do? Try using this equation to determine the number of grays you'll get from the screen ruling and printer resolution you've chosen.

$$\text{number of grays} = (\text{printer resolution in dpi/screen ruling in lpi})^2 + 1$$

The key to this equation is that "number of grays" can't be greater than 256—that's the maximum number of grays a PostScript printer can render.

You can work the equation another way, and maybe this one's more useful.

$$\text{screen ruling} = \text{sqrt}(16 * \text{printer resolution})$$

Other people like to use this equation.

maximum frequency = printer resolution/16

If you come up with a line screen that's too coarse for your taste, think about it—is your publication one where you can sacrifice a few grays for a finer screen?

Spread Size

Together with ink-level overprinting, the Spread size option is one of FreeHand's global trapping options. "Spread size" enlarges the areas taken up by basic lines and fills (not PostScript, Tiled, Custom, Graduated, or Radial fills) by the value you specify in the text edit box. This automatic spreading feature does not apply to type, or to any element or ink which has been set to overprint.

If you want to see how spreads work, refer to the color section in this book, or see "Trapping" in Chapter 6, "Color").

"Spread size" is a good, basic trapping option that'll take care of many of your trapping needs, but don't think it'll everything for you. You'll still need to manually trap type, objects which cross color boundaries, graduated and radial fills, and a host of other things.

Also note that "Spread size" spreads items even if they *don't* overlap other colored objects. If you've noted objects in your publication printing larger than you think they should and can't figure out why, you've probably got a "Spread size" setting that's greater than zero.

Transfer Function

This option specifies how the printer's color densities correspond to the color densities you specify. Why do we need this? Because gray levels printed on 300-dpi printers look very different from gray levels printed on 2540-dpi printers (in general, lower percentages of gray, especially 10 percent, look darker at lower resolutions). If you choose "Default," FreeHand prints exactly the density you've specified, without reading any of the gray level adjustment information from the PPD.

Ordinarily, "Default" is the best choice for most tasks. If you want to compensate for the differences between printers with different resolutions (to get a more accurate proof), use "Normalize," which reads gray-level compensation information from the PPD.

"Posterize" creates special effects by converting the available gray levels into just four gray levels. "Posterize" works about the same way as the "Posterize" image preset. See "Bilevel and Gra;y-scale TIFFs and Image control," in Chapter 4, "Importing and Exporting," for more on posterization.

Crop Marks. Crop marks are lines, printed outside the area of your page, that define the area of your page. If your paper size is not larger than your page size, FreeHand won't print your crop marks.

Separation Names. FreeHand can print the name of each ink color for each separation or overlay on each printed page. This way, you'll have an easier time telling the magenta overlay from the cyan overlay. If you're printing a compsite, FreeHand prints the word "Composite."

Registration Marks. Registration marks are little targets for your commercial printer to use when they're lining up, or registering, your color separations for printing. If your paper size is smaller than your page size, FreeHand won't print registration marks.

File Name and Date. It's often handy to print the file name and date on your publications so that you can see which of two printed versions is the most current. It can also make it easier for your commercial printer to tell which pieces of film in a stack of separations go together (this might seem easy for you to tell, but put yourself in their shoes for a minute). If your paper size is smaller than your page size, Free-Hand won't print the file name and date.

Layers

The Layers option controls which layers print. It's pretty simple: choose "All foreground layers" to print the layers you've defined as foreground layers in your publication. If you only want to print the foreground layers you've made visible (that is, the ones with a check mark next to them in the Layers palette), click "Visible foreground layers."

Tip:
Print Only What
You Need

If you've already printed proofs of an illustration, and only need to alter one part of the illustration and proof that change, consider putting the change on another layer, then printing only that layer. This way, you won't have to wait for the entire publication to print.

Image Use the image options to print a negative of your publication or to choose whether your publication prints emulsion up (right reading) or emulsion down (wrong reading). In PageMaker (and other applications), the Negative option is called "Invert" and the Emulsion down option is called "Mirror."

In the United States, most printers prefer getting their film negative, emulsion down, unless they've got stripping to do, in which case they prefer it emulsion up. European printers like their film positive, emulsion up. Printers vary a lot, though, so the best way to find out which way you should print your publication is to ask your commercial printer how they'd like to receive the film.

The Ink List The ink list found in the lower-left of FreeHand's Print options dialog box is an important part of determining how your color separations are printed. Only color definitions and object-level overprinting instructions are more important. All of the inks defined in your publication are included in the ink list, and, if you're using process colors, cyan, magenta, yellow, and black appear in the list as well.

You can control the screen angle for a specific separation, whether an ink overprints (though object-level overprinting instructions will override the settings in this dialog box for the objects they're applied to), and whether an ink prints or not.

Screen Angle. FreeHand reads the screen angles from the PPD/PDX files. These are Adobe Systems' optimized screen angles which will prevent most moirés from occurring, so you shouldn't alter these unless you have a really good reason to do so. When PostScript level 2 comes out, we can start playing around with screen angles again.

Objects to which you've applied a particular halftone and images you've used image control on override the settings in the Print options dialog box.

Print This Ink. The Print this ink option controls whether the selected ink prints or not. What happens when you have objects containing percentages of process inks and turn off one of the process inks? Simple enough—you don't get any of that ink. Turning an ink off doesn't affect any of the other inks in the object.

Turning an ink off doesn't affect that ink's knockout/overprinting settings. If the ink was set to knock out other inks, it'll still knock them out—whether you print it or not.

The Print all inks and Print no inks buttons are shortcuts. The former sets all inks to print; the latter makes all inks nonprinting. Typically, you use these when you want to print all but one ink (click "Print all inks," then select the ink you don't want to print, and uncheck "Print this ink") or print only one ink (click "Print no inks," then select the ink you want to print, and check "Print this ink").

Overprint Ink. The Overprint ink option makes all of the objects with the selected ink applied to them overprint anything that's behind them. Any object-level overprinting instructions override this setting for the objects they're attached to.

Process colors (cyan, magenta, yellow, and black) bring up some interesting questions. If you've got an object that's colored 60C 30M 0Y 10K on top of an object that's colored 10C 40M 10Y 0K, what ink percentages do you get in the areas where the objects overlap? It's simple—the process colors on top win. Even if you set cyan to overprint, you'll still get 10 percent cyan in the areas where the top object overprints the bottom object.

To see what overprinting looks like, refer to the Color Figure 1 in the color pages in this chapter.

Printing PostScript to Disk

If you want to examine or edit FreeHand's PostScript, you'll need to print your FreeHand publication to disk. Printing to disk creates a text file containing all of the PostScript definitions and commands needed to print the publication. If you want to print your publication at a service bureau, printing PostScript to disk can make life easier for both you and your service bureau (see "Preparing a FreeHand File for Imagesetting," later in this chapter).

Printing a FreeHand publication to disk as PostScript can take a while, and can produce huge files if you've got any images (paint or TIFF) in your publication, because FreeHand has to include all of the information in the form it would normally send to the printer.

In the case of a TIFF, FreeHand sends image data as hexadecimal numbers written out in ASCII. A 1-inch square, 300-dpi gray-scale TIFF takes up more than 700K in a PostScript file. A 1-inch square, 300-dpi gray-scale TIFF takes up 180K in a PostScript file. By pointing out these file sizes, I'm not trying to scare you away from including TIFFs in your FreeHand files, or even to scare you away from printing publications containing TIFFs to disk; I think both are reasonable and desirable things to do. Just be prepared.

Once you've printed your publication to disk as PostScript, you can open, view, and edit it with a word processor, because it's a text file.

Tip:
Attach Notes to
Objects You
Want to Find

Finding single objects in a PostScript text file can be difficult, so make your life easier by attaching notes to objects in FreeHand before you print PostScript to disk. To attach a note to an object, select the object and choose "Set note" from the Attributes menu. Type your note of up to 255 characters in the dialog box that appears and press Return, and the note's attached to the object. When you print PostScript to disk, the notes are placed, as PostScript comments, immediately before the object in the PostScript text file. For more on attaching notes to objects, see "Attaching Notes to Objects," which, for some reason, I put in Chapter 2, "Drawing."

Tip:
Include TIFF
Images

You should always link to TIFF and paint-type images when you're printing PostScript files to disk. If you don't link to them, they won't print. In many cases, the whole page won't print.

Printing to
Disk with the
LaserWriter 6.1
Driver

If you've updated to Macintosh System 7, printing to disk using the new LaserWriter driver is much easier than it was with previous versions (see "Printing to Disk with LaserWriter Drivers Prior to 6.1," below). If you haven't, can't, or don't want to update to System 7, you can still use the version 6.1 LaserWriter driver with System 6.

When you're using LaserWriter driver 6.1 (or greater), a new option appears in your Print dialog box: "PostScript file." Click this button to print PostScript to disk. The Print button changes to the Save button. Click the Save button, and the Save disk file as dialog box appears. Type the name you want for the file in the text edit box in the Save disk file as dialog box and direct the file to the folder you want and press Return. FreeHand prints the file to disk.

Printing to Disk with LaserWriter Drivers Prior to 6.1

To print a FreeHand publication to disk as PostScript, go through the Print and Print options dialog boxes as you normally would, choosing all of the printing options you want and press Return (or click the OK button). Immediately hold down the F key. If you've pressed the key quickly enough, FreeHand displays the message, "Creating PostScript file." If FreeHand doesn't display this message and behaves as if it's printing to your printer, you didn't get to the key quickly enough. Press Command-. to cancel printing and try again. This doesn't work if you have background printing turned on under MultiFinder (it's an option in the Chooser).

Printing to disk creates a PostScript file called PostScript*n* in your FreeHand folder, where *n* is the lowest number from 0–9 not already taken by a pre-existing PostScript file.

If you want to include your copy of the Apple LaserPrep PostScript dictionary in your PostScript file, hold down the K key instead of F. You shouldn't have to do this unless you've hacked your LaserPrep and want to include the hacked version with your file. FreeHand mostly ignores LaserPrep and the LaserWriter driver.

Tip: Adding the Disk File Option

If you don't like printing to disk by holding down F or K after you press Return in the Print dialog box, and you *still* don't want to start using LaserWriter version 6.1 (or higher), you can add a check box to your Print dialog box that'll print your files to disk when it's checked. This option does not add the ability to name the file; it's still going to be named PostScript*n* (where *n* is the smallest number between 1 and 9 not taken by another PostScript file), and it's still going to be printed to disk inside the printing application's folder (for a way to change the folder it goes to, see "Directing PostScript Files to a Specific Folder" later in this chapter). To alter your LaserWriter driver to add the Disk file option, follow these steps (see Figure 7-6).

1. Start ResEdit.

2. Locate and open your LaserWriter driver. The examples shown in this procedure use LaserWriter driver version 6.02.

3. Type DITL to select the DITL resource class (DITLs contain dialog box items such as buttons and text edit boxes) and press Return.

FIGURE 7-6

Adding the
Disk File option

*Start ResEdit and open DITL ID -8191 in your
LaserWriter driver (it'll be inside your system folder).*

*Once you've got the DITL open, choose "Select
Item Number" from the DITL menu.*

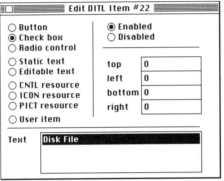

*ResEdit opens a DITL item
that's not visible in the DITL
window.*

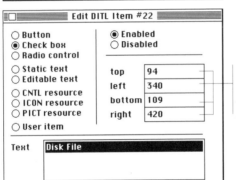

*Type these coordinates
in these text edit boxes and
press Command-S to save
your work.*

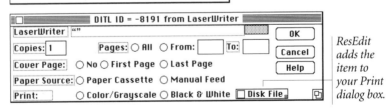

*ResEdit
adds the
item to
your Print
dialog box.*

4. ResEdit displays a list of DITL resources inside the LaserWriter
driver.

5. Select DITL ID number -8191 and press Return to open the
DITL.

6. Choose "Show All Items" from the DITL menu.

7. Choose "Select Item Number…" from the DITL menu. ResEdit displays the Select which item? dialog box. Type "22" in the text edit box and press Return.

8. Choose Open as Dialog Item from the Resource menu. ResEdit opens a view of the DITL item "Disk File." Click the Enabled check box and type "94" in the Top text edit box; "109" in the Bottom text edit box; "370" in the Left text edit box; and "460" in the Right text edit box. Press Return. ResEdit moves and expands the "Disk File" DITL item.

9. Press Command-S to save your changes to the LaserWriter driver, and then Press Command-Q to quit ResEdit.

The next time you open the Print dialog box (in FreeHand or in any other application using the LaserWriter driver), you'll see the Disk File check box. Check this box, and the application will print a PostScript file to disk in the printing application's folder. This PostScript file is the same file as you get when you hold down F after pressing Return (or clicking OK) in the Print dialog box.

Tip:
Directing
PostScript Files
to a Specific
Folder

If you're tired of looking through your FreeHand folder for PostScript files you've printed to disk, or if you just want to send your PostScript files to a specific folder or disk, and you *still* don't want to update your LaserWriter driver to version 6.1 (or higher), you can redirect the PostScript files to another folder. Follow the steps below to change the folder your PostScript files are sent to when you print to disk (see Figure 7-7).

1. Start ResEdit.

2. Locate and open your LaserWriter driver (in your system folder).

3. Type "STR#" to select the STR# resource class and press Return.

4. ResEdit displays a list of STR resources inside the LaserWriter driver.

5. Select STR ID number -8191 and press Return to open the STR# resource.

FIGURE 7-7
Directing PostScript
files to a specific folder

Start ResEdit and open your LaserWriter driver.

*Locate and select the STR# resource class. Press
Return (or double-click) to open the resource class.*

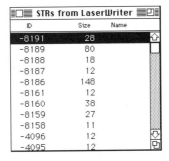

*Locate and open
STR# resource number -8191.*

*Type the volume and folder name
where you want your PostScript
files sent, and press Command-S
to save your changes to the
LaserWriter driver.*

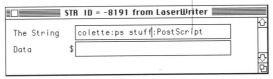

6. Type the full path name for the folder you want your PostScript
files directed to when you print to disk. You enter path names as
*diskname:foldername:*PostScript. To direct your files to a folder
named "postscript files" on a disk named "colette" you'd type
"colette:postscript files:PostScript." If you wanted to change the
name of the files to something else, just replace PostScript with
the file name you want. Make sure that the folder already exists
on the specified drive and that the drive and folder names are
identical to the names as they appear in the Finder.

7. Press Command-S to save your work and Command-Q to quit
ResEdit.

The next time you print to disk, the file will be directed to the
folder you specified.

Learning About FreeHand's PostScript

The best way to learn about how FreeHand makes images using PostScript is to create simple files, print them to disk as PostScript, and then look at the PostScript file with a word processor. How does FreeHand draw a line? A box? Text? It's all easy to see in the PostScript FreeHand prints to disk. Having good PostScript books around is good, but FreeHand has its own dialect, and the best way to learn that dialect is to look at lots of examples of FreeHand's own PostScript.

How is a printed-to-disk PostScript file different from an EPS file? The former contains all of the instructions needed by a PostScript printer to render the page, including all of FreeHand's crop marks, page size information, and, specifically, the PostScript page-printing operator *showpage*. The EPS file, on the other hand, counts on the application it's placed into for things like crop marks and page-positioning information. Basically, an EPS file is a FreeHand file without any options you've chosen in FreeHand's Print and Print options dialog boxes, while the printed-to-disk PostScript file includes all of those options. Further, the EPS file can include an attached PICT resource (Macintosh EPS) or TIFF (MS-DOS) for screen preview, while the printed-to-disk PostScript file is straight text.

FreeHand, PPDs, and APDs

PPDs and APDs are printer description files. PPD stands for PostScript Printer Description and APD stands for Aldus Printer Description. PPDs and PDXs are always used in pairs, and you can't use a PDX without a PPD. In general, PPDs contain general information about a specific printer; PDXs contain information application developers (like Altsys/Aldus) want to add to the PPD (such as page sizes, new spot functions, etc.).

Printer description files are not, and should not be confused with printer drivers. Printer description files work in conjunction with printer drivers to give the application information about the printer (what page sizes are available?; what's the resolution of the printer?; what do the printer error messages mean?) and to customize the printer's operation for the application (what PostScript routine does the application use to render halftones?).

FreeHand uses its built-in printer driver (for most things) and the Apple LaserWriter printer driver (for very little), and uses PPDs/PDXs, and APDs to optimize printing for a specific printer.

Which Should You Use?

Should you use APDs or PPDs/PDXs? Use PPDs/PDXs. If you've added custom page sizes to your APDs, it's pretty easy to add them to a PDX. APDs don't have the optimized screen angle information that FreeHand needs to be able to print without creating moiré patterns.

Rewriting PPDs and PDXs

You can edit your PDXs to add custom page sizes, to add new sets of screen angles, to download PostScript routines automatically, and to do a variety of other things.

In general, you should make changes to PDXs rather than PPDs. PPDs are much trickier animals to work with, and leaving them alone provides a solid base from which you can experiment with PDXs. Adobe Systems, in particular, recommends that you leave your PPDs alone; they don't want you messing with the optimized screen angles they've provided in the PPDs. You can always add new sets of screen angles to PDXs, if you have a burning desire to do so.

What's in a PPD/PDX?

Table 7-4 shows a listing of some of the keywords you'll see when you open a PPD/PDX file. I haven't tried to cover every keyword and entry you'll find in a PPD/PDX, mainly because FreeHand doesn't use all of them. I've included keywords you might want to change, as well as keywords you shouldn't change.

TABLE 7-4 Keywords in a PPD/PDX

Keyword	Example	What is it?
*PSVersion	*PSVersion: "52.0"	Version of PostScript in the printer's ROMs. Change this value if your printer has a different PostScript version than that listed in the PPD/PDX.

TABLE 7-4 *Continued*

Keyword	Example	What is it?
*Product	*Product: "LaserWriter II NT"	The name of the printer, as returned by the printer itself. You can use as many "*Product" keywords in a PDX file as you want. Make this value null (which you'd enter as "") if you don't like messages telling you you've got the wrong PPD/PDX selected for the current printer.
*Include:	*Include "LWII_NT.PPD"	Includes a file at this point in the PDX. Usually, this is used to include the PPD that the PDX is attached to, but it could be used to include a file containing your own PostScript code. You can have any number of "*Include" keywords in a PDX.
*DefaultResolution	*DefaultResolution: 1270dpi	Default resolution of the printer. This is the variable that shows up in the Resolution text edit box in the Print options dialog box. Don't change this setting.
*SetResolution	*SetResolution 2540dpi: " count 0 eq { % is the password on the stack? true }{dup % potential password statusdict begin checkpassword end not} ifelse { % if no password or not valid (WARNING : Cannot set the resolution.) = (Password supplied is not valid.) = (Please contact the author of this software.) = flush quit} if	Sets the resolution of the printer, for those printers capable of switching resolutions via software commands (imagesetters, mostly). If you don't know the routine to change the setting on an image-setter (they're all different), leave this value alone and change the resolution from the imagesetter's control panel.

TABLE 7-4 *Continued*

Keyword	Example	What is it?
	256 string statusdict begin li5backendparams end length 0 eq { (WARNING : Cannot set the resolution through software) = flush quit } if serverdict begin exitserver statusdict begin 2540 setresolution end" *End	
*ColorDevice	*ColorDevice: False	Tells FreeHand whether the selected printer is a PostScript color printer or not.
*PatchFile	*PatchFile: "MyPSPatches"	Includes a file in the PostScript output. This is a great place to enter PostScript code that changes global printing parameters.
*FreeVM	*FreeVM: "992346"	Amount of the printer's memory FreeHand can work with before having to flush fonts, etc.
*Password	*Password: "0"	Provides a password for the printer. Do not change this, or if you do, make sure you remember the password. If you don't know the password, you might have to replace chips on your motherboard to be able to use your printer again. There have been reports of viruses that reset your password and make your printer unusable. I cannot think why Adobe put this into their interpreter. In fact, I'm vaguely upset by the notion you'd want to keep someone on your network from printing on your printer.

TABLE 7-4 *Continued*

Keyword	Example	What is it?
*FileSystem	*FileSystem True	Lets FreeHand know if the selected printer has a hard disk attached to it. If this value is "True," FreeHand will check the printer's hard disk for downloadable fonts before looking for them on the current system. If you have a hard disk attached to your printer, set this keyword to "True"; otherwise, leave it at "False." If you have a printer that can be attached to a hard disk, FreeHand queries the printer to see if it has a hard disk attached. If you change this setting to "True," FreeHand doesn't have to ask.
*DeviceAdjustMatrix	*DeviceAdjustMatrix: "[1 0 0 1 0 0]"	Don't change this variable unless your printer chronically distorts the pages you're printing. If your printer does distort images, you'll have to calculate the percentage of distortion vertically and horizontally and enter it in the matrix. If you found that your printer was always stretching an image by 5 percent vertically, you'd change the matrix to [.95 0 0 1 0 0]. Don't even think about changing for 300-dpi printers—they're not accurate enough for it to make a difference. See the *PostScript Language Reference Manual* for more (lots more) information on adjusting matrices.

TABLE 7-4 *Continued*

Keyword	Example	What is it?
*ScreenFreq	*ScreenFreq: "120"	Sets the screen frequency the printer uses to print halftones. If you don't like it, change it. Any setting you make in the Halftone screen dialog box overrides this value.
*ScreenAngle	*ScreenAngle: "45"	Sets the screen angle the printer uses to print halftones. Change this value if you want a different default screen angle for your printer. Any setting you make in the Halftone screen dialog box overrides this value.
*DefaultScreenProc	*DefaultScreenProc: Dot	Sets the default halftone screen drawing procedure for the printer. This procedure is defined in the "*ScreenProc" keyword listing.
*ScreenProc	*ScreenProc Dot: "{abs exch abs 2 copy add 1 gt {1 sub dup mul exch 1 sub dup mul add 1 sub }{dup mul exch dup mul add 1 exch sub }ifelse }" *End	Halftone screen drawing procedures for the printer. You could enter "*ScreenProc Line: "{ pop }"" or "*ScreenProc Ellipse: "{ dup 5 mul 8 div mul exch dup mul exch add sqrt 1 exch sub }"" instead, but you've got to remember to call them from the "*DefaultScreenProc" keyword to get them to work. I've found that it actually works a little better to add new halftone screen procedures to FreeHand by entering them in FreeHand's Scrn resource (see Chapter 8, "PostScript," for more on how to do this).
*DefaultTransfer	*DefaultTransfer Normalized	Sets the default transfer function for the printer.

TABLE 7-4 *Continued*

Keyword	Example	What is it?
*DefaultPageSize	*DefaultPageSize: Letter	Sets the default paper size for your printer. The keyword for the paper size corresponds to the name of a defined paper size existing either in the printer's ROMs or in the PPD or PDX file. For more on creating custom paper sizes, see the section "Adding Custom Page Sizes to PDXs," later in this chapter.
*PageSize	*PageSize Letter: "letter"	Sets up a paper size. If your printer has variable page sizes (imagesetters usually do; 300-dpi printers usually don't), this entry could be: ""*PageSize Letter.Extra: "statusdict begin 684 864 0 1 setpageparams end""
*DefaultPaperTray	*DefaultPaperTray: None	Do you have a printer with more than one paper tray? I thought not. Leave this alone. If you really do have a printer with two paper trays, change this to the tray you want as your default. The tray selection for your printer is defined in the "*PaperTray" section of the PPD.
*PaperTray	*PaperTray Letter: "statusdict begin lettertray end"	Defines available paper trays for your printer.
*DefaultImageableArea	*DefaultImageableArea: Letter	Sets the default imageable area (the area inside a page size that the printer can actually make marks on) for the printer. The available imageable areas for your printer are set up using the "ImageableArea" keyword.

TABLE 7-4 *Continued*

Keyword	Example	What is it?
*ImageableArea	*ImageableArea Letter.Extra: "0 1 684 864"	Sets up the imageable area for a defined page size (in the example, a page size named "Letter.Extra").
*DefaultPaperDimension	*DefaultPaperDimension: Letter	Sets the default paper dimension for the printer. You set up paper dimensions are set up using the "*PaperDimension" keyword.
*PaperDimension	*PaperDimension Letter.Extra: "684 864"	Sets up the paper dimension for a specific page size (in the example, a page size named "Letter.Extra"). Enter the width and height of the paper, in points.For a wide orientation page, the entry would read "*PaperDimension Letter.Extra.Wide: "864 684""
*VariablePaperSize	*VariablePaperSize: True	Tells FreeHand whether your printer can accept variable paper sizes. Most imagesetters can; most 300-dpi laser printers can't. If your printer can accept variable paper sizes, the Paper size pop-up menu in FreeHand's Print options dialog box will include "Other." If you choose "Other," you'll be able to enter a custom paper size in the Page size dialog box and print to whatever size of paper you want (within the bounds of the imagesetter's capabilities). You can also add your own custom page sizes to PDXs of printers capable of accepting variable page sizes. Changing this value from "False" to "True" does not give your printer the ability to accept variable page sizes.

TABLE 7-4 *Continued*

Keyword	Example	What is it?
*DefaultInputSlot	*DefaultInputSlot: Lower	Sets the default paper feed for your printer, if your printer has more than one input slot (a NEC LC 890 Silentwriter is an example of a printer with two input slots). The available input slots are set up by the entries in the "*InputSlot" keyword.
*InputSlot	*InputSlot Lower: "statusdict begin 1 setpapertray end"	Defines the available input slots for your printer.
*DefaultManualFeed	*DefaultManualFeed: False	Makes manual feed the printer's default paper feed. Don't change this unless you habitually use your printer's manual feed.
*ManualFeed	*ManualFeed True: "statusdict begin /manualfeed true store end"	Sets up the printer's manual feed mechanism, if it has one.
*Font	*Font Times-Bold: Standard "(001.002)"	Lets FreeHand know that a font is resident in the printer. Add fonts to this list if you're sure they're going to be on your printer's hard disk or memory. FreeHand will ask your printer if it has a certain downloadable font installed, unless it finds the font in this list. If you enter the font in this list, FreeHand doesn't have to ask and prints faster. You add a font to the list by typing:

Font *PostScriptFontName*: Standard "(001.001)"

The PostScript name of the font can be a bit tricky to figure out. The best way to do it is to create a text block containing the font in FreeHand and print the file to disk as PostScript or create an EPS. Then open the file with a text editor and |

TABLE 7-4 *Continued*

Keyword	Example	What is it?
		look at the way FreeHand names the fonts near the start of the file.
		The numbers following the font name are the font type and the font version. Most fonts, these days, are Type 1 (or "001"). Unless you know the font version, just enter "001" for the version.
*DefaultFont	*DefaultFont: Courier	Defines the default font for your printer. This is the default font that gets used if FreeHand can't find the downloadable font used for text in your publication. If you're tired of looking at Courier, you can change it to any other printer-resident font you want.

Adding Custom Page Sizes to PDXs

The main reason to edit PDXs is to add custom paper sizes. If you find yourself entering the same numbers in the Page size dialog box over and over again, it's a job for custom page sizes. Once you've added a custom page size to a PDX file, the new page size appears on the Paper size pop-up menu when the PDX file is selected.

If, instead of using the Page size dialog box, you're creating your publications on page sizes other than the paper size of the printed piece, stop (unless you're creating signatures, or have some other good excuse). Remember that paper size equals printer RAM. Your jobs will print faster if you use a paper size that's no larger than your publication's page size plus crop marks (which adds about 60 points in each dimension).

You can add custom paper sizes to PDXs for any printer that can accept variable page sizes. Usually, imagesetters can accept variable page sizes and 300-dpi laser printers can't.

To add a custom paper size to a PDX file, follow these steps.

1. Back up the PDX file you intend to edit. Remember that if you make a backup copy of the file you'll be able to return to where you started if you make a mistake. Without the backup, you'll have to go beg a copy of the PDX from your friends, who'll laugh at you.

2. Open the PDX with your word processor.

3. Anywhere after the "*Include" line, enter three lines defining your new page size. The lines are shown below. Variables you enter are shown in italics.

   *PageSize *PageSizeName*: "statusdict begin *x y offset orientation* end"
   *ImageableArea *PageSizeName*: "0 0 *x y*"
   *PaperDimension *PageSizeName*: "*x y*"

   PageSizeName is the name you want to use for your custom page size. This name should not have spaces in it. *x* is the width of the custom page size, in points (if you're an inch monger, just multiply the inch measurement by 72 to get the distance in points) and *y* is the height of the custom page size, in points. *Offset* is a value used to offset the paper size from the edge of the imagesetter's paper (or film) roll. This value should almost always be 0. *Orientation* is either 1 or 0—0 means normal orientation (with the height of the paper being measured along the length of the imagesetter's paper roll); 1 means transverse (where the width of the paper is measured along the length of the imagesetter's paper roll). Here's a custom page size for a 576-by-1152-point (8-by-16-inch) paper size with a normal orientation.

   *PageSize PageSizeName: "statusdict begin
   576 1152 0 0 end"
   *ImageableArea PageSizeName: "0 0 576 1152"
   *PaperDimension PageSizeName: "576 1152"

4. Save your edited PDX file to the Altsys PPDs folder in the Aldus folder (in your system folder) as text only.

5. Open FreeHand.

6. Press Command-P to display the Print dialog box. Press the Change… button to display the Print options dialog box. If you edited the PDX file you currently have selected, you'll have to select another PDX, and then select the edited PDX to read the new page size information into FreeHand. Once you've selected the edited PDX file, your new page sizes should appear in the Page size pop-up menu.

If the new page sizes didn't appear in the Page size pop-up menu, or if the PDX can't be opened, you probably forgot to save the file as text only. Return to your word processor and try that.

Preparing a FreeHand File for Imagesetting

I've listened long and carefully to the grievances of imagesetting service bureau customers and operators. I've heard about how this designer is suing that service bureau for messing up a job, and I've heard imagesetter operators talking about how stupid their clients are and how they have to make changes to the files of most of the jobs that come in. I've listened long enough, and I have one thing to say.

Cut it out! All of you! There's no reason that this relationship has to be adversarial. Don't throw the book across the room—I don't mean to sound harsh. I just think that we can all cooperate, to everyone's benefit.

Designers and illustrators, you have to learn the technical chops if you want to play. That's just the way it is. The technical challenges are no greater than those you mastered when you learned how to use an airbrush, X-Acto, or a rapidograph. Your responsibility to your imagesetting service bureau is to set your file up so that it has a reasonable chance of printing (the guidelines in this book should help) and to communicate to your service bureau exactly how it is you want your publication printed (or, if you're creating a PostScript file, to make sure that the settings in the publication are correct).

Service bureau folks, you've got to spell out the limits of your responsibility. If you don't think you should be fixing people's files, don't do it. If you do think it's your responsibility, tell them up front you'll do so, fix the files, and charge the customer for the time. And if you get a customer who knows what they're doing, give them a discount. This will encourage everyone else.

Okay, back to the book.

If you know what you're doing, the best way to prepare your publication for printing at an imagesetting service bureau is to print a PostScript file to disk. If you've set up your printing options correctly, the file will include everything that is needed to print the publication. This way, all your service bureau has to do is download the file, instead of having to open the file, set the printing options, link to any images included in the file, and print. The only things that can go wrong are related to film handling and processing—the wrong film's used, the film's scratched, or the film's processed incorrectly.

This means, however, that you have to be dead certain of the printing options you want before you print to disk, because it's difficult or impossible to change things after that.

What are the most critical things you have to look out for?

Links to Images. Make sure any images you want to print (any that aren't on the background layer) are linked.

Tiling. If you're not tiling, make sure this is off. If you are, make sure you're tiling the way you want to. If you're tiling manually, you'll have to print a separate PostScript file to disk for each tile you want to print.

Scaling. It's easy to forget that you've scaled things for printing on your proof printer. Make sure that this is set to the scaling you want (generally 100 percent).

Separations/Composite. If you want to get separations back from your service bureau, make sure you choose "Separations" in the Print dialog box. An obvious point, but I've forgotten it at least once.

Printer Type. If you don't choose the right printer type, your publication may not print, and may even crash the service bureau's imagesetter. They hate this, so pick the type of imagesetter they use from the pop-up menu.

Page Size. Pick a page size at least large enough to contain your page. If you're printing separations, pick a page size that's at least 60 points wider and taller than your page size so that printer marks can be printed. Also make sure that you understand the page orientation you're working with—wide or tall; normal or transverse.

Screen Ruling. If you haven't set a screen ruling for each item in your publication using the Halftone screen dialog box, enter the screen ruling you want here. Any screen ruling you entered in the Halftone screen dialog box overrides any entry you make here.

Spread Size. If you're using FreeHand's automatic trapping, enter a value for your spreads here. Don't guess; ask your commercial printer what sort of spread their equipment requires.

Printer Marks. If you're printing separations, you can live without separation names and the file's name and date, but you've got to have the crop marks and registration marks if you want your printer to speak to you again. I turn them all on most of the time.

Negative/Emulsion Up. Are you printing negatives or positives? Emulsion up or down? Set it here.

Inks. What inks do you want to print? If you don't set them to print here, don't look askance at your service bureau when you don't get an overlay/separation for the ink. If you don't want an ink to print, make sure you turn it off or expect to pay for an additional piece of film.

You could make yourself a checklist of all of these items to go through every time you create a PostScript file.

The Golden Rules

These rules are mentioned elsewhere in this book, but all of the service bureau operators I know think I should repeat them again here. The times I mention here are averages, based on a series of benchmarks.

Use Blends, Not Graduated Fills. Blends that are created to match your printer's resolution and the line screen you intend to use print more than two times faster than graduated fills covering the same area. This assumes that you're not pasting the blend inside another object, which takes longer. For more on creating blends instead of graduated and radial fills, see Chapter 2, "Drawing."

Use Filled Objects, Not Clipping Paths. Illustrator users are used to creating fountains (what FreeHand calls "graduated fills") by creating a blend and then placing the blend objects inside a clipping path. In FreeHand, you should avoid doing this whenever possible, because it takes over five times as long to print as a simple graduated fill of the same path.

Use Duplicated Objects, Not Tiled Fills. Tiled fills are a wonderful thing—as long as you're basing them on objects with basic lines and fills. As soon as you create a tiled fill containing a graduated or radial fill, watch out! Our benchmarks show that tiled fills containing complex objects take more than twice as long to print as an identical series of duplicated objects.

Remember that Page Size Equals Printer RAM. The size of your page corresponds directly to the amount of printer RAM consumed when you try to print the publication. A 4-by-4-inch card centered on a letter-size page takes almost twice as much time to print as the same card laid out on a 4-by-4-inch page. For more on page setup and page size, see "Printing and Page Setup," earlier in this chapter.

Increase Flatness Whenever Possible. When you're printing to high-resolution imagesetters, the difference between a flatness setting of 3 and a flatness setting of 0 isn't noticeable, but the path with a flatness of 3 prints almost four times as quickly as the same path with a flatness setting of 0. For more on flatness, see "Flatness" in Chapter 2, "Drawing."

Don't Draw What You Can't See. Your printer has to process everything on your publication's page, so why make it work rendering objects that'll never be seen on the printed publication?

Simplify Your Paths. If you're working with complex paths created by autotracing images, you should consider splitting the path into smaller segments.

Scan Gray-scale and Color Images at No More Than Twice Your Line Screen. When you're scanning images, it's natural to assume that you should scan them at the highest resolution available from your scanner to create the sharpest possible scans. In fact, image data scanned at a resolution greater than two times the screen frequency you intend using to print your publication does not add significantly to the sharpness of the images, and may even harm the image's quality. For more on scanned image resolution, see "TIFFS, Line Screens, and Resolution" in Chapter 4, "Importing and Exporting.".

Don't Import Things When You Don't Have To. Whenever possible, always "Paste," from one FreeHand publication to another, rather than exporting and importing EPS graphics. If you have a FreeHand EPS, go to the original file and copy the elements you want out of it. If you're working with an Illustrator EPS, open the file (if possible), rather than placing it. In my tests, placed EPSs took up to 16 times as long to print as the same images pasted from another FreeHand file or converted from an Illustrator EPS.

Printing Troubleshooting

It's going to happen to you. Files are going to take hours to print, and some aren't going to print at all. Or they're going to print in some way you hadn't expected. While this book can be viewed as an extended treatise on printing troubleshooting, this section deals with a few of the most common printing problems and how to fix them.

First of all, what makes a file hard to print? TIFFs, PostScript fills and lines, custom fills and lines, graduated fills, radial fills, and paths with lots of points and curves all do their part to increase the amount of time your publication spends churning around in a printer's RIP. When I say paths with lots of points, I mean paths with more than 100 points—the kind you get when you autotrace the scanned picture of Aunt Martha. Don't forget composite paths, either. At some point, one of these is going to trip you up. When that happens, you'll see a Post-Script error message.

PostScript error messages can be cryptic in the extreme, and, best of all, seldom say what they really mean. Almost all of the PostScript errors that have the word "VMError" in them mean that your printer's run out of memory while processing the document. If you see error messages with the word "limitcheck" in them, something in your document is pushing your printer (or PostScript) past an internal limit. If you see these errors, you're going to have to apply some or all of the golden rules to your publication. In particular, try splitting some of the more complex paths in your publication and increasing the flatness of some or all of the paths in your publication.

There are two errors that have to do with downloadable fonts that are easily fixed.

- PostScript error: "limitcheck" Offending command: "framedevice"

- PostScript error: "VMError" Offending command: "array"

If you get these error messages, go to the Page setup dialog box and click the Unlimited downloadable fonts option. This should fix the problem.

If you see an error containing the word "syntaxerror," you've made a mistake in one of the custom PostScript fills or lines you're using. Generally, these are misplaced brackets or parentheses. Look through your code and see what you've missed. If you're using Nisus, you can search for unmatched pairs of brackets or parentheses.

Tip:
When TIFF Images Look Terrible

If your job prints, but your bilevel TIFF and paint-type images look terrible, you probably need to magic-stretch them to match them to the printer's resolution. See "Resizing Images to Your Printer's Resolution" in Chapter 4, "Importing and Exporting," for more on magic-stretching.

Tip:
When TIFF Images Don't Print

If your job prints, but lacks a TIFF image or paint-type graphic, you probably lost your link to the image. This often happens when you take the FreeHand file to an imagesetting service bureau for printing (rather than giving them a PostScript file). Remember to take any linked TIFF or paint-type files along when you go to your service bureau, or print your file to disk as PostScript while the files are still linked; they'll be included in the PostScript file.

Calibrating Your Imagesetter

There's an excellent section in the *Aldus FreeHand User Manual Version 3.0* on imagesetter calibration, so I won't spend much time on it here. What the manual doesn't tell you, though, is that Aldus PrePrint 1.5 ships with an excellent HyperCard stack for calibrating imagesetters (better than the one that came with PrePrint 1.0). This stack does almost all of the work of rewriting a PDX file for you, and even makes adding new paper sizes painless.

If you have PrePrint, use the stack to calibrate your FreeHand PDXs. If you don't have PrePrint, find someone who does and borrow the stack.

Tip:
Image Polarity
and Calibration

Lots of people (including me) have said that the polarity of your image (whether it's positive or negative) should be controlled at the image-setter. We said this because we'd had problems with old versions of PostScript ROMs not inverting images. At this point, PostScript ROMs and software developers' image polarity controls are in sync, and calibration routines for several color separation programs require that you use the application's image polarity controls. Use the image controls in your printing application, instead of setting the polarity at your imagesetter, unless you're working with PostScript ROMs 47.1 or earlier.

You can calibrate your imagesetter using the HyperCard stack mentioned above for the image polarity you typically use, while the instructions for calibrating your imagesetter in the *Aldus FreeHand User Manual* force you to calibrate your imagesetter with a positive image polarity.

Printing to Non-PostScript Printers

FreeHand 3's printing to QuickDraw printers has been improved from that of version 2, which would print only the screen representation of your publication. Lines now print as smoothly as is possible at the QuickDraw printer's resolution, and, if you're using ATM, you can even use type. You can print text that's been altered by most of FreeHand's transformation tools, but you won't be able to print FreeHand's PostScript text effects.

In spite of these improvements, FreeHand is a PostScript printing program, and you shouldn't expect to get more than the roughest proofs from a non-PostScript printer.

Fortune Cookie

I love fortune cookies. "Look afar, and see the end from the beginning," one fortune told me. It could've been talking about printing with FreeHand. You really should be thinking, How am I going to print this thing? from the time you press Command-N to create a new file.

Whenever possible, examine the processes you use to create publications in the light of the "golden rules" presented earlier in this chapter. You can almost always make something simpler from your printer's point of view without compromising the appearance of your publication.

Finally, as I always say, if something doesn't work, poke at it.

RUDDI GORE

PostScript

is the engine that makes desktop publishing go. If you already know all about PostScript and how your printer uses it, and/or just want to know how to use it in your FreeHand publications, skip the next section. I'm about to explain PostScript and laser printing as I understand them, in as few words as possible. Everyone else, take a deep breath.

What Is PostScript?

PostScript is a page-description language—a programming language for describing graphic objects. It's been said that page-description languages tell your printer how to make marks on paper. This isn't quite true—your printer already knows how to make marks. Page-description languages tell your printer *what marks to make.*

PostScript has emerged as the best of the commercially available page-description languages (other page-description languages being Hewlett-Packard's PCL, Imagen's Impress, and Xerox's Interpress). This doesn't mean it's perfect—just that it's the highest standard we've got. PostScript Level 2, an upgrade to the PostScript language, is making its way into printer controller circuitry even as I write this.

Inside your PostScript printer, there's a computer dedicated to controlling the printer. This computer interprets the PostScript sent to it by your Macintosh, and turns it into a bitmap the size of the printer's current page. The combination of printer hardware (processor and memory) and software (the version of the PostScript language in the printer's ROMs) is often called a RIP, or Raster Image

Processor, because it turns a set of drawing commands into a raster image, or bitmap.

When the printer receives and processes all of the information for a specific page, the printer transfers the bitmap from its memory to a photosensitive drum with a laser beam. The areas where the drum is charged attract the powdered toner in the printer. When it's time to print the page, paper is pulled into the printer so that the bits of toner are transferred from the drum to the paper. In an imagesetter, the laser beam directly exposes photographic film.

What's PostScript Got to Do with FreeHand?

You can almost think of FreeHand as PostScript wearing a user interface. This isn't to say that FreeHand's internal database is PostScript (it's not), but that FreeHand approaches drawing objects the same way that PostScript does. And then there's printing. Try printing a FreeHand publication on something other than a PostScript printer, and you're in for a disappointment.

So if FreeHand is PostScript, how can you write your own PostScript to alter and extend FreeHand?

- You can use the PostScript lines and fills that are built into FreeHand (the Custom lines and fills).

- You can attach your own PostScript code to FreeHand objects by choosing "PostScript" in the Fill and line dialog box and typing up to 255 characters of code.

- You can write your own EPS files.

- You can create your own PostScript effects, save them as USERPREP, activate them by choosing "PostScript" from the Fill or Line pop-up menus in the Fill and line dialog box, and typing the names of procedures you've defined in the file. This gets you around the 255-character limit.

- You can create your own PostScript effects and turn them into FreeHand external resource files. Once you do this, they'll appear when you choose "Custom" from either the Fill or Line pop-up menu in the Fill and line dialog box.

Using FreeHand's Custom Lines and Fills

The first method is to stick with FreeHand's Custom lines and fills. In FreeHand 2, these were the lines and fills you invoked by typing commands and variables in the PostScript dialog box. When you sent the publication to your printer, FreeHand 2 would download UserPrep, a PostScript dictionary containing the code that told the printer how to print the custom lines and fills. These lines and fills are now stored inside FreeHand 3, and their use is covered in Chapter 2, "Drawing."

Typing PostScript in the Fill and Line Dialog Box

When you choose "PostScript" from either the Fill or Line pop-up menu in the Fill and line dialog box, a large text edit box appears. You can type up to 255 characters of PostScript code in this text edit box. FreeHand applies the code you enter here to the selected object as a PostScript fill or line effect.

In some ways, this is the easiest way to get PostScript you've written into FreeHand, provided the code fits in the text edit box. The trouble is, 255 characters isn't a lot of code. You can cut down the number of characters used by making your variable and procedure names shorter ("ls" instead of "lineStart," for example), but this only works to a certain point.

There are three ways around this limitation. You can rely on procedures you know are already defined in FreeHand and use them in your PostScript code, you can create your own UserPrep file containing routines you want to use, or you can create your own external resource files. These three techniques are covered later in this chapter.

The following steps show you enter a apply a simple PostScript line effect (see Figure 8-1).

1. Draw a line.

2. Press Command-E to display the Fill and line dialog box.

3. Choose "PostScript" from the Line pop-up menu. A large text edit box appears.

FIGURE 8-1

Specifying a
PostScript line effect

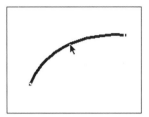

Select a line and press Command-E
to display the Fill and line dialog
box.

In the Fill and line dialog box,
choose PostScript from the Lines
pop-up menu.

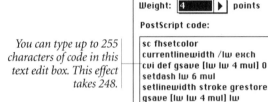

*You can type up to 255
characters of code in this
text edit box. This effect
takes 248.*

Type the following code in the PostScript
code text edit box (note that some of the
code is not visible in the text edit box
shown at left).

sc fhsetcolor currentlinewidth /lw
exch cvi def gsave [lw lw 4 mul] 0
setdash lw 6 mul setlinewidth
stroke grestore gsave [lw lw 4 mul]
lw setdash lw 3 mul setlinewidth
stroke grestore gsave [lw lw 4 mul]
lw 2 mul setdash lw setlinewidth
stroke grestore

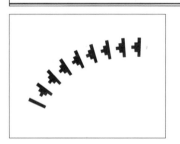

When you print, you get this cool
PostScript line.

4. Type PostScript code in the text edit box.

5. Press Return to close the dialog box.

The selected line won't look any different, but when you print to a
PostScript printer, the effect you've typed is applied to the path.

Here are a few more line effects you can enter. I've formatted these
so that they're a bit easier to read, but you should enter the code without carriage returns (like the code shown in Figure 8-1).

All three example line effects use PostScript's *setdash* operator (you
can use "d," which FreeHand defines to mean "setdash") in peculiar
ways to do some things you can't do using FreeHand's dashed lines.

```
/T
{
sc length 4 eq
{
sc
{
nx
} forall 4 array astore /sc xdf
}
{
sc 0 get
{
nx
} /nt xdf sc 0 nt put
} ifelse
} def
/nx
{
.8 mul
} def
currentlinewidth /lw xdf
0 1 4 {q /c xdf [lw lw 3 mul] lw c mul d lw w T S Q /lw lw 2 div
def} for
```

PostScript line effect created by the PostScript code example above

```
currentlinewidth /lw xdf
/A [.5 lw mul lw 4 mul] def
q A 0 d S Q
1 1 6
{
/c xdf q A .5 c mul lw mul d
sc length 4 eq
{
sc
{
.7 mul
} forall 4 array astore /sc xdf
}
{
```

```
sc 0 get .9 mul /N xdf sc 0 N put
} ifelse
lw c mul w S Q
} for
```

PostScript line effect created by the PostScript code example above

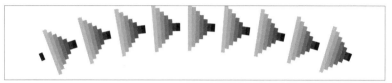

```
0 1 50
{
/c xdf
q
[1 49] c 2 add d
sc length 4 eq
{sc {.01 sub} forall 4 array astore /sc xdf}
{sc 0 get .01 sub /N xdf sc 0 N put}
ifelse
S
Q
} for
```

PostScript line effect created by the PostScript code example above

PostScript fill effects work just like PostScript line effects. You can type up to 255 characters in the text edit box (see Figure 8-2).

1. Draw a rectangle.

2. Press Command-E to display the Fill and line dialog box.

3. Choose "PostScript" from the Fill pop-up menu. A large text edit box appears at the bottom of the fill section of the dialog box.

4. Enter PostScript code in the text edit box and press Return to close the Fill and line dialog box.

The rectangle fills with PSs. When you print, FreeHand applies the PostScript fill you've entered to the rectangle.

FIGURE 8-2

Creating a PostScript
fill effect

*Select the object you
want to fill and press
Command-E.*

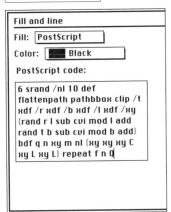

*In the Fill and line dialog box,
Choose "PostScript" from the
Fill pop-up menu, choose a
color, and then type the code
you want in the PostScript code
text edit box.*

*Press Return to close the Fill and
line dialog box.*

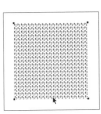

*FreeHand displays
the PostScript fill
with a pattern of
"PS."*

*When you
print, you'll
see your
PostScript
fill.*

Here are a few more PostScript fill effects you can enter. Once again, I've formatted the code so that it's a little bit easier to read, but you should type it into the PostScript code text edit box without adding carriage returns or any extra spacing. I've also added a few comments—anything to the right of a "%" is a comment. Don't type any of the comments into your PostScript fills, or they won't work. They're just here to show you how to vary the fills.

```
6 srand %%This line sets the random number generator
%%You can enter any number you want in
%%place of the "6," or you can delete this line entirely
%%for a totally random fill.
/nl 10 def %%Number of iterations of the drawing loop
flattenpath pathbbox clip %%put the coordinates of the
```

```
%%selection's bounding box on the stack
/t xdf %%get the topmost coordinate
/r xdf %%get the right side coordinate
/b xdf %%get the bottom coordinate
/l xdf %%get the leftmost coordinate
/xy %%this procedure randomly places a point inside path
{rand r l sub cvi mod l add
rand t b sub cvi mod b add}
bdf
q %%FreeHand shorthand for "gsave"
n %%FreeHand's way of saying "newpath"
xy m %%move to a random point
nl
{xy xy xy C} %%random "curveto"
repeat %%repeats the curve "nl" times
f %%close and fill the path
n
Q
```

PostScript fills produced by the PostScript code above

I don't know how useful you'll find these, but I like them.

6 srand

14 srand

10 srand

45 srand

```
1 srand %%This routine works almost exactly the
%%same way as the routine above
/nl 20 def
flattenpath pathbbox clip
```

```
/t xdf
/r xdf
/b xdf
/l xdf
/xy
{rand r l sub cvi mod l add
rand t b sub cvi mod b add}
bdf
q
n
xy m
nl
{xy L} %%random "lineto"
repeat
f
n
Q
```

PostScript fills produced by the PostScript code above

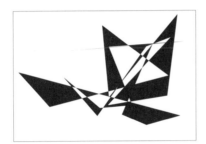

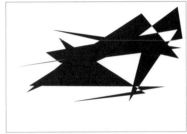

1 srand   *12 srand*

Tip:
Registration
Color

Lots of FreeHand users have asked for a "registration" color—a color which prints on all separations, regardless of whether you're using process colors, spot colors, or both. If such a color existed, they argued, they'd be able to draw their own printer marks and crop marks wherever they wanted them.

As it turns out, applying a registration color to lines and fills is easy (see Figure 8-3). Select the line or fill you want, and press Command-E to display the Fill and line dialog box. In the Fill and line dialog box, choose "PostScript" from the Fill (or Line) pop-up menu. In the PostScript code dialog box, type "0 setseparationgray fill" for a fill that prints on all separations, or ".2 setlinewidth 0 setseparationgray stroke" for a line (you can enter any line weight you want, of course). If what you want is a "white" registration color (that is, a color that knocks out everything behind it on all separations), enter "1 setseparationgray" instead of "0 setseparationgray."

FIGURE 8-3
Registration color

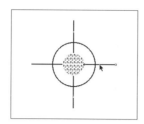

Select the line you want to print on all separations and press Command-E.

FreeHand displays the Fill and line dialog box.

In the Fill and line dialog box enter a line weight for your line. Then type "0 setseparationgray" to specify that it prints as solid on all separations.

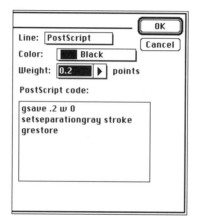

The dialog box on the right shows what you'd type if you were setting a fill to print solid on all separations.

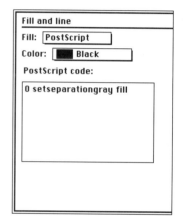

Writing Your Own EPS Files

If you want to write your own PostScript files and place them in Free-Hand, you'll have to convert them from "raw" PostScript to EPS. Your PostScript code should not include the following PostScript operators.

banddevice	exitserver
initclip	letter
nulldevice	setsccbatch
legal	renderbands
setmatrix	stop
erasepage	grestoreall
initmatrix	copypage
note	framedevice
setpageparams	initgraphics
quit	

Beyond these restrictions, all you need to do is add the following few lines to the beginning of your file.

```
%!PS-Adobe-2.0 EPSF-1.2
%%BoundingBox: lowerLeftX lowerLeftY upperRightX upperRightY
%%EndComments
```

The variables following "%%BoundingBox" are the measurements of the image your PostScript code creates, in points. Usually, *lowerLeft* and *lowerLeft* are both zero. If you're not sure what the size of your image is, print the file and measure it.

Here's an example EPS file (see Figure 8-4).

```
%!PS-Adobe-2.0 EPSF-1.2
%%BoundingBox: 0 0 612 792
%%Creator:(Greg Stumph)
%%Title:(Fractal Tree)
%%CreationDate:(9-25-90)
%%EndComments
%% set up variables
/bdf
    {
    bind def
    } bind def
/depth 0 def
%% maxdepth controls how many branchings occur
%% exceeding 15 will be VERY time consuming
/maxdepth 10 def
%% after branching "cutoff" times, the branch angles increase
%% set cutoff higher than maxdepth to supress this
/cutoff 4 def
/length
    {
    rand 72 mod 108 add
    } bdf
/ang
    {
    rand 10 mod 10 add
    } bdf
/sway
    {
    rand 60 mod 30 sub
    } bdf
/NewLine
```

```
        {
        sway length 3 div sway length 3 div
        0 length rcurveto currentpoint
        depth 1 sub maxdepth div setgray
        stroke translate 0 0 moveto
        } bdf
/down
        {
        /depth depth 1 add def
        depth cutoff gt
            {
            /ang
                {
                rand 30 mod 20 add
                } bdf

            } if
        } bdf
/up
        {
        /depth depth 1 sub def
        depth cutoff le
            {
            /ang
                {
                rand 10 mod 10 add
                } bdf
            } if
        } bdf
%% FractBranch is the loop that does all the work,
%% by calling itself recursively
/FractBranch
        {
        gsave .8 .8 scale
        down NewLine
        depth maxdepth lt
            {
            ang rotate FractBranch
            ang 2 mul neg rotate FractBranch
            } if
        up grestore
        } def
gsave
306 72 translate 0 0 moveto
```

```
10 setlinewidth
1 setlinecap
currentscreen 3 -1 roll
pop 65 3 1 roll setscreen
FractBranch
grestore
%%End of file
```

FIGURE 8-4
Example EPS graphic

Tip:
Using SmartArt
to Convert Raw
PostScript to EPS

You can use SmartArt from Adobe Systems to turn a raw PostScript file into an EPS file (with or without a screen preview).

1. Start SmartArt.

2. Choose "Open" from the SmartArt menu.

3. Locate and open the PostScript file you want to convert. If you can't see your file, make sure that "EPSF and TEXT" is checked in the Open dialog box.

4. Choose "Export…" from the SmartArt menu.

5. Choose "Macintosh EPS" or "Generic EPS" and press Return.

SmartArt exports your file as an EPS. Now you can place the file in FreeHand and use it in your publications.

Looking at FreeHand's PostScript

If you've gone about as far as you can go typing short snippets of PostScript code into the Fill and line dialog box, you can call on the PostScript routines already defined by FreeHand. With more routines defined outside of the text edit box, you'll be able to fit more effects in fewer characters, thereby stretching the effectiveness of the text edit box (see Table 8-1).

If you're creating your own USERPREP file or external resource file, you should also take a look at FreeHand's PostScript to see if there's something there you can use. Otherwise, you'll just end up reinventing the wheel.

What routines can you make use of? The best thing to do is to take a look at a FreeHand PostScript file. After you've printed a PostScript file to disk from FreeHand (see "Printing PostScript to Disk" in Chapter 7, "Printing"), you can open it with any word processor. What is all this stuff? Immediately following several comment lines stating the creator, creation date, and some code setting up the page size, there's a FreeHand user dictionary (beginning with the line "%%BeginProcSet: FreeHand_header 3 0").

Everything between "%%BeginProcSet: FreeHand_header 3 0" and "%%EndProcSet" is one or another of FreeHand's subdictionaries. Specifically, though, you should look at the PostScript definitions following "/supdict 65 dict def" and "/ropedict 85 dict def." These are the support routines for FreeHand's custom PostScript lines. If you can't see these dictionaries, make sure the file you've printed to disk contains at least one custom line or fill.

Don't be scared—you don't have to know this stuff to enter most of the new PostScript lines and fills in this chapter. The code is pretty well annotated with comments (by software engineering standards) and you should be able to understand some of it just by looking at it. PostScript comments are preceded by a "%" and are ignored by the printer.

If you're having trouble making sense of the PostScript file, remember that procedures begin with a "/" and end with a "}def" or "}bdef." Here's an example of a procedure.

```
%procedure for picking a random integer
/randint {
rand exch mod } def
```

Name	Example	What it does
F	F	Fills the current path with the current color.
f	f	Closes the current path, then fills it with the current color.
S	S	Strokes the current path with the current line weight, color, and dash pattern.
s	s	Closes the current path using the current line weight, color , and dash pattern.
q	q	Saves the current graphic state. Same as PostScript's "gsave" operator.
Q	Q	Restores the most recently-saved graphic state. Ssame as PostScript's "grestore" operator.
d	[5] d	Sets the dash pattern of a line. Same as the PostScript operator "setdash."
xdf	/top xdf	Defines the current variable name ("top" in the example) as whatever's on top of the operand stack. Same as "exch def."
bdf	/top {.5 mul} bdf	Same as PostScript's "bind def."
fc	fc fhsetcolor	Current fill color
sc	sc fhsetcolor	Currnet line (stroke) color

TABLE 8-1
Selected FreeHand
PostScript procedures

	Name	Example	What it does
TABLE 8-1 *Continued*	randint*	10 randint	Returns a random integer between 10 and zero. If you wanted a number between 5 and 15, you'd enter 10 randint 5 add.
	newrope*	{roman} 10 10 0 [0 0 0 1] newrope	Draws the procedure "Roman" along a line. The variables preceding "newrope" are the height, width, spacing, and color of the line pattern.
	newinside*	{randomBox} newinside	Fills the selected shape with the contents of the procedure "randomBox."

*These procedures are only included in FreeHand's PostScript when you use a custom line or fill.

Creating Your Own PostScript Effects

There are several different ways to enter your own PostScript code.

- Add a patch file to a PPD or PDX file. FreeHand adds this file to the PostScript output immediately before FreeHand's PostScript dictionaries. This makes patch files good for changing printer environment variables. For more on working with PPD/PDX files, see "Rewriting PPDs and PDXs" in Chapter 7, "Printing."

- Create a FreeHand patch file. If you save a file as text-only with the file name FREEHAND POSTSCRIPT PATCHES to either the Aldus folder or the folder containing your FreeHand application, FreeHand adds the file to the PostScript stream immediately after the dictionaries and immediately before %%EndSetup.

- Create a USERPREP file. If you create a file named USERPREP and place it either in the Aldus folder or the folder containing your FreeHand application, FreeHand adds the file to the PostScript output stream immediately after the FreeHand's PostScript dictionaries and before %%EndSetup (but before any FREEHAND POSTSCRIPT PATCHES file).

- Create your own FreeHand external resources. External resource files found in FreeHand's search path (in the Aldus folder in the system folder or in the folder containing FreeHand) are actually loaded into FreeHand when the program starts. These resources can alter, augment, or replace resources already inside FreeHand.

Creating FreeHand PostScript Patches

When FreeHand prints your publication, it'll send along two PostScript files if it finds them inside the FreeHand folder: USERPREP and FREEHAND POSTSCRIPT PATCHES.

In general, you use UserPrep to define routines you'll invoke using PostScript lines and fills you enter in the Fill and line dialog box; and you use FREEHAND POSTSCRIPT PATCHES when you want to redefine something in one of FreeHand's PostScript dictionaries ("FHIODict," "FreeHandDict," and "FreeHandSepDict" are the main ones).

Creating a FreeHand Patch File. When FreeHand finds a text file named FREEHAND POSTSCRIPT PATCHES, it inserts the patch file into its PostScript output stream after setting up the various dictionaries and before the start of the drawing instructions for the publication's contents. This is a great place to redefine existing procedures in the FreeHand PostScript dictionaries.

At the point the patch file enters FreeHand's PostScript, your PostScript dictionary stack contains the PostScript dictionaries md (the AppleDict), and userdict and systemdict (these last two are the default—more or less—dictionaries for any PostScript interpreter). Here's what a very basic patch file would look like.

```
FHIODict begin %%FHIODict is a kind of dictionary "preamble"
for FreeHand's dictionaries
FreeHandDict begin %%Opens the main FreeHand dictionary
/law (NOT TO GO ON ALL FOURS) def %%Defines the string
variable "law"
end %%Closes the main FreeHand dictionary
end %%Closes FreeHand's FHIODict
```

Improving FreeHand's Registration Marks. Here's something a little more useful. This patch file improves FreeHand's registration marks and adds color bars to FreeHand separations (see Figure 8-5). You can type this code in your word processor, save it as text-only with the file name FREEHAND POSTSCRIPT PATCHES, and put it in your FreeHand folder. You'll have registration marks that'll make your printer happier. You can omit any comments as you type the file.

```
FHIODict begin %%Open the setup dict
FreeHandDict begin %%Open the main FreeHand dict
%%The next definition sets up a new variable. It's just a counter.
%%Okay, so I started with BASIC
/firstTime 0 def
%%The next section replaces FreeHand's
%%default alignment marks ("am")
/am
    {newpath gsave
    %%This next procedure draws the color boxes across the top
    /doBoxes
        {gsave
        /xpos -8 def
        /ypos 6 def
        /drawBox
            {xpos ypos moveto
            -12 0 rlineto
            0 -12 rlineto
            12 0 rlineto
            0 12 rlineto
            closepath
            fill
            newpath
            /xpos xpos 12 sub def
            }
            def
        0 .1 1
        {setseparationgray
        drawBox
        } for
    grestore
    }
    def
%%This next procedure prints some advertising for this book
%%And also gives your printer some type to register to
```

```
/doType
    {
    gsave
    /Times-Roman findfont 5 scalefont setfont
    8 -1.5 moveto
    (REAL WORLD FREEHAND 3) show grestore
    } def
%%This part draws a single registration mark
%%Note that I'm using "setseparationgray," not normal
%%"setgray" to get my marks to print on all colors
3 0 360 arc currentpoint 0 setseparationgray fill grestore
/ypos exch def
/xpos exch def
xpos 3 sub ypos translate
0 0 moveto
gsave newpath 0 0 5 0 360 arc .3 setlinewidth
    0 setseparationgray stroke grestore
gsave -3 0 moveto 3 0 lineto .3 setlinewidth
    1 setseparationgray stroke grestore
gsave 0 3 moveto 0 -3 lineto .3 setlinewidth
    1 setseparationgray stroke grestore
gsave -3 0 moveto -7 0 lineto .3 setlinewidth
    0 setseparationgray stroke grestore
gsave 0 3 moveto 0 7 lineto .3 setlinewidth
    0 setseparationgray stroke grestore
gsave 3 0 moveto 7 0 lineto .3 setlinewidth
    0 setseparationgray stroke grestore
gsave 0 -3 moveto 0 -7 lineto .3 setlinewidth
    0 setseparationgray stroke grestore
%%If this is the first time we've been through this
%%routine for this color, draw the type and the color bars
firstTime 0 eq {doType doBoxes} if
%%Increment our kludgy counter
/firstTime firstTime 1 add def
%If the counter's up to three, reset it
firstTime 3 eq {/firstTime 0 def} if
grestore} bdf
end %%Close FreeHandDict
end %%Close FHIODict
```

If you want to make your registration marks even better (so that FreeHand prints registration marks vertically centered on both sides of your page), see "Improving FreeHand's Registration Marks (Even More)," later in this chapter.

FIGURE 8-5
Improved registration
marks and color bars

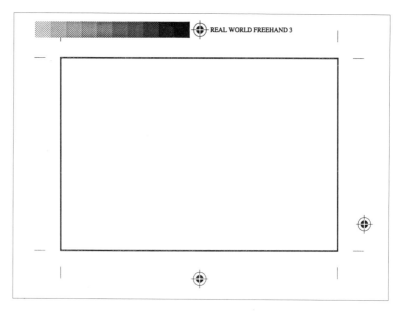

**Creating and Using
a UserPrep File**

If you've created some PostScript line or fill effects or have borrowed them from some other source (such as this book, other PostScript books, or the text files you found on someone's Corel Draw disks) and want to use them in FreeHand, the simplest thing to do is to create a PostScript dictionary of your own. The following steps give you an overview of the process.

1. Using a word processor or a PostScript programming tool such as LaserTalk from Adobe Systems, create a series of procedures you want to use.

2. Save the procedures as a text-only file named USERPREP and place the file in either the Aldus folder in your system folder or inside the folder containing your copy of FreeHand.

3. In FreeHand, select a path to which you want to apply one of your new PostScript effects.

4. Press Command-E to display the Fill and line dialog box.

5. Choose "PostScript" from the Fill or Line pop-up menu.

6. Type the name of your procedure in the PostScript code text edit box, preceding it with any variables it requires.

7. Close the dialog box and print your publication. If you get a PostScript error or if nothing prints, you've made a mistake in either your USERPREP or the way you entered the procedure in the Fill and line dialog box. Find it and fix it. Errors containing the words "nostringval," "nocurrentpoint," and "stack underflow" are usually caused by entering a variable improperly before the procedure name in the Fill and line dialog box.

Figure 8-6 shows how you'd use an example USERPREP.

FIGURE 8-6

Using USERPREP

A sample USERPREP file. This file defines one PostScript fill effect, "scribble."

```
%%UserPrep
/scribble
%%on stack: random number seed, line weight, number of lines
    {/ns xdf /lineWeight xdf /seed xdf /SC sc def
    seed srand lineWeight w
    flattenpath pathbbox clip /top xdf /right xdf /bottom xdf /left xdf
    fc length 4 eq
        {/colorChange
            {fc {newTint} forall 4 array astore /sc xdf} def}
        {/colorChange
            {fc 0 get {newTint} mul /tint xdf sc 0 tint put} def
        } ifelse
    /randint
        {rand exch mod} def
    /newTint
        {/random {100 randint .01 mul} def random mul} def
    /xy
        {rand right left sub cvi mod left add rand
        top bottom sub cvi mod bottom add
        } bdf
    ns {n xy m xy xy xy C S colorChange} repeat
    /sc SC def} def %%end UserPrep
```

Type the parameters your new fill effect expects (in this example, you'd type a seed for the random number generator, the line width, and the number of lines you want), followed by the name of the procedure.

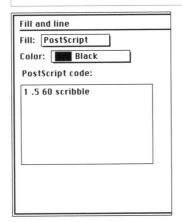

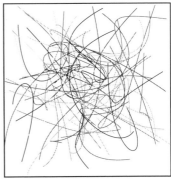

"scribble" PostScript fill effect

Looking at FreeHand's PostScript Resources

The Post and STR# resources inside FreeHand contain all of Free-Hand's PostScript code. If you're creating your own PostScript code, or if you're creating external resource files, you'll probably find it helpful to take a look at these resources.

What's the difference between the PostScript that's in the Post resources and the PostScript that's in the STR#s? Most of the Post resources contain PostScript variable definitions, procedures, and dictionaries—the PostScript that gets downloaded *before* your publication. The PostScript in the STR# resources contains the PostScript that's sent to your printer (or file) to describe what's inside your publication.

To open FreeHand's Post resources, follow the steps below (see Figure 8-7). If you haven't created a template for the Post resource class, you might want to skip ahead to "Creating External Resource Files," to find out how. It's much easier to look at and edit these resources if you use a template (the POST template in ResEdit won't work).

1. Start ResEdit.

2. Locate and open your FreeHand application. Always work on a copy of FreeHand so that you don't inadvertently damage the application.

3. Type "Post "to select the Post resource class and press Return to open the class.

4. ResEdit displays a list of all of the Post resources in FreeHand.

5. When you're through looking at the resources, close the file or quit ResEdit.

The resources are labelled by number, and it can take a while to locate the code you want. Since I've already gone through the resources, I can tell you where things are (see Table 8-2).

What's the point of all of this? If you know where something is, you can change it, which is what most of the rest of this chapter is about. If you're happy with everything about the way FreeHand prints, or don't feel the urge to create your own PostScript effects, or aren't curious, you can skip the rest of the chapter. If you want to change the way

FIGURE 8-7

Looking at FreeHand's

Post resources

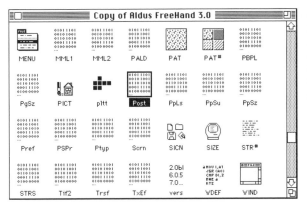

Locate and open a copy of FreeHand using ResEdit. Select the Post resource class and press Return to open it.

ResEdit displays a list of the Post resources inside FreeHand. Select one and press Return to open it.

If you haven't yet created a resource template for the Post resource class, you'll see something like this. The text to the right of the columns of hexadecimal numbers is the actual PostScript code FreeHand sends to your printer (or to an EPS file).

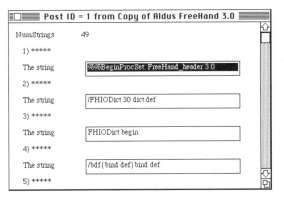

If you've skipped ahead and created a Post resource template, you'll see something like this. As you can see, it's quite a bit easier to read than the view of the same resource shown above.

This resource contains the start of FreeHand's user dictionaries.

TABLE 8-2	Resource ID	What's in it
Selected FreeHand Post resources	10000	ropedict, the PostScript dictionary containing support routines for drawing custom PostScript lines
	10006	texturedict, the PostScript dictionary containing code for rendering FreeHand's custom Post-Script textured fills (coquille, sand, denim, etc.)
	10007	random leaves fill effect
	10008	random grass fill effect
	10009	new noise fill effect
	10010	bwnoise fill effect
	10011	topnoise fill effect
	10012	neon line effect
	10013	burlap fill effect
	10014	denim fill effect
	10015	sand fill effect
	10016	coarse gravel fill effect
	10017	fine gravel fill effect
	10018	light mezzo fill effect
	10019	medium mezzo fill effect
	10020	coquille fill effect
	10021	supdict. support dictionary for custom Post-Script fill and line effects
	10022	arrow line effect
	10023	braid line effect
	10024	crepe line effect
	10025	snowflake line effect

	Resource ID	What's in it
TABLE 8-2 *Continued*	10026	tiger teeth fill effect
	10027	two waves line effect
	10028	three waves line effect
	10029	wedge line effect
	10030	star line effect
	10031	cartographer line effect
	10032	checker line effect
	10033	dot line effect
	10034	diamond line effect
	10035	right diagonal line effect
	10036	left diagonal line effect
	10037	rectangle line effect
	10038	ball line effect
	10039	squiggle line effect
	10040	swirl line effect
	10041	zigzag line effect
	10042	roman line effect
	10043	heart line effect
	9002	heavy text effect
	9003	oblique text effect
	9004	shadow text effect
	9005	stroke/fill text effect
	9122	zoom text effect
	9123	inline text effect

FreeHand prints your registration marks, or add new PostScript line and fill effects, or really know what's under the hood, read on.

Tip:
Making Textured
Fills Transparent

If you want FreeHand's textured fills ("Burlap," "Denim," "Coquille," etc.) to print with a transparent background, you can edit the Post resource that controls the way that they print. This is one of the simplest, easiest, and most useful changes you can make to FreeHand's Post resources.

First, if you haven't already skipped ahead to build yourself a Post resource template, do so now. The example screens I'll show use the template, not the hexadecimal display.

To make FreeHand's textured fills transparent, follow these steps (see Figure 8-8).

1. Start ResEdit. Locate and open a copy of FreeHand.

2. Locate and select the Post resource class and open it by pressing Return (or by double-clicking on the icon). ResEdit opens FreeHand's Post resource class and displays a list of all the Post resources inside FreeHand.

3. Select and open the Post resource number 10006.

4. Scroll through the resource until you reach String number 56.

5. Type "%%" in front of the first character in strings 56, 57, 58, and 59.

6. Press Command-S to save your work. Quit ResEdit.

FIGURE 8-8
Making textured fills
transparent

Type "%%" before
the first characters
in these strings.

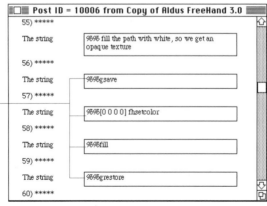

When you print textured fills from this copy of FreeHand, they'll print with transparent backgrounds. If you want an opaque background behind one of your textured fills, draw an opaque shape behind the object containing the textured fill.

FreeHand's STR# resources contain text that FreeHand uses in dialog boxes, menus, the info bar, and lots of other places, including the PostScript that FreeHand generates to describe a page. The procedure for viewing STR# resources is identical to that described for viewing Post resources above, except that you don't need to create a template for STR#s—ResEdit already has one.

I haven't snooped through the FreeHand's STR# resources as much as I have the Posts, but Table 8-3 shows you some interesting things I've found.

	Resource ID	What's in it
TABLE 8-3 Selected FreeHand STR# resources	20314	Code that tells your printer how to draw FreeHand's crop marks (called "cut marks" in this resource).
	20315	Code that tells your printer how to draw FreeHand's registration marks (called "alignment marks" in this resource).
	20318	Code for printing the names of your separations off of the page area when you print.
	20410	PostScript document structuring comments (file name, creator, creation date, bounding box, etc.).
	20441	Code for specifying a change in font.
	20538	Code telling your printer to draw an opaque box behind TIFFs when printing color separations. This makes it difficult to create duotones by stacking up TIFFs. You can change this, as shown in "Overprinting TIFFs," later in this chapter.

Changing FreeHand's PostScript

Earlier in this chapter, in "Looking at FreeHand's PostScript Resources," I talked about the PostScript inside FreeHand's STR# resources. Did you ever wonder how FreeHand knew to send the following code to your printer or file to change to a new font, scale the font, and draw a string of text? If you used ResEdit to open STR# 20190 inside Free-Hand, you'd see the resource shown in Figure 8-9.

```
/f1 /|_____Sabon-Roman dup RF findfont def
{
f1 [24 0 0 24 0 0] makesetfont
176.225555 658.196564 m
0 0 32 0 0 (Rapture!) ts
```

FIGURE 8-9
STR# 20190

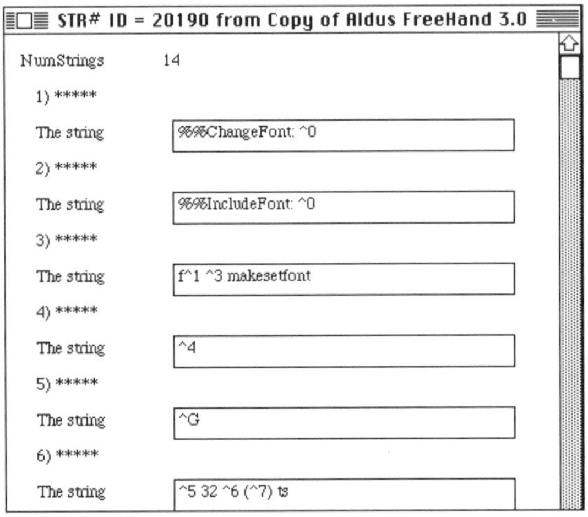

STR# ID = 20190 from Copy of Aldus FreeHand 3.0	
NumStrings	14
1) *****	
The string	%%ChangeFont: ^0
2) *****	
The string	%%IncludeFont: ^0
3) *****	
The string	f^1 ^3 makesetfont
4) *****	
The string	^4
5) *****	
The string	^G
6) *****	
The string	^5 32 ^6 (^7) ts

Does the gibberish in the figure look familiar? It's a blank form for the PostScript above. The characters preceded by a caret (^) are FreeHand's internal representations of the data it'll use to fill out the form. Some of the tags are pretty easy to figure out—in this example, ^1 equals "1" and ^5 and ^6 represent "0 0." But it's not all that simple. Look at ^4, which combines ^1 and ^3 with other data.

In many cases, only FreeHand knows what's going on. Still, you can do quite a bit with the simple stuff. Following are two of my favorite STR# modifications.

Overprinting TIFFs. If you read Chapter 4, "Importing and Exporting," you remember that I complained about FreeHand 3's habit of always knocking out anything under a TIFF, regardless of that TIFF's overprinting specifications. Having TIFFs knock everything out makes it tough to do duotones (where you want to be able to position one TIFF on top of another).

While I was snooping around in FreeHand's STR#s late one night, I found a resource that started with the comment "%draw a box behind the TIFF." There it was: the grail. And all you have to do is comment out the last line (which sets the color of the box). The following steps show you how (see Figure 8-10).

1. Start ResEdit.

2. Locate and open a copy of FreeHand.

3. Type "STR#" to select the STR# resource class.

4. Press Return to open the STR# resource class. ResEdit displays all of the STR# resources in FreeHand.

5. Select STR# resource number 20538 and press Command-C.

6. Press Command-N to create a new resource. Name it "no knockout.fhx3" (or something like that) and press Return. ResEdit creates your new, empty resource.

7. Press Command-V to paste the STR# you copied out of FreeHand into your new resource.

8. Open the STR# resource class and open the single STR# resource inside. Scroll to the end of the resource and type "%" at the start of the last line in the resource.

9. Choose "Get info about *filename*" from the File menu. In the Type text edit box, type "FHX3." Type "FHA3" in the Creator text edit box. Save your file and quit ResEdit.

Put the FHX3 file you've just created in your Aldus folder. The next time you start FreeHand, FreeHand will use this resource instead of its own STR# 20538. When you print, your TIFFs won't knock out. When you want your TIFFs to knock out again, just move the FHX3 file out of the Aldus folder (or draw a box behind them).

FIGURE 8-10

Making TIFFs overprint

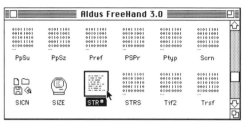

Start ResEdit. Locate and open FreeHand, and select the STR# resource class. Double-click the icon to open the resource class.

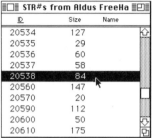

Select STR# resource number 20538 and press Command-V to copy it to the Clipboard.

Press Command-N to create a new resource file. Paste the STR# resource into the new file.

Open the STR# resource. Scroll to the last string in the resource and type "%" before the first character of the string.

Choose "Get info about filename" from the File menu and change the file's type and creator.

Press Command-S to save your work. Quit ResEdit.

Put the new resource file in your Aldus folder.

Improving FreeHand's Registration Marks (Even More). The FREE-HAND POSTSCRIPT PATCHES file shown earlier in the chapter improves the appearance of FreeHand's registration marks, and adds a color bar. That's great, but what if you want to position the registration mark on the right side of the publication at the vertical center of the page, rather than near the lower-right crop marks. And what if you want to add a registration mark on the left?

It's easy to do using a replacement STR# resource. First, copy STR# 20315 out of a copy of FreeHand and into a new resource file using the procedure described in Steps 1 through 7 of the previous section. After you've completed those steps, you should have a new resource file with a single STR# resource in it. Then follow these steps (see Figure 8-11).

1. Open the STR# resource class and open the single STR# resource inside.

2. Scroll to the sixth string in the resource. It should look like this:

   right bleed add ^P sub abs xs mul 1 le {right bleed add 9 xs
   div add 20 ys div bottom add am} if

3. Change the resource so that it looks like this:

   right bleed add ^P sub abs xs mul 1 le {right bleed add 9 xs
   div add top bottom add 2 div am} if
   %%left reg mark
   left bleed sub ^O sub abs xs mul 1 le
   {left bleed sub 9 xs div sub
   top bottom add 2 div am} if

4. Press Command-W to close the resource.

5. Choose "Get info about *filename*" from the File menu. Type "FHX3" in the Type text edit box and "FHA3" in the Creator text edit box. Save your file and quit ResEdit.

6. Open your word processor and type in the FREEHAND POST-SCRIPT PATCHES file shown in "Improving FreeHand's Registration Marks," earlier in this chapter (or open the file, if you created it earlier). Change the line that starts with "firstTime 3 eq" and change it to read "firstTime 4 eq" (after all, we're working with four registration marks now).

FIGURE 8-11
More improved
registration marks

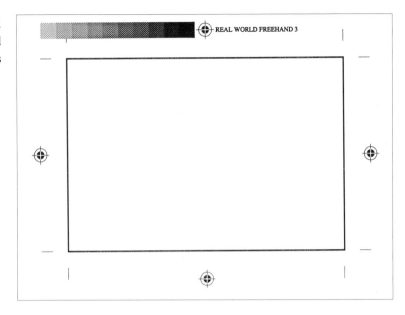

Put your new FHX3 in your Aldus folder. When you next launch FreeHand, it'll use this resource instead its internal STR# 20315. And when you print, you'll get your improved registration marks.

Creating External Resource Files

One of FreeHand 3's most significant new features is that you can extend the program using external resource files. Almost any preexisting resource in FreeHand can be replaced by an external resource file, and whole new resources can be added to FreeHand. Before you go off half-cocked and start trying to add charting modules to FreeHand, let me point out a few practical limitations. We can't easily get at *how* FreeHand works, because most of the active part of FreeHand is compiled code. We can, however, get at *what* this active part of FreeHand works with.

We can, for example, easily add menu items to the pop-up menus in the Fill and line dialog box, but it's quite another matter to add another pop-up menu. FreeHand wouldn't know what to do with it (unless you added new CODE resources—which is way beyond the scope of this book).

Don't take these limitations too hard. The number of things you can do with external resource files is mind-boggling. The additions that I find most exciting are the ones that extend FreeHand's printing abilities and the ones that add new PostScript lines, fills, and halftone screens. I've placed most of this book's discussion of external resource files in this chapter because these exciting modifications and additions have to do with PostScript.

Why use external resource files to add PostScript effects instead of creating a USERPREP file? Because it's too easy to make mistakes entering variables for an external USERPREP. External resources make it easy to remember what variables a procedure needs, because you can display a dialog box containing buttons, text edit boxes, and pop-up menus. Creating external resource files is much more difficult than creating a USERPREP file, but it's worth it.

Creating FreeHand 3 Resource Templates. Before you can create any external resources for FreeHand, you've got to create four resource templates in ResEdit. Don't let that deter you, though. This part is easy. You don't have to know the theory of how this stuff works—I don't. I just know what to do to get the results I want, and I'm happy to share the results of my trial and error experimentation with you.

We'll be creating templates named FlEf (Fill Effects), LnEf (Line Effects), Post (PostScript; this resource type differs from the built-in POST resource, so don't think you can skip creating this one), and Scrn (Halftone Screens). We'll add the templates to a copy of ResEdit, which we'll then use to create our external resource files.

I used ResEdit 2.1 to create my templates, and I strongly suggest you use ResEdit version 2.1 or higher. Version 2.1 is light-years ahead of earlier versions in stability, capability, and ease of use. If it gets much better, they'll have to start charging money for it. As it is, you can get ResEdit from your local Apple user group, or even from computer stores (though they often want you to pay them for the disk). I cannot thank Apple Computer enough for this tool, which makes it (relatively) easy for Macintosh users to augment and customize their system software and applications. Nothing like ResEdit exists on any other platform.

We'll create the Post resource template first, following the steps below (see Figure 8-12).

1. Make a copy of ResEdit and open the copy with ResEdit.

2. Locate and select the TMPL resource (you can just type "T" to move to the resource). Double-click to open it. A listing of available templates appears.

3. Press Command-K to create a new template. We're going to use Command-K again several different times in this procedure, to do several different things. What Command-K does varies depending on the context you're in (usually changing based on what you've got selected). Command-K generally means "create another one," with the object being created determined by what window you're in or what you've got selected. In this case, a new, empty template appears.

4. Select the field tag ("1)*****") in the template window and press Command-K to create a new field. Two new text edit boxes, "Label" and "Type" appear, along with another field tag ("2)*****").

5. In the Label text edit box, type (exactly as shown) "Num-Strings" and in the Type text edit box, type "OCNT" (that's the letter "O," not a zero).

6. Select the next field tag and press Command-K to create another new field. Again, a new field tag and two text edit boxes appear. Type "*****" in the Label text edit box and type "LSTC" in the Type text edit box.

7. Select the next field tag and press Command-K to create a third new field. Type "The string" in the Label text edit box, then type "PSTR" in the Type text edit box.

8. Select the next field tag and press Command-K to create the fourth and last field in the resource template. Type "*****" in the Label text edit box and type "LSTE" in the Type text edit box.

9. Press Command-I to display the Info window for the template. Type a fairly high number (I use 2000) in the ID text edit box. You do this to keep the new resource ID from conflicting with the preexisting templates. Press Tab to move to the Name text edit box. Type "Post" in the Name text edit box and press

FIGURE 8-12
Creating ResEdit
templates

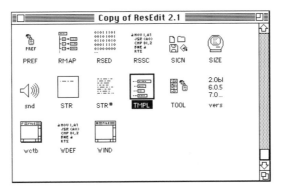

*Make a copy of ResEdit,
and then open the copy
with ResEdit.*

*Select the TMPL
resource class, and press
Return to open it (or
double-click the icon).*

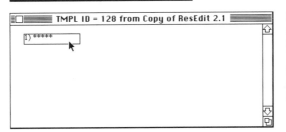

*ResEdit displays a list of all of the
template resources inside the copy of
ResEdit.*

*Press Command-K to create a new
resource template.*

*ResEdit creates and
opens a new resource
template.*

*Select the first field
("*****") and press
Command-K.*

*Two text edit
boxes appear.*

*Type "NumStrings" in
the Label text edit box
and type "OCNT" in
the Type text edit box.*

FIGURE 8-12
Continued

Create more fields and fill them in as shown.

TMPL ID = 128 from Copy of ResEdit 2.1

1) *****
Label   NumStrings
Type   OCNT
2) *****
Label   *****
Type   LSTC
3) *****
Label   The string
Type   PSTR
4) *****
Label   *****
Type   LSTE
5) *****

Press Command-I to display the info window for your new resource.

Info for TMPL 2000 from Copy of ResEdit 2.1

Type: TMPL   Size: 0
ID: 2000
Name: Post

Owner type

Owner ID: DRVR
Sub ID: WDEF
                           MDEF

Attributes:
☐ System Heap   ☐ Locked   ☐ Preload
☐ Purgeable   ☐ Protected   ☐ Compressed

Type "2000" in the ID text edit box and type "Post" in the Name text edit box.

Press Command-S to save your work. Press Command-W twice to close the two top-most windows.

TMPLs from Copy of ResE

ID	Size	Name
267	16	"CMDK"
268	25	"RVEW"
269	416	"fval"
270	118	"resf"
271	193	"CMNU"
272	126	"hwin"
273	146	"sect"
274	138	"ppcc"
2000	50	"Post"

Your new template appears in the list of templates.

Command-W twice to close both the Info window and the TMPL window.

Your new resource template appears in the listing of templates.

Follow the same procedure to create two more templates, entering the values shown in Table 8-4 in each field as you create it.

Name	Field	Label	Type
Scrn	1	Screen display 0 = default 1 = dot 2 = line	DWRD
	2	STR# res. id	DWRD
	3	STR# index (menu text)	DWRD
	4	PostScript spot function	PSTR
LnEf	1	STR# res. id	DWRD
	2	STR# index	DWRD
	3	POST 1	DWRD
	4	POST 2	DWRD
	5	POST 3	DWRD
	6	POST 4	DWRD
	7	DLOG res id	DWRD
	8	parameters	OCNT
	9	*****	LSTC
	10	param type	DWRD
	11	DITL item #	DWRD
	12	min	DWRD
	13	max	DWRD
	14	default	DWRD
	15	*****	LSTE
	16	PS parsing string	PSTR

TABLE 8-4
Template parameters

The FlEf resource is identical to the LnEf resource in every way except for its name and ID number, so can save yourself a little work by following these steps.

1. Select the LnEf template you've created and press Command-C to copy it to the Clipboard.

2. Without deselecting the LnEf template, press Command-I to display the Info window for the template. Change the ID number and press Command-W to close the Info window.

3. Press Command-V to paste the template from the Clipboard.

4. Without deselecting the LnEf template you've just pasted, press Command-I to display the Info window for the template. Change the name of the template from LnEf to FlEf, and press Command-W to close the Info window.

We've just built four new ResEdit tools for creating FreeHand 3 external resource files. Save your changes and quit out of this copy of ResEdit. We'll be using the copy of ResEdit we've modified, so you can throw away the original copy of ResEdit (just kidding—back it up so that you'll always be able to retrace your steps if something doesn't work).

To make sure that you've correctly created the templates, follow these steps (see Figure 8-13).

1. Open the modified copy of ResEdit.

2. Press Command-N to create a new file. Type a name for the file and press Return. A new file window opens.

3. Press Command-K to create a new resource. ResEdit displays the Select New Type dialog box. Scroll through the list of templates until you find one of the templates you added to this copy of ResEdit. Select one and press Return to close the dialog box.

FIGURE 8-13
Testing the templates

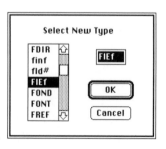

If everything's gone well, you'll see your new resource templates in the Select New Type dialog box.

If you've built the new templates successfully, ResEdit creates a new resource and opens a view of the resource that's formatted according to the template's instructions. If this doesn't happen, go back to the steps above and try to figure out what went wrong. Are you sure you're using the copy of ResEdit you modified?

Test all four of the templates. When you're through, you can throw this dummy resource file away.

Creating New PostScript Lines and Fills. If you don't know Post-Script, this section will show you how to add a variety of new PostScript lines and fills to FreeHand. If you do know PostScript, the examples in this section will show you how to fit your code into FreeHand's scheme of things. There are really three ways to add Post-Script lines and fills to FreeHand.

- Add new lines and fills based on support routines already inside FreeHand.

- Add new lines and fills based on support routines outside of FreeHand.

- Mixing and matching the two above methods.

What's the big deal about support routines? While you can create a simple PostScript line by typing PostScript code in the PostScript dialog box, remember that you're limited to 255 characters. If you want an effect which repeats some shape along a path, or changes shape randomly, you'll probably need more room. Most PostScript is based on pieces of code that are used over and over again to do some particular function (picking a random integer, for example). These pieces of code are called support routines. They can't create the effect you want by themselves, but they keep you from having to reinvent the wheel each time you want to create a new PostScript effect.

Why would you want to use FreeHand's existing routines? Free-Hand's PostScript user dictionary contains routines for repeating an object along a path (line effects), for filling a path with a repeated shape (fill effects), and for filling a path with a randomly rotated and scaled shape (more fill effects). I don't know about you, but it would take me literally years to write PostScript code that'd do these things alone. And there's more good stuff inside FreeHand for you to take advantage of. The drawback to using FreeHand's support routines? You have to know what they are and how to use them.

Why would you want to use your own routines? You know them better. If you're a PostScript hack like David Blatner of PSpatterns fame, you've already written totally different routines for doing the same things (and different things, too), and have a certain number of PostScript effects you created for FreeHand 2 you want to convert to FreeHand 3 external resources. The drawback to using your own support routines? It can take a while to copy them all into a Post resource, because you've got to cut them into 255-character chunks.

Clearly, mixing and matching has the potential to give you the best of both worlds. Whenever possible, you can use the code that Altsys and Aldus spent blood, sweat, and person-years creating. And then, when necessary, you can create your own support dictionary to do things beyond the scope of the built-in code.

Creating Custom PostScript Lines Using FreeHand's Built-in Routines. You can use FreeHand's built-in custom line drawing routines to create virtually any line pattern you can imagine. Here's how it works. The PostScript routines found in FreeHand's newrope procedure take values from a subroutine containing instructions for drawing one iteration of the pattern you want to repeat along the line. The procedures then scale, space, and color the pattern according to the values you enter in a dialog box (see Figure 8-14).

The heart of the subroutine is a kind of cell—like a tiny FreeHand page that's one unit square. The size of the unit itself doesn't matter, because the scale of the cell gets determined later by the values you enter in the line's associated dialog box. The zero point of this line-drawing cell is placed at its center, and all of FreeHand's line drawing commands (which you use to construct the line pattern) get their coordinates relative to this zero point.

You can create an enlarged version of this cell to use in plotting the placement of line segments and paths inside the cell, as shown in Figure 8-15.

1. Open FreeHand and press Command-N to create a new file.

2. In the Document setup dialog box, type "0p144" for both the width and height of the page, and enter a bleed amount of

FIGURE 8-14
How FreeHand draws
custom PostScript lines

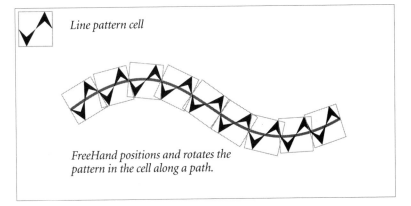

Line pattern cell

FreeHand positions and rotates the
pattern in the cell along a path.

FIGURE 8-15
Coordinate matrix for
creating custom lines

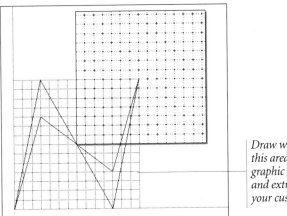

Draw whatever you want in
this area, then export the
graphic as "Generic EPS"
and extract the pattern for
your custom line.

0p100. Enter "0p10" in the Visible grid text edit box. Enter "0p5" in the Snap-to grid text edit box. Press Return to close the dialog box.

3. Create a grid that's 100-points square, with grid lines every 5 points.

4. Select the grid, press Command-G to group it, and press Command-I to display the Group dialog box.

5. Type "-50" in both the Vertical and Horizontal text edit boxes and press Return. FreeHand moves your grid so that its center point is precisely above the bottom-left corner of your publication's page.

6. Create a background layer, select the grid, and send the grid to the background layer.

Now that you can use the grid as a guide for creating your new line style, draw anything you want inside the grid. When you've got something you think would make a good line pattern, export the file as a "Generic" EPS file, and then use a word processor to extract the line pattern from the EPS graphic.

1. Open the file with your word processor. If you're using Microsoft Word, you can open the file by holding down Shift as you choose "Open..." from the File menu or press Shift-F6 and choose the file from the list of files in the Select a Document dialog box.

2. Delete everything preceding the first line ending with an "m" ("moveto") instruction.

3. Delete everything from the start of the line "%%Trailer" to the end of the file.

4. Delete any occurrence of "vmrs," "vmr," "vms," "u," or "U" in the file.

At this point, the file contains only the commands for drawing and filling the shape (or shapes) you drew.

Once you've got the line pattern, you can plug it into a couple of PostScript routines. Type the code shown below, replacing the variables shown in italics with the names you want your routines to use and with the line pattern you extracted from the EPS graphic in the previous section.

```
ropedict begin  %%FreeHand's set of line effect procedures
/linepatternname
{
gsave colorchoice initiallinewidth w n translate rotate scale
%%The next line scales the drawing instructions you extracted
%%from the FreeHand EPS to the scale of the line effect's cell
.01 .01 scale
drawingprocedures
grestore
} def
end
```

If your drawing procedures are very long (over 400 steps), you'll have to split them up into separate procedures. This relates to a PostScript limit—you can't place more than 500 operands on the stack at once. Never mind what this means; just don't do it. If you split the procedure, it would look like this.

```
ropedict begin
/drawingprocedure1
{drawinginstructions} def
/drawingprocedure2
{drawinginstructions} def
etc.
/linepatternname
{
gsave colorchoice initiallinewidth w n translate rotate scale
.01 .01 scale
drawingprocedure1 drawing procedure2, etc.
grestore
} def
end
```

Avoid procedures this complex, anyway, if you ever want to see your job print.

Here's an example line pattern.

```
/zigzag2
{
gsave colorchoice n translate rotate scale
.01 .01 scale
-15 0 m
-15 8.2844 -8.2844 15 0 15 C
8.2844 15 15 8.2844 15 0 C
15 -8.2844 8.2844 -15 0 -15 C
-8.2844 -15 -15 -8.2844 -15 0 C
f
n
-50 0 m
-25 50 L
25 -50 L
50 0 L
25 -35 L
-25 35 L
-50 0 L
```

```
f
n
grestore
} def
end
```

The shapes in this line pattern are filled but not stroked, so there's no need for the initial line width variable. There's also no need for any explicit color settings ("[0 0 0 1] ka") because the color of the object is set by the Color pop-up menu in the dialog box. (I haven't talked about the dialog box yet, but I will soon.)

Now that you've got the idea, let's create an external resource file that adds a new custom PostScript line pattern to FreeHand. First, create the Post resource containing the PostScript code for the example line (see Figure 8-16).

1. Under MultiFinder, start both your word processor and ResEdit.

2. Type the PostScript code shown above into your word processor.

3. Switch to ResEdit. Press Command-N to create a new resource file. Type a name for your resource file and press Return. ResEdit opens a new, empty window. Press Command-K to add a resource to the open resource file. In the text edit box in the Select New Type dialog box, type "Post" (not "POST") and press Return to close the dialog box. ResEdit opens the new Post resource. Select the field number ("1)*****") and press Command-K to create a new field.

4. Switch back to your word processor. Select the first 255 or fewer characters (you can use your word processor's character count feature, if it's got one, to see how many characters you have selected) and press Command-X to cut them to the Clipboard.

5. Switch to ResEdit. Click inside "The string" and press Command-V to paste the PostScript code from the Clipboard. ResEdit pastes the code into the text edit box. Select the next field number and press Command-K to create a new field.

6. Repeat Steps 4 and 5 until you've copied all of the PostScript code into the Post resource.

FIGURE 8-16

FreeHand custom line dialog box

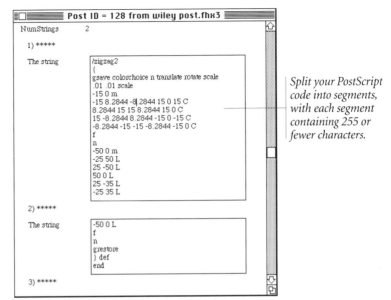

Split your PostScript code into segments, with each segment containing 255 or fewer characters.

7. Press Command-W to close the Post resource. If ResEdit displays a warning that one of the strings is too long, you'll have to go back and figure out which field in the Post resource holds more than 255 characters. You can probably cut and paste text inside the Post resource to make everything come out right.

8. Without deselecting the Post resource, press Command-I to display its Info window. Give the resource a high ID number (over 25000) so that it won't conflict with any existing Free-Hand resources. Save your work.

If you were creating an external resource file from scratch, or if you wanted to create a line with some nonstandard properties, you'd have to create a new dialog box using DLOG and DITL resources. (DLOGs are resources that create the dialog boxes. DITL resources contain the text, buttons, etc., that go inside dialog boxes. The information that's found in a DITL is displayed inside a DLOG.) But you're not—you're creating a custom line that uses the same variables as most of FreeHand's internal custom lines: color, pattern width, pattern height, and distance between patterns. This means that you can use a dialog box that already exists inside FreeHand. This dialog box is DITL (and DLOG) ID 20930 inside FreeHand (see Figure 8-17).

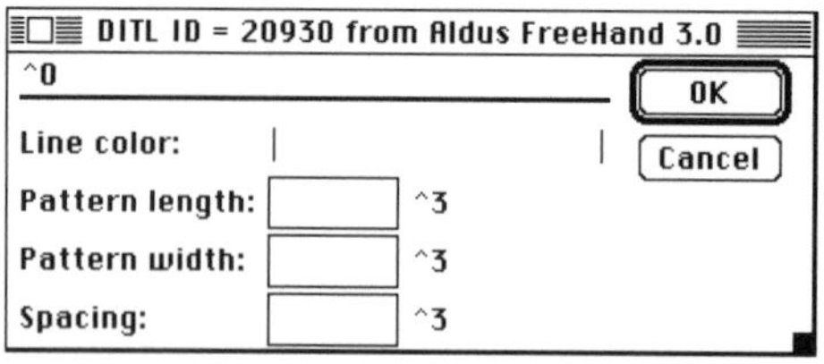

FIGURE 8-17
FreeHand custom line
dialog box

We don't need to copy this dialog box into our external resource file in order to use it, we just enter the right ID numbers in the LnEf resource.

Now we'll use one of ResEdit's stock templates, STR#, to add the name of the line as we want it displayed on the Effect pop-up menu.

1. In ResEdit, with the external resource file open, press Command-K to create a new resource. The Select New Type dialog box appears. In the text edit box, type "STR#" and press Return to close the dialog box. ResEdit creates and opens a resource.

2. Select the field number ("1)*****") and press Command-K to create a new field. Click inside the new text edit box.

3. Type the name of the line as you want it to appear on the Effect pop-up menu and press Command-W to close the STR# resource.

4. Select the STR# resource and press Command-I to open the Info window for the resource. Type the same ID number as you typed for the Post resource. Press Tab, type the name of the line effect, and then press Command-Option-W to close all of the open windows on the STR# resource.

Next, you'll create an LnEf resource for our external resource file. The LnEf resource ties everything together. It tells FreeHand where to look for the PostScript code and where to find any support routines that the code requires. It also points to the DLOG and DITL resources so that FreeHand knows what dialog box to display. Parameter types help FreeHand make sense out of the information you enter in the dialog box. Finally, the PostScript string field determines the order in which the variables are sent during printing. The following steps create an LnEf resource for your example line effect.

1. If you're not still in ResEdit, start ResEdit and open the external resource file you've been working on. Press Command-K to cre-

ate a new resource. In the Select New Type dialog box, type "LnEf" in the text edit box and press Return to close the dialog box. ResEdit creates and opens a new LnEf resource.

2. In the STR# res. id field, type the ID number of the STR# resource you created above. In the STR# index file, type the number of the field in the STR# resource containing the string you want FreeHand to use in the Effect pop-up menu for this line effect. In this case, type "1."

3. In the Post 1 field, type "10021," which is the ID number of a Post resource inside FreeHand containing the support routines used to create custom PostScript line effects. In the POST 2 field, type "10000," which is the ID number for a resource in FreeHand containing more support routines. In the POST 3 field, type the ID number for the Post resource in the external resource file. Leave the POST 4 field blank. These fields tell Free-Hand where to find all of the PostScript code needed to render the custom line effect.

4. In the DLOG res id field, type the number of the DLOG corresponding to the dialog box we want FreeHand to display when we choose our new line effect from the Effect pop-up menu. In this case, type "20930."

5. Select the field number following the parameters field and press Command-K to create fields to enter parameter information. Five new text edit boxes appear. In the Param type text edit box, type "0"; in the DITL item # text edit box, type "7." Type "0" in the min text edit box and "1" in the max text edit box. Type "1" in the default text edit box. The DITL item # text edit box tells FreeHand what text edit box, button, or pop-up menu in the dialog box provides the value for this parameter. In the example dialog box, the pop-up menu for the color of the line is DITL item # 7; the Pattern height text edit box is DITL item # 9; the Pattern width text edit box is DITL item # 10; and the Spacing text edit box is DITL item # 11.

6. Repeat Step 5 three more times, entering the values shown in Table 8-5 as you create each new field.

TABLE 8-5

Filling in parameters

Field number	Param type	DITL item #	Min	Max	Default
2	3	9	0	1000	0
3	2	10	0	1000	10
4	3	11	0	1000	0

7. Now enter the PostScript string you want FreeHand to send to your printer (or to a file) in the PSTR resource. Type in the procedure name you've just created, and the variables you want to get back from the dialog box, preceded by carets (^), in the order in which they appear in the dialog box, followed by the word "newrope". Here's how a generic PSTR for a line effect would look, with variables you'd plug in shown in italic.

{nameOfEffect} patternLength patternWidth spacing lineColor newrope

For the example code shown above, you enter the following.

{zigzag2} ^1 ^2 ^3 ^0 newrope

8. Press Command-W to close the LnEf window. Select the new resource and press Command-I to display the Info window for the resource. Type the same ID number as you did for the Post and STR# resources and whatever name you want.

Only one more thing to go before you save, close, and test the file, and that's to change its file and creator type.

1. Choose "Get Info about *filename*" (where *filename* is the name you gave the file when you created it) from the File menu. ResEdit displays the Info dialog box for the file.

2. In the Type text edit box, type "FHX3." In the Creator text edit box, type "FHA3."

3. Press Command-W to close the dialog box. ResEdit asks if you want to save the changes to your file. You do, so click Yes.

4. Quit ResEdit.

Move the external resource file you've just created to the Aldus folder in your system folder.

Test the external resource file by opening FreeHand 3, drawing a path, and pressing Command-E to display the Fill and line dialog box. Can you see your example line effect on the Effect pop-up menu after you choose Custom on the Lines pop-up menu? If so, select it. If not, run through the procedures above and try to see where you made an error.

When you select the custom line from the Effect pop-up menu, does the dialog box appear? If so, choose a color and type some values into the text edit boxes. Press Return twice to close both the custom line's dialog box and the Fill and line dialog box.

Now try printing the file. If it prints, congratulations! You've just added a line effect to your copy of FreeHand 3. If it doesn't print, it's most likely you've either typed something wrong or have made an incorrect entry in one of the Post text edit boxes in the LnEf resource (suspect this first if you get an "undefined" PostScript error).

Creating an external resource requires considerable attention to detail, because the LnEf resource you create has to keep track of the IDs of six other resources and other information inside those resources. Figure 8-18 should help you sort it out.

FIGURE 8-18
The LnEf resource keeps
track of other resource
locations

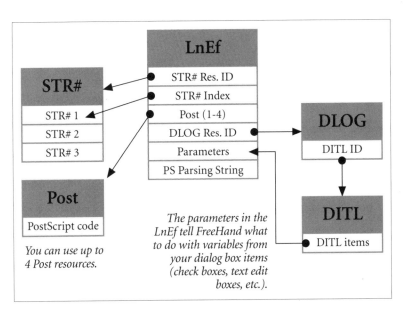

Once you've got everything working, why not add some more line effects to the external resource? The only difference is that, this time, we won't have to create new resources from scratch. This time, the steps will be a little bit more general, so refer back to the procedures earlier in this section if you're having a hard time following along.

First, add a section to the existing Post resource (see Figure 8-19).

1. Start both ResEdit and your word processor.

2. Type the following PostScript code into your word processor.

```
ropedict begin
/helix1
{
gsave colorchoice n translate rotate scale
-.50 .0 m
-.30 .0 -.25 .35 -.25 .35 C
-.20 .70 .0 .0 .0 .0 C
0 .0 .20 -.70 .25 -.35 C
.25 -.35 .30 .0 .50 .0 C
.30 .0 .25 -.20 .25 -.20 C
.20 -.55 .0 .0 .0 .0 C
0 .0 -.20 .55 -.25 .20 C
-.25 .20 -.30 .0 -.50 .0 C
f
n
grestore
} def
end
```

3. In ResEdit, open the external resource file you created earlier and open the Post resource. Press Command-K to add a new Post. Cut and paste the PostScript code into the new Post.

4. Press Command-I to display the Info window for the new Post. Type an ID number for the new line effect (make it higher than the ID number of the line effect you created earlier), press Tab, and type a name for the effect.

5. Press Command-W to close the Post resource.

Next, create a new STR# resource to hold the name of the line effect as you want it to appear in the Effects pop-up menu.

1. Open the STR# resource.

2. Press Command-K to create a new STR#.

3. Press Command-I to display the Info window for the new STR#. Type the ID number of the STR# (it's a good idea to make it match the ID of the Post), press Tab, and type the name of the effect as you want it to appear on the Effect pop-up menu in the Fill and line dialog box.

4. Press Option-Command-W to close the STR# resource.

Because these line effects are so similar, you can copy and paste the LnEf resource.

1. Open the LnEf resource, select the LnEf resource we created earlier, and press Command-D to duplicate the resource. ResEdit creates a new resource and assigns it a new ID number.

2. Without deselecting the new LnEf resource, press Command-I to display the Info window on the resource. Type the ID number you entered above for the Post resource for the second line effect in this resource file, press Tab, and type the name of the new effect. Press Command-W to close the Info window.

4. Double-click the new LnEf (or press Return) to open it.

5. In the LnEf window, type the ID number you assigned to the STR# for this line effect, press Tab, and type "1" in the STR# index text edit box (because the name of the new line effect is in the second field in the STR# resource). Type the ID number of the new Post resource in the Post 3 text edit box. In the PS parsing string text edit box, type the name of the new PostScript procedure between the brackets. Leave everything else the same.

6. Close, save, and test the edited external resource file.

FIGURE 8-19
"Helix 1" line effect

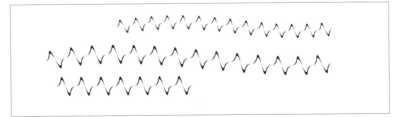

You can continue adding new custom line effects resources to this file. The only thing you have to remember is that you must keep the IDs of the Post resources straight and you must keep on updating the location of the line effect's name in the STR# resource.

Creating Custom PostScript Lines Using Your Own Support Routines. If you have your own PostScript line drawing procedures you want to use, you can create your own Post resource and add it to your external resource file. Then, in your LnEf, enter the resource ID of the Post containing your procedures—just as you entered the resource ID of the FreeHand resource containing the FreeHand's line drawing procedures (ropedict) in the examples above.

Creating Custom Fill Effects. Because you can create tiled fills inside FreeHand, there's not much need to create fill effects that simply repeat one pattern over and over again. If you want a fill effect that randomly resizes, scales, or skews a pattern inside a filled object, or if you want to create a tiled effect using an image (a paint-type graphic or a TIFF file), custom fills are just the ticket.

You can draw an object in FreeHand, and then create a fill that randomly positions some number of scaled and rotated copies of that object inside a filled path. FreeHand comes with two fills that do this: Random leaves and Random grass. Any object you can draw in Free-Hand can be turned into this type of fill effect.

You can use the 100-point-square matrix you created earlier to create the objects we want to use inside the fill, but we'll have to change it a bit first (see Figure 8-20).

1. Open the FreeHand file containing the 100-by-100 drawing matrix you created earlier, or create a new one from scratch (see "Creating Custom PostScript Lines Using FreeHand's Built-in Routines" earlier in this chapter).

2. Select the matrix of guidelines and press Command-M. The Move elements dialog box appears.

3. Type "50" in both the Vertical and Horizontal text edit boxes and press Return. FreeHand moves the guides, positioning the lower-left corner on the publication's zero point. You do this

FIGURE 8-20

Creating guidelines for
drawing fill objects

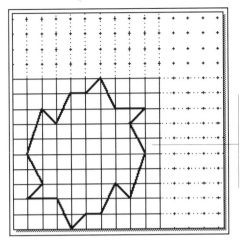

*Draw the shape you want to use
in your PostScript fill effect
inside this grid. When you've
finished, export the graphic as
"Generic EPS" and extract the
shape from the EPS file with
your word processor.*

because the coordinate system for creating fill objects is measured from the lower-left corner (this is the way PostScript
usually measures coordinates).

4. Save this file under another name so that you'll have one file for
creating line effects and one file for creating fill effects.

5. Draw an object inside the guidelines to use inside the fill. For
now, use only basic fills in this object. You can work your way
up to graduated and tiled fills later (and be forewarned—they'll
take forever to print when they're used inside a custom fill
effect). Once you've created the object, export the file as a Generic
EPS file.

Next, extract the commands from the EPS file that draw the object.

1. Open the EPS file with your word processor.

2. Delete everything preceding the first line in the file that ends
with an "m" (moveto) command.

3. Delete everything from the start of the "%%PageTrailer" line to
the end of the file.

4. Delete any occurrence of "vmrs," "vmr," "vms," "u," or "U" in
the file.

5. Delete any line ending with "Ka" or "ka."

Now you can graft the code into the PostScript routine for drawing one copy of the object.

```
supdict begin
/name of fill effect
{
brandxy translate
degrees randint rotate
/randscale size randint offset add def
randscale 100 div randscale 100 div scale
drawing commands
} def
end
```

degrees is a number you can use to limit the object's random rotation. If you don't want to limit the object's rotation, enter 360. *size* is the maximum size of the object, in points. FreeHand's existing *randint* routine will pick a number between the number you enter here and zero. To keep our printer from spending time rendering zero-sized objects, we add the value *offset* to the result of the random number. If you want objects between 10 and 50 points, therefore, you'd enter 40 for *size* and 10 for *offset*.

Here's a sample routine that draws a randomly sized (from 10 to 50 points), randomly colored, randomly rotated square each time it's called. This routine, by itself, isn't enough to create a fill effect.

```
supdict begin
/randomsquare
{
brandxy translate
360 randint rotate
/randscale 40 randint 10 add def
randscale 100 div randscale 100 div scale
0 0 moveto
0 100 L
100 100 L
100 0 L
closepath
/randomcolor [100 randint .01 div 100 randint .01 div 100
randint .01 div 100 randint .01 div] def
randomcolor setcmykcolor
f
```

```
n
} def
end
```

At this point, what we need is a routine that calls the above routine over and over again, as many times as we want. In this case, there are only two variables for you to fill in, so I've filled in the name of this routine ("randomsquares") and the name of the routine we created above ("randomsquare").

```
/randomsquares
{
supdict begin
newinside
{
gsave randomsquare grestore
} repeat end
} def
```

That's all the code, so now it's back to ResEdit to create the Post, FlEf, STR#, DITL, and DLOG resources. You have to create a DITL and a DLOG because there's no generic dialog box for fill effects inside FreeHand, as there is for line effects. You'll be able to steal one from there, though, so we won't have to start from scratch.

1. Start ResEdit without quitting your word processor. Press Command-N to create a new resource file. Type a name for the resource file ("fill effects") and press Return. ResEdit opens a window on a new, empty resource file.

2. Press Command-O to open another file. In the list of files, locate and select your FreeHand application and press Return. ResEdit opens your copy of FreeHand and displays icons representing the resource types inside FreeHand.

3. Type "DITL" to select the DITL resource type. DITLs hold the buttons, text edit boxes, and static text you see inside dialog boxes.

4. Open the DITL resource type by double-clicking on its icon. Res-Edit opens a window displaying all of the DITL resources inside

FreeHand. Select the DITL with the ID number 20925 and press Command-C to copy the resource to the Clipboard. Close the DITL resource type by pressing Command-Option-W.

5. Make the window for the new resource file (the one you created in Step 1) active by clicking on it. Paste the DITL resource from the Clipboard into the new resource file.

6. Make the window for FreeHand's resources active. Type "DLOG" to select the DLOG resource type. Open the DLOG resource type by double clicking on its icon. ResEdit displays a window showing all of the DLOGs inside FreeHand.

7. Select DLOG number 20925 and press Command-C to copy the DLOG to the Clipboard. Press Command-W to close the DLOG resource type window.

8. Make the window for the new resource file (the one you created in Step 1) active by clicking on it. Paste the DLOG resource from the Clipboard into the new resource file.

9. Click on the FreeHand window to make it active and press Command-W to close the file. If ResEdit prompts you to save any changes, click No. Remember, this is your FreeHand application and you don't want to change anything in it—at least not yet. Press Command-S to save your work.

At this point, you've got one DITL and one DLOG from FreeHand in your new resource file. Next, you need to make a few changes so that you'll be able to use these resources.

1. Double-click the DITL icon to open the DITL resource type. ResEdit opens a window displaying the one DITL resource inside this file. Select the DITL resource and press Command-I to open the Info window for the resource. Type a new ID number for the DITL. Make sure the number's over 25,000 and does not match any of the ID numbers you assigned to any line effects you created earlier in the chapter. Press Tab and type a name for the fill effect (the example code shown earlier is called "randomsquares"). Press Command-W to close the Info window.

2. Double-click the DITL resource to open it. ResEdit displays the contents of the DITL as they'd appear inside a dialog box. Don't be alarmed if the bold outline of the OK button looks weird. Just leave it alone.

3. Double-click the static text "Random leaves." ResEdit opens a window on the static text. In the Text field, type "^0." Press Command-Option-W to close all of the DITL windows you've opened. When you enter "^0" in the DITL resource for this dialog box, you direct FreeHand to plug the name of the fill effect (chosen from the Effect pop-up menu) into the title of the dialog box. This means you'll be able to use this DITL/DLOG combination for more than one fill effect. Change the static text "Number of leaves" to "How many?".

4. Double-click the DLOG icon to open the DLOG resource type. ResEdit opens a window showing the DLOG resource you copied into this file. Select the DLOG resource and press Command-I to display the Info window for this resource. Type a new number for the resource's ID that matches the number you entered for the DITL resource in Step 1. Press Tab and type the name of the fill effect you're creating ("randomsquares"). Press Command-W to close this window.

5. Double-click the DLOG resource to open it. In the DITL ID text edit field, type the ID number of the DITL you entered in Step 1. Press Command-Option-W to close all of the windows on the DLOG resource type.

6. Press Command-S to save your work.

Now that you've got the DITL and DLOG taken care of, create a Post resource to hold the PostScript code for your fill effect.

1. Press Command-K to create a new resource type. ResEdit displays the Create New Type dialog box. Type "Post" in the text edit box and press Return. ResEdit creates and opens a new Post resource type.

2. Select the first field tag ("1) *****") and press Command-K to create a new field. Click inside the new field.

3. Switch back to your word processor, where the document containing the code for the fill effect,"randomsquares," should still be open. If you've closed the document, open it.

4. Copy the first 255 or fewer characters of your PostScript code from your word processor to the Clipboard. Do not break individual lines of the code.

5. Switch to ResEdit. Press Command-V to paste the PostScript code from the Clipboard into the field you selected. Create a new field by selecting the next field tag and pressing Command-K. Click inside the new field. Switch back to your word processor and copy the next chunk of code to the Clipboard, always selecting fewer than 255 characters at a time. Repeat this step until you've copied all of the PostScript code from your word processor into the Post resource you've got open in ResEdit.

6. Press Command-I to display the Info window for this Post resource. Type the same ID number as you assigned to the DITL and DLOG resources you created earlier, press Tab, and type the name of the fill effect ("randomsquares").

7. Press Command-Option-W to close all of the windows of the Post resource type.

Three resources down (DITL, DLOG, and Post); two to go (FlEf and STR#). Create the STR# next.

1. Press Command-K to create a new resource. ResEdit displays the Create New Type dialog box. Type "STR#" in the text edit box and press Return. ResEdit creates and opens a new STR# resource.

2. Select the field tag ("1) *****") and press Command-K to create a new field.

3. Click inside the field and type the name of the fill effect as you want it to appear on the Effect pop-up menu in the Fill and line dialog box inside FreeHand (for the example fill effect, type "Random squares").

4. Press Command-I to display the Info dialog box for this resource. Type the same ID number as you've typed for all of the other resources for this effect. Press Tab and type the same name as you've typed for all of the other resources for this effect.

5. Press Command-Option-W to close all of the windows for the STR# resource type.

6. Press Command-S to save your work.

The last step in this process is to create an FlEf resource to tie all of the other resources together.

1. Press Command-K to create a new resource. ResEdit displays the Create New Type dialog box. Type "FlEf" in the text edit box and press Return. ResEdit creates a new FlEf resource and opens it.

2. Fill in the fields as shown in Table 8-6.

3. Press Command-W to close all of the windows on the FlEf resource.

Change the resource file's file type and creator type.

1. Choose "Get Info about *filename*" (where *filename* is the name you gave the file when you created it) from the File menu. Res-Edit displays the Info dialog box for the file.

2. In the Type text edit box, type "FHX3." In the Creator text edit box, type "FHA3."

3. Press Command-W to close the dialog box. ResEdit asks if you want to save the changes to your file. Click Yes.

4. Quit ResEdit.

Place the file you've just created somewhere in FreeHand's search path (either in the Aldus folder or in the folder containing your copy of FreeHand) and start FreeHand. The new fill effect appears in the Effect pop-up menu in the Fill and line dialog box. When you print, you'll see your new "randomsquares" fill (see Figure 8-21).

Text edit box	What you enter	Why you enter it
STR# res. id	ID number	To direct FreeHand to the STR# for the fill's name as you want it to appear in the Effect pop-up menu in the Fill and line dialog box
STR# index	1	Where the name of the fill is inside the STR# resource
POST 1	10021	Location, inside FreeHand, of the start of a dictionary containing PostScript routines you need
POST 2	10000	Location, inside FreeHand, of the start of a dictionary containing more PostScript routines you need
POST 3	ID number	Directs FreeHand to this resource for the code for this fill effect
POST 4	blank	
param type	0	Enters the parameter type for a particular DITL item
DITL item	6	Where the item is inside the DITL. This one's the How many? text edit box.
min	1	Set the minimum value
max	1000	Set the maximum value
default	100	Set the default value
PS parsing string	^0 randomcubes	PostScript string you want passed to your printer

TABLE 8-6
Filling in the FlEf

Now that you've got a resource file for PostScript fill effects created, why not add more fills to it? As with line effects, you've got to make sure that each succeeding fill effect has its own unique ID number for all of its resources.

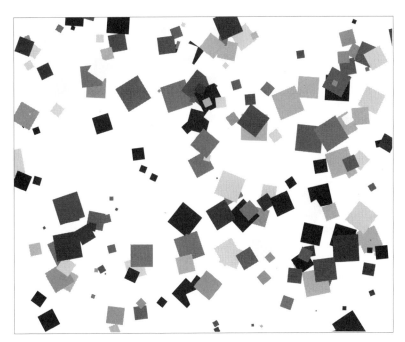

Creating Your Own Dialog Boxes. The best way to create dialog boxes for your FreeHand external resource files is to steal them from Free-Hand and modify them for your own use with ResEdit. This is especially true if you want to use the FreeHand color pop-up menu in your dialog box. These little buggers are tough to make from scratch. If you look at one in ResEdit, you'll see that it's a user item (in this case, a pop-up menu) stacked on top of a static text field. Don't bother creating one of these on your own—just copy it out of FreeHand.

If you've worked through the procedures above for creating LnEf and FlEf resources, you're probably curious about what the numbers you type in the Variable type text edit box mean. Table 8-7 should clear things up a bit.

Finally, make sure that the OK button in your dialog box is DITL item number 1 and that the Cancel button is DITL item number 2.

Number	Parameter type	What it is
0	FreeHand pop-up menu	Color
1	FreeHand pop-up menu	Line dash pattern
2	Text edit box	Line width (in current units)
3	Text edit box	Distance (in current units)
4	Text edit box	Angle in degrees
5	Text edit box	Fixed point number
6	Text edit box	Integer
7	Check box	Boolean value (true/false)
8	Text edit box	Percentage

PostScript PostScript

This has been the hardest chapter in the book to write, and I feel I've only scratched the surface of what you can do with FreeHand and PostScript. Once I figure out how to do text effects, I may even have to create an addendum to this book. Or, this being a book by Peachpit Press, maybe we can do *The Little FreeHand Text Effects Book*. Now there's an idea!

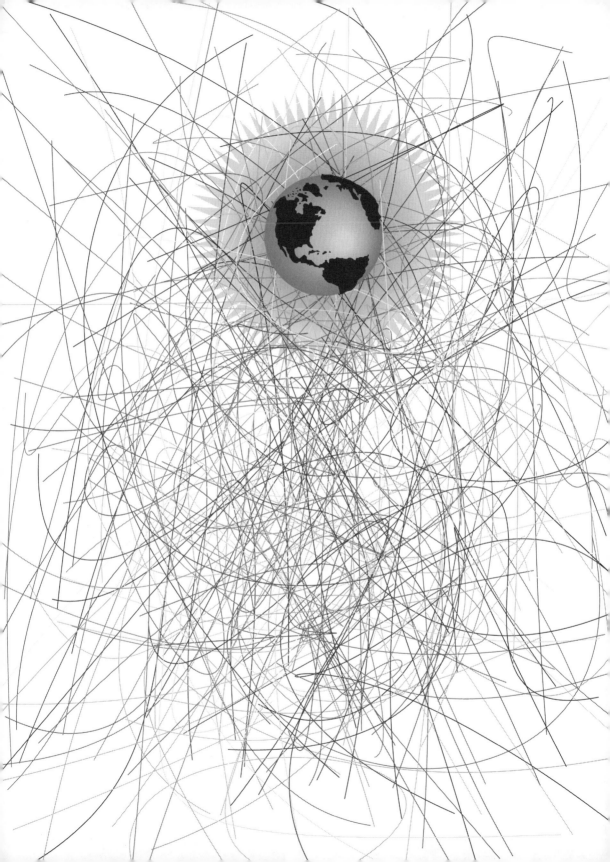

Like other desktop publishing tools, FreeHand does not exist in a vacuum. Sure, you can use it to create entire documents without needing a single other program—but the power and usefulness of FreeHand can be multiplied many times by having an array of utilities and System resources available.

Sometimes these additional tools perform just one, limited function; sometimes they're entire applications in their own right. In either case, having them around either improves your FreeHand productivity or (essentially) adds capabilities to FreeHand.

The first thing you need is a system configuration that is both reliable and that fits you like a glove. Your Macintosh should respond to your directions exactly the way you want it to, without crashing in mid-operation or doing anything else you didn't expect.

System

Your Macintosh system is made up of the System file itself and the INITs, cdevs, fonts, and desk accessories you use. The INITs and cdevs are memory-resident software that gets loaded into your System when you start your Macintosh. Part of an INIT or cdev is in RAM all the time, waiting for you to do whatever it is that activates that cdev or INIT. Fonts and DAs are resources you load into your System file either permanently using the Font/DA Mover or temporarily using a suitcase management utility such as MasterJuggler or Suitcase II. Once these resources are installed in your System, applications (such as FreeHand) can call on and use them.

A few rules about your System:

* Have only one System file per Macintosh.

   You can use a utility to "bless" one of several Systems on a Macintosh, but I've never seen it work well. The only reason to try this is if you're working with a KanjiTalk or Chinese System and need to switch back and forth between localized Systems. Otherwise, don't. If you need to store unused fonts and DAs somewhere, store them in suitcase files, not in an unused System file.

* Don't switch to the most current System version until it's been around for a couple of months.

   Some System versions are buggy, and are withdrawn by Apple after they've been in circulation for awhile. What you really need is an idiot friend who always installs the newest System version as soon as possible—even before they're released (I'm this way, actually). Let them lose work because of incompatibilities and bugs. Then ask them about the new System software. Once their level of bitching and whining declines, you know it's safe to upgrade (by this time they're on to a new version, anyway).

* When you update your System, check all of your INITs and cdevs for compatibility.

   Check your applications, too, but you'll generally have more problems with the items that live inside the System.

* Don't work on a live System file with ResEdit.

   I lose work all the time doing this. It's a stupid thing to do.

* When you update your System, make sure that the installer copies all of the files you need.

   For some reason, Apple's Installer utilities have trouble copying all of the files you need to update your System. Apple assumes that you shouldn't bother copying things you might not need, and this is a good approach, but I'd rather copy everything that's been updated, then delete the stuff I don't need. Specifically, you should make sure that 32-bit QuickDraw and the most current version of AppleShare get installed.

- Approach the System 7 update with caution.

    I don't know much about System 7. I expect there'll be serious compatibility conflicts with many of the applications, INITs, cdevs, and utilities mentioned in this book, if not with FreeHand itself. System 7 offers some tremendous new features, but make sure that the software you know and use works with it before you update your System. There's nothing worse than missing deadlines because you've updated your System and none of the things you need to work are working.

- Less is not more, but can be less trouble.

    Every INIT and cdev you use takes up RAM, and the more INITs and cdevs you have, the more likely it is that they'll conflict with each other or with your applications. Do you really need to have a rainbow-colored cursor? A rotating globe instead of a watch? Like the tree in the garden of Eden, the Macintosh gives us the ability to make our systems as weird and stupid as we want. Rule of thumb: If you're running more than ten INITs/cdevs on an 8MB Macintosh, it's time to exercise some restraint. Tell the snake you're not interested.

- Before you blame the application, check your System.

    As far as I can tell, 50 percent of the technical support calls to Macintosh application developers are about funky Systems, multiple Systems, corrupted font files, etc.

- Your system is more than your System.

    As wonderful as the Macintosh System is, a real desktop-publishing system includes other applications: word processors, other page-layout tools, font-editing software, utilities, and image-editing programs. The whole of the software on your Macintosh should be greater than the sum of its parts.

Your FreeHand Installation

FreeHand comes with several disks' worth of subsidiary files, most of which end up on your hard drive when you install FreeHand. What is all of this stuff? Where does it all go? Table A–1 shows you what's where, and why, for a standard FreeHand installation. If you change folder names, or drag files around after you've installed them, things will look different.

Tip:
Use the Default
Installation

Why ask for trouble? Leave your FreeHand files where FreeHand's installer thinks they should go. Ideally, of course, FreeHand could find the files wherever you put them, with whatever names you cared to give them. Ideally. We don't live in an ideal world, and neither does FreeHand. FreeHand looks for specific files in specific folders. If it can't find them, it can't use them.

Always install your copy of FreeHand from copies of the original product disks, rather than by dragging the files off another drive or file server. It's too easy to miss all of the subsidiary files that aren't inside the application folder.

In spite of this admonition, it's okay to change the name of your FreeHand folder and put it anywhere you want.

Tip:
Converting
Characters to
Paths

If you're trying to convert characters to paths and keep getting a message that the font is in a format that can't be converted—even though you know that it's an Adobe Type 1 font (or a Type 3 font created using Fontographer)—you've probably lost your FreeHand filters file. Locate the file and put it inside the Aldus folder in your system folder and restart FreeHand. In fact, whenever you see a message like this when you're trying to convert a file—whether it's a PICT or an EPS—you've probably misplaced your FreeHand filters file.

INITs, cdevs, and DAs

As I mentioned earlier, INITs and cdevs are little applications that are loaded when your system starts up. Part of an INIT or cdev is always active in your Macintosh's memory, waiting for you to do something it needs to respond to.

TABLE A−1
What's installed when you install FreeHand

Folder	File	What it is
Aldus*	Aldus FreeHand Defaults	FreeHand default settings
	Aldus Installer/Utility	The program you used to install FreeHand. If you want to use any of the diagnostic checks it performs (fonts, system version, etc.), or if you want to decompress any of the FreeHand files you didn't install, keep this around. If you don't, you can throw it away.
	FreeHand filters	The filters that tell FreeHand how to import files from other applications, including converting characters into paths. Don't throw this file away. Don't put it in the Aldus filters folder (if you've got PageMaker, you'll have an Aldus filters folder). Don't move it to another folder. Just leave it alone.
	PANTONE colors	FreeHand's Pantone color library.
	PPDs	A folder containing the PPDs and PDXs you chose to install.
	TeachText	Like every other installer in the world, FreeHand's gives you a copy of TeachText, Apple's simple text viewing utility. You probably already have 20 or 30 of these, so you can throw this one away.
Aldus FreeHand 3**	Aldus FreeHand 3	You know, FreeHand.
	Aldus Installer Diagnostics	A text file created by the installer during installation. If you weren't watching the installer screens, and something went wrong, you can find it in this file. It's a log of the installation. If nothing went wrong, you can throw this file away.

TABLE A–1
Continued

Folder	File/folder	What it is
Aldus FreeHand 3	Aldus Installer History	Another text file created by the installer. If you ever plan to call Aldus Technical Support, keep this file. They'll be able to use it to help you troubleshoot your system. Otherwise, throw it away.
	Aldus FreeHand 3 KEYS	A QuicKeys set for FreeHand. If you didn't get the QuicKeys demo with your copy of FreeHand, this file won't be present.
	Blend Table.EPS	A file containing a table of optimal blend steps for various printer resolutions. Print this file out and refer to it when you're creating blends.
	Color templates folder	This folder contains a set of FreeHand templates, each template having its own color scheme. I always throw this folder away. There are some good color schemes in the templates, though, so you might want to keep it around.
	Calibration Editor	A HyperCard stack you can use to calibrate your imagesetter, if you've got one. If you don't, you can throw this file away.
	Calibration File	A FreeHand file you can use to help calibrate your imagesetter. You use this file in conjunction with the Calibration Editor. If you don't want or need to calibrate your imagesetter, you can throw this file away. If you have PrePrint 1.5, use PrePrint's calibration file and editor.
	CrayonLibrary.clib	A color library containing 64 color definitions. Keep this file around, if only as an example of how to create color libraries.

TABLE A-1
Continued

Folder	File/folder	What it is
Aldus FreeHand 3	FreeHand 3 Help	FreeHand's online help file. FreeHand has a very good context-sensitive online help system, so you might want to save this file. If you never use online help, you can throw this file away.
	Read Me	A text file full of last-minute information on FreeHand, additions and corrections to the documentation, etc. Print this file, read it, and throw the file away.
	Registration card	Your product registration card. You can print this, fill it out, and send it in to Aldus. Then throw it away.
	Sample illustrations folder	A folder full of sample FreeHand illustrations. Check it out—some of these publications are pretty good. Do not assume, however, that the creators of these files have the final word in good publication construction (though most of the files are set up well).
	Tracing files folder	A file full of tracing examples. If you're new to FreeHand, you might want to open a few of these and practice your path-drawing skills. Otherwise, you can ditch this folder.
	Tutorial files folder	You use the files in this folder as you work your way through the FreeHand tutorial. If you've done that, or if you don't intend to do that, you can throw these files away.

*in your system folder
**wherever you put it; whatever you named it

ATM and TrueType. In the early days of Macintosh, you had to have a screen font for every size of type you used—unless you didn't mind your type looking jagged on screen. These days, Adobe Type Manager (ATM) produces smooth-looking characters on your screen (as smooth as they can be at your screen's resolution) from your Type 1 PostScript printer fonts. If you don't have the printer fonts, ATM won't produce better-looking type. Apple's TrueType, which is included with System 7, also produces smooth type on screen from TrueType outline fonts.

Should you buy lots of TrueType fonts? Or should you get ATM and use PostScript Type 1 fonts? Which is better from FreeHand's point of view? While FreeHand supports TrueType, ATM and Post-Script Type 1 fonts are your best bet. For me, the deciding factor is that FreeHand can convert PostScript Type 1 fonts to paths. FreeHand can't do that with TrueType fonts.

Tip:
Where You
Should Put
Your Fonts

If FreeHand's having trouble finding your printer fonts, put the fonts into your system folder. Not inside some other folder; not inside another folder inside your system folder. I understand that this is an inconvenience for people who like to keep their fonts in other folders, in other places. But this is the real world, and reality encompasses certain unpleasant facts. What's more important—keeping the fonts in another folder, or being able to use them? You choose.

ATR. Adobe Type Reunion (ATR) combines your font families into groups on your font menus. Instead of having a separate menu choice for Helvetica Condensed and Helvetica Compressed, ATR shows you a menu item for "Helvetica," and lists "Condensed" and "Compressed" on a submenu attached to the (roman) font family's name.

Is this a good thing? Most of the merging of font families (so that they show only the roman name of the family on your font menus) has already been done by NFNTs, so there's no longer any excuse for anyone having "B Times Bold" or "CBI Helvetica Condensed Bold Italic" on their font menus. (Besides, if you choose those screen font names, you probably won't get what you expected back from your image-setting service bureau.)

As I write this, ATR doesn't work very well with System 7, and has known problems working with FreeHand. I'd give it a miss.

MasterJuggler and Suitcase II. These two INITs make everything about working with fonts and DAs easier and quicker, because you can add fonts to your system without opening the Font/DA Mover (pre-System 7) or dragging them into your System icon (System 7). With either MasterJuggler or Suitcase II, you can load and unload fonts in seconds, without having to click and drag your way around in the Finder. System 7 was supposed to make these INITs obsolete. It didn't.

That said, these two INITs do about the same things. I like MasterJuggler better, because it's got a better user interface and a great application launcher, but Suitcase is made by a larger company and might be updated to System 7 sooner.

Boomerang. Boomerang is a cdev that is active only when you're in a "standard file" dialog box (these are the dialog boxes where you see a listing of files you can open, save, or place). When Boomerang's running, a new icon appears in those dialog boxes. Click this icon, and you'll see a menu of files and folders you've been working with recently. You can use this menu to switch from file to file, folder to folder, and volume to volume quickly, or you can use Boomerang's keyboard shortcuts to move even more quickly (see Figure A-1).

FIGURE A-1
Boomerang's menus

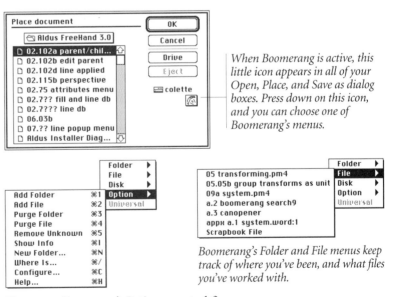

When Boomerang is active, this little icon appears in all of your Open, Place, and Save as dialog boxes. Press down on this icon, and you can choose one of Boomerang's menus.

You can use Boomerang's Option menu to define keyboard shortcuts for specific files and folders.

Boomerang's Folder and File menus keep track of where you've been, and what files you've worked with.

Do you frequently go to an Open or a Place dialog box and forget what file name you wanted—or where you left the file? If you do, you'll love Boomerang's Where is… feature. Press Command-? or choose "Where is…" from Boomerang's Options menu, and Boomerang displays a nifty little dialog box that'll help you find your file. Whatever you named it. Wherever it is (see Figure A-2).

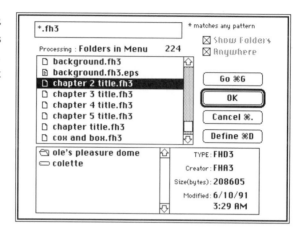

FIGURE A-2
Boomerang's
Where is…
dialog box

DiskTop. DiskTop, from CE Software, is a DA replacement for the Finder. What's so great about that? DiskTop has some capabilities still lacking in the Finder (even in System 7), and you don't have to leave your current application to use it. You can search for all of the files you created on a particular day or range of days, and copy them (as a group) to another disk. This is a great feature for making quick, informal backups. You can change the file type and creator of files without having to open ResEdit or a file editor. System 7 was supposed to make DiskTop obsolete. It didn't.

CanOpener. CanOpener, from Abbott Systems, is a great little DA (actually, there's also an application, but I always use the DA) that'll open just about any kind of file. Once you've got the file open, CanOpener can save text and graphics it finds in the file. Obviously, this makes CanOpener just the thing for extracting graphics and text from files you've lost to bad disks (see Figure A-3).

Cheshire. Cheshire is an INIT made by Abbot Systems, the makers of CanOpener. Cheshire makes charts and graphs form text you've typed

FIGURE A-3

CanOpener

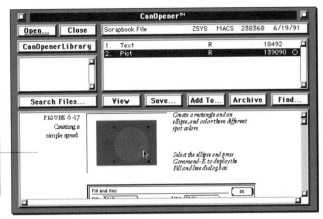

In this example, I've opened a group of PageMaker items that I copied to the Scrapbook. CanOpener can copy them to the Clipboard, or save them as PICT or a variety of other formats.

in PageMaker, Word, or MacDraw. While Cheshire doesn't work directly with FreeHand, it's a great thing to have around when you need to make a simple chart from text you've typed in one of the supported programs. You can save these charts as PICTs, which you can, of course, open and edit using FreeHand.

QuicKeys. QuicKeys, from CE Software, is an INIT that you use to create keyboard shortcuts and macros (a macro is a series of tasks performed in a sequence). If you find yourself wishing for more keyboard shortcuts in FreeHand (like a shortcut for "Export," or "Blend," or "Split elements," to name but a few of the most needed), get yourself a copy of QuicKeys and add them. You might even have a demo version of QuicKeys in your FreeHand package—all of the packages shipped as I'm writing this book have included the demo, but I understand that the demo won't be bundled with FreeHand indefinitely.

Utilities

While I might caution you against large numbers of INITs and cdevs, utilities are another thing. You can never have too many utilities.

ResEdit. I talked about ResEdit back on page 413. Simply put, you cannot do without this utility if you want to modify the way that your programs behave to better fit the ways that you work. And if you want to add external resources to FreeHand, it's essential.

In the old days, ResEdit was a terrifying and unstable product—more prone to demolish any file it touched than make it more useful. These days, ResEdit is still a little rough around the edges, but it's safe enough for your kids to play with.

FreeHand's resources are set up beautifully from a ResEdit hacker's point of view—usually one resource does only one thing. Heck, some of them are even labelled. Get yourself a copy of ResEdit and start investigating a copy of FreeHand (see Figure A-4).

FIGURE A-4
FreeHand,
as seen by ResEdit

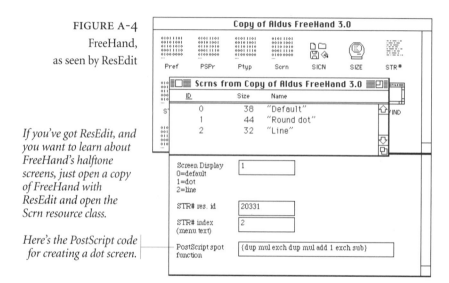

If you've got ResEdit, and you want to learn about FreeHand's halftone screens, just open a copy of FreeHand with ResEdit and open the Scrn resource class.

Here's the PostScript code for creating a dot screen.

StuffIt and DiskDoubler. Like work expanding to fill the time available for it, your files expand to fill the amount of space you have on your hard drive. StuffIt and DiskDoubler compress files so that they take up less space on your disk (now if I could only find a work compression utility!). Both programs compress FreeHand PostScript files to about a third of their original size, which is a great thing to do when you're taking your file to an imagesetting service bureau. Your service bureau may even prefer getting compressed files—ask them.

PostScript Tools

If you're creating your own PostScript dictionaries or external resource files for line and fill effects, or if you're just trying to find out why your last publication didn't print, you need some tools for working with PostScript. Here are a few of my favorites.

LaserTalk. LaserTalk is the essential PostScript utility. With LaserTalk, you can communicate directly with the PostScript interpreter in your printer, and, better yet, *you can see what's going on* (see Figure A-5). If you're serious about creating PostScript effects for FreeHand, you've got to get LaserTalk.

Which brings up a problem. LaserTalk was originally made by Emerald City Software. Emerald City was acquired by Adobe Systems, the makers of PostScript. After the acquisition, Adobe stopped developing LaserTalk. They might not even be selling the program, at this point, and they certainly haven't updated it for System 7 (which means that you've got to go back to LaserWriter driver 5.2 to use LaserTalk).

This is a shame. Adobe should update LaserTalk or make available some other program like it. Write them, send them a fax, or give them a call and tell them so.

Meanwhile, find a copy of LaserTalk and start writing PostScript.

FIGURE A-5
LaserTalk

*LaserTalk
(late? lamented?)
puts you in direct
contact with the
PostScript interpreter
in your printer.*

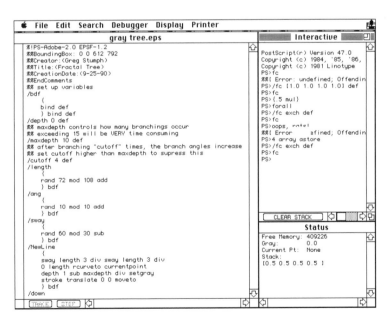

LaserStatus. LaserStatus is a Desk Accessory PostScript downloader from CE Software. Though it's a DA, it's better than many of the

PostScript downloading applications. The great thing about Laser-Status is that you can create sets—lists of files you want downloaded. When you want to send a series of files to your printer, just choose the set you've created with those file names in it (see Figure A-6).

FIGURE A-6

LaserStatus

Use LaserStatus to download PostScript files without leaving your current application.

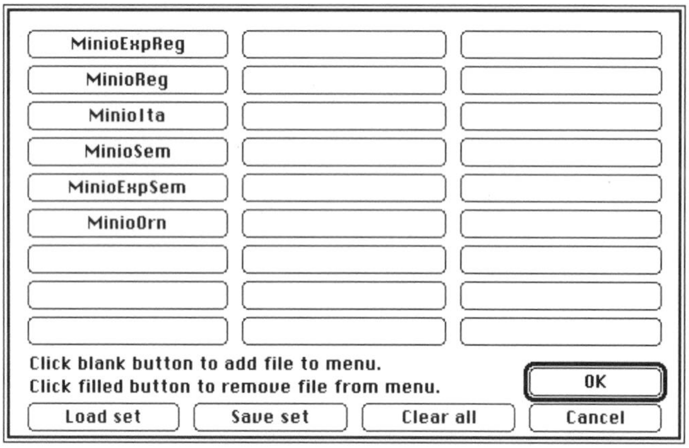

Use LaserStatus sets to download groups of PostScript files (including fonts, as shown in this example).

This appendix tells you where to get the things mentioned in this book. First of all, you can write to me or send me a message on Compuserve. I'd love to know what you thought of the book (even if you didn't like it—I took my best shot, but I can't correct my aim unless I know I've missed). I'd also love to hear about any fabulous FreeHand tips and tricks you've come up with (so I can steal them for the next editon).

Olav Martin Kvern
4021 Aurora Avenue North
Seattle, Washington
98103
(206) 634-0153 (fax)
CIS: 76636,2535
or visit Section 2, "Dr. Kvern's Office," in the Aldus Forum

David Blatner/Parallax Productions
PSPatterns (PostScript line and fill effects)
4021 Aurora Avenue North
(yes, David and I share a beautiful office above a gun shop)
Seattle, Washington
98103
(206) 633-4030

Greg Stumph
Custom PostScript programming
4240 South Findlay Street
Seattle, Washington

98118
(206) 723-2177
(206) 343-3335

Abbott Systems
CanOpener, Cheshire
62 Mountain Road
Pleasantville, New York
10570
(800) 552-9157

Adobe Systems, Incorporated
Adobe Illustrator, Adobe Photoshop, Adobe Type Manager, Adobe Type Reunion, Adobe TypeAlign, PostScript, LaserTalk (?), SmartArt (?), Fonts
1585 Charleston Road
Mountain View, California
94039
(415) 961-4400

Aladdin Systems, Incorporated
StuffIt Deluxe
Deer Park Center, Suite 23A-171
Aptos, California
95003
(408) 685-9175

Aldus Corporation
PageMaker, FreeHand, Persuasion, PrePrint
411 1st Avenue South
Seattle, Washington
98104
(206) 622-5500

AlSoft
MasterJuggler
P.O. Box 927

Sprint, Texas
77383
(713) 353-4090

Altsys Corporation
EPS Exchange, Fontographer, Metamorphosis Pro
269 West Renner Road
Richardson, Texas
75080
(214) 680-2060

Apple Computer
MacDraw, ResEdit
20525 Mariani Avenue
Cupertino, California
95014
(408) 996-1010

Bantam Books
Real World PageMaker 4; Industrial Strength Techniques
by Olav Martin Kvern and Steve Roth
666 Fifth Avenue
New York, New York
10103

Brøderbund Software, Incorporated
TypeStyler
17 Paul Drive
San Rafael, California
94903

CE Software
QuicKeys, DiskTop, LaserStatus
1854 Fuller Road, P.O. Box 65580
West DesMoines, Iowa
50265
(515) 224-1998

Fifth Generation Systems
SuitCase II
10049 North Reiger Road
Baton Rouge, Louisiana
70809
(504) 291-7283

ISDC
Studio Convert
545 Academy Drive
Northbrook, Illinois
60065

Letraset Corporation
ColorStudio, DesignStudio, LetraStudio
40 Eisenhower Drive
Paramus, New Jersey
07653

Microsoft Corporation
Microsoft Word, Microsoft Excel
One Microsoft Way
Redmond, Washington
98052
(206) 882-8080

PC Quik-Art
The Graphics Link Plus
394 South Milledge Avenue, #200
Athens, Georgia
30606
(404) 543-1799

Peachpit Press, Incorporated
Lots of great books, especially—from this book's point of view—
Learning PostScirpt; A Visual Approach, by Ross Smith.
2414 Sixth Street
Berkeley, California

94710
(800) 283-9444

Salient Software, Incorporated
DiskDoubler
124 University Avenue
Palo Alto, California
94301
(415) 321-5375

Seattle Gilbert & Sullivan Society
Thespis, Trial by Jury, The Sorcerer, H.M.S. Pinafore, The Pirates of Penzance, Patience, Iolanthe, Princess Ida, The Mikado, Ruddigore, The Yeomen of the Guard, The Gondoliers, Utopia Limited, The Grand Duke, and, yes, even Sullivan & Burnand's *Cox and Box*
P.O. Box 15314
Seattle, Washington
98115

Silicon Beach Software, Incorporated
(a subsidiary of Aldus Corporation)
Super 3-D, SuperPaint
9770 Carroll Center Road, Suite J
San Diego, California
92126
(619) 695-6956

ZetaSoft
Boomerang
2425 B. Channing Way
Suite 492
Berkeley, California
94704
(415) 658-7213

tape here (also tape the sides if you've enclosed a check)

fold here

place
stamp
here

PEACHPIT PRESS
2414 SIXTH STREET
BERKELEY, CALIFORNIA
94710

REAL WORLD FREEHAND 3 ♪ THE DISK

If you'd like to get your hands on a disk full of FreeHand fun, here's your chance. *Real World FreeHand 3: The Disk* contains all of the PostScript lines and fills shown in this book, plus more lines and fills I didn't have space to show you (plus a few I've only just thought of). Besides that, you'll find FHX3 files for supercharging your copy of FreeHand, "ColorMaker," an application for generating color libraries, several useful color libraries, ResEdit templates for creating your own FHX3 files, FreeHand templates containing tiling and latticework patterns seen in this book, and even more FreeHand tips and tricks.

ORDERING INFORMATION

COPIES		PRICE	TOTAL
	REAL WORLD FREEHAND 3 ♪ THE DISK	$20.00	

You can order by phone by calling Peachpit Press at (800) 283-9444; or faxing an order to (415) 548-5991	SHIPPING		$4.00
	CALIFORNIA RESIDENTS PLEASE ADD 8 PERCENT SALES TAX		
	TOTAL		

NAME

ADDRESS

CITY	STATE	ZIP

CHECK ENCLOSED ☐	VISA ☐	MASTERCARD ☐	COMPANY PURCHASE ORDER NUMBER: _____

CREDIT CARD NUMBER	EXPIRATION DATE

Satisfaction unconditionally guaranteed or your money cheerfully refunded!